GULF TO GLOBAL

SANSOM MILTON
GHASSAN ELKAHLOUT

Gulf to Global

The Rise of Qatar in Conflict Mediation

OXFORD
UNIVERSITY PRESS

OXFORD
UNIVERSITY PRESS

Oxford University Press is a department of the
University of Oxford. It furthers the University's objective
of excellence in research, scholarship, and education
by publishing worldwide.

Oxford New York
Auckland Cape Town Dar es Salaam Hong Kong Karachi
Kuala Lumpur Madrid Melbourne Mexico City Nairobi
New Delhi Shanghai Taipei Toronto

With offices in
Argentina Austria Brazil Chile Czech Republic France Greece
Guatemala Hungary Italy Japan Poland Portugal Singapore
South Korea Switzerland Thailand Turkey Ukraine Vietnam

Oxford is a registered trade mark of Oxford University Press
in the UK and certain other countries.

Published in the United States of America by
Oxford University Press
546 Fifth Avenue, New York, NY 10036, United States of America

Library of Congress Cataloging-in-Publication Data is available
Sansom Milton and Ghassan Elkahlout.
Gulf to Global: The Rise of Qatar in Conflict Mediation.
ISBN: 9780197852118

Printed and bound in Great Britain by Bell and Bain Ltd, Glasgow

CONTENTS

ABOUT THE AUTHORS

Sansom Milton is a Senior Research Fellow at the Center for Conflict and Humanitarian Studies, within the Arab Center for Research and Policy Studies.

Ghassan Elkahlout is the Director of the Center for Conflict and Humanitarian Studies and Associate Professor at the Doha Institute for Graduate Studies.

ACKNOWLEDGEMENTS

This book is the culmination of years of dedicated research and engagement on Qatar's role in conflict mediation, undertaken at the Center for Conflict and Humanitarian Studies, Doha, Qatar. It would not have been possible without the support and encouragement of many individuals and institutions.

We would like to acknowledge the contribution of the team that worked on the Documentation and Archiving of Qatari Mediation project that conducted many of the interviews with Qatari mediators and conflict parties utilized in the book. This includes Mohammed Alsousi, Khalil Osman, Amena El Ashkar, and Rana Barout. We are also deeply grateful to the Diplomatic Institute and Ministry of Foreign Affairs of the State of Qatar for facilitating interviews and access to archival material utilized in the writing of the book. Special appreciation is reserved for Dr Abdulaziz Al-Horr for coordinating this methodical data-gathering process. We also remain deeply grateful to the interviewees who generously shared their insights and experiences, enhancing our understanding of Qatari mediation.

We extend our thanks to Mohammad Al-Hamawi, Irina Andriiuc, Haythem Dellai, Maya El Jundi, Rabbia Saeed, Taj Hussain, and Sara Elkhatib for providing research assistance. Special acknowledgement is due to the individuals who reviewed and commented upon draft versions of various chapters, in particular Arne Strand, Hameed Hakimi, Sean Deely, Anna Hess, Mouin Rabbani, Bassel Salloukh, and Sana Tariq. Finally, we would like to thank Michael Dwyer for his excellent editorial advice and assistance.

LIST OF ABBREVIATIONS

AMIS	African Union Mission in Sudan
AU	African Union
DDPD	Doha Document for Peace in Darfur
DDR	Disarmament, Demobilization, and Reintegration
DDS	Darfur Development Strategy
DPA	Darfur Peace Agreement
DRA	Darfur Regional Authority
DRC	Democratic Republic of Congo
EU	European Union
IAEA	International Atomic Energy Agency
JCPOA	Joint Comprehensive Plan of Action
JEM	Justice and Equality Movement
LJM	Liberation and Justice Movement
MOFA	Ministry of Foreign Affairs in the State of Qatar
NATO	North Atlantic Treaty Organization
NGO	Non-governmental organization
PLO	Palestine Liberation Organization
RNT	Republic Negotiation Team
RSF	Rapid Support Forces
SLA	Sudan Liberation Army
SLM/A-AW	Sudan Liberation Movement/Army (Abdel Wahid faction)
SLM/A-MM	Sudan Liberation Movement/Army (Minni Minawi faction)
UAE	United Arab Emirates

UK	United Kingdom
UN	United Nations
UNAMID	United Nations–African Union Hybrid Operation in Darfur
UNSC	United Nations Security Council
U.S.	United States

1

INTRODUCTION

In recent years, Qatar has emerged as a leading global mediator in conflict and crisis. This remarkable journey to the centre of international peacemaking has played out over several decades, overcoming many challenges on the way. Qatar's first stride into conflict mediation was its successful brokering of negotiations between Eritrea and Yemen over the Hanish Islands dispute in 1995. This minor episode was peripheral not just to conflict resolution at a global level but also within the Gulf's sub-regional security complex. By contrast, in the early 2020s, Qatari mediation shifted to high-profile crises at the global level, including the landmark agreement between the United States (U.S.) and the Taliban, the 7 October War on the Gaza Strip, and talks between Russia and Ukraine. This three-decade transformation is addressed in this book, which traces the ascendancy of Qatar from the Gulf to the global in conflict mediation.

Qatar's ascent as a mediator has taken place in a global context marked by increasing levels of conflict and polarization. In 2024, there were fifty-six active conflicts worldwide, the most since the Second World War, with ninety-two countries involved.[1] There has also been a dearth of successfully negotiated solutions to conflict in recent years, which underscores the importance of analyzing mediation and the factors affecting successful conflict resolution. Qatar's emergence as a global mediator is also remarkable considering the trend towards mediator proliferation, with many international organizations, small states, private individuals, and faith-based groups, to name a few, increasingly offering mediation services in a saturated field.[2] In short, Qatar has emerged as a mediator at a point in history at which there has been a growing demand for effective engagement in conflict mediation along with greater competition between prospective mediators.

In the early 2010s, a number of scholars produced research on Qatar's intensifying engagement in conflict mediation.[3] However, this strand of research was quickly eclipsed by real-world events, such as Qatar's role in the Arab Spring and the regional blockade imposed in 2017, during which its mediation role was curtailed.[4] Most studies on Qatari mediation are based on generalizations from few cases focusing on the period 2006–10—particularly the Lebanese political crisis of 2008, the Houthi conflict in Yemen during the 2007–08 period, the Darfur peace process culminating in 2011, and, to a lesser extent, the 2012 Hamas–Fatah reconciliation agreement.[5] Moreover, these analyses are largely based on secondary sources and do not interrogate the specifics of Qatari mediation by utilizing original, primary material. Whilst early studies on Qatari mediation were significant, they have become outdated and fail to reflect Qatar's evolution as a mediator.

As Qatar continues to attract global attention for its expanded mediation efforts, there is a clear need for rigorous, comparative research that transcends surface-level observations of Qatari mediation. Despite a rise in academic interest, systematic and contemporary studies on Qatar's mediation remain scarce, particularly concerning Qatar's recent re-emergence as a major global mediator. This book offers the first in-depth, comparative empirical analysis, blending historical and contemporary cases based on Qatar's track record from the 2000s to the 2020s. Besides providing a nuanced analysis of Qatar as a small-state mediation actor, the book also aims to contribute to the burgeoning research interest in the rise of non-traditional peacemaking actors and the roles of the Gulf States in contemporary conflict resolution at large.

Methodology

The book aims to advance collective understanding of Qatari mediation through systematic analysis based on original research and analysis. As such, the research underpinning the book draws on an eclectic range of methods. The professional engagement of the co-authors as researchers and practitioners engaged in peace research and mediation support within Qatar provides a wealth of first-hand observation that informs the analysis. Furthermore, a key element of the methodology is a qualitative dataset produced by the Center for Conflict and Humanitarian Studies, which includes interviews with senior Qatari officials, representatives of various conflict parties, and individuals who have engaged in Qatar's mediation efforts. The dataset also includes an archive of primary documents, offering unprecedented access to Qatari mediation efforts. In so doing, the book unpacks the complexities inherent to Qatari mediation, with a view to engaging with and explaining the modalities through which Qatar approaches conflict mediation.

Whilst Qatari mediation has gained significant attention in media and academic circles, much of the existing analysis remains speculative, relying heavily on outsider perspectives. By securing trusted access and maintaining academic rigour, this book offers first-hand insight into Qatar's mediation model and its evolution over time, thus demonstrating the methodological utility of an approach rooted in in-depth, primary research. Most importantly, there is a methodological advantage in studying and understanding individual mediators, at least partially, in their own words and perspectives. This approach is particularly vital for mediators less inclined to openly discuss their activities.

Over the past few decades, the field of conflict mediation has expanded significantly. A wide range of actors—from state-based mediators to international organizations and private actors—have emerged, resulting in a crowded and increasingly complex field. This expansion has been accompanied by standardization of practices, with an emphasis on training and accreditation, development of specialized tools and normative guidance notes, as well as integration of monitoring, evaluation, and knowledge management into mediation processes.[6] One dimension of this professionalization is the documentation and archiving of mediation processes, which enhances methodological rigour and is vital for the professionalization and institutionalization of mediation actors.[7] Despite all this, there remains a distinct lack of in-depth research on the mediation practice of the Gulf States. Much of the literature remains focused on Western actors, and often overlooks the institutional dynamics, diplomatic styles, and evolving strategies of Gulf-based mediators. This book aims to fill this gap by offering a systematic documentation and analysis of Qatari mediation as a state actor.

Traditionally, mediation research takes an exogenous approach, focusing on the external factors shaping mediation procedures, such as the conflict context, the political setting, the structural components of the international setup, the geopolitical environment, or third-party involvement. An endogenous viewpoint, on the other hand, underscores the importance of the mediation process's internal features, including the modalities, tactics, and styles of the mediators, as well as how these factors interact with the conflict parties and the agenda of the mediation.[8] This book primarily adopts an endogenous approach to analyzing Qatari mediation and underlines the importance of mediator characteristics. Concurrently, it is recognized that internal dimensions of mediation do not exist in a vacuum, but are instead dynamically shaped by, and in turn respond to, the contexts and processes in which they are embedded. By examining Qatar as both an individual actor and one embedded in broader geopolitical dynamics, this study aims to offer a more comprehensive understanding of its mediation practice. This perspective enhances analytical and practical insight into process design, and contributes to greater methodological diversity in mediation studies by combining qualitative and empirical approaches. It also has relevance for practitioners seeking to adapt mediation strategies to the characteristics of both the mediator and the conflict environment.

Case Selection

Thus far, studies of Qatari mediation have largely focused on general impressions or analyses of single cases, leaving a significant gap in systematic research that would offer generalizable insights. Few attempts have been made to conduct a thorough evaluation of Qatar's mediation efforts across various contexts. This book presents five case-study chapters that provide an empirical and comparative examination of Qatari mediation. The cases of Lebanon, Darfur, Afghanistan, Gaza, and multiple post-2020 crises have been selected not only for their geopolitical importance, but also for the distinct insights they offer into Qatar's mediation style, institutional learning, and adaptation across diverse contexts.

Lebanon represents a key early success that was foundational for Qatar's trajectory as a mediator. Darfur offers an instructive study in Qatar's multi-party mediation that showcases its long-term commitment to the peace process. Afghanistan is a critical case, signifying the maturation of Qatar's mediation approach and its emergence as a major mediator in complex conflict contexts. The Gaza Strip following the war from 7 October 2023 stands out as the most high-profile context of Qatari mediation, whilst also contextualizing the roots of its engagement in long-term involvement in Palestine. Finally, the post-2020 mediation cases are selected to illustrate the progressively wider geographic reach and geostrategic significance of the contexts in which Qatar has engaged in facilitation and mediation. Collectively, these cases provide a comprehensive overview of Qatar's evolving role in conflict mediation.

Another dimension of the case selection rationale is explaining the changes in Qatari mediation over time. The contexts of Lebanon and Darfur offer insights into Qatari mediation in the 2000s; Afghanistan and the Gaza Strip illustrate Qatar's long-term strategy of laying the groundwork during the 2010s that culminated in major mediation roles in the early 2020s; and the post-2020 contexts address contemporary dynamics. As such, the book offers a diachronic account of Qatari mediation which is grounded in multi-year research and a longitudinal view of both Qatar's mediation within individual cases and its wider evolution as a mediator.

This methodological approach helps avoid the pitfalls of synchronic, time-sliced analyses in which key findings and conclusions are generalized based on specific and contingent moments. Traditionally, academic and policy circles have paid attention to Qatari mediation following the signing of notable agreements, often producing snapshot analyses based on immediately available accounts that are unable to track long-term outcomes. Research on Qatari mediation has also been generated from specific temporal phases (for example, the 2006–10 period) that had quite specific, localized drivers. Qatar's renewed third-party role offers a powerful case that enables analysis of how this particular state's mediation approach has evolved over time. This longitudinal perspective is vital for grasping the specificities of Qatari mediation, its long-term outcomes in individual cases, and the strategic linking between Qatari mediation and sustained humanitarian and development support. This case selection thus addresses a gap in comparative mediation research, which has paid scant attention to the temporal dimension of the changing forces shaping mediation approaches and the strategies employed by individual mediators.

Structure of the Book

This book is structured into three sections. Section One comprises an introduction and three chapters that trace Qatar's background, contextualize its ascent as an actor in conflict mediation, examine its extensive mediation profile, and synthesize the existing research on the topic.

Chapter One, *Introduction*, contextualizes and rationalizes the book. Chapter Two, *The Rise of Qatar as a Mediator*, offers an overview of Qatar's historical, socioeconomic, and political landscape, tracing its journey from a newly independent state to a dynamic, transformative power in the region. The chapter then provides a chronological and comprehensive summary of the emergence of Qatar as a key player in conflict mediation from the early 1990s to its subsequent phase of highly active mediation in the 2000s. The narrative then explores the retreat of Qatari mediation during the tumultuous Arab Spring and the resumption of mediation as a central tool in Qatari foreign policy in the early 2020s.

Chapter Three, *Conceptualizing Qatari Mediation*, surveys the prevalent theoretical lenses applied in existing studies of Qatari mediation and outlines the theoretical foundations of this book. The chapter begins by outlining the predominant theoretical underpinnings within competing schools of international relations, small-state mediation literature, and reductive critiques of Qatari mediation as 'chequebook diplomacy'. It then introduces novel theoretical lenses through which

Qatari mediation can be best understood, including the paradigms of non-traditional actors in the plural global landscape of peacemaking and, specifically, the role of the Gulf States.

Section Two, which forms the core of the book, presents detailed empirical analyses of Qatari mediation in Lebanon, Darfur, the Gaza Strip, and Afghanistan, as well as in recent cases such as between Russia and Ukraine, between the U.S. and Venezuela, and between the U.S. and Iran. These case-study chapters were chosen to represent some of the most consequential and illuminating instances of Qatari mediation.

Chapter Four, *Stepping Back from the Brink: Lebanon's 2008 Doha Agreement*, analyses Qatar's mediation during the May 2008 crisis in Lebanon—a breakthrough moment in Qatari mediation. This analysis traces the methods and strategies employed by Qatar to harmonize the conflicting agendas within the political landscape of Lebanon. It finds that these mediation efforts stand as one of Qatar's most successful cases of mediation, with implications for their emerging reputation as a peacemaker. Insights from this case study shed light on Qatar's mediation effectiveness amidst a critical period characterized by regional tensions.

Chapter Five, *Brokering Peace in Darfur: The Doha Document and its Legacy*, analyzes Qatar's multi-party mediation efforts in the Darfur region of Sudan, which culminated in the signing of the Doha Document for Peace in Darfur. The chapter explores Qatar's collaborative approach with the African Union and the United Nations to address the sub-regional conflict. It provides an in-depth analysis of Qatar's modalities of mediation and its post-agreement role. By examining Qatar's long-term commitment to the peace process in Darfur, the chapter offers valuable insights into the challenges and successes of sustaining peace agreements, thereby contributing to a deeper understanding of the longevity and impact of Qatari mediation.

Chapter Six, *Afghanistan at a Crossroads: The 2020 U.S.–Taliban Agreement and Beyond*, explores Qatar's facilitation of talks between the U.S. and the Taliban, which culminated with the signing of the 2020 agreement that reshaped the Afghan geopolitical landscape. The chapter outlines how Qatar laid the groundwork through years of strategic engagement and quiet diplomacy. It then shifts to Qatar's role in the ensuing intra-Afghan talks between the Taliban movement and the former Afghan government, and its engagement following the Taliban takeover in 2021. The chapter is key to understanding the evolution of Qatari mediation, demonstrating its growing strategic weight and ability to navigate complex diplomatic scenarios.

Chapter Seven, *Diplomacy Amidst Devastation: Qatar's Mediation in the 7 October War on Gaza*, analyses the role of Qatar as a mediator in the context of the Gaza Strip. It begins with a documentation of Qatar's diplomatic entry into this file, unpacking the controversies and mutually irreconcilable interpretations of Qatar's roles and objectives in Palestine. Here, Qatari mediation is analyzed in a case study of the intra-Palestinian reconciliation process between rivals Fatah and Hamas. It then examines Qatar's efforts to mediate multiple ceasefires in the Gaza Strip between Israel and the different Palestinian factions. This will provide the necessary contextualization for the crux of the chapter: a contemporary case study of Qatar's attempts to mediate multiple ceasefires and prisoner swap deals in the 7 October War in the Gaza Strip.

Chapter Eight, *Qatari Mediation at the Heart of Global Crises*, analyzes Qatar's resurgence as the go-to mediator on the global stage since 2020. It examines their engagement in a range of African crises, including Chad, Libya, Somalia, as well as its mediation in U.S.–Venezuela, U.S.–Iran, and Russia–Ukraine negotiations. It then explores the changing regional and global landscape that facilitated Qatar's re-emergence as a global mediator in the post-2020 era.

Section Three offers a comparative analysis of the case studies, incorporating insights from Qatari mediators and reflecting on the wider significance of in-depth analyses of Qatari mediation.

Chapter Nine, *Pillars of Qatari Mediation*, presents the key elements of Qatari mediation. In so doing, it briefly outlines each pillar of Qatari mediation, including strategic reach, impartiality, pragmatism, long-term commitment, and multifaceted approaches. The chapter synthesizes key findings from the case-study chapters and first-hand accounts from key figures closely associated with Qatar's diplomatic efforts.

Chapter Ten, *Conclusion*, synthesizes the major findings of the book and summarizes the identified themes which have come to characterize Qatari mediation.

2

THE RISE OF QATAR AS A MEDIATOR

Since the 1970s, Qatar has undergone a remarkable transformation, evolving from a small pearl-trading Gulf state into one of the world's wealthiest nations and an influential global actor. This evolution has been driven by its vast natural gas resources, leadership committed to long-term development, strategic investments in education, culture, and sports, and an ambitious foreign policy. This chapter explores the critical events, frameworks, and policies that have shaped Qatar's trajectory—from its post-independence history to its emergence as a stable and influential nation. The chapter then focuses on the rise of Qatar as a mediator. It traces this rise chronologically, providing a narrative of Qatari mediation across multiple phases: the early forays into mediation in the 1990s; the proactive period of mediation from 2006 to 2010; the low-profile role during the Arab Spring and Gulf Crisis (2017–21); and the return of Qatari mediation to the diplomatic spotlight in the 2020s. This stylized account of Qatar's trajectory as a mediator provides the historical backdrop against which the case studies presented in this book can be contextualized. By tracing these developments, this chapter sets the stage for understanding Qatar's diplomatic efforts in the late 2010s and early 2020s, particularly its role as a mediator in regional and international conflicts.

State Formation and Post-Independence Rise

Until the 1930s, Doha was a small fishing and pearling village, with modest development and limited infrastructure. Qatar's domestic modernization and economic development, which accelerated in the second half of the twentieth century, was catalyzed by the discovery of hydrocarbon resources and the development of the North Field, the world's largest non-associated natural gas field. Although oil exploration in Qatar began in the late 1930s, it was not until the 1960s that hydrocarbons became the driving force behind Qatar's economic and political transformation. Under Sheikh Ahmad bin Ali Al Thani's rule (1960–72), control over oil revenues was consolidated through the establishment of the Ministry of Finance and the Department of Petroleum Affairs.[1] Shortly after Qatar declared its independence from British rule in 1971, the North Field was discovered. Sheikh Khalifa bin Hamad Al Thani (1972–95) took critical steps to secure greater state control over Qatar's oil and gas resources, including overseeing the creation of Qatar Petroleum Company (now QatarEnergy) in 1974. The country's global economic presence grew significantly, with the first gas exports from North Field beginning in 1996 under His Highness Emir Sheikh Hamad bin Khalifa Al Thani. This economic boom led to Qatar becoming one of the world's largest liquefied natural gas producers and achieving one of the highest per capita incomes globally.[2] The rapid development enabled Qatar to become a major financial investor, donor, and importer of foreign labour, with strategic investments made abroad through the Qatar Investment Authority, founded in 2005.[3]

This rapid, resource-fuelled modernization prompted analysis of Qatar's transformation through the lens of rentier state theory. However, over time, rentierism alone became insufficient to explain the developmental trajectory of the Gulf States, overshadowing specific features of their political and socioeconomic structures.[4] Yet, Qatar's growth as a state in the decades that followed cannot be attributed to resources alone but also to the transformative vision of its leaders and a high level of domestic political stability.

This stability and growth within Qatar is often attributed to a small and apolitical population, the absence of sectarian tensions, and a cohesive ruling elite.[5] During the earlier years of state formation, the population of Qatar did not exceed 150,000 people, with 20,000 of them being members of the Al Thani family, who had been leading Qatar's political and economic development since the mid-nineteenth century.[6] And whilst the 1960s witnessed an increased influx of expatriate labour to Qatar to accommodate the rapidly developing economy, the proportion of the local population remained small.[7]

The vision of Qatar's leadership was a central driving force in its long-term transformation. Under Emir Sheikh Hamad bin Khalifa Al Thani, the state's foreign policy shifted from a relatively insular approach to a more assertive and influential role on the global stage.[8] Building on the legacy of domestic advancement under his predecessors, Sheikh Hamad leveraged the country's vast natural resources to pursue an ambitious internationalization strategy. This established Qatar as a regional powerhouse through an increasingly bold foreign policy, strategic investments, and the establishment of Al Jazeera, the influential global media network.[9] Moreover, the leadership's commitment to the National Vision 2030, which serves as the cornerstone of the country's long-term transformation, has driven significant progress across multiple sectors and enabled Qatar to make remarkable developmental progress.[10]

During this early stage of Qatar's formation as an independent state, the country underwent three leadership changes. Nevertheless, each of these rulers demonstrated a continuous commitment to transforming their abundant resources into a base for stability and national wealth. In doing so, Qatari leadership crafted a developmental model that successfully transitioned Qatar from a 'tribal confederacy to a modern state'.[11] As such, the rapid ascent from the periphery to the centre stage of global affairs was significantly shaped by the long-term vision of its national leadership, which ultimately enabled the country to maintain its transformative trajectory amidst a shifting and uncertain regional and international environment.[12]

Domestic Transformations

Over the course of several decades, Qatar has undergone a major transformation at the domestic level. This has involved progressive reforms aimed at economic diversification, addressing labour market challenges, and strengthening domestic institutions. Moreover, investments in education, sports, and culture form a central pillar of the state's long-term developmental strategy, which is laid out in the Qatar National Vision 2030.[13] This vision aims to reduce the country's dependency on hydrocarbons by creating a knowledge-based economy, fostering innovation, and positioning Qatar as a hub for global cultural and sporting events.[14] However, some have been critical of these major investments, reductively labelling them as part of place branding strategies aimed at gaining reputational benefits.[15] Whilst these often high-profile initiatives have indeed helped place Qatar on the map, framing such initiatives primarily as place branding overlooks their deeper significance, namely the fact that these efforts are integral to Qatar's long-term nation-building strategy.[16]

In the education sector, Qatar's transformation has involved substantive investments, such as the creation of Education City, incentivizing branch campuses of leading universities to open in Qatar, and the establishment of region-leading research infrastructure.[17] These institutions aim to cultivate a new generation of highly skilled professionals and researchers, preparing Qatar to compete in the global knowledge economy. In sport, by hosting major events, most notably the 2022 FIFA World Cup, and investing in high-profile sports franchises, Qatar has also placed itself on the sporting map globally.[18] In these cases, Qatar's investments were not merely for place branding but rather led to the development of significant domestic infrastructure, including stadiums and sports complexes. Sport is viewed internally as a means to improve public health and foster social cohesion, and internationally as an opportunity to enhance its reputation through sports diplomacy.[19] Culture complements Qatar's education and sports initiatives, with institutions like the Museum of Islamic Art and Qatar Museums' global art engagements advancing the country's vision of cultural diplomacy and fostering a vibrant, internationally connected society.[20]

Evidently, Qatar's approach to public diplomacy is guided by a broader strategy that includes domestic development and international image-building. Many of the aforementioned initiatives served dual purposes, projecting a narrative of modernity, progress, and openness to the world whilst simultaneously enhancing Qatar's infrastructure, cultural landscape, and contributing to nation-building. They represent a cohesive strategy aimed at building a sustainable, diversified economy that is globally integrated and resilient in the post-hydrocarbon era. These sectors are key to the country's ambitious long-term project of national transformation, providing the infrastructure and human capital needed to sustain Qatar's growth well into the future.

Security amidst Regional Rivalries

The emergence of Qatar as a global mediator must be understood in relation to the prerogatives of foreign policy within the regional security environment of the Gulf. In the post-independence era, Qatar faced a volatile regional context marked by geopolitical rivalries (such as those between Iran and Saudi Arabia) and regional conflicts. After the withdrawal of British protection in 1971, Qatar came to depend on Saudi Arabia for security matters.[21] Following this, Qatar, along with the other Gulf States, was under the political influence of Saudi Arabia as the pre-eminent major power in the Gulf. The Gulf Cooperation Council—formed in 1981 and comprising Bahrain, Kuwait, Oman, Qatar, Saudi Arabia, and the United Arab Emirates (UAE)—provided a collective framework for security and economic cooperation,[22] and was primarily driven by the Gulf States' concerns over the 1979 Iranian Revolution, its potential to spread revolutionary ideology across the region, and Iran's perceived hegemonic ambitions. It was also significantly influenced by fears over the spread of the Iran–Iraq War and broader regional spillover effects.[23] The council's Joint Defence Agreement emphasized that an attack on one member would be considered an attack on all, thereby providing a security guarantee to a small state like Qatar during uncertain times.[24] Yet, despite these sub-regional arrangements, Iraq invaded and occupied Kuwait in 1990, which was followed by the Gulf War in 1991.[25] These failures of the Council's regional security mechanisms prompted Qatar to rethink its geopolitical strategy.[26]

Qatar's need to maintain relations with Iran—which was locked in a regional rivalry with Saudi Arabia—was another key feature of this increasingly independent foreign policy. Qatar and Iran share both a maritime border and the world's largest natural gas field.[27] The first export of liquefied natural gas occurred in 1997, which necessitated increased cooperation and communication between Qatar and Iran. Additionally, Qatar and Saudi Arabia have longstanding mutual dependencies, including transportation routes for the export of oil and gas.[28] Thus, Qatar's shared borders and geographical location means that maintaining cordial relations with its neighbours is crucial for its security and prosperity.

Qatar's adoption of 'low profile and official neutrality' as a hallmark of its foreign policy was notable in the early phases of its state formation.[29] Nonetheless, the major strategic realignment in the early 1990s led the country to place greater emphasis on the pursuit of an independent foreign policy. Since 1991, Qatar has pursued broader security interests, reducing its overdependence on Saudi protection, and opting for more diverse and reliable security arrangements instead.[30] Over time, Qatar balanced tensions between Saudi Arabia and Iran, developing new strategic alliances that strengthened its sovereignty and autonomy.[31] Additionally, in 1992, Qatar signed a formal Defence Cooperation Agreement with the United States (U.S.), which established the American security guarantee.[32] This was followed by the construction of the Al Udeid Air Base in 1996, which grew to become the largest American air base in the Middle East.[33] Hosting the U.S. military base signalled Qatar's closer strategic alignment with the U.S. as the foremost global superpower in the twenty-first century and served as a deterrent against potential threats from regional powers.[34] It thus formed a key pillar of the state's security strategy, reducing its reliance on traditional Gulf partners and enabling it to engage more actively in broader Middle Eastern security dialogues.

Qatar's independent foreign policy is encapsulated by the fact that it maintains relations and channels of communication with a wide range of states and organizations that appear diametrically opposed. For instance, prior to the Arab Spring, Qatar served as a bridge between the two regional camps of Iran and Syria on one side and Saudi Arabia on the other within the 'Arab Cold War'.[35] This stance is also apparent in its hosting in Doha of controversial individuals and groups, such as Islamic scholar Yusuf Al-Qaradawi, Egyptian President Mohamed Morsi, Hamas, several Taliban leaders, and heads of their political offices.[36] Qatar has grown in its ambitions and regional role, transitioning from a stance of 'strategic followership' to more active 'leadership', which has caused tensions with the traditional powers in the region, such as Saudi Arabia, Iran, Syria, and Egypt.[37]

Maintaining an independent stance and cultivating diverse diplomatic relationships—hallmarks of Qatari foreign policy since the 1990s—was central to the emergence of Qatar as a mediator in conflict-affected and crisis zones. Qatar's diplomatic strategy evolved gradually, with mediation becoming a key pillar of its foreign policy approach, which emphasizes dialogue and peaceful conflict resolution.[38] By acting as a third party in brokering peace deals, Qatar bolstered its diplomatic credibility and global standing, and established a distinctive role in promoting regional stability.[39] The chapter now turns to consider Qatar's emergence as a mediator, tracing its rise from the earliest episodes of regional diplomacy to the heights of Qatar's global mediation efforts in the 2020s.

Early Mediation Efforts

Qatar's emergence as a mediator in regional disputes dates back to the mid-1990s, when it first took on a substantive diplomatic role in resolving international conflict. A much earlier (though largely symbolic) gesture of support for peace efforts occurred during the 1962 Evian Accords negotiations between Algeria and France. At that time, the Emir of Qatar, Sheikh Ahmad bin Ali Al Thani, hosted the Algerian delegation at his residence in Geneva.[40]

Whilst Qatar's mediation efforts were comparatively limited during the 1990s, this era laid the foundation for its expanding influence in global peacemaking moving forward. The first contemporary episode arose in 1995, in the dispute between Eritrea and Yemen regarding claims to sovereignty over the Hanish Islands.[41] That dispute boiled over into a brief military confrontation, resulting in hundreds of casualties and the raising of geopolitical tensions in the Red Sea.[42] In response, Qatari Foreign Minister Sheikh Hamad bin Jassim Al Thani was involved in mediation, brokering direct negotiations and wider consultations between Eritrea and Yemen.[43] Ultimately, Qatari mediation efforts succeeded and led to the resolution of the dispute through the establishment of an arbitration agreement. In 1998, the Permanent Court of Arbitration in The Hague ruled in favour of Yemen, granting it sovereignty over the Hanish Islands—a decision that was respected by Eritrea.[44]

The timing of the Hanish Islands dispute was notable in that Qatar's mediation came just months after Sheikh Hamad bin Khalifa Al Thani became the Emir of Qatar on 27 June 1995. As one Qatari diplomat explained, 'prior to 1995, there were efforts, but they were scattered. The genuine strategic orientation towards mediation began that year and has continued to this day'.[45] Under Emir Hamad's rule, the direction of foreign policy changed to be more open and outward-looking. This reflected a departure from the more insular and domestic-focused strategy adopted by Emir Sheikh Khalifa bin Hamad Al Thani. Qatar thus established its reputation as an emerging third party capable of mediating complex disputes. It also reinforced belief within the state's leadership under Sheikh Hamad in the virtues of a foreign policy focused on conflict resolution and diplomatic engagement.[46] Moreover, the resolution of the dispute was crucial for maintaining stability in Red Sea oil shipping routes that are vital to the Gulf States.[47]

A year later, in 1999, Qatar brokered another agreement aimed at restoring diplomatic ties between Sudan and Eritrea.[48] In 1994, Eritrea severed diplomatic relations with Sudan, with the two countries issuing mutual accusations of supporting rebel groups within their borders. This arose within the context of a wider struggle for regional power in the 1990s, with both Eritrea and Sudan competing for influence across the Horn of Africa.[49] In 1998, Qatar entered as a mediator between the two African nations. These efforts culminated in a May 1999 summit meeting in Doha between Presidents Omar Al-Bashir and Isaias Afwerki, during which a six-point agreement was signed, leading to the resumption of diplomatic relations.[50] Qatar's successful mediation of the Sudan–Eritrea conflict laid the groundwork for subsequent peace efforts in various regions, including its prominence in the Darfur peace talks from 2008.

Notably, Qatar's first steps into the conflict mediation arena took place amidst the proliferation of comprehensive peace agreements in the early 1990s, following the fall of the Soviet Union and the birth of the United Nations (UN) peacebuilding framework. This period saw landmark deals, including the Oslo Accords in Israel–Palestine (1993), the Dayton Accords in Bosnia (1995), the fragile Arusha Accords in Rwanda (1993), the Paris Peace Agreements on Cambodia (1991), the Chapultepec Peace Accords in El Salvador (1992), the Guatemala Peace Accords (1996), the Good Friday Agreement in Northern Ireland (1998), and many others across the world, which marked the peak of international mediation efforts since 1945.[51] Qatari mediation thus emerged at a time when the peace industry was flourishing. As such, whilst these early episodes were significant in Qatar's transformation into a regional peace broker, they did not garner much global attention. Nevertheless, over time, this groundwork facilitated the state's growing role as a distinct and high-profile mediator in response to regional crises in the Middle East during the new millennium.[52]

Qatar's Rise to Prominence in Mediation between 2006 and 2010

In the early 2000s, Qatar took further steps to assert itself as a conflict mediator and move towards the forefront of global politics. The shift from the periphery was marked by the assumption of leadership and chairmanship roles at the regional and international levels, including the organization of the Islamic Conference in 2000 and 2003, the chairmanship of the G77 + China grouping at the UN in 2004, and gaining a two-year seat on the UN Security Council (UNSC) from 2006 to 2007.[53] Furthermore, in 2009, Qatar hosted the 21st Arab League Summit in Doha, later assuming the League's leadership. Collectively, these multilateral initiatives 'provided a regional and international platform for the assertion of Qatar's mediation ambitions and foreign policy ideals'.[54]

These leadership roles, particularly the term on the UNSC, came at a time when the Arab region was highly securitized following the events of 11 September 2001 and fraught with conflicts, thereby making the need for a neutral mediator of heightened importance. Accordingly, Qatar's rise as a new actor in international politics gained prominence, assuming multiple roles in conflict mediation, humanitarian aid, early recovery, and post-conflict reconstruction.[55] For instance, between 2006 and 2010, the country undertook its most high-profile mediation files, including those of Yemen, Lebanon, and Darfur, which earned it the reputation of the 'non-stop mediator'.[56]

By June 2007 and February 2008, His Highness Emir Sheikh Hamad bin Khalifa Al Thani and diplomats from the Ministry of Foreign Affairs succeeded in mediating and reaching a joint ceasefire agreement between the Houthis and Ali Abdullah Saleh, which was then followed by a peace agreement signed in Doha.[57] That agreement initially brought hope for peace in Yemen as it outlined cessation of military operations, the release of prisoners, the disarmament of Houthi forces, the extension of state authority in conflict-affected areas, and a Qatari-funded reconstruction and compensation initiative for those affected by the war.[58] However, the agreement began to unravel amidst deep-seated mistrust, divergent interpretations of key provisions, and weak mechanisms for sustained dialogue between the parties. As progress stalled, hostilities resumed, and regional tensions grew, Qatar withdrew from the mediation process, highlighting the complexities of peacemaking in Yemen's fragmented political landscape.[59]

In parallel to its efforts in Yemen, Qatar closely monitored the Lebanese political crisis of May 2008, which nearly resulted in a civil war between Hezbollah and the government of Prime Minister Fouad Siniora. Qatar hosted the negotiations between the Lebanese parties and successfully brokered the Doha Peace Agreement on 21 May 2008, defusing the political feud and restoring stability to the country.[60]

In Darfur, Qatar launched a formal mediation process in 2008, supported by the Arab League, African Union, and UN. Qatar also hosted representatives from Omar Al-Bashir's government, various rebel groups from Darfur, and civil society members, successfully reaching a series of framework and ceasefire agreements, ultimately brokering the Doha Document for Peace in Darfur (DDPD) in 2011.[61]

These three instances of proactive diplomacy—Yemen, Lebanon, and Darfur—facilitated Qatar's 'rise to prominence as a heavyweight power in the Middle East and a neutral mediator'.[62] Qatar's meteoric ascent and success as a mediator in this period can be attributed to the personal involvement of the Emir along with senior Qatari officials, the ripeness of the conflict and feasibility of negotiations, as well as the strategic use of financial inducement. The means through which this was achieved are explored in greater detail in the case-study chapters, particularly on Lebanon and Darfur. In brief, these regional crises allowed Qatar to showcase its diplomatic skills, project an image of neutrality, and enhance its reputation as a reliable peace broker in the Arab region.

Qatari Mediation amidst the Arab Spring and the Gulf Crisis

The outbreak of the Arab Spring in late 2010 was a tumultuous set of events that had a profound impact on Qatari mediation.[63] During this period, Qatar proactively supported the Arab public's aspiration for fundamental socioeconomic and political change. Qatar's role in setting the tone for regional politics became more pronounced, as it actively mobilized support for the uprisings and shaped the narrative of the unfolding Arab Spring through its Al Jazeera media network. For instance, during the 2011 Syrian uprisings, Qatar was amongst the first Arab states to break its ties with the Assad regime, to advocate for suspension of the Syrian membership from the Arab League,[64] and to provide an estimated USD 3 billion in arms and training to Syrian revolutionary forces.[65] Additionally, Qatar was amongst the most influential actors supporting the international community's decision to implement the doctrine of the Responsibility to Protect in support of the uprising in Libya.[66]

Qatar's neutrality and non-intervention policy were challenged by major regional events, leading to a significant shift in its foreign policy.[67] In contrast to the neutrality that enabled its rise as a mediator in the 2000s, Qatar increasingly adopted a proactive and interventionist approach to regional conflict response.[68] Its open support for opposition movements, especially in Syria and Libya, meant that it was no longer perceived as neutral in relation to regional conflicts.[69] Meanwhile, Qatar's participation in the Saudi-led Peninsula Shield Force intervention in Bahrain in 2011 contrasted with the assertive, unilateral approach that defined several of Qatar's other Arab Spring policies.[70] The post-Arab Spring phase thus limited its role as a mediator, curbing the momentum of its rise to the forefront of global politics.[71] As the peaceful demonstrations of the early Arab Spring evolved into deeply polarized proxy civil wars, scepticism and division amongst various conflict parties grew significantly towards competing Gulf States.[72] Consequently, a complex web of alliances further complicated the resolution of the emergent conflicts, with growing regional polarization between rival camps backed by Qatar on the one side, and Saudi Arabia and the UAE on the other.[73]

This state of affairs formed the roots of the Gulf Crisis, which started as a diplomatic rift in 2014, and sharply escalated into a land, air, and sea blockade of Qatar imposed by Saudi Arabia, the UAE, Bahrain, and Egypt (known as the Quartet) in June 2017.[74] The initial 2014 crisis stemmed from multiple factors, in particular Qatar's support for political Islam, which was vehemently opposed by Saudi Arabia and the UAE due to the threat that democratically elected Islamism posed to their authoritarian legitimacy.[75] The Gulf Crisis (2017–21) unfolded on a much larger scale and posed an unparalleled existential threat to Qatar. Yet, rather than bow to external pressure, Qatar responded to the regional blockade by contesting its status in international law, such as through a case at the International Civil Aviation Organization—a move that was challenged by the Quartet but ultimately allowed by the International Court of Justice.[76] Additionally, Qatar enhanced its self-reliance capacities through a national resilience strategy,[77] strengthening major security alliances, particularly with Türkiye in relation to defence cooperation and investment.[78] As a result, Qatar increased domestic support for its leadership, despite the Quartet's attempts to sow divisions between the people and the government.[79] This national unity and the leadership's crisis response enabled Qatar to swiftly implement adaptive measures and strengthen strategic partnerships, bolstering national resilience in the face of geopolitical pressure.

In the midst of the Arab Spring, some observers suggested that Qatar's mediation efforts had been permanently curtailed. It was questioned whether an inward shift 'may herald the end of Qatar's high-profile interventions and temper its strong drive to mediate conflicts in the Middle East'.[80] Given this, the subsequent Gulf Crisis only strengthened the narrative that Qatari mediation may have been halted altogether. Moreover, from mid-2017, Qatar shifted from its role in mediating conflicts to needing external mediation to resolve its dispute with regional neighbours.[81] Although this changing regional landscape led to a decline in Qatar's high-profile initiatives, the country's leadership did not abandon its foreign policy ambitions. Instead, recognizing the strategic impact of the earlier efforts, it opted for 'a quieter, lower-key approach to mediation'.[82]

Qatar continued to leverage the skills, resources, and expertise it had acquired from previous successful engagements in a range of conflicts and crises. It sustained its role as a diplomatic provider of good offices, facilitating dialogue and supporting negotiated settlements, most notably the DDPD in 2011. In a lesser-noted mediation effort, on 23 November 2015, the Tuareg and Tebu tribes signed a reconciliation agreement in Doha, under the auspices of His Highness the Emir Sheikh Tamim bin Hamad Al Thani, to end fighting in Ubari, south-western Libya. In this case, Qatar's mediation efforts were endorsed by both tribes and included a permanent ceasefire, the return of displaced residents, the reopening of public roads, and the cessation of armed conflict.[83]

Likewise, around that time, Qatar's skill in negotiating complex deals was called upon in Syria, even despite its role in supporting Syrian revolutionaries. In 2017, Qatar and Iran brokered an agreement to evacuate civilians from four besieged Syrian towns: Foua, Kafriya, Madaya, and Zabadani; Qatar facilitated the evacuation from rebel-held Madaya and Zabadani, whilst Iran oversaw the evacuation from government-held Foua and Kafriya. This deal allowed around 7,350 civilians to be safely relocated and facilitated the delivery of humanitarian aid.[84] Qatar was also involved in the Astana Process, chiefly mediated by Russia and Türkiye, by attending talks in Lausanne in October 2016, and later complementing negotiations with the Doha Process in March 2021.[85] It continued supporting peace talks even in this geopolitically charged context.

Importantly, this period of Qatari mediation laid the foundations for its later diplomatic successes in the 2020s. At the institutional level, Qatar consolidated its capacities in 2016 through the establishment of the Office of the Special Envoy for Counterterrorism and Mediation in Conflict Resolution. The Special Envoy gained responsibility for multiple mediation portfolios, in particular Afghanistan and Darfur. This was a key organizational development through which Qatar 'expanded the foreign policy apparatus to enable more intensive handling of individual conflicts'.[86]

Notably, Qatar accepted the requests to host the Hamas Political Bureau in 2012 and the Taliban Political Commission in 2013, both of which were established in coordination with the U.S. These moves solidified the role of Doha as a diplomatic convening space, opening opportunities for subsequent Qatari mediation. Qatar also brokered the Fatah–Hamas Doha Agreement in 2012 and the 2014 ceasefire in the Gaza Strip. It also immediately enabled Qatar to enter the Afghan peace process as a facilitator and broker of prisoner and hostage releases. For instance, Qatar secured the release of U.S. Sergeant Bowe Bergdahl in exchange for five Taliban leaders detained in Guantanamo Bay in 2014, as well as the release of four Tajik soldiers in June 2015, who had been captured by the Taliban.[87] Qatar's collaboration with international actors in these cases has been interpreted as a sign of the increasing institutionalization of its mediation practices. This approach was explained by a Qatari diplomat:

> Whilst our approach to mediation can be described as 'Qatari', it is grounded in established international legal and scientific frameworks. Qatar has matured in this field. It has always strived to make mediation part of an institutional system rather than an individual or ad hoc process. Qatar does not act as a solo mediator; it works through international organizations and regional blocs, which contributes to generating international legitimacy and effective operational mechanisms.[88]

The diplomatic actions in Afghanistan and the Gaza Strip were a highly formative experience. Through long-term, quiet facilitation, Qatar gained vital experience of multi-party mediation in two of the most high-profile contemporary conflicts while fostering relationships with a wide range of states and international players. The lower-profile engagements in the post-Arab Spring era thus enabled a consolidation and professionalization of Qatar's mediation infrastructure, supporting its re-emergence as a key global mediator.

Qatar's Post-2020 Re-emergence as a Mediator

Qatar's return to the mediation arena was made apparent to a global audience with the signing of the Doha Agreement between the

U.S. and the Taliban in February 2020, which was the result of years of facilitation by Qatar and other third parties. Following this agreement, Qatar repositioned itself as a go-to mediator capable of operating in a wide range of conflict zones and political crises.[89] This was a remarkable turnaround given the more low-key approach adopted just a few years earlier in response to the restrictions of the post-Arab Spring and Gulf Crisis environment. By the early 2020s, the scope and visibility of its already proactive third-party diplomacy in the 2000s had evolved into far more central and recognized achievements.

The post-2020 efforts included the 2021 Somalia–Kenya border agreement, the 2022 Chad transitional agreement, the 2022 Libyan political proposal, and the 2025 reconciliation talks between Rwanda and the Democratic Republic of Congo. Furthermore, Qatar brokered the release of Ukrainian children through the facilitation of mediation efforts between Ukraine and Russia in 2023 and May 2024.[90] Additionally, Qatar successfully facilitated a high-profile prisoner exchange between the U.S. and Iran in 2023. This negotiation spanned several months, culminating in the mutual release of five prisoners from each side, and involved the unfreezing and transfer of USD 6 billion in Iranian assets to banks in Qatar and Switzerland.[91] Although it was received critically in various international circles, particularly within the U.S., this agreement marked another strategic diplomatic step in Qatar's mediation track record. Furthermore, in June 2023, Qatar arranged a secret meeting where it hosted officials from both the U.S. and Venezuela for negotiations between the two countries,[92] leading to a mutual prisoner release agreement in December 2023.

Qatar's renewed prominence as a mediator was markedly on display when it emerged as a key broker between Israel and Hamas in the 7 October War that erupted in Gaza in late 2023. In the midst of the devastating war, Qatar alongside Egypt—and, at times, the U.S.—worked to secure the exchanges of captives on both sides and enable the flow of humanitarian assistance. These multi-party mediation efforts yielded a temporary seven-day truce in November 2023 and a more comprehensive ceasefire in January 2025. It was achieved by building upon Qatar's longstanding diplomatic and humanitarian involvement in Palestine and underscored its growing stature as a trusted facilitator capable of handling high-stakes negotiations.[93]

This series of mediation episodes reflects Qatar's renewed emphasis on conflict mediation, which lies at the centre of its foreign policy. In this post-2020 phase, its diplomatic efforts evolved, rising to prominence in many regions globally and increasingly in high-profile disputes at the heart of geopolitics.

Conclusion

Qatar's rise in conflict mediation—from the periphery in small-scale regional disputes to the centre stage in Afghanistan and Gaza—was nothing short of turbulent. Its transition to global mediator was a two-pronged process. First, the vast financial resources and forward-looking leadership, coupled with internal stability, shaped the development trajectory of modern Qatar, turning it from a small pearl-trading country to a modern state boasting an advanced education system, state-of-the-art health infrastructure, diverse cultural and sports facilities, and a dynamic workforce. As a modern state, facilitated by a foreign policy that sought to place the country outside the orbit of the traditional powers of the Gulf, Qatar's leadership forged key alliances and brokered significant peace agreements in Yemen, Lebanon, and Darfur, garnering international attention.

These early successes in resolving regional disputes laid the groundwork for Qatar's expanding role in mediation and peacemaking. Despite setbacks during the Arab Spring and Gulf Crisis, Qatar continued engaging in crucial behind-the-scenes efforts and supporting various peace initiatives. Qatar then re-emerged to the fore by facilitating the U.S.–Taliban Agreement in 2020 and mediating between Israel and Hamas amidst the 2023 escalation, cementing its status as a leading mediator in protracted and geopolitically sensitive conflicts. This trajectory, marked by both achievements and challenges, has solidified Qatar's position in global diplomacy and conflict mediation.

3

CONCEPTUALIZING QATARI MEDIATION

Qatari mediation has been subject to increasing levels of academic and policy attention, yet its mediation approach remains theoretically under-explored. Rather than be reducible to a single explanatory model, Qatari mediation can be analyzed through a wide range of theoretical lenses.[1] This chapter critically engages with existing literature on Qatari mediation, situating it within broader debates in international relations, conflict resolution and mediation research, and recent scholarship on non-traditional actors in peacemaking. It begins by synthesizing several leading theoretical lenses applied to the rise of Qatar in conflict mediation—in particular, interpreting its motivations and interests through realist, constructivist, and liberal lenses, and focusing on the use of leverage, soft power, and small-state mediation theory. It then outlines the backdrop against which Qatari mediation is evolving, shedding light on the changing landscape of peacemaking, including 'emerging' Global South actors and the growing role of Gulf States in mediation. In so doing, the chapter advances an integrated conceptual framework for understanding Qatari mediation and charts novel directions for future research.

Conventional Framings of Qatari Mediation

Qatar's growing role in conflict mediation has been extensively analyzed through the lenses of competing schools of international relations theory. Realist explanations of individual mediators tend to emphasize how states pursue their strategic interests through the tool of conflict mediation, particularly through the power-based mediation model, which was most notable during the Cold War period.[2] Some of the major criticisms of the realist approach to conflict mediation arose from its focus on the short-term settlement of disputes and lack of tools to address deeper issues, such as identity, state failure, and economic underdevelopment—often the basis of many modern conflicts.[3] Nevertheless, and amidst the geopolitical shifts of the twenty-first century, the realist and neorealist lenses remain useful in analyzing the mediation and peacemaking efforts of rising states like China or Brazil.[4] Constructivist theories, by contrast, explain states' involvement in mediation in terms of their internal social constructs, identities, beliefs, and ideas. For instance, Norway's commitment to peacemaking has been analyzed as central to its national identity formation.[5] Sweden offers another example of how a state was able to change its foreign policy identity, adjusting to a multi-polar post-Cold War world through its role as a mediator and norm entrepreneur.[6] Liberalism, meanwhile, holds that states engage in mediation out of a commitment to cooperation through global institutions, with the aim of tackling the shared global challenges of conflict and crisis.[7] Amongst many other schools of thought surrounding international relations, as well as the nuances within each school, the realist, constructivist, and liberal strands shed light on the main theoretical lenses that have framed existing research on Qatari mediation.

The realist lens views Qatar's engagement in conflict mediation as being primarily motivated by its strategic interests. Qatari mediation has thus been analyzed in terms of pursuing economic interests through trade, investments, and food security,[8] achieving national security in a turbulent region beset with conflict risks, or cultivating alliances and networks of influence across the world for its own strategic advantage.[9] Such strategic imperatives are all pertinent, with Qatar's involvement in high-stakes mediation explained as related to the need to remain economically competitive, establish security and trade partnerships, and maintain domestic political stability.[10]

In parallel, Qatari mediation has also been explained through a soft-power rationale, a concept embedded in both liberal and constructivist traditions. Soft power is defined as the ability to persuade and co-opt rather than coerce, relying on cultural appeal, political values, and foreign policies that are perceived as legitimate.[11] Much research has focused on Qatar (and Gulf States more broadly) through the lens of place branding, charting how the state utilizes a mixture of major sporting events, media channels, cultural initiatives, and other tools to bolster its international reputation. Qatari mediation has thus been analyzed in this paradigm as a tool of place branding and soft power.[12] For instance, it is held that a combination of soft power diplomacy and mediation enabled Qatar to become 'an innovative, dynamic actor with the capacity to mediate in the various conflicts in the region, and to project itself onto the world stage'.[13] Qatari officials have also reiterated their soft-power rationale, arguing that Qatar's rise as a global mediator was motivated by the adoption of a resilient policy based on soft power, international law, positive neutrality, and international reputation.[14]

Constructivist theory has emphasized conflict mediation as a practice embodying Qatar's national identity, cultural and religious values, and normative ethics.[15] Additionally, Qatari mediation has been analyzed as a normative expression of the state's constitutionally enshrined commitment to global peace and security.[16] Mediation as a practice is deeply rooted in Arab culture and related to both Islamic teachings and tribal customs. As such, Qatari mediation embraces this heritage as a reflection of its own culture and society.[17] Qatari leaders often express a self-understanding that engagement in mediation is out of moral, civic, and religious duties.[18] However, analyses of Qatari mediation have often overlooked the normative and ethical dimensions that also play a significant role.[19]

Whilst leading to sustained reflection on Qatar's motivations and interests in mediation, the overemphasis on international relations theoretical frameworks has somewhat limited the collective understanding of Qatari mediation. This has produced more research on the interests and ideas driving Qatari mediation, with much less analytical attention paid to concrete mediation practices and patterns embedded in Qatari cultural traditions.

Another key theoretical lens applied within research on Qatari mediation—one which is rooted in international relations theory but drawing more on conflict resolution perspectives—is the role of small states in conflict mediation, which will be explored in the following section.

Small-State Mediation

Qatari mediation has often been analyzed through the conceptual lenses of small-state theory. In the realm of international relations, nation-states have long been viewed through a hierarchical lens in which a state is classified as either small, middle, great, or super, based on its power and resources. In many scholarly works, Qatar is depicted as a small state by virtue of its diminutive geography—'the tiny peninsula of Qatar'—when it in fact has a land mass approximate to that of Lebanon, Jamaica, and Montenegro, whose supposedly diminutive geography is not similarly foregrounded as a trope in academic research.

Within international relations theory, it was long assumed that only great powers could serve as effective mediators in armed conflict. Great powers are distinguished in mediation by their power or leverage over conflict parties in an attempt to influence or control outcomes. In order to achieve their goals, great powers often control or influence peace processes in terms of mediation design, procedures, and content.[20] They employ a 'carrot and stick' approach, offering positive inducements like financial, military, and political support, and negative inducements such as political pressure, sanctions, military action, or diplomatic isolation.[21] Their substantial economic and military resources, along with their influence over global bodies such as the United Nations (UN) and the North Atlantic Treaty Organization, enable them to pressure states and non-state groups through sanctions or threats, including terrorist designations.[22] A notable example is the United States (U.S.) and its partners ending the Bosnian War (1992–95) through air strikes, sanctions, and political pressure on the conflict parties, leading to the Dayton Accords.[23]

The geopolitical shifts in the twenty-first century have had major impacts on the field of conflict mediation, including the rise of small states and middle powers in this process. Traditional mediators have, in part, driven this shift, often seeking out smaller states to engage in collaborative mediation efforts and share the burdens whilst benefiting from the comparative advantages they offer.[24] These new actors brought an increasingly sophisticated set of conflict management strategies, which made such actors more appealing to the conflict parties.[25] This marked a pendulum swing away from the more plural set of mediators in previous decades, such as non-governmental organizations and faith-based organizations, with states increasingly viewing mediation as their prerogative.[26] Qatari mediation since 2020 has been bolstered by this transformation of the mediation space, which widened to include a plural range of states whilst simultaneously narrowing to state-based mediation.

The acceptance of small states as mediators is often enabled by their perceived neutrality, non-interference, and 'no legacies of foreign excess'.[27] Additionally, small states can have a 'buffer effect' between great international and regional powers, as they tend to project neutrality in their interactions, pursuing sustainable, friendly, and equidistant relations with greater powers.[28] The lack of coercive power and resources can also boost the acceptability of small states by conflict parties. As Randa Slim puts it eloquently: 'For the powerful party, a small state can provide a face-saver to whom capitulations can be made without threatening the public-bargaining posture of the powerful party. For the weaker party, a smaller state can provide a sympathetic ally who can understand what it means to negotiate from weakness'.[29]

In contrast to the 'hard power' of much larger states, small states typically have no significant sources of leverage over conflict parties. Rather, small states tend to utilize facilitative or procedural strategies—sometimes described as 'pure' mediation—which emphasize neutrality and a hands-off approach. For example, Switzerland, lacking the military might of high-powered mediators, has extensively used its 'good offices' to provide space for negotiation, such as in the Sudan-Nuba Mountains mediation in 2002, Armenia–Türkiye talks in 2008–09, and the Syrian peace process in 2016.[30] These approaches aim to create a two-way communication channel or platform, improving the flow of information, and fostering a working level of trust and common understanding between the conflict parties.[31] Such strategies often produce more durable agreements with stronger buy-ins from conflict parties.[32] Moreover, by virtue of their stature and lack of hard power, small states tend to champion negotiated solutions over military intervention, thereby enhancing their perception as impartial and their credibility as mediators.[33]

Within this context, Qatari mediation offers an important hybrid case in that its sources of leverage in mediation, particularly its strategic use of its resources, entail that it does not fit the classic typology of a small-state mediator. Often classified as a small state, Qatar has been applying mediation approaches traditionally exercised by big powers. It is therefore important to analyse Qatar's leverage and utilization of resources in mediation and peacemaking.

Leveraging Peace

Qatari mediation has often been reductively described as focusing on short-term financial inducements to conflict parties in order to reach agreements. This has become a common trope in research that reduces Qatar's multifaceted conflict response to 'chequebook diplomacy', characterizing Qatar's leverage in mediation as rooted only in financial power.[34] Scholarly accounts from the early 2010s perceived this approach as 'business diplomacy', 'dollar diplomacy', and 'reward power'.[35] The dominant view of Qatar's approach as employing financial 'carrots' to incentivize peace deals[36] implies that Qatari mediation is often short-term in nature and unsustainable. Qatari mediation is often characterized as beset by structural limitations in terms of low capacity for agreement monitoring and implementation that compound these limitations in sustaining agreements.[37]

More recently, theories of transactional power have conceptualized Qatar's political clout and mediation as fundamentally built on its vast financial and oil resources. Although similar in many ways to other Gulf States, Qatar's rentier-state dynamics, its economic history, royal family politics, and strategic global positioning have led to a distinctive model of 'late rentierism', entrepreneurial state capitalism, and activist microstatism, where energy wealth continues to drive political stability, economic diversification, and international branding.[38] Advancing the existing literature on rentier state theory and developing an alternative theory of 'rented power', Galeeva's analysis of

Qatar's rise as a regional power further explores how the state projects its power through engagement with non-state actors, such as political Islamists, Gulf tribes, the media, and sports organizations, which allows it 'to rent the well-established influence' of those actors due to their 'transnational nature'.[39] Notably, its mediation initiatives—which involved strategic alliances with political Islamic movements and financial incentives, yet also positioned Doha as a neutral broker—are seen as 'the key to Qatar's scope of rented power'.[40]

Beyond Transactionalism—Qatar's Multifaceted Conflict Response

The 'checkbook diplomacy' and transactionalist critiques of Qatari mediation are analytically one-dimensional and therefore reductive. Qatari mediation is best grasped through long-term and in-depth empirical examination of its practice and evolution within real-world conflict contexts and through direct engagement with Qatari mediators. Understanding the modalities of Qatari mediation requires a multifaceted framework that identifies the use of leverage and the strategic linking of mediation with humanitarian and development assistance to conflict-affected societies through all phases of peacemaking.

Understanding the interplay between mediation, humanitarian action, and development in Qatar's foreign policy requires a long-term perspective. Much of the reductive characterization of Qatari mediation is based on research that generalizes from several high-profile conflicts in the 2000s—notably Yemen, Lebanon, and Darfur—failing to keep up with Qatar's re-emergence and growth as a global mediator in the 2020s. Qatar's role as a mediator has changed substantially over the past few decades, with the country possessing more institutionalized and professionalized capacities than in the 2000s. Compared to the 2000s, when Qatar was primarily a financial donor in humanitarian assistance, by the 2020s, it had evolved to become a multifaceted humanitarian actor[41] engaged in various forms of sophisticated conflict response, such as development cooperation, humanitarian diplomacy, and crisis management.[42] Following this, Qatar increasingly has far more tools in its repertoire to strategically link with mediation than mere financial inducements for short-term agreements.

Given this, there is a need for new theoretical frameworks to re-evaluate Qatar's early phases as a mediator and also to best understand the transformations it has undergone in recent years. One theoretical lens through which this book analyzes Qatari mediation is the integration of third-party roles with other forms of conflict response. It thus aligns with recent research that has explored this under-examined facet of Qatar's mediation practice.[43]

Non-Traditional Mediators

To better understand the evolving characteristics of Qatari mediation, it is necessary to place it within the broader category of non-traditional mediators—a growing cohort of Global South state-based mediators that increasingly challenge the dominance of Western-led models.

The rise of new mediators from the Global South has created a more pluralistic global landscape of conflict mediation. Countries such as Brazil, China, India, South Africa, Türkiye, and the Gulf States have increasingly taken active roles in mediating conflicts, challenging the traditional dominance of Western powers in this field. For instance, in 2023, China facilitated the landmark agreement between Saudi Arabia and Iran to restore diplomatic relations, and in 2024 played a significant role in mediating an intra-Palestinian reconciliation agreement.[44] Similarly, Türkiye has established 'a distinctive Islamic ethical approach to international mediation' and has been actively engaged in Somalia, Ethiopia, Libya, and the Russia–Ukraine agreement on grain exports through the Black Sea.[45] Furthermore, Russia and Türkiye co-brokered the Astana Process in Syria, providing an alternative platform for peace negotiations outside Western-led initiatives.[46]

This transformation is marked by a growing scepticism of mediation embedded in the Western liberal peace paradigm and the rise of Global South actors who advocate alternative approaches to conflict response.[47] Many countries across the Global South, including the Gulf monarchies, prioritize principles such as solidarity, cooperation, non-interference, and mutual support in their engagements.[48] Their peace efforts emphasize cultural and contextual sensitivities, and favour solutions that are nationally owned and led, rather than externally imposed programmes.[49] These actors also invest in establishing institutions outside traditional Western frameworks in order to enhance collaboration and provide less intrusive support (for example, the BRICS' New Development Bank and the Asian Infrastructure Investment Bank, which offer alternative financial platforms).[50] Within this evolving context, Qatar contributes to the diversification of peacebuilding activities by integrating these emerging principles into its own conflict response strategies. Furthermore, Qatar is actively engaging in mediation efforts that leverage its regional influence, cultural ties, and nuanced understanding of local dynamics, thereby positioning itself as a significant actor within this rapidly changing landscape.

The 'non-traditional mediator' theoretical lens offers a new perspective through which small-state mediation could be understood. In general terms, the dominant, Western-centric frameworks in peacemaking and peacebuilding overlook the diverse, non-Western approaches that rose to prominence on the global stage since the 2010s. Non-Western actors like Gulf States employ distinct strategies and priorities, often emphasizing unilateral, development-focused, and locally driven methods, that challenge the conventional liberal peacebuilding approach. This calls for more nuanced research to fully understand these alternative models and their implications in a shifting multipolar world.[51] With its distinct cultural conception of peace and nuanced understanding of conflicts, Qatar has operationalized a multifaceted approach to mediation that balances between humanitarian aid, diplomacy, dialogue, and development. By leading intricate and sensitive mediation processes, Qatar exhibits characteristics typical of high- or middle-powered mediators, challenging those typologies of small-state mediation advanced by international relations schools.

Qatar's re-emergence as a mediator in the post-2020 period was thus catalyzed by its occurrence in a historically ripe moment marked by accelerated shifts towards multipolarity and an increasingly uncertain global landscape of peacemaking. Qatari mediation has, to many observers, become emblematic of these wider transformations that have broadened the spectrum of credible peacemakers beyond traditional Western powers. For instance, Pierre Hazan, referring to the

Hamas–Israel ceasefire in November 2023, writes that 'Qatar's mediation is a crystal clear example of the end of Western hegemony over the international system'.[52] Moreover, 'the struggle of traditional mediators to adapt to the complexities of an increasingly multipolar, interconnected, and networked world'[53] have also set the stage for the greater prominence of Gulf States as mediators.

Gulf States as Mediators

The evolution of Qatari mediation is best understood by situating it within the broader landscape of regional mediation practices across the Gulf. Over recent decades, several Gulf States have played increasingly prominent roles in conflict mediation, both regionally and globally. Whilst their approaches vary, these states have emerged as distinct and influential actors in contemporary diplomacy, often combining facilitation, brokerage, and soft-power strategies with broader foreign policy objectives.

Oman has been evocatively referred to as an 'interlocutor state' or the 'Switzerland of the Middle East', aiming to bridge East and West. The most prominent file mediated by Oman was its facilitation of secret talks between the U.S. and Iran that led to the nuclear deal in 2015.[54] In 2025, Oman again emerged as the principal mediator in renewed indirect negotiations between the two nations, as both sides sought to address Iran's advancing nuclear program amidst regional tensions and threats of military action.[55] Likewise, Kuwait was involved in mediation attempts to settle the 2014 diplomatic rift and the 2017–21 Gulf Crisis. Whilst it lacked traditional leverage,[56] its positive engagement showed how small states can achieve balance in regional affairs without having to pick sides or 'winners'.[57] Less prominent in the 2010s and 2020s, Bahrain's mediation involvement included the Kosovo process (1999), where it mediated through the UN, and it's support for the post-intervention processes in Iraq (2004) and Afghanistan (2006, 2011).[58] The United Arab Emirates (UAE), meanwhile, has been referred to as a 'consensus builder'[59] in the rapprochement between Ethiopia and Eritrea in 2018. Additionally, in 2023, it attempted to mediate the decades-long hostilities between India and Pakistan, and also facilitated prisoner-of-war exchanges between Russia and Ukraine in 2024.[60] Furthermore, the transformation of Saudi Arabia's regional profile in the early 2020s involved a major role for mediation as a tool of foreign policy, notably hosting the Jeddah talks aimed at resolving the 2023–25 war in Sudan, as well as meetings in February 2025 between U.S. and Russian officials regarding the Ukraine war.[61]

It should be qualified that these peacemaking roles have come alongside interventionist roles in conflict. In particular, the Saudi–UAE coalition drew much international condemnation for pursuing the war in Yemen from 2015.[62] More recently, whilst Saudi Arabia has brokered peace talks in Sudan since 2023, the UAE has drawn international scrutiny for its material support to Sudan's Rapid Support Forces,[63] which has significantly fueled the war.[64] Similarly, Qatar played a proactive role in support of rebel forces in Syria and Libya during the Arab Spring.[65] These forms of military involvement have drawn controversy around the Gulf States, which have played complex roles in contemporary conflict response—serving as influential brokers of peace agreements whilst also asserting greater military and economic power.

As their mediation services become more commonly sought after—as facilitators, hosts of negotiations, messengers, trust-building experts, and donors—the Gulf States occupy an important position as new and distinctive actors in the conflict mediation arena. Their growing involvement in the field has attracted heightened scholarly interest. Various accounts explore individual approaches of countries in the Gulf Cooperation Council to mediation (along with the challenges they face and their potential) that should be recognized in contemporary peacemaking and peacebuilding.[66] The engagement by Gulf States in mediation should also be understood in relation to a wider research agenda examining their multiple roles in humanitarian action and development assistance, in which they have evolved as major bilateral donors and multilateral actors.[67]

Emphasis has also been placed on the shared cultural attributes of the Gulf States as a commonality across their mediation approaches and styles. One such cultural dimension is that Gulf States' mediation is framed within wider Arab peacemaking approaches (such as *sulh*) and is generally influenced by Islamic principles that emphasize justice, peace, and the restoration of social harmony.[68] Whilst *sulh* is traditionally used in resolving disputes at community and tribal levels, its underlying values inform the mediation styles of Gulf States in international conflicts. Another aspect specific to the Gulf is the culturally rooted concept of the *majlis*, which involves playing a critical role in resolving disputes between tribes and addressing sensitive issues related to religion, trade, resources, and security.[69] Through the integration of such culturally significant practices into the mediation efforts, the Gulf States advance and shape new perceptions about the effectiveness of culturally rooted methods in conflict resolution.[70]

A closer examination of individual Gulf States reveals diversified mediation practices that reflect each country's distinct capacity, economic leverage, and evolving strategic priorities. For instance, one point of divergence is that whilst some Gulf States are solely focused on local and regional conflicts, others are more internationally oriented and multilateral in their approach, notably Qatar and the UAE.[71] Further comparison has revealed differences in motivation for mediation between these two nations, with religious duty and Arab nationalism, respectively, acting as drivers of state engagement.[72] The systematic and in-depth analysis of Qatari mediation presented in this book aims to contribute substantively towards this emerging research agenda that explores the changing practices of Gulf State mediation in an evolving global landscape.

In short, whilst each Gulf actor exhibits idiosyncratic understandings of conflict mediation, there are also unifying traits that mark Gulf mediation as a distinctive set of practices. The Gulf States' approach to mediation has proven to be unique in its ability to leverage resources, bridge gaps, and remain flexible to address fast-changing conflict contexts. Moreover, Gulf States have strategically integrated mediation into their foreign policy doctrines in response to various external pressures, regional challenges, and as a way to gain an increasingly influential role in the international community. Nonetheless, there has been variation in how the six Gulf States approach or undertake mediation, with Qatar's mediation efforts becoming the most prominent internationally.

Conclusion

Over the past few decades, Qatar's role in mediation has transformed from largely reactive or ad hoc diplomacy to strategic and multifaceted conflict mediation. This evolution of its mediation profile poses a methodological and theoretical challenge to existing analytical frameworks. This chapter has critically evaluated the mainstream theoretical frameworks, framing much of the research on Qatari mediation, whilst, more importantly, setting out the novel and innovative research contributions of this book.

Realist and constructivist theoretical frameworks shed valuable light on the role of small states in conflict mediation, yet they fail to capture the significant characteristics of Qatari mediation and the complexity of its engagement in conflict contexts in the long run. Described as a 'small state', Qatar boasts political, diplomatic, cultural, structural, and financial capacities that have rendered its conflict-mediation approach into one that is integrative and highly in demand by global powers, small states, or non-state armed groups alike. Earning the titles of the 'go-to mediator' and the 'high-stakes mediator' has been the outcome of continuous learning, resilience, and adaptation to rapidly changing contexts. Consequently, these variables render the Qatari mediation profile a hybrid case that does not align with established international relations theoretical frameworks.

This chapter also contextualizes the contribution of this book towards debunking the prevalent assumption of Qatar's mediation as merely 'chequebook diplomacy' or 'rented power'. Through a comparative and diachronic analysis of Qatari mediation, this book demonstrates that Qatar's conflict response has become more integrative, to now include mediation, humanitarian aid, and post-conflict reconstruction. This marks a shift from the established view of Qatari mediation being tied to short-term engagement or of financially incentivizing conflict parties. Rather, Qatar is now seen as engaging in more sustained, long-term diplomatic initiatives, focusing on deeper and more strategic forms of conflict resolution and relationship building. Within the context of a rapidly changing mediation landscape, Qatar, along with other Gulf States, is spearheading the practical and theoretical shifts in the field of conflict mediation and peacemaking at large. Through an analysis of Qatari mediation in different cases in the following chapters, this book also significantly contributes to the theoretical debate on the state of art in the Global South peacemaking.

4

STEPPING BACK FROM THE BRINK

LEBANON'S 2008 DOHA AGREEMENT

In May 2008, Lebanon faced a crisis that placed the country at risk of a renewed civil war. The alarming political situation arose following the 2005 Cedar Revolution, the consequent Syrian withdrawal from Lebanon, and the July War with Israel in 2006. This period in contemporary Lebanese history was extremely volatile, considered as serious a threat to stability in Lebanon as the 1958 crisis and the events that led to the outbreak of the civil war in 1975.[1] With no president, and the country divided along deep political and sectarian lines, tensions reached a boiling point. Whilst agreements to overcome Lebanon's fractious political crises had until then been brokered by powers such as France, Saudi Arabia, Syria, and the United States (U.S.), the 2008 crisis saw Qatar enter the fold as a mediator.

Following proactive regional diplomacy and a week of intense talks in Doha, the Lebanese factions signed the 2008 Doha Agreement, which defused tensions and laid out a new political framework. This chapter tells the story of how Qatar, as a small yet ambitious Gulf State, emerged as a mediator in Lebanon and analyzes the 2008 Doha Agreement, which stands out as one of the most significant episodes of Qatari mediation to date. The analysis in this chapter is also based on extensive interviews with politicians who were either directly involved in the negotiations or the signing of the agreement, as well as those who were active in the political arena at the time and were in close contact with key participants throughout the entire process.

Historical Background on Lebanon

The Lebanese political landscape is complex and deeply fragmented, characterized by its consociational system of governance that identifies the Lebanese populace along sectarian lines. Lebanon's political system, which has been rooted in the principles of proportional confessional representation, dates back to the government of the Mutasarrifiyya of Mount Lebanon under Ottoman rule in 1861. This system, established in the administrative council of the Mutasarrifiyya period (1861–1918) and the 1926 constitution, distributes political power along sectarian lines.[2] Article 95 of the Lebanese Constitution (1926) stipulates that public sector employment and cabinet positions should be proportionally distributed amongst the sects.[3] Another critical turning point in the institutionalization of the sectarian power-sharing system was the 1943 National Pact, an unwritten agreement that laid the foundations of the confessional structure in Lebanese politics. It established a sectarian allocation of the highest offices of the state: the presidency to a Maronite Christian, the premiership to a Sunni Muslim, and the parliamentary speakership to a Shi'a Muslim. This arrangement was intended to be a compromise to balance communal interests in the newly independent state.[4]

Lebanon's confessional political system has perpetuated societal divisions and resulted in recurrent periods of instability and conflict. The most prominent of these conflicts was the 1975–90 Lebanese Civil War, which unfolded largely along sectarian lines. In response, the 1989 Taif Agreement was formulated to end hostilities and introduce political reforms. The agreement succeeded in halting the fighting, and called for the disarmament of militias and the withdrawal of foreign forces. It also explicitly identified the abolition of political sectarianism as a 'fundamental national objective', to be achieved through a phased plan. However, its objective remains unrealized, leaving the political landscape fragmented by confessionalism and the country vulnerable to renewed unrest.[5] This legacy set the stage for the 2008 crisis, which, like other post-war political deadlocks, revolved around contestation over the terms and balance of this sectarian power-sharing.

The Roots of the 2008 Crisis

The immediate root causes of the 2008 crisis can be traced back to several significant political events. The assassination of former Prime Minister Rafic Al Hariri on 14 February 2005 triggered the Cedar Revolution, resulting in the withdrawal of Syrian troops from Lebanon in April 2005. This withdrawal exposed unresolved divisions along sectarian lines and power struggles amongst wartime factions, intensifying political tensions in Lebanon.[6] Thereafter, in July 2006, tensions on the Lebanon–Israel border dramatically escalated into a highly destructive war.[7] Israel's strikes in Lebanon targeted not only Hezbollah-controlled areas in the south, but also inflicted heavy damage on major civilian infrastructure.[8] The thirty-four-day war resulted in significant casualties and destruction on both sides, and ended on 14 August 2006 with a ceasefire brokered by the United Nations (UN) under UN Security Council Resolution 1701, which Hezbollah claimed as a victory.[9]

These events were coupled with a growing political crisis, namely the failure to elect a successor to President Émile Lahoud in November 2007, whose term had been unconstitutionally renewed in 2004.[10] The country was left without a head of state, as Prime Minister Fouad Siniora's government and the Hezbollah-led opposition failed to reach an agreement on the election of a new president. This presidential vacuum deepened the existing political deadlock, with the Lebanese parliament unable to convene for over a year and presidential votes repeatedly postponed.[11] During 2006–08, Hezbollah and its allies held a prolonged sit-in in downtown Beirut, calling for increased representation for the opposition in the government, which contributed to the broader paralysis of political institutions.[12] Although foreign powers seemed to agree on the need to keep the situation under control, the country faced deep divisions on a level not witnessed since the 1975–90 civil war.[13] According to one former minister, the national political divide that occurred after the

2006 war contributed to the clashes in 2008, as not all Lebanese factions perceived the war similarly.[14] In addition, an arms race between the various factions also increased the possibility of an eruption of a civil war amidst a fragile political system.[15]

The crisis escalated sharply on 5 May 2008 when the Siniora government decided to dismantle Hezbollah's covert telecommunications network, which had been set up all over the country, allegedly extending to Beirut's airport.[16] Hezbollah leader Hassan Nasrallah equated this move to a 'declaration of war',[17] and the group retaliated by deploying armed forces across Beirut. As a result, clashes broke out in multiple neighbourhoods,[18] mainly between Hezbollah and Sunni forces in Beirut, who at that point were loyal to Saad Hariri, as well as with Druze forces loyal to Walid Jumblatt in the Chouf mountains. Notably, Hezbollah very quickly achieved total military dominance and took control of Beirut through armed confrontation'.[19]

Hezbollah's actions were deemed by its detractors to be 'a clear attack on the state and its sovereignty in Lebanon'.[20] Ashraf Rifi, former General Director of the Internal Security Forces, remarked that the 'Shia duo [a reference to the alliance between Hezbollah and the Amal Movement] aimed to take over everything and entered the capital Beirut' as part of 'an Iranian project'.[21] Meanwhile, political allies of Hezbollah argued that the crisis was primarily a result of disagreements around the vacant presidency and the deep divisions between the various factions within the existing political system.[22] These opposing views around the origin of the crisis are emblematic of the deep rifts that had festered between the different actors in Lebanon. Other analysts argue that the root cause of the May clashes lay in Hezbollah's growing fear that the March 14 Alliance, backed by the U.S., was preparing to elect a president with a simple parliamentary majority—a move that Hezbollah strongly opposed[23] despite the fact that the Lebanese constitution requires a two-thirds quorum for the first round of voting and an absolute majority in subsequent rounds.[24]

The emergent crisis pushed Lebanon to the brink of renewed civil war. Many media outlets described the situation as unprecedented since the 1975–90 war, whilst several political figures described these incidents as a 'mini civil war' or compared the situation to the previous conflict. As tensions worsened, the need for mediation became more urgent. By May 2008, escalating tensions had 'created pressure on everyone to reach an agreement'.[25] As the threat of open armed conflict loomed, high-level talks were held in Doha.[26] The Doha Agreement highlighted the importance of foreign mediation in, and support for, Lebanon due to the overlap of domestic, regional, and international interests in Lebanese internal affairs, thereby saving 'Lebanon from the possibility of civil war during that period'.[27]

Acceptance of Qatar as a Mediator

The acceptance of Qatar as a mediator in the Lebanese crisis was rooted in several key factors, most notably its neutrality, capacity to communicate with all sides, and its legacy of humanitarian efforts, particularly with its major contribution to post-2006 reconstruction efforts. Qatar's lack of prior involvement in Lebanese politics was to its advantage, allowing it to maintain its reputation as a neutral party.[28] Moreover, its ability to keep an 'equal distance from all parties'[29] facilitated its acceptance as a mediator and enabled it 'to position itself effectively in a region marked by rivalries, particularly with Saudi Arabia, which traditionally played a dominant role in Lebanon'.[30] Whilst other Arab states, such as Saudi Arabia, were viewed as having biased agendas and divergent interests in Lebanon, Qatar was perceived as a fair player with no 'ulterior motives'.[31] For example, for Hezbollah (as the main opposition party), Qatar was a preferred choice over Egypt and Saudi Arabia, both of which the group had poor relations with. This sentiment was echoed by Gebran Bassil, who said that 'everyone saw Qatar's role as positive and didn't consider it an enemy or biased'.[32]

In the opinion of Mustapha Allouch, Qatar's rivalry with Saudi Arabia and its strategic relationship with the U.S. helped shape its diplomatic approach.[33] Nonetheless, Qatar's mediation efforts were publicly backed by support from regional and international powers, notably Saudi Arabia, Syria, and the U.S., which further enhanced its legitimacy. This support was crucial, as 'the Doha Agreement wouldn't have succeeded without the support of Saudi Arabia and the U.S.'.[34] Importantly, the endorsement of Saudi Arabia was particularly significant due to its considerable leverage over key Lebanese parties, such as the Future Movement and the Lebanese Forces. Most of the politicians interviewed also believed that Qatar had U.S. backing and support to engage in this file. This endorsement allowed Qatar to assume a more assertive role, with both local and international stakeholders encouraging it to advance proposals under a shared desire for resolution.[35]

Qatar's diplomatic strategy was also characterized by its ability to 'maintain good relations with many different parties', allowing it to 'communicate with everyone, whereas other parties didn't have that ability'.[36] Qatar's high level of contextual knowledge and familiarity also strengthened its position as a mediator. As noted by Abou Faour, 'Qatar's understanding of Lebanon's structure, contradictions, and way of thinking [...] enabled them to play this role'.[37] This epistemic proximity was also credited with bolstering diplomatic success, enabling 'Qatar to mediate effectively and to bring political viewpoints closer together in hopes of achieving broader security'.[38]

Qatar's acceptability as a mediator was also built upon the goodwill generated through its humanitarian and reconstruction efforts in Lebanon. Following the July 2006 war, Qatar pledged USD 300 million for rebuilding through the Qatar Rehabilitation Program of South Lebanon, which was implemented in several southern Lebanese villages.[39] Furthermore, the Qatar National Relief Committee had implemented an 'adopt a village' programme, which directly funded impacted individuals and collaborated with local partners. By February 2008, USD 121 million had been disbursed for housing compensation and various projects, with USD 80.9 million of this allocated specifically for housing compensation in the adopted villages.[40] Qatar also refrained from justifying the Israeli war on Lebanon—a position that reinforced its credentials as a mediator in this file. As such, Qatar's support boosted its reputation in Lebanon, with many villages displaying 'Thank You Qatar' banners and flying the Qatari flag during the Emir Sheikh Hamad's visit to the region in 2010—the first visit by a head of state to Lebanon since the start of the war.[41] Many Lebanese factions recognized Qatar's contributions in the aftermath of the 2006 war, with Jarrah stating, 'Why did they have so much respect for Qatar? Because in 2006, Qatar stood by them, rebuilding villages, schools, and spending money. [...] Qatar rebuilt entire villages after the war'.[42] Thus, Qatar's mediation role in Lebanon did not emerge from a vacuum. Rather, it built a strong foundation of trust through its longstanding diplomatic ties and humanitarian aid, which fostered goodwill amongst both the political leaders and the general population.

Qatar's engagement in Lebanon was driven by both a normative commitment to peace and a strategic ambition for a more influential regional role. A member of the Free Patriotic Movement, Alain Aoun, commented: 'Qatar wanted to play a regional role [...]. It's a capable state with the means to help countries like Lebanon. Qatar didn't invest its resources selfishly; instead, it helped Lebanon'[43] and did not ask for any control or leverage in return.[44] Member of Parliament Ashraf Rifi similarly emphasized that 'Qatar had no personal ambitions, focusing instead on creating a platform for dialogue'.[45] Michel Pharaon referred to it as a 'Gulf moral responsibility',[46] suggesting that Qatar's mediation was rooted in a commitment to Arab political stability.

Whilst many ordinary Lebanese held a positive view of Qatar's mediation efforts, there was some hesitation amongst certain political factions, with some politicians believing Qatar's mediation efforts were part of its geopolitical strategy.[47] Based on the interviews conducted, factions that were hesitant were mainly those affiliated with the March 14 bloc—in other words, those who oppose Hezbollah. They particularly felt that this agreement allowed Hezbollah to further exert its influence by retaining its weapons. Pierre Bou Assi specifically said: 'the Doha Agreement didn't address Hezbollah's capabilities'.[48] Various politicians also proposed that Qatar aimed to expand its influence and become a key regional actor in the Middle East.[49] Ultimately, it was Qatar's neutrality, and the trust it had established over several years, that positioned it to be widely accepted by the various Lebanese factions as a mediator.

The 2008 Doha Agreement

On 11 May 2008, in response to widespread clashes across Lebanon, Egypt called for an emergency Arab League session that led to the issuance of Resolution 69/15 to form a ministerial committee headed by Secretary-General of the Arab League Amr Moussa and the Qatari

Prime Minister and Foreign Minister Sheikh Hamad bin Jassim Al Thani.[50] The purpose of this Committee was to call for dialogue between Lebanese politicians to end the hostilities that had wreaked havoc on Beirut and threatened the outbreak of civil war.[51] In this endeavour, 'Qatar's involvement was crucial, as it had built strong credibility with all Lebanese factions, making its role in mediation much easier'.[52] After three days, the Committee arrived in Beirut and held several late-night meetings with key political figures, including Speaker of Parliament Nabih Berri, Prime Minister Fouad Siniora, Commander of the Lebanese Armed Forces, General Michel Suleiman, and other leaders representing various religious sects. Here, Qatar demonstrated a sense of urgency and decisiveness as it swiftly moved beyond preliminary discussions and immediately began speaking to all groups. On 15 May 2008, and based on an Arab League-sponsored agreement, the Committee announced that talks between the various Lebanese factions would commence in Doha the next day.[53]

With the mediation effort led by Sheikh Hamad bin Jassim Al Thani and Amr Moussa, fourteen negotiators representing the various Lebanese political factions gathered in Doha from 16 to 21 May 2008 to resolve two issues: to elect a president, and to redraft the electoral law for the upcoming parliamentary elections.[54] Although there were fourteen representatives present, the principal disputants were Hezbollah (part of the March 8 Alliance) and the Future Movement (part of the March 14 Alliance), which was led by then Prime Minister Fouad Siniora. The talks also included negotiations on forming a unity government, electoral reform, and ending the clashes in Beirut.[55]

The Qatari mediation team successfully ended the crisis with the signing of the Doha Agreement on 21 May 2008.[56] The agreement comprised several components. The first component was the consensus decision to elect General Michel Suleiman as president. It was also agreed that the Speaker of Parliament would call a session within 24 hours to facilitate this election, taking into consideration that this approach was deemed to be the most appropriate constitutional solution under the exceptional circumstances at the time. The newly elected president was tasked with initiating national dialogue, forming a national unity government, and building trust amongst Lebanese citizens.[57]

The second component was the formation of a national unity government of thirty ministers. This government would include sixteen ministers from the majority bloc (the March 14 Alliance), eleven from the opposition (the March 8 Alliance), and three appointed by the president.[58] With this, the opposition secured its desired blocking third through a one-third-plus-one representation in the cabinet—a point of contention for the opposition since 2005.[59] This effectively granted the March 8 Alliance veto power,[60] and Hassan Mrad, Member of the Lebanese Parliament (affiliated with the March 8 Alliance), believed that this 'allowed for a balance of power'.[61] The president was also given a ministerial share,[62] which effectively created a centrist bloc in the cabinet that was neither with the majority nor with the opposition in order to promote consensus and collegiality in decision-making.[63] In addition, all parties agreed not to resign or obstruct the government's operations, with this aspect of the agreement lasting three years.

The third component mandated the adoption of the 1960 electoral law as a framework for the 2009 parliamentary elections, with electoral constituencies premised on districts.[64] Specific districts such as Marjayoun-Hasbaya, Baalbek-Hermel, and West Bekaa-Rachaya were to remain unchanged, whilst Beirut would be redrawn into three districts. This was a highly contentious issue, as electoral district boundaries directly influence political representation and sectarian balance. During negotiations over this matter, 'Lebanese participants were shocked with the detailed knowledge of the Qatari delegation regarding the electoral districts'.[65]

The fourth component prohibited the use of weapons or violence for political gain or dispute resolution. All signatories further pledged to enhance the Lebanese state's authority over its territory to ensure the security of both the state and its citizens.[66]

The agreement was signed by the leading power brokers and decision-makers representing the largest political parties in Lebanon: Nabih Berri, Fouad Siniora, Amine Gemayel, Michel Aoun, Michel Murr, Saad Hariri, Walid Jumblatt, Boutros Harb, Ilyas Sakkaf, Ghassan Tueni, Muhammad Al Safadi, Muhammad Raad, Hagop Pakradounian, and Samir Geagea. The signing was witnessed by then Qatari Prime Minister and Foreign Minister Sheikh Hamad bin Jassim Al Thani and Secretary-General of the Arab League Amr Moussa.

Some critics argued that this consensus stemmed from pressure to accommodate the Arab League rather than to address the root causes of the crisis—a forced approach that often led to policy stagnation or delays in resolving the 2008 crisis.[67] However, 'the successes of Qatari mediation in this file could also be attributed to the fact that all parties needed an exit, a leeway the Doha talks provided'.[68] In other words, Qatar's diplomatic prowess was evident in its successful mediation of the 2008 Lebanese crisis, as it managed to convince Gulf states to influence their Lebanese allies, ultimately leading to the Doha Agreement and Michel Suleiman's election as president.[69] By steering the negotiations to a settlement, Qatar brought an end to a longstanding political deadlock and demonstrated the depth of its growing diplomatic reach within the region.[70] The following subsections will build on this with a discussion of Qatar's mediation modalities and motivations as a third-party actor in the Lebanese file.

Modalities of Qatari Mediation in Lebanon

Qatar's approach to mediating the Lebanese conflict entailed a structured process of 'providing the venue and the environment for dialogue',[71] which was designed to achieve a peaceful resolution. By fostering an atmosphere of trust, Qatar encouraged open dialogue and a willingness to compromise. This neutral space was crucial in reducing tensions and fostering open communication amongst the conflicting parties. These efforts led to significant political agreements, particularly in terms of power-sharing arrangements. Jreissati noted that: 'The Emir hosted them, called them together, and facilitated dialogue [...]. They paved the way for what became known as political power-sharing'.[72] Various politicians see Qatar's role as not only mediating but also establishing a framework for ongoing governance.

At the outset, the participants were brought to the Sheraton Hotel in Doha on two chartered flights, where they were essentially sequestered for five days to ensure focus and minimize external distractions.[73] The mediation process began with a brief welcoming ceremony, setting the tone of the talks and emphasizing the significance of the negotiations. Following this, various committees were established, each tasked with addressing specific aspects of the conflict.

Qatari mediators 'employed shuttle diplomacy', actively moving 'from wing to wing in the hotel', between the committees and the different factions to facilitate communication, clarify positions, and 'ensure agreements were reached'.[74] This modality allowed the mediators to bridge the gaps and build trust. As the negotiations progressed and the necessary groundwork was laid, the mediators organized direct meetings at the negotiation table when it was deemed most effective. By carefully timing these face-to-face discussions, the mediators maximized the potential for productive dialogue in order to reach a consensus.

Efforts to reduce tensions and finalize the agreement in Doha were highly challenging. Michel Moussa remarked that 'the key was getting the factions to the table and having them trust the mediator, which allowed them to put their concerns on the table and find common ground'.[75] Establishing this level of trust necessitated the personal involvement of the then Emir Sheikh Hamad bin Khalifa Al Thani and then Prime Minister and Foreign Minister Sheikh Hamad bin Jassim Al Thani in the mediation process.[76] Their direct engagement with this file also enhanced the credibility and weight of the proposals later submitted by the Qatari mediators. Although the negotiations took place under the auspices of the Arab League, it was the Qatari team led by Sheikh Hamad bin Jassim that was instrumental in guiding the process. The Arab League provided essential regional legitimacy but did not play an active role in the mediation itself, instead supporting Qatar's leadership in resolving the crisis. Sheikh Hamad bin Jassim worked to maintain a positive atmosphere at the negotiating table and was able to prevent the talks from collapsing, including by proposing new solutions.[77] It was evident that he aimed for a fair and honourable agreement, and, unlike previous mediators, he maintained an impartial stance in the negotiations.[78] His role was initially to facilitate the election of a new president, but this role rapidly grew to include mediation.[79] This personal involvement of senior Qatari leaders was crucial in helping Lebanese leaders reach a consensus.[80]

When the talks ground to a halt, the Emir personally communicated with then Syrian President Bashar Al-Assad to enlist his help in persuading Hezbollah to adopt a more lenient approach to reach a compromise.[81] This proved successful, as Hezbollah's negotiators subsequently shifted their position and agreed to a settlement.

Additionally, the Qatari mediators maintained lines of communication with other dominant regional actors with interests in Lebanese political issues and affairs, such as Iran and Saudi Arabia, who also shared an interest in resolving the stalemate.[82] This proved challenging as Qatari senior officials themselves simultaneously mediated between the Lebanese factions and indirectly managed the interests of their foreign backers, such as France, Iran, and Saudi Arabia. Qatar's 'personal and insistent intervention'[83] with the Emir of Qatar, even 'calling each leader one by one',[84] was a crucial factor in persuading the fractious political leaders, who were generally unable to come around on critical domestic issues, to resolve the deadlock.[85]

Evidently, Qatar adopted a hands-on approach throughout the mediation process, remaining in 'constant communication with foreign parties' and facilitating coordination between 'the Americans and the Iranians'.[86] This illustrates Qatar's role in expediting broader international involvement and the importance of its pragmatic foreign policy, leveraging its existing relationships with both Lebanese factions and regional and international actors to navigate the complex dynamics of this file effectively.

Qatar's approach to Lebanon was characterized by a blend of neutrality and strategic engagement, setting it apart from other regional powers. Unlike Iran, Syria, or Saudi Arabia, which have historically aligned themselves with specific Lebanese factions, Qatar has maintained a more balanced stance towards all political blocs. This neutrality, coupled with Qatar's substantial investment in post-conflict reconstruction in southern Lebanon following the 2006 war with Israel, significantly enhanced its credibility and acceptability amongst Lebanese factions. Moreover, Qatar's non-partisan involvement in Lebanon's affairs, focusing instead on economic support and development initiatives, further strengthened its image as a trustworthy mediator.[87] This was particularly evident during the 2008 crisis, wherein Qatar's diplomatic efforts led to the successful Doha Agreement, thereby ending an eighteen-month political impasse.

Chequebook Diplomacy

Qatar's mediation in the 2008 Lebanese crisis has faced scrutiny for allegedly using financial incentives to encourage conflict parties to reach an agreement. This aligns with Qatar's broader pattern of offering substantial post-conflict reconstruction funding, which can motivate participation in Doha-hosted negotiations.[88] However, claims about such incentives in the 2008 agreement are often exaggerated in academic literature and lack solid supporting evidence.

As has been established in this chapter, Qatar's contributions towards rebuilding villages in southern Lebanon after the 2006 Lebanon War were important in boosting the country's reputation and acceptability as a mediator. However, the causal relation between this reconstruction funding and Qatar's subsequent mediation of the 2008 agreement has been confused in much of the literature. Most notably, critics have characterized Qatari mediation in Lebanon as a form of 'chequebook diplomacy', mobilizing claims that reconstruction funding in 2006 was provided to promote power-sharing between Hezbollah and the Fouad Siniora government.[89] For instance, one source has stated that 'the promises of further investment totalling around USD 300 million provided much-needed leverage on the parties to deliver an agreement'.[90] However, this is a factual inaccuracy that erroneously attributes the USD 300 million pledge from 2006 as a source of Qatar's leverage in 2008. Given that two years passed between this reconstruction support and the Doha Agreement, it is clear that the historic funding allocation itself played no causal role in shaping the behaviour of the Lebanese factions in May 2008. A more nuanced version of the chequebook diplomacy critique would hold that the promise or expectation of further Qatari investment in Lebanon following any agreement served as leverage in securing the Doha Agreement. However, this remains speculative and is not supported by available evidence.

A prevalent interpretation of Qatari mediation in Lebanon most often emphasizes the role financial dividends allegedly played in influencing the parties' decisions during the negotiations. That is, Qatar's success in mediation and conflict resolution, including in Lebanon's 2008 political deadlock, is believed to be largely dependent on its financial incentives rather than political and diplomatic prowess.[91] Such views were, for instance, shared during the data collection process. As Bechara Khairallah, an advisor to President Michel Suleiman, claimed, 'the Qataris gave him [Michel Aoun] incentives, and they gave him the electoral law [...]. This all happened after midnight'.[92] Whilst Qatar's financial leverage remains a peculiar feature of its diplomatic strategies and may serve strategic roles in political stalemates, it is reductionist to characterize Qatari mediation as merely chequebook diplomacy.

At that time, Parliament Speaker Nabih Berri acknowledged Qatar's goodwill towards Lebanon through its efforts in support of stability and reconstruction, wherein it maintained financial support for the embattled Lebanese state and economy.[93] As Karami noted, 'Qatar continues to fund the Lebanese army [...] giving them support every six months to pay the soldiers',[94] thus demonstrating a sustained commitment that strengthens Qatar's role in the Lebanese context. Jbeily reinforces this idea, stating that 'Qatar is the only Arab country still putting money into Lebanon [...]. They are giving to the army and providing some other forms of aid',[95] which highlights Qatar's unique position in supporting Lebanon compared to other regional actors. Given this context of wider Qatari support, it is plausible that the expectation of the continuation of such funding could have shaped the decisions of key actors during the 2008 talks. However, this connection remains highly speculative and is not supported by any credible evidence.

Despite these weak evidentiary foundations, there persists a general impression amongst many Lebanese observers that Qatar's financial leverage was influential in reaching the 2008 agreement. For instance, Karami reflects, 'People ask me—what is Qatar's power? We all know Qatar's power is financial', despite admitting he had no information about any payments during the Doha talks.[96] Similarly, critics such as Mustapha Allouch argue that Qatari mediation was founded upon financial leverage to facilitate a short-term agreement, yet lacked the depth required for a long-term sustainable solution.[97] However, these views often reduce the complexity of Qatar's mediation efforts to a transactional model, ignoring the broader diplomatic strategies at play.

By contrast, other Lebanese observers emphasize diplomacy rather than financial leverage as the cornerstone of Qatar's success. Michel Moussa counters claims of chequebook diplomacy, asserting that 'Qatar's good relationship with all factions allowed the Doha

Agreement to happen'.[98] Gebran Bassil similarly highlights Qatar's non-transactional approach, stating that, 'they didn't ask for something in return like an oil well or a power plant contract'.[99] Jreissati also counters claims of financial leverage by stating, 'there are malicious tongues that say money played a significant role, but that's not true [...]. They didn't buy the presidency'.[100] Taken together, these accounts illuminate Qatar's cultivation of trust and dialogue amongst adversaries, which was critical to its effectiveness as a mediator.

Ultimately, whilst Qatar's financial power undoubtedly bolstered its standing in Lebanon, its success in mediating the 2008 Doha Agreement was rooted in its ability to engage diplomatically and build relationships amongst deeply divided factions. This achievement challenged perceptions of Qatar as a minor player in international diplomacy. The Doha Agreement averted a potential civil war and solidified Qatar's status as a credible and effective mediator in the region.

Outcomes

The Qatari-sponsored agreement was successful in ending the crisis, and led to the election of the former Lebanese Armed Forces Commander, Michel Suleiman on 25 May 2008 as a consensus president, the formation of a thirty-member national unity government, and the adoption of the revised 1960 election law.[101] Many analysts characterized Qatari mediation in Lebanon as a major success, particularly given the failures of past mediation efforts.[102] Despite its initial success, there is almost a consensus in the literature that the agreement was insufficient for long-term peace because it did not address the root causes of the country's flawed and fragile consociational political system.[103] However, for a country that rarely witnessed peaceful episodes, this neither undermined the agreement nor discounted its successes.

It can be argued that, in the short term at least, the Lebanese factions were content with the outcomes of the 2008 Doha Agreement, viewing it as the last resort to prevent another civil war.[104] Even the national unity government it established enjoyed relative stability for two and a half years, before collapsing in January 2011.[105] Walid Jumblatt, a Druze leader and a member of the March 14 ruling coalition, expressed that his coalition saw that the agreement was a fair compromise and claimed that Hezbollah in particular was satisfied because it achieved its goal, namely veto power in the cabinet.[106] As such, the agreement was able to decrease the tensions between the fighting parties.

However, Lebanon's peculiar and complex political scene, as well as changing power dynamics and relationships across sectarian lines, have often posed significant challenges to the sustainability of peace or political agreements.[107] Maintaining political consensus beyond the 2008 agreement within this sectarian setting proved a burdensome task. The collapse of the government in 2011, after Hezbollah and its allies resigned over disagreements regarding the Special Tribunal for Lebanon, testifies to the complexity of Lebanese national politics.[108] Yacoubian points to this development as evidence that the 2008 Doha Agreement did not provide long-term resolutions, and it is evident 'that Lebanon's political leaders continued to operate as they did prior to the 2008 agreement as the underlying issues were left unaddressed'.[109] Similarly, Najat Aoun Saliba emphasized that the deeper issue lies within Lebanon's political elite, who remain more interested in securing their own personal gains rather than advancing the country's long-term interests.[110]

Whilst the Doha agreement successfully defused the political tension that almost triggered another destructive civil war in Lebanon, it did not succeed in transforming the conflict parties' behaviours and attitudes towards peaceful and long-term negotiated political settlements that would break away from the zero-sum thinking that has dominated the country's national politics.[111] In part, the agreement was designed with the objective of crisis management rather than to tackle Lebanon's political institutional structure or enhance relations between its main powerholders.[112] Thus, the 2008 Doha Agreement was focused on ending the immediate clashes and resolving the presidential vacuum, rather than fundamentally transforming the root causes of the country's protracted political crisis.

Further, critics highlighted the lack of a follow-up mechanism to monitor the implementation of the agreement. Kamrava notes that Qatar's mediation in Lebanon lacked mechanisms to ensure that the parties adhered to the agreement's terms.[113] That is, the post-agreement follow-up, despite its importance for long-term conflict resolution and transformation, seemed to have been neglected.[114] For instance, the 2008 agreement did not address Hezbollah's military arsenal—a critical aspect of the conflict. Instead, it left this issue for future discussions amongst Lebanese political leaders, which never materialized, proving to be a contentious matter long after the agreement. Moreover, it was clear that the group was uncompromising on its arsenal, which it considered vital for its continued existence as a 'resistance force'. In the years that followed, 'The issue of Hezbollah's arms and the question or the strategy of the Lebanese state control over these arms was not implemented'.[115] This has been described as one of the consequences of the absence of a follow-up mechanism, which proved detrimental to the agreement's sustainability.

Foreign meddling and geopolitical interests also undermined the positive political momentum that the 2008 Doha Agreement sought to build. For example, the Syrian intelligence apparatus under the Ba'athist regime remained a powerful political backer of Hezbollah and was thus able to maintain its influence in Lebanese politics.[116] Additionally, regional powers, including Iran and Saudi Arabia, continued to influence Lebanese politics through their support for Hezbollah and the Sunni-dominated March 14 Alliance, respectively. Thus, although Qatar maintained its neutrality as a mediator after 2008 vis-à-vis the parties, the agreement was not immune to the impacts of regional and geopolitical competition amongst the traditional power blocs, including Iran, Saudi Arabia, and Syria.[117]

The 2008 agreement succeeded in outlining the pathways for peaceful conflict resolution. However, the complex political landscape, including the political will of the parties involved and the broader regional dynamics, consistently undermined its practical execution. Ultimately, it is important to note that the 2008 Doha Agreement was designed with the objectives of crisis management, establishing a minimum level of political compromise, and securing inter-elite settlement to save Lebanon from a relapse to violence. This means that the agreement, by creating some form of consensus between the parties, was a successful and concrete step towards long-term conflict resolution and transformation. Nevertheless, the lack of follow-up support and enforcement mechanisms, particularly from regional organizations such as the Arab League,[118] and the complex structural build-up of both the formal and informal political structures of Lebanon, curbed the potential of further developing the positive outcomes of the agreement.[119]

Conclusion

The 2008 Doha Agreement played a crucial role in preventing the outbreak of another civil war in Lebanon. Although its success was largely short-term, addressing immediate political and security concerns, it accomplished its intended outcomes. The agreement successfully led to the election of Michel Suleiman as president, the formation of a national unity government, and, most importantly, defused the mounting political tension that nearly resulted in another episode of sectarian conflict. However, the agreement to resolve the 2008 crisis had its limitations. The insufficient follow-up mechanisms meant that implementation depended on the political will of factions entrenched in post-war rivalries, which was evident in the collapse of the unity government in 2011. The agreement also lacked regional and international support, which weakened enforcement and hastened its collapse.

Nevertheless, these shortcomings cannot overshadow the central achievements of the Doha Agreement. Through de-escalating a mounting crisis, the accord demonstrated Qatar's ability to convene opposing factions through neutral facilitation, drawing upon personal and diplomatic relations with many stakeholders, as well as the strategic use of leverage. The involvement of high-level Qatari officials, including the Emir and the Foreign Minister, helped to sustain momentum and prevent talks from collapsing. Finally, in bringing together Lebanese factions to de-escalate the 2008 crisis, the Doha Agreement marked a major success in Qatar's emerging role as a mediator, paving the way for subsequent mediation efforts in Darfur and elsewhere.

5

BROKERING PEACE IN DARFUR

THE DOHA DOCUMENT AND ITS LEGACY

Qatar played a key role in the multi-party mediation efforts that culminated in the signing of the Doha Document for Peace in Darfur (DDPD) in 2011. This chapter addresses Qatar's role in the mediation process, providing an overview of its engagement in terms of preparatory groundwork, facilitation of multi-track dialogue, humanitarian aid, and follow-up mechanisms. It discusses the challenges confronted on the path to peace in Darfur, including balancing regional rivalries and managing a peace process with myriad rebel factions. The analysis also considers and counters several leading critiques of Qatari involvement in Darfur negotiations, providing a balanced perspective on the peace process and its long-term legacy.

Darfur in Context

In 2003, rebels in Darfur rose against Omar Al-Bashir's government, triggering a devastating conflict. This conflict was sparked by the formation of the Sudan Liberation Army (SLA) and the Justice and Equality Movement (JEM), each representing marginalized non-Arab communities.[1] These groups launched military attacks, assaulting the El Fasher airport and challenging the government's authority. The regime's response was to mobilize military forces and Arab militias known as the Janjaweed, which provoked widespread violence, including village burnings, looting, and human rights abuses. The Janjaweed were accused of ethnic cleansing and genocide against non-Arab Darfuris. The war quickly generated a severe humanitarian crisis and large-scale civilian displacement. Under President Al-Bashir, Sudan faced international isolation and sanctions, including its designation by the United States (U.S.) as a state sponsor of terrorism from 1993 to 2020, which rendered it a pariah state.[2]

Scholars offer various perspectives on the origins of the conflict. Many argue it stems from longstanding grievances over political marginalization, underdevelopment, and inequitable resource distribution. Since the mid-nineteenth century, Arab elites from Sudan's Nile region have monopolized governance, implementing policies that neglected Darfur and other peripheral areas.[3] Regional instability in southern Sudan and Chad, coupled with arms proliferation, further aggravated security challenges.[4] Although the mainstream narrative focuses on inter-ethnic conflict between Arab herders and African farmers, others emphasize local-level clashes between nomadic pastoralists and sedentary agricultural communities over land and water, compounded by drought and desertification.[5] In a critical and revisionist interpretation, the violence in Darfur cannot be understood without examining the colonial invention of tribal homelands (*dars*), environmental degradation, and the politicization of tribal authority through colonial and post-colonial statecraft.[6] These competing perspectives are essential to understanding the contextual complexities of the conflict.

The outbreak of the war in Darfur compounded the humanitarian crisis, leaving devastating human, economic, and political impacts. Between 2003 and 2008, over 300,000 were killed and around 2.7 million Darfurians were displaced.[7] By 2007, approximately 4.2 million people in Darfur depended on humanitarian assistance.[8] Darfur was already amongst Sudan's least developed regions, and this increased due to the war, with poverty rates exceeding 60 per cent in Western and Central Darfur.[9] The conflict exacted a substantial developmental toll, costing Sudan USD 30.5 billion and diverting much public expenditure from development to security.[10] Darfur's history of famines and vulnerability to climatic shocks—including floods, droughts, and locust infestations—compounded this humanitarian and developmental crisis. Since 2003, Darfur has experienced multiple conflicts beyond the initial crisis, including inter-communal and inter-tribal resource disputes, systematic violence targeting local ethnic communities, and cross-border tensions with Chad.

Sudan has endured decades of conflict, from national civil wars to sub-national insurgencies. Darfur and South Sudan have witnessed systematic oppression and resource exploitation by successive Sudanese governments, which have historically marginalized non-Arab populations. Both regions share a history of systemic neglect and exploitation by the Sudanese state, resulting in cycles of violence, mass displacement, and civilian suffering. These conflicts are intertwined; for example, instability in Darfur has led to spillover effects in South Sudan through refugee flows and cross-border ethnic ties. Furthermore, both conflicts echo broader themes of political exclusion, ethnic identity, and resource competition that continue to shape Sudan's sociopolitical landscape and peripheries. Such conflicts required extensive mediation efforts aimed at different levels, ultimately producing over sixty agreements, declarations, and protocols across decades of instability.[11]

Previous Mediation Attempts

Early mediation efforts failed to resolve the conflict. The Abeche Peace Talks, led by the Chadian government, culminated in the first ceasefire agreement between the government and the SLA on 3 September 2003.[12] Although not formally implemented, these talks marked the first explicit recognition of the conflict's roots amidst rising international concern. The discussions also signalled the African Union's (AU) early steps towards a leading role in the crisis. However, continued military mobilization in Sudan indicated minimal commitment to a negotiated peace. In December 2003, the rebels refused to resume negotiations, citing the regime's offensive and their 'lack of faith' in Chad's President Idriss Déby as a mediator.[13] Meanwhile, President Déby called the rebel's terms for substantive negotiations 'unacceptable' and unilaterally ended the process.[14]

With the Arab League advocating Arab unity yet taking a relatively neutral position in the process,[15] a wider circle of external actors was needed to facilitate talks. Later negotiations, hosted by Chad and facilitated by the European Union (EU), the AU, and the United Nations (UN), produced a forty-five-day humanitarian ceasefire.[16] On 13 April 2004, the AU Peace and Security Council requested an urgent reconnaissance mission to prepare the Ceasefire Commission and assess the need for a protection force.[17] This led to the African Union Mission in Sudan (AMIS) becoming operational on 19 June 2004 after securing its headquarters in El Fasher and negotiating its status with Sudan's government.[18] Over time, the AMIS expanded, with the AU taking a proactive role in mediation support and advocating for African-led solutions.

In July 2004, the AU initiated Inter-Sudanese Peace Talks in seven phases, culminating in the Darfur Peace Agreement (DPA), signed in Abuja on 5 May 2006. The DPA—signed by the Sudanese government and Sudan Liberation Movement/Army led by Minni Minawi (SLM/A-MM)—focused on power-sharing, wealth distribution, and security arrangements. Despite its potential, the DPA soon floundered due to continued fighting and a lack of support from Darfur's communities, evidenced by protests and deteriorating security.[19] According to the JEM's leader, the Abuja platform allowed parties to seek solutions, but they were unable to end the war peacefully, and the crisis continued.[20] The DPA's collapse underscored significant implementation problems, particularly its lack of public acceptance. In June 2006, Jan Pronk, the UN Secretary-General's Special Representative in Sudan, explained that the DPA did not resonate with Darfur's populace but rather strengthened the positions of the regime and the minority Zaghawa tribe, who were represented by Minawi.[21] Moreover, the negotiation process was critiqued for its 'deadline diplomacy', which pressured parties into agreements without sufficient time for internal discussion or consultation, eroding ownership and commitment.[22]

In 2007, in a bid to revive peace efforts, the AU and UN shifted mediation to Libya, hoping Muammar Gaddafi's involvement would advance talks under the AU–UN Special Envoys.[23] However, this initiative also faltered due to the absence of key rebel groups.

Subsequently, the UN–AU Hybrid Operation in Darfur (UNAMID), active from 2007 to 2020, was established to restore security and support peace. Despite being the largest peacekeeping operation at inception, UNAMID struggled to mitigate the conflict or achieve a comprehensive solution in Darfur.[24]

These mediation and peacebuilding efforts were consistently hindered by major challenges, notably the absence of key rebel groups in talks, limited commitment by conflict parties to previous accords, and insufficient regional and international support. Thus, when Qatar entered the peace process in 2008, it did so amidst calls to reform the multi-party mediation approach and adopt a more inclusive peace process—one led by a mediator acceptable to all warring parties and regional or international stakeholders.

Qatar's Entry as a Mediator

In September 2008, Qatar was appointed by the Arab League to mediate peace in Darfur. Unlike previous attempts, Qatari mediation gained broader regional and international backing from the AU, Türkiye, Syria, the UN Secretariat, Security Council Permanent Five, and the U.S.[25] Qatar's entry into the mediation process was also facilitated by other international actors, including the United Kingdom (UK) and France. The latter offered behind-the-scenes diplomatic support, endorsing Qatar's mediation and its Darfur plan.[26] During mediation, a Sudanese diplomat pointed out France's capacity and willingness to assist Qatar in bringing parties to the table by leveraging rebel movements, such as the SLM/A and its leader, Abdel Wahid Al-Nur (SLM/A-AW), who had resided in Paris under a special permit granted in 2006.[27] Regarding France's leverage on the JEM faction, one senior Western diplomat explained:

> Sarkozy is a personal friend of the Emir of Qatar, and during a visit to Paris, there was a direct, and personal request to the Emir, that Qatar, having been successful in Lebanon and as an Arab country, should get involved. They [France] promised them [Qatar] help [...] the thinking was that if the French could influence the Chadians, then the Chadians could deliver Khalil [the leader of JEM], and this was probably what the French promised to the Qataris.[28]

Khalil Ibrahim, the founding leader of the JEM, was initially cautious about Qatar's candidacy due to its close links to Khartoum and support for Sudan in the UN Security Council. Ultimately, however, France persuaded him after a JEM delegation—who met French officials at the Élysée with Qatar's ambassador present—was reassured that the new initiative 'was not about reviving the DPA' and was supported by 'key international actors'.[29]

Sudan's ambassador to Qatar framed this involvement through the lens of bilateral relations and the Arab concept of 'brotherly ties'.[30] The Sudanese diplomat disclosed that the initiative for mediation in Darfur came from His Highness Sheikh Hamad bin Khalifa Al Thani.[31] He emphasized that the Emir viewed the conflict as rooted more in developmental disparities rather than in religious, ethnic, or sectarian divisions and as a viable opportunity for resolution.[32] Although Khartoum welcomed Qatar's initiative, there is scant evidence that Darfur's rebel groups invited Qatar to mediate. Nevertheless, some interviews suggest that JEM members later viewed Qatar's role positively: 'It became clear to us from the very first moment the desire of the State of Qatar and those in charge of the file to earnestly push the conflicting parties to sit down and understand how to solve the raging crisis in Darfur'.[33]

Qatar's acceptability as a mediator stands in contrast to other states aspiring to a third-party role in Darfur. Egypt, for instance, engaged early in the crisis, driven by its view of Sudan as a key ally essential to its security interests. Despite Egypt's diplomatic efforts, including an international conference in Cairo, Al-Bashir's regime remained sceptical due to concerns over Egypt's neutrality.[34] Saudi Arabia was also considered but faced reluctance from various Sudanese factions, who questioned Riyadh's experience in mediation and feared that its regional ambitions could affect the mediation process.[35]

Before Qatar's involvement, many Darfurians were sceptical of its proposed candidacy, 'having already become weary of previous or ongoing mediation attempts by Egypt and the Arab League, most of which they had come to view as biased in favor of Khartoum'.[36] Many rebels also perceived any Arab mediator as a means 'to protect Sudanese President Omar Hassan Al-Bashir from the possibility of indictment for war crimes by the International Criminal Court'.[37]

Nevertheless, broader endorsement from regional and international stakeholders set Qatar apart as the preferred facilitator in Darfur's peace process.[38]

From Qatar's perspective, the motivation to mediate the Darfur conflict stemmed from humanitarian concerns, enduring cultural respect for Darfur's role in Islamic history, and strategic considerations. According to Ambassador Ali Bin Hassan Al-Hammadi, Qatar's response to the Darfur crisis was driven by a deep-seated connection with Sudan (a country with which Qatar has maintained good relations throughout the past regardless of the regimes ruling in Khartoum), as well as with all Darfur tribes, which generated trust amongst those tribes regarding Doha's role as a mediator.[39] Ambassador Ahmed Al Mahmoud also linked Qatar's mediation in Darfur to a historical and cultural sense of gratitude, highlighting Darfuri contributions to Mecca—such as the annual caravans that delivered the Kiswa and copies of the Qur'an—and recalling that Muhammad Ali Dinar, Sultan of Darfur (1898–1916), built wells (Abyar Ali) to aid pilgrims, framing Qatar's efforts as a moral duty rooted in shared heritage.[40] This relationship, along with a genuine concern for Sudan's stability, propelled Qatar to initiate mediation. Strategically, Qatar's engagement was aligned with its longstanding ties with Omar Al-Bashir's government and the large Sudanese diaspora in Doha.[41] It was also an attempt to promote stability in the Horn of Africa by mitigating the risk of escalation in Darfur and the potential subsequent destabilization in its neighbouring states.[42]

The Doha Document for Peace in Darfur

Between 2008 and 2011, the Qatar-led multi-party mediation aimed to resolve the protracted conflict in Darfur. These negotiations initially included the government and JEM, with notable involvement from the U.S.[43] A critical juncture was reached in December 2010 when negotiations expanded to incorporate other rebel movements in Darfur. The discussions focused on wealth distribution, compensation for victims, a ceasefire, prisoner releases, and the political recognition of rebel groups. The process faced a setback when the JEM, the largest rebel faction, walked away from the table, citing inadequate progress and increased aggression from the Sudanese Armed Forces. This departure led to the creation of the Liberation and Justice Movement (LJM)—a rebel coalition comprised of eleven factions—encouraged by international mediators to represent Darfur's myriad armed groups. Despite the LJM's weak connection to the realities on the ground in Darfur, it grew to be the main negotiating body with the government.[44]

The negotiations culminated with the DDPD, signed on 14 July 2011, between the regime and LJM.[45] The DDPD established a comprehensive framework for peace, covering critical areas such as a permanent ceasefire, the protection of human rights, arrangements for power-sharing, wealth distribution, and justice and reconciliation. It also set up the Darfur Regional Authority (DRA) to manage governance until a definitive administrative status for Darfur could be determined through a referendum. The UNAMID supported the multi-party mediation structure, providing technical expertise and promoting the inclusion of movements that did not sign the agreement. Following its signing, the DDPD continued to offer the primary framework for peacemaking in the Darfur crisis.

Modalities of Qatari Mediation

This section examines modalities of Qatari mediation, including preparatory work, hosting high-level negotiations, inclusive stakeholder engagement, leveraging peace through investment, and post-mediation follow-up and support.

Laying the Groundwork through Preparation

The initial mediation phase entailed a preparatory process to lay the groundwork for forthcoming talks. This included initial contacts, context exploration, identifying shortcomings of previous mediation attempts, and gathering additional information.[46] Qatar's familiarity with the conflicting parties served as a foundation for its diplomats in addressing the file. A key first step involved confirming the genuine intent of all parties and their backers to end the Darfur conflict.[47]

In 2008, the Minister of State for Foreign Affairs, His Excellency Minister Ahmad bin Abdullah Al Mahmoud, conducted extensive diplomatic efforts to prepare for Qatari mediation. He visited multiple capitals to engage with international and regional political stakeholders and institutions. He also undertook an exploratory mission in Khartoum and Darfur, where, according to a Sudanese diplomat, his exceptional familiarity with the Darfur region even exceeded the knowledge of some local officials.[48] This was particularly evident from the time he spent living and interacting within the refugee camps.[49] Based on those direct interactions with people on the ground, Minister Al Mahmoud compiled a list of their demands, brought the document back to Qatar, and later shared it with Djibril Bassolé, who had been appointed as the Joint AU–UN Chief Mediator for Darfur.[50] He also engaged in factfinding in Djibouti, which had been involved in previous mediation efforts, in addition to Kenya and Chad, both of which were host countries for Darfuri refugees. Ultimately, Qatar sought to gain a comprehensive understanding of the conflict, and the perspectives of local, regional, and international stakeholders.[51]

Minister Al Mahmoud's visits and direct engagement with the conflict stakeholders illustrated one of the modalities through which Qatar positioned itself as a mediator in this context and how it built goodwill amongst Darfur's myriad groups. This proved decisive in easing Darfuris' scepticism towards Arab interventions, encouraging a more open attitude towards Qatari mediation. Where previous mediators showed regard for local context, Qatar's sustained diplomatic investment in the pre-mediation phase, especially first-hand consultations with displaced communities and prior mediation actors, set it apart and laid a stronger foundation for future dialogue.[52]

Hosting Track I Talks

Qatar employs a range of mediation modalities, utilizing classic Track I diplomacy in some cases, and combining Track I and Track II dialogues in others (depending on the context of each mediation effort). The latter characterized Qatari engagement in Darfur, where it operated under a tripartite multilateral mediation structure involving both the UN and AU.

Whilst the international community previously opted for threatening the Al-Bashir regime with economic sanctions, Qatar offered a multilateral dialogue platform for government-rebel talks. Observers noted that, by then, Khartoum was inclined to accept any peace process that would relieve international pressure.[53] Officials eventually recognized Darfur as a burden on the state—especially given International Criminal Court indictments against the Sudanese president and others—thus making a diplomatic resolution more politically feasible.[54]

From 2008 to 2011, Qatar hosted several Track I talks. In early December 2008, the JEM delegation—comprising Tahir Al-Faki, Jibril Ibrahim, Ahmed Hussein Adam, and Khatab Widaa—met with Minister Al Mahmoud to deliver the JEM's message.[55] Additionally, this visit facilitated the JEM's meeting with Djibril Bassolé, along with the French and Norwegian envoys to Darfur, allowing for more productive engagement amongst the parties to the peace process. A series of important meetings in Doha occurred between 10 and 17 February 2009, the first formal engagement between the Sudanese government and JEM since the 2007 Abuja talks. These meetings also included behind-closed-door sessions, such as a personal meeting between the Qatari Emir and President Al-Bashir's close adviser Nafie Ali Nafie.[56] The process, however, lacked other major Darfur rebel factions, such as the SLM/A-AW, SLM/A-MM, Sudan Liberation Army-Unity, and United Resistance Front.

The negotiations culminated in the signing of an agreement of goodwill and confidence-building between the Sudanese government and JEM on 17 February 2009.[57] With advancements in the progress achieved, Khartoum signed another series of documents in Doha, including framework agreements with JEM and LJM on 23 February and 18 March 2010, respectively.[58] Qatar's efforts to engage other key Darfur rebel factions at this stage continued. The first official meeting between the leader of SLM/A-AW, Minister Al Mahmoud, and Bassolé occurred in July 2010 in Paris, where parties focused more on the issue of civilian protection and the return of the internally displaced persons and refugees to their villages.

During this stage, Qatar assumed responsibility for facilitating negotiations, upholding neutrality, and ensuring a conducive environment for dialogue. It hosted multiple rounds of peace talks in Doha, providing diplomatic support and a neutral venue for negotiations, ensuring that the parties could engage in constructive dialogue to resolve the conflict.

Inclusive Peace Process

Qatar's mediation approach engaged a broad spectrum of stakeholders—from rebel leaders and rank-and-file members to the wider Darfur community. This strategy was instrumental in bringing reluctant leaders to the negotiation table. Ongoing dialogue, maintained by Djibril Bassolé, then Qatari Prime Minister Sheikh Hamad bin Jassim Al Thani, and His Excellency Minister Ahmad bin Abdullah Al Mahmoud, was crucial. Although this inclusive approach took up to three years, it highlighted the mediators' patience and commitment to overcoming the reluctance of several key rebel leaders to participate in the peace process.

In order to reach out to the wider Darfur community, Minister Al Mahmoud and Djibril Bassolé met with civil society representatives in Zalingei University, West Darfur, in December 2010, where they presented a document reflecting the community's demands, which had been collected earlier by Al Mahmoud during the exploratory visits to Darfur.[59] As the meeting proceeded, a protest broke out outside the university. Despite serious security risks, the Qatari diplomat recalled that he insisted upon exiting the building and addressing the gathered crowd, a step supported by Djibril Bassolé.[60] Minister Al Mahmoud viewed that as an important act of respect towards the people of Darfur and a reaffirmation of the mediators' courage and sincerity.[61]

In May 2011, the All Darfur Stakeholders Conference convened in Doha with almost 500 attendees from across Darfur.[62] Attendees included civil society organizations, traditional leaders, refugees and internally displaced persons, and representatives of multiple factions and political groups. Collectively, they called for a comprehensive peace agreement and addressed key concerns, including militia disarmament and victim compensation. Qatar's strategy of mobilizing civil society to pressurize armed movements proved critical, as hosting representatives of various elements of Darfurian society generated an inclusive environment for peace negotiations.[63] This engagement helped shift existing perceptions that rebel groups were the main barrier to peace, whilst intensifying public pressure on armed movements. This inclusive mediation strategy became a distinguishing feature of the DDPD compared to previous peace processes, paving the way for a more comprehensive peace agreement.

Leveraging Mediation through Aid and Investment

Qatar supported the Darfur Development Strategy (DDS) by pledging investments during its involvement in the initiative. In March 2010, the Darfur donors conference in Cairo approved Qatar's proposal to establish the Darfur Development Bank.[64] Ultimately welcomed by the parties to the DDPD, the proposal included Qatari plans to invest USD 2 billion.[65]

During the International Donor Conference for Reconstruction and Development in Darfur in April 2013, held in Doha and organized under the guidance of His Excellency Dr Ahmed bin Mohammed Al Muraikhi, Qatar provided USD 88.5 million in immediate cash support from its overall contribution to launch the implementation of recovery and reconstruction projects in Darfur.[66] Additionally, Qatar pledged USD 500 million to rebuild Darfur and support the DDS. This prospect of major inward investment in reconstruction constituted a form of leverage for Qatari mediation, acting as a 'carrot' to incentivize rebel groups to agree to the negotiated settlement.[67] Qatar's approach to mediation included culturally relevant initiatives, such as offering gifts during Muslim holidays, which some observers interpreted as reflective of its emphasis on fostering goodwill and trust amongst the parties.[68] Furthermore, Qatar's financial resources made it possible to host a large-scale Track II peace process in Doha for many months, with hundreds of guests hosted at the expense of the government.[69]

This has led to the charge that Qatari mediation in Darfur only bridged short-term divisions without tackling the deep-lying conflict causes.[70] However, by contrast, Qatar maintained a longer-term commitment to Darfur through diplomatic channels and provision of humanitarian and development assistance, with the latter acknowledged to be a facilitating factor in signing the agreement.[71] Qatari charitable and humanitarian frameworks, active in Sudan even before the negotiations, also shaped the trust placed in Qatar. They continued on-the-ground work beyond the negotiations, incentivizing the parties to reach peace, as these efforts could be sustained and expanded in the post-conflict phase.[72]

Overcoming Challenges in the Peace Process

The Darfur peace process faced multiple interlocking challenges that threatened to derail negotiations and limit the scope of any agreement. This section examines how Qatari mediators addressed two of the most complex and persistent obstacles—namely rebel factionalism and regional interference—and the strategies they used to keep the process on track.

Navigating Rebel Factionalism

The reluctance of key rebel factions to join the peace talks posed a major hurdle throughout the peace process. Central figures such as Khalil Ibrahim (the JEM's founding leader) and Abdel Wahid Al-Nur (head of the SLM) remained resistant to engaging with mediators. Djibril Bassolé emphasized that their ongoing reluctance to enter into dialogue with the regime impeded mediation efforts.[73]

Their absence was not merely a procedural oversight, but underscored the difficulty of achieving a comprehensive peace without the participation of all major parties. The JEM's disengagement illustrated a profound scepticism towards the peace process, although such disengagement was anticipated in the earlier stages of the peace process. In 2009, His Excellency Minister Ahmed bin Abdullah Al Mahmoud acknowledged the danger of other rebel groups refusing to join the process if the JEM met with the Sudanese government first. However, he judged that the other advantages of moving forward outweighed this concern. He reportedly likened the Doha Agreement to a train journey, emphasizing the need to 'start putting the train on the track', encouraging passengers (i.e. future signatories) to join at later stations (i.e. talks).[74] As the process began, His Excellency Minister Al Mahmoud explained:

> [T]he train has moved and the peace process started. The Darfurian people want peace and we will support them in achieving this, just like the international community. The Sudanese president assured that he will honour the peace document and the LJM said that it will abide by it. We are working with them in this sense and the train of peace is ongoing in its journey. We respect the opinion of those who do not want peace, but the sufferings of the Darfurian people cannot continue because of the opinions of someone here and there.[75]

This initial challenge was compounded by rebel disunity and factionalism.[76] Ambassador Zayed bin Rashid Al-Mansour Al-Nuaimi noted that Darfur's tribal society accelerated the rapid splintering of rebel groups.[77] What started as a manageable number of factions quickly doubled, complicating negotiations and raising questions about the legitimacy of emergent groups. Many adopted hardline stances without substantial military involvement in the conflict, prompting doubts about their actual influence. The proliferation of splinter groups posed a dilemma for Qatari mediators: ignoring smaller entities risked alienating their tribal support bases, potentially exacerbating the conflict; conversely, larger factions often refused to acknowledge these groups as legitimate negotiating partners, dismissing them as opportunists.

Qatar's mediation efforts resolved several areas of disagreement between the parties. Nevertheless, the multiplicity of armed movements and continuing divisions amongst them prolonged negotiations.[78] For instance, although JEM and the SLM were the largest two movements by 2008, Qatari mediators still required about seven months to gather these actors, communicate with them, and formulate an agreement to begin negotiations.[79] At the outset of the mediation, around seventeen different factions existed, each with unique positions and interests.[80] Another example is the LJM, formed from a mosaic of various groups and individuals under one banner. Although initially aligned with the agreement, each LJM faction sought its own share during implementation, resulting in a lack of consensus.[81] Some factions refused to comply, others opposed the terms, and some assumed different roles, forming more splinter factions.

This situation created a complex negotiation landscape, where inclusivity and pragmatism had to be balanced carefully. In managing this multiplicity of rebel groups, Qatar relied on careful preparatory work, notably seven months of meticulous planning and negotiation.[82] Commenting on the strengths of Qatari diplomacy in managing the issue of rebel divisions and shifting alliances, Ali Suleiman Al-Burjo argued:

> First of all, the patience of the Qataris, their patience with the Darfurian actors—this was crucial. I am telling you, if it had been any other country, I might have been kicked out from the start! But their patience and wisdom gave ownership of the process to the concerned parties themselves.[83]

Additionally, Qatar employed strategies to undermine the splinter groups' financial bases whilst also accommodating their aspirations. Ambassador Al-Nuaimi noted that identifying sources of external or internal support for the movements and then negotiating with their backers was critical to encouraging these groups towards peace.[84] By 2010, the Doha negotiations were marked by inter-rebel tensions, shifting allegiances, and a lack of transparency, as various international actors continued to exert pressure both publicly (often through cash pledges) and behind the scenes.[85] Time was of the essence throughout the talks, since any delays would likely fuel further factionalism and reduce the prospects for a negotiated agreement.[86]

Managing Regional Tensions

From the outset, one of the key challenges to mediating the Darfur conflict was the complex web of regional rivalries and external interests that risked undermining any cohesive peace process. Tensions between Sudan and its neighbours, especially Chad and Libya, were particularly destabilizing. Cross-border dynamics, including ethnic linkages, support for opposition groups, and proxy warfare, threatened to derail negotiations and contributed to persistent fragmentation amongst Darfuri rebel groups. Addressing these regional dynamics became a core component of Qatar's mediation strategy.

Rather than acting solely as a neutral platform, Qatari mediators actively worked to prevent competing mediation tracks from taking hold. In one early episode, following the February 2009 goodwill agreement between the Sudanese government and JEM, Qatari officials learned that JEM was considering engagement with an alternative platform in Cairo.[87] To address the growing risk of mediation fragmentation, Al Mahmoud contacted Scott Gration, the U.S. Special Envoy to Sudan, using his personal connection. He briefed Gration on the new developments and, after a day of verification, it was confirmed that the Cairo platform had been shelved.[88] This stands as one illustrative example of a contextually grounded strategy for managing regional relations that Qatar adopted throughout the multi-year mediation process.[89]

Regional geopolitics were further complicated by Sudan's modern borders with its neighbours, which left many tribes straddling both sides.[90] The Sudanese and Chadian governments issued mutual accusations that the other was supporting opposition forces. One notable instance of such proxy conflict dynamics was the JEM's Chad-backed incursion into Khartoum in May 2008. Such events deepened the discord between the two countries. The roots of the Darfur crisis were also seen to have begun with 'exporting the Chadian crisis to that region and ended with exporting the Darfur problem to the rest of Sudan and from there to the world'—a progression that necessitated 'reconciling the people of Darfur, restoring matters in Chad to their proper place, or isolating the Chadian problem from the situation in Darfur'.[91] Achieving this would have required a level of wider political consensus and coordination that was difficult to attain on the ground, especially with the high level of internationalization of the crisis.

Nevertheless, in this challenging regional environment, Qatari mediation prompted de-escalation of tensions and facilitated a détente between Sudan and Chad, with the Doha Accord signed in May 2009.[92] Qatar's diplomatic efforts proved crucial in normalizing relations between the two countries and establishing a solid groundwork for continued negotiations. The chief negotiator of the JEM, Ahmed Tugud Lisan, noted that initial discussions between the JEM and the Sudanese government in N'Djamena paved the way for a subsequent framework agreement in Doha.[93]

Likewise, Libya's involvement in the migration and military training of Darfur residents showed the interconnection of local and regional elements in the crisis. For instance, during negotiations with the movements in early 2010, the Qatari side found that the JEM, upon arriving at the platform, was accompanied by two major groups—one from Tripoli and the other from Addis Ababa—who aimed to become part of the peace process. Later on, mediators achieved some success in merging the two groups into a single movement under the leadership of Tijani Sese, forming the LJM. Yet, Libya covertly sought to influence the Darfur peace talks by dispatching a security officer to sway those rebel factions that it hosted in Tripoli, leading to agreements reached in the evening often unravelling by the next morning as new disputes kept emerging.[94] Minister Al Mahmoud recounted that, upon discovering this interference, he spoke to the head of Libyan intelligence, thanked him for facilitating the group's presence in Doha, but requested that Libya ease its interference and leave the group undisturbed during the talks.[95]

Qatari mediators' knowledge of the ethnic, tribal, and political dynamics within Darfur and the wider region informed their strategy for engaging in dialogue with the Central African Republic, Chad, Egypt, Eritrea, Ethiopia, Libya, and South Sudan.[96] Each engagement was carefully calibrated to address historical connections, safe havens for opposition, geographic proximity, shared conflict zones, and ethnic connections. In many instances, overcoming the external interference in the Darfur mediation process involved accurately identifying the real decision-makers and engaging with them through direct, high-level meetings, often in informal settings.[97]

One high-stakes example involved the UN Security Council. As efforts progressed to formalize the DDPD, the Qatari delegation was initially told that no session could be scheduled due to Syria and Yemen dominating the agenda. In response, His Excellency Al Mahmoud personally lobbied individual Security Council members, presenting the agreement and urging support. A meeting was hastily convened, but strong resistance from South Africa threatened to derail endorsement. According to Al Mahmoud, a tense exchange followed, during which he appealed directly to the ambassador's moral responsibility, ultimately leading to South Africa lifting its reservation.[98] The DDPD was subsequently adopted as an official UN document, representing a major diplomatic victory for Qatar.

These two interlinked challenges—rebel fragmentation and regional interference—shaped not only Qatar's approach to the Darfur peace process but also the contours of its post-mediation engagement. When the DDPD was announced, the absence of two major rebel signatories made implementation particularly fragile. This difficulty was compounded by the turbulent regional backdrop of the Arab Spring and the Gulf Crisis.[99] Despite these headwinds, Qatar sustained its diplomatic role during the follow-up phase, advocating for expanded inclusion of non-signatory groups and supporting post-agreement mechanisms aimed at reinforcing the peace process.

Post-Mediation Institutional Frameworks and Development Initiatives

Whilst rebel fragmentation and regional interference posed serious obstacles, the signing of the DDPD marked a critical turning point, shifting the focus from negotiation to implementation. In the aftermath of the agreement, Qatar transitioned from mediator to post-conflict partner, assuming a central role in the institutional and developmental efforts designed to consolidate peace. The following section examines how post-agreement mechanisms were established, and how Qatar sought to translate political commitments into tangible gains for Darfur's long-term recovery.

Monitoring and Verification Mechanisms

Under the DDPD, Qatar became a member of the Joint Commission, which, together with the Ceasefire Commission, was established as a ceasefire monitoring and verification mechanism. The Joint Commission's objective was to resolve disputes amongst parties referred to it by the Commission and ensure implementation of DDPD security provisions. The Joint Commission conducted multiple meetings during the post-agreement phase, where some limited progress was made in the verification of forces and disarmament plans. During these meetings, the members continuously emphasized the need for parties' commitment and timely completion of peace arrangements to ensure stability and development in Darfur.[100]

Additionally, Qatar chaired the Implementation Follow-up Commission, which monitored and assessed the DDPD implementation in accordance with the timelines, providing funding and technical assistance to bodies established by the agreement. This mechanism, despite having some structural weaknesses, became one of the distinct features of the DDPD compared to the DPA.[101] The meetings continued to take place multiple times in the years following the signing of the agreement. The thirteenth and fourteenth sessions—amongst the latest meetings—were held in 2018, in Doha and Khartoum, respectively.

Reconstruction and Development Efforts

The DDPD also galvanized international aid and investments in Darfur, which allowed for the implementation of some large-scale development projects. Qatar provided substantial financial support and encouraged other donors to contribute to Darfur's reconstruction. For instance, Qatar's commitment of USD 88.5 million to the UN multi-partner trust fund underscored its dedication to the region's development.[102] This influx of aid facilitated the implementation of essential services and infrastructure projects, including the construction of water stations, model villages, schools, healthcare facilities, police stations, and roads.[103] Various humanitarian and development Qatari organizations implemented projects for the resettlement of displaced people in several locations.[104] These efforts addressed immediate humanitarian needs and aimed at laying the groundwork for long-term economic growth in Darfur.

During the post-mediation phase, Qatar actively supported bilateral and multilateral reconstruction and development efforts in the Darfur region. In accordance with the provisions of the DDPD, the Darfur Joint Assessment Mission was conducted in late 2012, which developed and outlined the DDS.[105] Following this, Qatar's involvement expanded considerably in relation to the DDS' activities. For instance, the 2016 Qatar Fund for Development report presented its work towards the 'Reconstruction of Darfur Program' under three categories: (1) construction of model services centres in each of the Darfur's states; (2) supporting the Early Recovery Program in cooperation with the United Nations Development Programme in Darfur; and (3) a project for providing clean drinking water to the Southern and Central Darfur states.[106] One of the diplomats highlighted that Qatar, despite being the only proactive actor in this file, did everything it could to set up development projects in Darfur.[107] The key development project—with a notable USD 70 million investment—included the construction of ten integrated villages, aimed at benefiting over 300,000 people.[108] Other projects included multi-service complexes in Sisi and Abu Soruj villages in West Darfur, and a Taiba Education City for orphans, with the aim of enhancing education and healthcare access.[109] Additionally, Qatar Charity's broader efforts encompassed agricultural training and infrastructure improvements to support sustainable livelihoods in the region.

Outcomes of the DDPD

The DDPD led to multiple short- and long-term outcomes, both positive and negative, that shaped Darfur's political and developmental landscape. Signing the agreement was intended to resolve a multidimensional conflict. This agreement was built on earlier initiatives, including the DPA, and was shaped by Qatar's mediation efforts, substantial financial contributions, and a focus on integrating peace with development.

The DDPD yielded several positive outcomes in the immediate post-agreement phase. Under the auspices of the DPA and the DDPD, Disarmament, Demobilization, and Reintegration (DDR) programmes were revitalized. Prior to the agreement, the first DDR programme in Darfur, carried out in 2006 by the Sudanese government, demobilized 4,027 former combatants.[110] However, only 315 of these fighters received reintegration support. By 2015, following the DDPD, the programme had demobilized over 31,000 ex-combatants and fighters.[111] By 2016, the armed movements had been weakened militarily, and the fighting was confined to the Jebel Marra area.[112]

Another achievement was the incorporation of former armed group leaders into the political process through the establishment of the DRA.[113] The DRA was designed to oversee the implementation of the peace agreement and manage development projects in Darfur.

This step aimed to foster a sense of political representation and legitimacy amongst previously marginalized groups, contributing to a more inclusive governance structure. By integrating these leaders into formal political roles, the DDPD sought to reduce the appeal of armed rebellion and promote transition towards peaceful political engagement.[114] Several interviewees noted that Qatar was the primary, if not sole, donor behind the DRA's formation, providing it with more than USD 15 million in financial support.[115]

Conflict Continuation

Despite these achievements, the war in Darfur continued to escalate in the years following the DDPD. In 2013, new conflict trends emerged, the most notable being resource-based disputes over the control of artisanal gold mining and trade in the Jebel Amir area of North Darfur State. The resurgence of violence resulted in the displacement of 90,000 to 100,000 civilians in Darfur in 2012, with the following year witnessing even higher numbers, as 480,000 civilians were newly displaced.[116] In 2014 and 2015, the Rapid Support Forces (RSF)—a paramilitary group that evolved from the Janjaweed militias—carried out two counterinsurgency campaigns in Darfur, including one in Jebel Marra, during which the forces attacked villages, burned and looted homes, raped and beat villagers, extrajudicially executed civilians, and caused massive civilian population displacement.[117] By 2016, one of the most acute issues—namely the return of internally displaced persons and refugees to the places of their origin—was hindered as their lands were occupied by RSF and some Arab tribes from Chad and West Africa.[118] The conflict trends escalated after the signing of the DDPD and brought its efficacy into question.

Critiques and Counter-Arguments

Given these realities of continued conflict, the DDPD has been subject to various critiques that seek to account for the weak outcomes in terms of halting violence and bringing peace to Darfur and Sudan. Whilst not claiming that the DDPD was successful in bringing about peace in Darfur, this section also considers several notable themes that collectively constitute a nuanced reflection upon the outcomes and legacy of the agreement.

The Technocratic Peace Thesis

The DDPD has been subject to a critique that it did not constitute a conventional peace agreement involving all major parties, but was rather a technocratic framework aimed at leveraging peace through development. Qatar's financial commitments that underwrote the DDPD are held to be an aid package and governance framework that operates with a theory of change, strategically linking enhanced development in Darfur with peace consolidation. Assuming that the DDPD functioned as a hybrid framework leveraging peace through development, it is important to evaluate the success of the agreement on those terms. Ahmed Tugud Lisan, head of the JEM delegation, explained that the 'Qatari government exerted significant efforts in peacebuilding in Darfur, based on the outcomes of the Doha Peace Agreement. The initial steps involved constructing settlements, buildings, and institutions to enable the previously conflicting parties to establish a foothold for living and accommodation'.[119]

From a critical perspective, Alex De Waal states that 'the Doha Document for Peace in Darfur was an experiment in an internationally validated template, backed by Qatari funds, to incentivise peace, but it was incompetently managed'.[120] He also writes that: 'Rather than an agreement among combatants, or a consensus position drawn from consulting Darfurians, the Doha Document for Peace in Darfur, adopted in 2011, is a blueprint for a technocratic governance of Darfur, made possible by Qatari patronage and legitimized by the UN'.[121]

Despite the validity of the claim that the DDPD did not achieve peace in Darfur through the intended mechanism of promoting development, it should be recognized that the agreement was consistent with global policy towards fragile states at the time. This developmental approach to peacebuilding must be understood in the context of the security and development nexus rationale in the early 2000s. The international intervention in Darfur, alongside Iraq and Afghanistan, was seminal in advancing this new approach.[122]

Moreover, although the realization of the agreement's full potential to leverage peace through development was constrained by the unresolved security challenges, it nonetheless provided substantive support that attempted to address humanitarian and development issues whilst fostering peace and stability.

Addressing Darfur in Isolation from the Sudan Conflict

Another critique holds that the peacemaking strategy in the DDPD treated the Darfur issue in isolation from Sudan's broader conflict. The 2010–11 Darfur-focused mediation efforts followed the landmark 2005 Comprehensive Peace Agreement, which brokered South Sudan's independence. Notably, various actors urged a more comprehensive approach to Sudan's multiple, overlapping conflicts.[123] Such calls included the 2009 AU High-Level Panel on Darfur, led by Thabo Mbeki, which framed the issue as 'Sudan's crisis in Darfur'.[124] Another attempt to integrate Darfur into a national framework emerged through the Sudan Consultative Forum, established in May 2010 and lasting until 2013.[125] From its inaugural meeting in Khartoum in July 2010, the Forum served as a platform for Sudan's international partners to implement the Comprehensive Peace Agreement provisions. It coordinated international support for Sudan's democratic transformation, enabling parties to exchange views on peace, justice, and reconciliation in Darfur. Critics argue that isolating the Darfur conflict was a missed opportunity to tackle national-level challenges comprehensively. Only in 2014 did the UN Security Council begin addressing the Darfur conflict within Sudan's broader crisis.[126]

However, mediators persisted in handling Darfur separately at that time. Responsibility for this approach lay with the broader multiparty mediation framework—encompassing the AU, UN, Qatar, and key states advising in the background—rather than any single actor. By 2011, the peace process itself was marked by competition between mediators (metaphorically described as 'too many cooks').[127] Thabo Mbeki and Djibril Bassolé each championed distinct approaches, with Bassolé favouring a separate Darfur track and Mbeki supporting the Doha peace talks. This strategy had positive advantages in tackling a more manageable, localized issue first—one Darfuris could potentially resolve themselves—thereby laying groundwork for peacemaking in Sudan at large. Whilst a comprehensive approach seems ideal in theory, Sudan's political realities rendered it impractical at the time. A telling example was the EU's reluctance to accept the Darfur-based political process, advocated by Thabo Mbeki, citing its exclusion from the 'quartet' (that is, the AU High-Level Implementation Panel, UNAMID, the U.S. and Sudan).[128]

Critics contend that compartmentalizing Sudan's conflicts aligned with Khartoum's strategy of granting the Bashir regime a strategic victory in peacemaking.[129] Some perceived the DDPD as favouring the Sudanese government, leading to charges that mediator bias undermined the agreement. For instance, it was claimed that the DDPD 'lacked credibility because the State of Qatar was supporting the regime in Khartoum and helping it achieve political stability with the intention of placing Sudan within the regional political alliance supported by Qatar'.[130] Such perceptions were reinforced by practitioners who noted that Al-Bashir, initially refusing talks with the JEM following its Omdurman attack in May 2008, accepted the Arab League proposal to appoint Qatar as a mediator, due to Sudan's close political and economic ties with the Gulf state and the international Islamic movement headquartered in Doha.[131]

The critiques of mediator bias, however, overlook the need for reliable ties with Khartoum, whose central role in the conflict and its ability to resist the international community made its cooperation essential for any agreement. For instance, in 2007, after repeatedly agreeing to the 2006 Addis Ababa Agreement's framework, President Al-Bashir effectively rejected the proposed hybrid UN–AU peacekeeping force in Darfur, citing violation of Sudan's sovereignty and eventually undermining the accord.[132] Additionally, Qatar's pre-mediation groundwork balanced its engagement, ensuring the DDPD's viability by involving other rebel groups (to the extent possible within the context of international support provided at the time). With no colonial baggage, Qatar was well-positioned to bring diverse parties to the negotiation table, using its financial resources and ability to convene actors on its neutral ground to advance the dialogue during political stagnation and high-stakes competition between international actors. Our interview data and the observable willingness of leading international actors to collaborate with Qatar throughout the peace process suggest recognition of Qatar's neutrality and credibility.

Grasping the contextual particularities and conflict dynamics in Darfur in the late 2000s is key to comprehending the DDPD's impact and legacy. Whilst the Doha Document did not address all conflicts in Sudan, some of its elements focused on interconnected issues that would otherwise be difficult to tackle in detail within a national process. These include provisions for reconstruction and development, the return of internally displaced persons, compensation for the war-affected population, local reconciliation, restoration of traditional land rights, and the role of the native administration. By 2011, rather than becoming a comprehensive peace agreement, the Doha Document emerged as 'a technical template on which peace theoretically could be built'.[133] Ultimately, as Natsios puts it:

> All efforts—Abuja, Addis Ababa, Serte, and Doha—failed because there are so many competing actors with so many conflicting agendas. The rebel groups tried to outdo each other with their demands to incorporate unachievable and widely unrealistic promises to their supporters in the agreement. [...] No successful peace process in recent history has included so many competing players or such exaggerated demands.[134]

Treating Darfur in isolation from Sudan's broader conflicts reveals a deeper tension in modern peacemaking, demonstrating a trade-off between addressing immediate, localized issues and tackling systemic, national-level crises. In Darfur, this dilemma was evident through the mediators' competing and constantly changing approaches to resolving the conflict.[135] Whilst the DDPD attempted to address the unfolding violence and political stalemate, it also showed the inherent risk of peace process fragmentation. The Darfur case suggests that tackling issues in isolation from the broader context requires further mechanisms to ensure the outcomes are integrated into a broader framework for national reconciliation.

Missing Rebel Groups and Follow-Up Mediation

The failure to bring the main rebel groups to the peace process meant that the potential for violence remained. Day writes that 'like its predecessor, the DDPD suffered from a lack of meaningful buy-in by the parties, many of whom continued to fight openly in Darfur over the next two years while others remained outside the process'.[136] Whilst creating momentum for further peacemaking efforts, it largely missed the opportunity to establish mechanisms that would bind parties to sustainable conflict de-escalation.[137] The persistent mistrust between signatories and non-signatories, and between local communities and the government, showed the limitations of reconciling national political interests with regional demands and grievances, reflecting the broader challenges of negotiating peace in a divided society.

After signing the DDPD, Qatari mediators continued their efforts to bring the two main rebel factions—the JEM and SLM—into the agreement, whilst simultaneously working with then President Al-Bashir's government on assuring the presence of the current regime representatives at the negotiation table.[138] At that point, Qatar's international partnerships facilitated dialogue between the conflicting parties.[139] Qatari mediators held meetings with Jibril Ibrahim and Minni Minawi in European capitals (some of the parties' leaderships were residing in Europe), aiming to secure their commitment to the agreement. Initial progress was achieved in December 2018, when the Sudanese government and the two rebel groups signed a pre-negotiation agreement, paving the way for resuming peace talks in Doha in 2019. The agreement was signed in Berlin after two years of informal talks facilitated by the German Federal Foreign Office and the Berghof Foundation.[140] Despite efforts to bring Germany, France, the UK, and the U.S. to facilitate negotiations in Doha in 2019, the planned discussions were halted by the fall of the Al-Bashir regime in Khartoum, which set Sudan towards a turbulent political transition.[141]

Legacy and Influence of the DDPD

The DDPD was amongst several bold yet ultimately unsuccessful attempts to resolve the Darfur conflict, reflecting the challenges in achieving sustainable peace in Sudan. Nevertheless, its legacy extends beyond Darfur in the 2010s, shaping subsequent mediation efforts. In 2014, peace talks convened in Addis Ababa with largely the same composition as the Abuja talks. Unlike the Doha negotiations, the Addis Ababa process involved key rebel leaders negotiating with government officials. Simultaneously, as Alex De Waal contends, the DDPD process altered the political marketplace in Darfur, thereby complicating efforts to reach a comprehensive agreement in Addis Ababa.[142]

Provisions set out in the DDPD influenced future attempts to negotiate peace in Darfur. Qatar's efforts in bringing peace helped to shape the 2020 Juba Peace Agreement, as evidenced by strategies carried over into the Juba talks. Furthermore, Minni Minawi stressed the iterative nature of the Darfur peace process, remarking that 'we were not an alternative to the roles played by Doha in Darfur, and the Juba Agreement is an extension of the role it played in the field of peace'.[143] Qatar also participated intermittently in the Juba talks.[144] Although ultimately failing to end the conflict, the Juba Agreement stood as the most significant accord reached since the DDPD, representing a renewed attempt to address Darfur's enduring challenges through a more inclusive and comprehensive framework.

Nonetheless, the greatest challenges facing Darfur persisted, carrying over into new negotiation phases. Unresolved issues included poor implementation of security arrangements, severe humanitarian crises, neglect of transitional justice, weak mechanisms for dialogue and tribal reconciliation, and foreign meddling. Addressing those issues in subsequent accords might have put Darfur on a trajectory towards greater stability. Yet what was once referred to as the 'Sudan crisis in Darfur' has since transformed into the 'Darfur crisis in Sudan', with the outbreak of the war between the Sudanese Armed Forces and RSF in April 2023.

Conclusion

This chapter highlighted Qatari mediation in the Darfur conflict, focusing on its approach and the challenges encountered. Its strategic engagement, use of diplomatic resources, and foreign aid stand out in the history of international efforts to address the protracted conflict in Darfur. Through meticulous groundwork, dedication to conducting inclusive negotiations, and leveraging aid and investment, Qatar made substantial contributions to the peace process. Its efforts were marked by extensive preparatory work and profound awareness of the conflict's local and regional dynamics. The inclusive peace process was instrumental in creating space for Darfur's civil society. Despite substantial challenges faced on the way to long-lasting peace, such commitment to complete the follow-up and support activities during the post-agreement phase pointed to its dedication to achieving political consensus in Darfur.

Although the refusal of major rebel groups to sign the agreement and the continuing violence highlighted the limitations of the peace process, Qatar's role as a mediator demonstrated the possibility of dialogue, where it brought short-term political stability and development aid to Darfur. This case exemplified Qatar's potential to operate in deeply divided societies where prolonged conflicts are complicated by continued division amongst conflict parties and extensive involvement of external actors with their changing approaches to conflict resolution over time. The lessons learned from this experience remain invaluable for future peace initiatives, emphasizing the need for comprehensive preparation, inclusive dialogue, and sustained post-mediation support. Whilst not fully resolving the conflict, Qatar's efforts contributed to a framework for ongoing peacebuilding and development in Darfur, reflecting its broader aspirations in regional and international diplomacy.

6

AFGHANISTAN AT A CROSSROADS

THE 2020 U.S.–TALIBAN AGREEMENT AND BEYOND

In the early 2010s, Qatar quietly assumed a mediating role in the protracted Afghan conflict, notably through hosting the Taliban's political mission in Doha. Whilst avoiding global public attention, Qatar's involvement faced low expectations and even cynicism amongst diplomatic and research communities, both globally and regionally. It was widely believed that mediating the multidimensional and geostrategically important conflict in Afghanistan, involving the world's foremost superpower and irreconcilably opposed Afghan conflict parties, would be a task too great for a 'small-state' mediator like Qatar. Yet the 2020 agreement between the United States (U.S.) and the Taliban, signed in Doha, was a watershed moment in perceptions of Qatari mediation and its facilitation of the peace process in Afghanistan, showcasing to a global audience the culmination of almost a decade of patient diplomatic groundwork.

Qatar's role in Afghanistan was multifaceted and complex, involving diplomatic endeavours to broker an agreement between the U.S.-led coalition and the Taliban, attempts to foster intra-Afghan talks, and efforts to act as an interlocutor since the Taliban's return in 2021. This chapter explores these various third-party roles played by Qatar, shedding light on the modalities and outcomes of the mediation and facilitation process, the management of the technical and geopolitical challenges, and the operationalization of the aid and diplomacy nexus in conflict mediation.

The case analysis in this chapter makes an original contribution to the literature by analyzing Qatari mediation in Afghanistan through a range of primary and secondary sources. This includes high-level access to the testimonies and experiences of Qatari mediators and the conflict parties in Afghanistan. It also draws on direct observational data from the co-authors' experience in scholarly and practitioner engagement with the Afghan peace process and their support for various Qatari initiatives in Afghanistan.

Context of Afghanistan

Afghanistan has endured over four decades of protracted conflict, beginning with the 1979 Soviet invasion, the Soviet–Afghan War, and the civil war in the 1990s. Following the 11 September 2001 attacks, which killed 2,977 people, Operation Enduring Freedom was launched, making Afghanistan, particularly the rural areas, the site of a large-scale international military intervention aimed at defeating Al-Qaeda and the Taliban whilst simultaneously seeking to stabilize the country.

Alongside the military operations, vast financial resources—around USD 4 billion in aid annually—were allocated towards building a modern Afghan state.[1] The goal of international efforts was to shape Afghanistan's governance system and promote peace and development. Afghanistan's post-Taliban political settlement was established through the Bonn Agreement on 5 December 2001. However, rather than an inclusive political arrangement, the agreement was more of a pronouncement of the U.S. military and security logic, which dictated conditions and presented a monolithic view of peace.[2] For example, the U.S. and its allies chose to exclude the Taliban from the conference and the resulting agreement. This was a major misstep—or, as Lakhdar Brahimi, the United Nations Secretary-General Special Representative for Afghanistan, framed it, 'the original sin or a big hole in the process',[3] which undermined the implementation of the provisions of the Bonn agreement.[4]

After 2001, the U.S.-led coalition followed an aggressive military rather than diplomatic strategy, aiming to eradicate the Taliban from Afghan soil. Whilst the Taliban was degraded in military capabilities and forced to seek shelter in Pakistan or hideouts within rural Afghanistan, it was not completely defeated.[5] Rather, by 2003, the group had regained ground and legitimacy, benefiting from an allegiance of disenchanted local tribes.[6] Subsequently, it mobilized thousands of recruits from underdeveloped villages, in particular those that were bombed and raided by both the Afghan government and international military forces.[7] In so doing, the Taliban consolidated a power base and became a meaningful force that would eventually have to be interacted with. In short, the exclusion of the Taliban from the post-war political order was a counterproductive decision that missed an opportunity to build the new Afghan political settlement on an inclusive foundation from the outset.

Positions of the Conflict Parties

The conflict in Afghanistan was characterized by complex and often divergent visions amongst the parties involved. President Hamid Karzai's government, the U.S., and the North Atlantic Treaty Organization (NATO) were constrained by certain non-negotiable principles regarding the Afghan constitution and government legitimacy, strongly maintaining that any political solution must preserve the core elements of the post-2001 constitutional order, including democratic elections and basic human rights. They were also adamant that the Taliban end its armed insurgency unconditionally and cut ties with Al-Qaeda and its affiliates. This stance limited the scope of potential compromises with the Taliban, who advocated for significant changes to the existing governmental structure.[8] For instance, the Taliban never recognized the post-2001 governance framework, viewing the government of the Islamic Republic of Afghanistan in Kabul as an 'impotent puppet manipulated by Western forces',[9] primarily referring to the U.S. Consequently, negotiating with Kabul was not a major objective the Taliban actively pursued. Instead, the U.S. represented a powerful enemy and the true authority in the country with whom the Taliban might negotiate some strategic issues in return for their total withdrawal from Afghanistan.

It is important to note, however, that there were attempts at dialogue and negotiation in the early 2000s, although these were limited. The Afghan government, supported by its international allies, had made overtures to insurgent groups, offering political inclusion in exchange for laying down arms and accepting the constitutional framework. These efforts achieved varying degrees of success but were complicated by ongoing military operations, shifting alliances, and deep-seated mistrust amongst the parties involved, particularly the U.S., which wanted a quick victory.[10]

As such, the initial talks occurred within a context of ideological and military stalemate. For President Karzai and the U.S.-led coalition, upholding the 2004 constitution and the republican nature of the political system in Afghanistan, combating international terrorism, and defeating the Taliban represented major strategic priorities. Conversely, the Taliban focused on liberating Afghanistan from foreign intervention and establishing an Islamic state.

Previous Mediation Efforts

After the Taliban's ouster from Kabul following the U.S. invasion in 2001, the notion of peace with the Taliban was out of the question for Washington. Nevertheless, as prospects of a swift military victory were fading, tentative interest in a political resolution was on the rise.[11] Various actors—including diplomatic, non-state, and intelligence strata—were involved in exploratory talks to test the feasibility of a negotiated political settlement that could accommodate the needs of the conflict parties. However, they were doomed to fail for multiple reasons, including the involvement of the mediators in military operations in Afghanistan, the imposition of preconditions deemed too demanding by the Taliban (such as publicly announcing their disassociation from Al-Qaeda), and the general lack of trust between the conflict parties.[12]

Following the stalemate of the early 2000s, various states attempted to play a role in mediation efforts in the Afghan conflict. In 2008 and 2009, President Hamid Karzai requested that the Saudi government facilitate high-level talks between the Afghan government and the Taliban. Although welcomed by the international community, the Saudi initiative did not achieve a breakthrough.[13] Riyadh, troubled by the involvement of Saudi nationals in the 11 September 2001 attacks, demanded that the Taliban publicly distance themselves from Al-Qaeda as a precondition for engagement in the Afghan peace process.[14] Moreover, Shiite groups and the leaders of the Northern Alliance (an anti-Taliban coalition of mainly non-Pashtun groups, including Tajiks, Uzbeks, Hazaras, and Turkmens) opposed the Saudi initiative.[15] Additionally, at the regional level, Iran openly criticized the initiative and insisted on having a role in any Afghan peace deal.[16]

Between 2007 and 2010, Norway secretly acted as a messenger between the Quetta Shura (the Taliban Leadership Council) and the Afghan government, arranging a meeting in Oslo on 28 February 2010. Mullah Abdul Ghani Baradar was supposed to attend, but his arrest in Pakistan led to the Taliban's withdrawal.[17] Another attempt in August 2010 also failed due to a last-minute cancellation by the Taliban. These setbacks, combined with direct threats from Al-Qaeda to Norwegian diplomats, forced Norway to abandon the Quetta Track. Despite increasing the Taliban's willingness for peace talks, Norway's efforts did not lead to official negotiations.[18]

In late 2009, Germany initiated contact with Tayyab Agha, Mullah Omar's former secretary, and initial meetings organized in Doha and Munich facilitated direct talks between Afghan and U.S. delegates.[19] The major outcome was the agreement to establish a Taliban political office in Qatar, contingent on the Taliban publicly dissociating from terrorism. The talks also included a prisoner exchange agreement involving five Taliban leaders and U.S. Sergeant Bowe Bergdahl.[20] However, the Taliban withdrew from these talks in March 2012 due to U.S. demands, and the absence of Afghan government representatives led to diplomatic tensions, prompting President Karzai to consider relocating the talks to Saudi Arabia.[21]

From 2007, the European Union (EU) and the United Nations (UN) endeavoured to establish contact and facilitate talks between the Taliban leadership and the international community. For instance, Michael Semple, the Deputy to the EU Special Representative for Afghanistan, organized secret exploratory talks with some Taliban commanders to identify opportunities for future interaction between the warring parties. Nonetheless, his efforts were halted when Karzai's government discovered there had been talks with the Taliban without its participation or knowledge.[22] Similarly, in 2009, Kai Eide, the head of the UN mission in Afghanistan, met with Taliban leaders to discuss venues and conditions for future talks. However, these efforts also failed after the 2010 joint U.S.–Pakistani security operation had captured Taliban leader Mullah Abdul Ghani Baradar in February 2010, who earlier endorsed the talks with the UN representatives.[23]

Over the years, other regional and international efforts aimed to revive the peace process. This included the Pugwash initiative and the Urumqi talks (both in May 2015), the Murree Peace Process in July 2015, the Heart of Asia-Istanbul Process Ministerial Conference in December 2015, the Quadrilateral Coordination Group in January 2016, the Russia–China–Pakistan Trilateral Dialogue on Afghanistan in December 2016, the Moscow Six-Party Talks in February 2017, and the Kabul Peace Process in June 2017—all of which failed to generate significant momentum between the conflict parties that could lead to a comprehensive political agreement. Common issues in these initiatives included a lack of coordination between tracks, heavily conditioned talks, the exclusion of the Taliban from participation, the influence of foreign meddling, and power asymmetry.[24]

Against this backdrop of unsuccessful mediation attempts and competition amongst potential hosts for peace talks, Qatar emerged as a major mediator and positioned itself as a trusted intermediary, thereby establishing a unique role in the diplomatic process.

Qatar's Mediation in Afghanistan

This section explains how Qatar's cultivated access to the Taliban evolved into a central diplomatic channel—from early informal exchanges with Taliban representatives, to hosting the U.S.–Taliban negotiations and the intra-Afghan dialogue, and later striking a difficult balance between humanitarian coordination and political legitimacy after August 2021.

Qatar's Entry as a Mediator

The killing of Osama bin Laden in Pakistan in May 2011 marked a significant turning point for the U.S. 'War on Terror' strategy in

Afghanistan, leading to increased efforts to negotiate with the Taliban and gradual military drawdowns.[25] Additionally, realizing the low possibility of a total military victory, the Obama administration approached Qatar in late 2011 to host the negotiations with the Taliban, recognizing its diplomatic acumen.[26] This request was driven by the need for a neutral and trusted mediator; as such, Doha was selected based on its acceptance of preconditions and non-involvement in the Afghan conflict.[27] Qatar accepted the role and agreed to formally host the Taliban's representation in a political office in Doha in 2011. After extensive preliminary arrangements and back-channel contacts under Qatari facilitation, this office was officially inaugurated in Doha in 2013, and became a focal point for diplomatic efforts aimed at resolving the longstanding Afghan conflict.[28]

Notably, Qatar's entry as a mediator to the U.S.–Taliban talks reflected its wider policy of engaging in mediation only when requested by negotiating parties. The importance of this strategy was underscored by the failed attempt of the United Arab Emirates (UAE) to intervene as a formal third party in the U.S.–Taliban negotiations and in the intra-Afghan process, when former President Ashraf Ghani sought to rotate the negotiation process around the Gulf region.[29] In both attempts, the UAE was eventually rebuffed by the Taliban, who were sceptical of the motives behind their offer. This point is further elaborated by Muhammad Suhail Shaheen, the head of the Taliban political office in Doha:

> Some countries wanted to host negotiations in their capitals instead of Doha, but Qatar had gained our trust and families of the members of the negotiation team were living in Doha, so we were not ready to change the avenue of negotiations. Furthermore, we believed that those countries may not be as impartial as Qatar, so we continued to opt for Qatar.[30]

Similarly, Zalmay Khalilzad, the U.S. Special Representative for Afghanistan Reconciliation, confirmed this competition amongst regional parties to host the U.S.–Taliban peace talks:

> There was significant interest from others, particularly because they believed it would be a high-profile negotiation that would attract considerable attention. Unsurprisingly, they wanted to host the

> event. But, after consulting and deliberating for a few weeks, I ultimately decided that we would conduct the talks here [Qatar], which I determined was the most realistic and appropriate location.[31]

Moreover, Qatar did not actively engage in Afghanistan's internal conflicts during the tumultuous 1980s and 1990s. Whilst other Gulf states supported various *mujahideen* factions during the Soviet–Afghan War and the subsequent civil war, Qatar maintained a relatively neutral stance.[32] Furthermore, from 1996 to 2001, Abu Dhabi and Riyadh played a crucial role in recognizing and supporting the Taliban government. However, after 2001, the UAE and Saudi Arabia severed ties with the Taliban, aligning with Washington's position and refraining from contact with the group.[33] In contrast, Qatar's unique position as an Islamic country that did not border Afghanistan, had no role in the conflict, and did not oppose the Taliban since 2001, made it an ideal venue for the Taliban political office and peace talks, thereby meeting the key criteria set by Mullah Omar.[34]

Moreover, through its experiences in Lebanon, Palestine, and Darfur, Qatar built a respectable diplomatic reputation, promoting its acceptability as a neutral mediator between different conflict parties. Since the 2000s, Qatar has established a reputation for mediating international conflicts and for advancing dialogue without imposing its agenda or threatening the conflict parties; these were critical factors that earned the Taliban's trust and acceptance.[35] This trust was not automatic but was also earned through diplomacy and patience. One leading Qatari official stated that 'before talks even began between the Taliban and the Americans, we spent more than seven months building trust with the Taliban. That gave us room to operate and earned us the movement's acceptance'.[36]

As such, Qatar's acceptability as a mediator can be attributed, inter alia, to its neutrality and non-threatening nature, its readiness to engage with actors of various viewpoints, and the capacity to mediate constructively and impartially rather than through coercion and the imposition of a predetermined agenda.[37] This point is also elaborated by Dr Mutlaq bin Majid Al-Qahtani, the Special Envoy of the Minister of Foreign Affairs for Counterterrorism and Mediation in Conflict Resolution:

> Qatar has led the mediation process, setting aside cultural, religious, or political bias toward any of the conflict parties. While previous mediators entered the mediation with hidden agendas, aiming, for example, to promote their bilateral relations with the U.S. or influence the outcomes of the peace agreements to their economic or political benefit, Qatar has neither favoured the U.S. for being a strategic partner, by labelling the Taliban a terrorist organization and increasing pressure on them during the process, nor did it favour the latter given its religious affiliation. Instead, the same distance was maintained with both parties, which promoted Qatar's credibility and transparency.[38]

Whilst the presence of the Taliban's office in Doha cultivated direct connections with Afghan leadership during negotiations and expedited decision-making, the direct relationships between the Qatari leadership and the U.S. President and senior American officials—thanks to the special ties between the two countries—were equally vital to the peace process. Qatar's embassy in Washington, led by His Excellency Ambassador Sheikh Meshal bin Hamad Al Thani, was instrumental in conveying diplomatic messages and building trust amongst U.S. officials and Congress in Doha's ability to host and mediate talks in a neutral and professional manner.[39]

In short, Qatar successfully entered as a facilitator in the early days of the Afghan peace process in 2011 following the official request of the conflict parties, particularly the American government. This was in part due to Qatar's profile as a highly credible, culturally sensitive, and flexible mediator. Importantly, Qatar's acceptance of the role was by no means impromptu, and the Ministry of Foreign Affairs was already prepared to assist and had examined conflict analyses of Afghanistan and lessons learned documents based on the experiences of other peace processes, including the Colombian case.[40] Consequently, rather than following the ad hoc style that characterized previous interventions, Qatar's entry was part of a balanced and evidence-driven policy of diplomatic engagement. As such, Qatar proved indispensable to the negotiation process, emerging as the go-to mediator between the U.S. and the Taliban.[41]

Qatar's Roles in the Afghanistan Peace Process

Qatar was a principal actor in the Afghanistan peace process—hosting, mediating, and facilitating the U.S.–Taliban and intra-Afghan negotiations and subsequently managing the post-2021 humanitarian challenges following the Taliban's return to power. These roles required vast financial resources and a combination of strategies and measures to build trust between the parties, maintain communication channels, facilitate negotiations, and ensure a less chaotic humanitarian evacuation.

Mediating U.S.–Taliban Talks

Talks between the U.S. and the Taliban were conducted over the course of eleven rounds spanning two years.[42] The first formal and direct negotiations over the withdrawal agreement between the U.S. and the Taliban commenced on 31 July 2018 in Doha. This initial meeting set the framework for further dialogue, leading to a second series of formal talks between 16 and 18 November 2018, wherein both parties engaged more substantively in negotiations. The fifth round of talks, from February to March 2019, was particularly notable as the two delegations engaged extensively in face-to-face discussions and with Qatari mediation over two weeks. This series of negotiations culminated in a landmark agreement on 29 February 2020 between the U.S. and the Taliban in Doha, witnessed by international representatives and marking a significant milestone in the pursuit of peace in Afghanistan.

Qatar's Third-Party Roles in U.S.–Taliban Talks

Qatar played a significant role throughout the multi-year negotiation process between the U.S. and the Taliban, serving as both a facilitator and a mediator at various points. For instance, before the 2018–20 peace talks, negotiations often stalled due to the intensity of the conflict and high death tolls on both sides. Meanwhile, Qatari diplomacy quietly worked to build common ground between the U.S. and the Taliban. This least reported episode is best captured by Qatar's chargé d'affaires for Afghanistan: 'His Excellency Sheikh Mohammed bin Abdulrahman Al Thani gradually broke this deadlock through tireless shuttle diplomacy. Since 2015, he worked relentlessly, proposing solutions and persuading both sides to meet face-to-face, taking the crucial first step towards a negotiated solution'.[43]

During the most intensive phase of the talks, the Taliban and U.S. met at the Sharq Hotel in Doha for sixteen consecutive days.[44] In this critical period, Qatar was not merely acting as a facilitator but was directly mediating between the two parties. Importantly, Qatar's role included the drafting of multiple versions of the U.S.–Taliban agreement text, with members of the Qatari mediation team producing the draft iterations during and between sessions to immediately reflect the positions expressed by the two sides during the discussions.

These efforts also helped overcome critical bottlenecks in the negotiation process, such as the withdrawal timeline of the foreign forces. Muhammad Suhail Shaheen, the head of the Taliban's political office, stressed the importance of Qatari involvement:

> The timeframe of withdrawal of foreign forces from Afghanistan was one of those sticking points. The timeframe asked by U.S. was initially three years, then decreased to eighteen months after long talks between the two sides. The U.S. side final word was eighteen months while we insisted on nine months. It was through the mediation of Qatar, particularly through the good offices of Sheikh Mohammed bin Abdulrahman Al Thani, that both sides agreed on a fourteen-month timeframe. So, their role was essential and constructive to keep negotiations on track for success.[45]

Moreover, Qatari mediators in Doha closely monitored the talks, stepping in to defuse tensions when needed. In the early meetings of 2018, U.S. General Austin S. Miller addressed the Taliban in a forceful tone, warning of destruction if they refused the agreement. Mullah Baradar, angered, insisted they were 'not here to sign a surrender agreement' and nearly walked out. At that point, the Emir's national adviser recalled, 'I held Baradar's hand and urged him to stay, relying on our trust and solid relationship. Afterwards, Khalilzad tried to ease the tension, and talks resumed productively'.[46]

On other occasions, when the conflict parties showed little flexibility during negotiations, Qatari mediators shifted from a technical to a humanitarian approach rooted in Islamic principles. This was echoed in the words of Qatar's chargé d'affaires for Afghanistan:

> During the negotiations, we were constantly aware that every day we reached a solution faster meant saving 300 lives in Afghanistan; a month's delay could cost around 9,000 lives. Using this humanitarian framing touched everyone—Americans, foreign forces, and the Taliban alike—and gave significant weight to the talks.[47]

Mediatory support also involved shuttle diplomacy between the two sides, particularly during difficult points in the negotiations; for example, when President Donald Trump cancelled talks with the Taliban after nine rounds of discussions in response to the killing of an American soldier, despite an agreement in principle being reached.[48] The Taliban reportedly believed Trump's withdrawal from the talks was due to their refusal to sign the deal at Camp David. However, this setback was overcome when Qatar brokered the release of a British and an Australian citizen in exchange for three high-profile Taliban prisoners, enabling the talks to resume.[49] This deal involved several prominent actors within the Qatari government, including the then Deputy Prime Minister and Foreign Minister, Sheikh Mohammed bin Abdulrahman Al Thani, and the Special Envoy, Dr Mutlaq bin Majid Al-Qahtani. Qatari mediation also addressed less-reported disputes, such as the Taliban's demand for a guarantor and the unwillingness of the U.S. to grant a monitoring role to a foreign government. This was eventually resolved by the U.S. arrangement for eleven Taliban members to be temporarily removed from the UN Security Council travel sanctions list.

Qatar also dedicated significant efforts and resources to incorporate trust-building measures as the negotiations advanced, cognizant of the fact that withdrawal from the negotiations was still an option for the parties. For instance, Special Envoy Dr Mutlaq bin Majid Al-Qahtani argued that in the preparatory phase of the U.S.–Taliban talks, Qatar aimed to maintain open communication channels by facilitating discussions that helped build trust between the parties. These discussions included topics such as U.S. sanctions and UN travel bans on Taliban leaders, prisoner releases, hostage exchanges, and the status of the Taliban's political office and commission in Doha.[50] Through these measures, Qatar established two-way communication channels, addressed perceptions of power imbalance, and built the necessary trust level to motivate the parties to negotiate.

Qatar's involvement in the negotiations also entailed providing technical assistance for Taliban leaders to travel to Doha for talks. The travel ban imposed in 2000 through the UN Security Council Resolution 1333 restricted the movement of Taliban leaders. However, Qatar's willingness to host groups proscribed by many conventional state mediators internationally, the establishment of the Taliban political office in Doha, and the logistical assistance through subsidized flights from Kabul to Doha were useful to both conflict parties.[51]

Qatari diplomats, especially the former Special Envoy Dr Mutlaq bin Majid Al-Qahtani, were actively involved in the Afghan case. He visited Kabul and various regional capitals multiple times to meet with key stakeholders and support the peace process, with 'this upbeat diplomatic activity aiming to establish Doha as a genuine platform on which international buy-in and efforts to find a peaceful resolution to the Afghan conflict could be streamlined and consolidated rather than having scattered endeavours pulling in different directions'.[52]

An important yet less-reported element of Qatar's role in the 2020 agreement was the underlying institutional and leadership structure that guided the mediation process. Dr Mutlaq bin Majid Al-Qahtani explains this point in detail:

> The diplomatic, political, logistical, and technical management of the U.S.–Taliban negotiations required highly coordinated efforts, a clear chain of command, and a focused vision between several vital institutions, such as the Amiri Diwan, the Ministry of Foreign Affairs, the General Intelligence Agency, the Security Advisor of His Highness the Emir, and the Qatari Embassy in Kabul. In addition, influential political figures—including His Highness Sheikh Tamim bin Hamad Al Thani; His Excellency Sheikh Mohammed bin Abdulrahman Al Thani; and His Excellency Mohammed bin Ahmed Al-Misnad, Advisor to His Highness the Emir for National Security—have drawn on their solid political expertise and acumen to push toward a peaceful settlement to the conflict.[53]

To frame the above point differently, Qatar adopted a whole-of-government approach in handling the Afghan case. The Qatari mediation team strategically ensured efforts were coordinated across various related institutions and departments. Accordingly, these joint efforts reduced the risk of conflicting policies and actions and allowed for resource optimization, ensuring that all available policy instruments and expertise were utilized efficiently. This ensured comprehensive and informed decision-making and a coherent strategy that addressed the complex, multifaceted nature of the conflict. This whole-of-government approach helped Qatar strengthen its credibility and trust amongst conflicting parties, demonstrating its commitment towards reaching a peaceful resolution.

Challenges during the U.S.–Taliban Peace Talks

The U.S.–Taliban peace talks occurred against the backdrop of the 2017–21 Gulf Crisis. In addition to facilitating the sensitive peace talks between the conflict parties, Qatari mediators had to build and maintain regional and global trust in their legitimacy as a neutral mediator and prevent attempts to derail the negotiations.

This context required incorporating spoiler management measures that contributed to the successful conclusion of the talks. Amongst the measures were a significant degree of professionalism, flexibility, and an open-door policy.[54] For instance, Qatar openly welcomed U.S. envoy Zalmay Khalilzad's decision to move the third meeting planned in Doha on 17 and 18 December 2018 between the U.S., the Taliban, and Ghani's government to Abu Dhabi. Additionally, although they were not invited to the Abu Dhabi meeting, Qatar still offered to take charge of the logistical arrangements for the Taliban, which the UAE rejected under the pretext of the Gulf Crisis.[55] Furthermore, Prince Khalid bin Salman Al Saud, the Saudi ambassador to the U.S., subtly alleged that Qatar was obstructing peace in the region by 'fueling terrorism and conflicts'.[56] However, in reality, both the Qatari leadership and the mediation task force maintained a self-distancing policy to abate the simmering tensions with Saudi Arabia and the UAE in order to avoid any disruptions to the ongoing negotiations.

In addition to political rivalries, Qatari diplomats faced some practical challenges. As one Qatari diplomat explained, 'one of the most prominent was logistical, especially in terms of communication between the negotiation team in Doha and the top leadership of the Taliban, which was scattered across Afghanistan, Pakistan, and other undefined areas due to the war and their security concerns'.[57] In response, Qatar developed new mechanisms for indirect communication, which included dispatching envoys to the countries of strategic significance for the mediation as well as hosting the key Taliban figures in Doha. The timely adjustment ensured continuity and responsiveness throughout the process, especially in the later stages of the negotiations.

Following the failure of the Abu Dhabi meeting, Pakistan proposed Islamabad as the new venue for negotiations, but this was rejected by the Taliban.[58] According to Rahimullah Yusufzai, the Taliban's decision was based on their concern about the pressure Islamabad would exert on them if any negotiations were to take place.[59] Yusufzai argued that the 'Taliban want to avoid Islamabad's pressure by holding meetings in Doha or somewhere else [except for Pakistan]. A neutral venue suits Taliban where they can negotiate independently'.[60] This was also confirmed by a Pakistani senior military official involved in the Islamabad proposal who stated that, 'we are in constant touch with the Taliban representatives, but they are reluctant to meet the U.S. delegation in Islamabad. Instead, they are insisting for Doha to be the venue of the meeting, where they have a political office and feel more comfortable'.[61]

The Taliban's response was likely driven by their apprehension that Pakistan may have had ulterior motives when proposing to host and lead the mediation process.[62] Additionally, Pakistan has long played a significant role in Afghanistan's internal affairs, often to the detriment of regional stability. Since the Soviet invasion of Afghanistan in 1979, Pakistan has sought to maintain diplomatic and military influence over its neighbour through support for various militant groups, including the Taliban.[63] This interference has often complicated efforts to stabilize Afghanistan and has strained relations with Islamabad, leaving the Afghan public sceptical about Pakistan's real motives. Moreover, the Taliban's relationship with Pakistan has evolved significantly, with the group asserting more independence and resisting Pakistani influence.[64]

In essence, the Taliban's leadership was aware of Pakistan's efforts to leverage the Afghanistan situation for political and economic gain, including repairing diplomatic ties with Washington and positioning itself as a key player in Afghanistan's future economic development and reconstruction projects.[65] As such, the Pakistani leadership failed to attract the Taliban and host negotiations in Islamabad due to concerns of neutrality and their apparent vested political and economic interests in Afghanistan.

Despite these challenges, Qatar succeeded in protecting its reputation and political capital as an impartial mediator by remaining non-confrontational towards its critics and refusing to engage. Instead, Qatari mediators pursued a policy of positive engagement with international and regional actors throughout the process. One creative measure of this positive engagement policy was the creation of a briefing platform through which states such as Germany and Norway (which had significant influence on Ghani's government), Türkiye, Indonesia, Pakistan, Saudi Arabia, and the UAE were regularly consulted and informed on the progress made in the negotiations and given a platform to provide their input and perspectives on the process.[66] This policy enabled Qatar to protect the mediation process from disruptions. Firstly, it gave partners a platform to access information and share perspectives on a potential peace agreement between the U.S. and the Taliban. Secondly, mitigating spoiler influence made it more difficult for them to obstruct the mediation efforts. As Dr Al-Qahtani stated: 'Ultimately, this briefing platform kept partners informed and neutralized spoilers, leading them to concede to the reality'.[67]

U.S.–Taliban Peace Agreement: Short-Term Outcomes

On 29 February 2020, the U.S. and the Taliban signed a landmark agreement in Doha—a breakthrough largely credited to Qatari mediation. During the official talks, Qatari mediators were able to resolve several high-priority concerns regarding counterterrorism obligations, details of the ceasefire between the U.S. and the Taliban, and the phasing of the U.S. withdrawal from Afghanistan. The agreement provided a roadmap for the safe withdrawal of U.S. troops from Afghanistan, a commitment from the Taliban to expel Al-Qaeda and other terrorist groups, and that the Taliban would enter intra-Afghan negotiations.

Within 135 days of the agreement's signing, the U.S. reduced its presence in Afghanistan from approximately 12,000 to 8,600 soldiers. Additionally, there was a significant drop in military engagements involving international forces, creating a temporary lull in the conflict's intensity. This reduction in violence, albeit limited, represented a tangible, if fragile, step towards the agreement's broader goals of peace and stability in the region.[68] However, the immediate post-agreement phase was also marked by a surge in insurgent attacks against Afghan security forces, with over 4,500 Taliban attacks conducted in the forty-five days following the deal—a 70 per cent increase compared to the same period in the previous year.[69] This spike in violence, coupled with the U.S. military's reduced support for Afghan offensive operations, significantly impacted the morale and effectiveness of the Afghan security forces.

Despite its unpopularity in some Washington and European circles, the agreement was vital to restoring Qatar's reputation as a key global mediator. Widespread coverage of Doha's diplomatic role in Afghanistan led to much greater recognition of Qatar's wider role in international diplomacy 'through its mediation-oriented foreign policy'.[70] The strong trust placed in Qatar by the U.S. was evident from multiple statements from U.S. officials who thanked Qatar for its 'decisive role' in the mediation and facilitation process.[71] Consequently, the 2020 agreement won broad approval from influential international actors, including the U.S. and the UN, for charting a path to end the Afghan conflict.

U.S.–Taliban Peace Agreement: Long-Term Outcomes

The general perception of the 2020 agreement shifted drastically following the return of Taliban rule to Afghanistan on 15 August 2021. It was argued that the Doha Agreement did not bring much-awaited peace to Afghanistan but rather that it incentivized the Taliban to take over Kabul.[72] The U.S.–Taliban agreement has even been described by some analysts as a 'case study in diplomatic disaster'.[73] David Petraeus, the former commander of U.S.–NATO forces in Afghanistan, called it 'among the worst diplomatic agreements to which the U.S. has ever been a party'.[74]

Whilst the Taliban's return to power was not an expected product of the agreement, the onus for this outcome falls squarely on the U.S. and its coalition partners. From a critical perspective, the U.S. sought to exit Afghanistan and cut its losses at its earliest convenience, having realized the impossibility of a military victory over the Taliban and the success of a liberal state in Afghanistan. The collapse of the republican system in Afghanistan was hastened by multiple factors, including the rapid tempo of the military withdrawal, the suspension of development funding, the economic sanctions on Afghanistan's banking sector, and the closure of various embassies in Kabul.[75] The Doha Agreement marked a milestone in international diplomacy and paved the way for a structured withdrawal from Afghanistan, yet its full potential remained unrealized. Building upon its framework to foster lasting peace and stability in Afghanistan was a collective responsibility, demanding sustained engagement and cooperation from all parties involved.

The return of the Taliban and the breakdown of the agreement tainted, to a minor extent, the reputational benefits that Qatar had accrued from the signing of the U.S.–Taliban agreement in 2020. Qatar's role led some experts and media outlets to question its motivations and strategies, particularly the hosting of the Taliban political office in Doha. Nonetheless, the facilitation led to the significant enhancement of Qatar's profile as a mediator, particularly in cases involving Islamist actors. Moreover, despite its shortcomings, the agreement offered a semblance of structure to the transition[76] by mitigating the risk of a more devastating conflict that could have resulted from an abrupt power vacuum. Without the Doha Process and the subsequent orderly U.S. withdrawal, the Taliban's takeover could have been far more chaotic and violent, potentially leading to protracted urban warfare in Kabul and other major cities.[77] Thus, whilst the withdrawal and power transition in Afghanistan remained challenging, the Doha Agreement averted a catastrophic scenario and saved numerous lives by supporting a swifter, less violent transition and preventing another cycle of destruction.

Intra-Afghan Peace Process

Following the U.S.–Taliban agreement signed on 29 February 2020, the stage was set for the intra-Afghan negotiations—an integral phase of the broader Afghanistan peace process. This section traces the development of Doha's engagement in those negotiations. The document signed in Doha effectively acknowledged the Taliban as a de facto state party, capable of engaging in bilateral discussions with the U.S.[78] This challenged the legitimacy of the Afghan government and elevated the Taliban's status in subsequent peace talks. The agreement, precise in its expectations from the U.S., was rather vague regarding the Taliban's commitments, leading to an imbalance in terms of clarity and accountability.[79] In Kabul, the political landscape was marred by deep divisions and a lack of consensus amongst the major political factions. President Ashraf Ghani's increasingly isolated administration faced challenges in forging alliances and consensus, which was vital for presenting a united front in the peace process.[80] This discord within Kabul's political elite was in stark contrast to the Taliban's unified and cohesive approach, further complicating the intra-Afghan dialogue. For illustration, Zalmay Mamozy Khalilzad, the U.S. Special Representative for Afghanistan Reconciliation highlighted this lack of cohesion and agreement between the Kabul-based political actors:

> I think there were obviously political issues that may have impacted the Kabul government. The last election that was held in Afghanistan was a very bad, poor election. The results were contested, and a lot of time was wasted on internal power struggles rather than focusing on peace and negotiations.[81]

Against this background, the negotiations, which were scheduled to begin on 10 March 2020, were delayed due to a disagreement over the release of 5,000 Taliban prisoners. This was one of the core conditions of the U.S.–Taliban agreement that the Kabul government acquiesced to due to pressure exerted by President Donald Trump's administration,[82] and after internal discussions between President Ghani and the political actors of Afghanistan about the objectives and the structure of the negotiation team that would represent the government in Doha. The intra-Afghan negotiations went through several critical stages in the period between the U.S.–Taliban agreement on 29 February 2020 and the Taliban's takeover of Kabul on 15 August 2021. On 29 March 2020, after a lengthy process of deliberations and consultations with key political actors in Afghanistan—including former President Hamid Karzai, Chairman of the High Council for National Reconciliation Dr Abdullah Abdullah, Marshal Abdul Rashid Dostum, the Jamiat Islamic Party, Hezb-e-Islami, the Islamic Front political party, and civil society members—President Ashraf Ghani introduced the Republic Negotiation Team (RNT) which comprised twenty-one members and represented different ethnic groups, such as Pashtuns, Tajiks, Hazara, and Uzbeks.[83]

The intra-Afghan negotiations lasted three rounds. The first one commenced in Doha on 12 September 2020 and concluded on 15 December 2020. During this period, both parties only agreed on the rules and procedures of the talks, leaving several agenda issues to be addressed in later rounds. The second round began on 5 January 2021 and ended in mid-May but yielded no significant progress. Both teams could only agree on 'preventing stoppages and targeting of people on routes they travel and Sharia and basic rights of captives and prisoners'.[84] The third round started on 1 June 2021, amidst a shifting power dynamic in favour of the Taliban following the U.S. troop withdrawal. As the security situation continued to deteriorate, the RNT entered the third round with three strategic objectives: including a facilitator during the discussions to help overcome impasses, agreeing on the principles of an inclusive government, and addressing a ceasefire alongside prisoner exchange arrangements. The Taliban, however, refused to engage constructively on these issues.[85] On 12 August 2021, the third round ended, sealing the fate of the intra-Afghan negotiations.

Initially, the RNT and the Taliban agreed that the intra-Afghan talks should be Afghan-led and Afghan-owned, an initiative that Doha and the international observers welcomed. However, the need for a facilitator over the three negotiation rounds in order to overcome impasses was evident. Qatar's role during the intra-Afghan negotiations, although limited when compared to its role during the U.S.–Taliban negotiations, was significant in terms of continued commitment to mediation and facilitation in the context of Afghanistan.

Qatar's Facilitation and the Challenges on the Path to Peace

Qatar's efforts to play a substantive role in the Afghan peace process were initially constrained by the Afghan sides themselves, who rejected significant involvement from an empowered mediator and confined Doha's function to logistical facilitation, such as securing travel arrangements and hosting the meetings. Therefore, the talks were Afghan-led, without the presence of a formal mediator (that is, no external party was present in the room during the negotiations). Qatar's role was to act as a host of negotiations between the Taliban and the RNT.[86] In other words, during the initial stages of the intra-Afghan negotiations, there was no official demand from the parties for a neutral authority to hold the parties accountable, facilitate dialogue, and provide objective guidance and direction.

However, as the negotiations proceeded, Qatari mediators were quick to spot the fundamental discrepancies in the process and the vast differences in the parties' positions, including issues such as seating arrangements, flag displays, and the official naming on stage banners, which led to disputes—with the Taliban demanding recognition equivalent to the Afghan government and insisting on the U.S.–Taliban agreement as the negotiation's foundation.[87] Accordingly, Qatar grew from its facilitation role to instead act as a mediator. Dr Mutlaq bin Majid Al-Qahtani took the lead to resolve the disagreement over procedural rules. His intervention in November 2020 was critical in bridging the gap between the parties, resulting in a procedural agreement on 3 December 2020. This agreement laid the groundwork for further negotiations and potential long-term solutions.

Aware of the impact of the absence of a mediator on the directions of the intra-Afghan talks, Qatar sought other means to engage with the Afghan political leaders and key international stakeholders to further the peace negotiations and overcome the impasse. As the second round of the negotiations was unfolding, Qatar, Türkiye, and the UN, as co-conveners, agreed to hold a conference from 24 April to 4 May 2021. The goal was to bring both parties together to discuss and agree on shared principles and a vision of peace in Afghanistan, develop a roadmap detailing the essential conditions of a political settlement, and reach consensus on a ceasefire.[88] However, although the conference did not take place as the Taliban negotiators were reluctant to participate, it demonstrated Qatar's ongoing commitment to facilitating dialogue and understanding amongst the Afghan parties.[89]

The intra-Afghan negotiations were fraught with multiple other challenges that significantly influenced the overall process. The talks, initiated to build on the U.S.–Taliban agreement, quickly revealed the parties' entrenched and inflexible positions. The Taliban, emboldened by their de facto legitimacy, adopted a zero-sum approach throughout the three rounds of the negotiations. They demanded the complete withdrawal of international forces and the re-establishment of a Sharia-based state, showing little willingness for compromise.[90] Moreover, they continuously rejected any calls for a Loya Jirga (an election council); they also resisted calls from the RNT to negotiate and agree on terms and conditions beyond those outlined in the Doha Agreement, including 'preserving the achievements of the period between 2001 and 2021, the principles of republicanism and the fundamental human rights, a comprehensive ceasefire, and a political settlement resulting from the intra-Afghan negotiations'.[91] This rigid approach was not driven by a desire for mutual understanding but rather by an expectation that their terms would be met, given their perceived upper hand.

On the other side, the Afghan government, led by President Ghani, struggled with internal political rivalries and a lack of cohesive strategy. The administration's inability to present a united and coherent stance was strategically exploited by the Taliban, who consistently dismissed proposals from the republic's side, significantly hindering the negotiation process. The lack of political consensus in Kabul manifested during the prolonged deliberations and consultations between the political actors over the membership, the leadership structure, and the objectives of the RNT, which was only formalized later in March 2020, nineteen days after the intra-Afghan peace process began.[92] As the negotiations unfolded, the weaknesses of the RNT's internal structure began to emerge. Although the RNT deliberately included women to represent and defend the interests and freedoms of Afghan women, many of its members had different political, ethnic, social, and religious orientations. Additionally, they lacked experience in peace negotiations, knowledge about the Taliban's negotiation style or strategy, and mutual trust amongst themselves. Moreover, it remained unclear whether decision-making authority rested with the chief negotiator, Mohammed Masoom Stanekzai, or with State Minister for Peace Syed Sadaat Mansoor Naderi. This led to delays in decision-making and a lack of direction.[93]

The structure of the negotiation process was another challenge, and the parties' choice for Afghan-led and Afghan-owned negotiations greatly impacted the overall process. Accordingly, the intermittent presence of an impartial mediator or facilitator set the necessary framework and rules to handle the process and helped the parties overcome stagnation.[94] The absence of a mediator throughout the negotiations pushed each party to advance its agenda and goals at the expense of the other, turning the entire process into a zero sum game. For example, during the third round, 'the Taliban did not respond to the Host-Country Peace Support Group's request to clarify their peace and war intentions and totally rejected the idea of a UN-Qatari facilitatory or mediating role'.[95] Overall, the Taliban left little room for flexibility or compromise. This unwavering ideological position was strategic, aimed at maintaining internal cohesion and capitalizing on their military and diplomatic advances. Additionally, both parties accused each other of lacking decision-making authority and undermining each other's legitimacy.[96] Muhammad Suhail Shaheen, the head of the Taliban's political office, reflects on the Taliban's perception of the RNT:

> The Afghan side's team believed the more they show no flexibility, the more they will have gains on the table. They insisted on reaching agreement on permanent ceasefire before discussing any other issue. This created mistrust in the eyes of our team, thinking that the Afghan side's team was not serious in negotiations but using stratagem. Everyone knew they just wanted to buy time by insisting on ceasefire in order to equip and reorganize their forces and then, when they are strong on the ground, withdraw from the negotiations.[97]

The contrasting perceptions of the U.S. presence in Afghanistan by key parties played a significant role in shaping the outcome of the intra-Afghan peace process. On the one hand, President Ghani exhibited an overconfident belief that American forces would maintain their presence in the country.[98] On the other hand, the Taliban accurately anticipated the U.S. withdrawal, which strengthened their resolve and unity. This divergence in understanding had profound implications. The Islamic Republic, reliant on American support, found itself in a state of anxious disarray as the reality of U.S. departure set in.[99] Meanwhile, the Taliban's correct assessment of the situation allowed them to present a more unified and determined front. This disparity in outlooks largely explains why the Taliban pursued a military means to reclaim control rather than engaging in meaningful negotiations with a government they correctly perceived as being on the brink of collapse without U.S. backing.[100]

Consequently, the RNT's lack of experience in peace negotiation and internal cohesion, the Taliban's unwillingness to make concessions or accept to negotiate conditions other than those agreed on in the Doha Agreement, and, finally, both parties' choice to lead the peace process on their own, limiting the role for an impartial mediator to help structure the process, led to a deadlock.

Moreover, a less-noted episode occurred one month prior to the Taliban takeover when the Islamic Republic initiated discussions with Taliban negotiators in Doha about a formal power transfer. In the week preceding the Taliban's advance towards Kabul, an agreement, facilitated by Qatar and involving the U.S., was formulated for the military elements of the transition of power in Kabul. This arrangement entailed the Islamic Republic managing Kabul's internal security and overseeing the civilian operations at Hamid Karzai International Airport. It was understood that President Ghani would resign and constitutionally hand over power to a Taliban-led transitional government within two weeks. Meanwhile, the U.S. and NATO were to oversee the military aspects of the airport for evacuations, mainly of foreign nationals. A key component of this agreement was deconfliction between the U.S. and the Taliban, with the latter committing to stay outside Kabul to avoid conflicts with international forces. However, this agreement collapsed following President Ghani's unexpected departure from Kabul on 15 August 2021.[101]

Whilst the deal did not hold because of Ghani's unilateral decision, it was a significant, albeit largely unknown, example that represented a missed opportunity for managing a more orderly, negotiated power transition. Ultimately, given the intransigence of the two parties and the weak formal structure of negotiations, the intra-Afghan peace process broke down, and the Taliban seized power.

Qatar's Post-2021 Engagement: From Evacuation to Aid and Diplomacy

When Kabul fell on 15 August 2021, Qatar swiftly mobilized its internal resources in response to the crisis and performed one of the largest civilian airlifts in modern history. The transit of over 70,000 evacuees through Doha to the U.S., Canada, and several European countries was successfully coordinated between the Qatari authorities, the U.S. military, international organizations, and the Taliban. Qatar deployed technical teams to restore operations and ensure security at Kabul International Airport, which operated in collaboration with Türkiye throughout 2021–22.[102] Upon arrival, evacuees were placed in temporary accommodation, including at the Al Udeid Air Base and repurposed sporting facilities.[103] Evacuee response also included establishing an emergency field hospital, additional temporary shelters, and portable sanitation units.[104] In so doing, Qatar mobilized a whole-of-government approach that involved institutional coordination between the Ministry of Foreign Affairs, the Qatar Emiri Air Force, the Ministry of Defence, and the Ministry of Public Health. It also mobilized charitable actors such as Qatar Charity, Qatar Red Crescent, and Qatar Foundation, which offered medical care, daily essentials, and holistic support for minors.[105] In August 2021, at least ten aircraft were provided by Qatar Airways to transport evacuees from Doha to other countries.[106] This episode stands out as a distinctive example of Qatar engaging as a flexible and responsive humanitarian actor, successfully orchestrating a complex operation that spanned humanitarian aid, technical cooperation, and dialogue. It also served to pave the way for Qatar to play a larger role in post-2021 humanitarian diplomacy in Afghanistan.

As Afghanistan faced an increasingly severe humanitarian situation in the post-2021 phase, Qatar also provided substantial humanitarian assistance. For instance, in March 2022, Qatar, the UN, United Kingdom, and others co-hosted a pledging conference to mobilize humanitarian aid for Afghanistan and raise awareness of the deepening crisis.[107] Qatari humanitarian entities also continued to play a role in aid provision across multiple sectors, including water, shelter, food assistance, and health.[108] Often working in tandem with UN organizations, Qatari charities launched projects to support the Afghan citizens hosted by Qatar.[109] Furthermore, reflecting the strong value that Qatar as a country has placed on education, much support was provided for education in emergencies programmes. This included delivering educational materials via the humanitarian airbridge,[110] supporting young female Afghan scientists to relocate to Doha,[111] and more systemic approaches such as partnering with the Ministry of Education under the de facto Taliban government to enrol 30,000 out-of-school children, half of whom were girls.[112] Across these multifaceted humanitarian roles, Qatar utilized a whole-of-society approach to mobilize its civilian capacities and play a constructive role in responding to the continued crisis in Afghanistan.

Alongside aid delivery, Doha became a venue for humanitarian diplomacy. As many diplomatic missions and donors suspended their presence in Afghanistan, the Qatari capital provided a neutral setting where governments could relocate their delegations and conduct 'over-the-horizon' diplomacy.[113] Various high-level meetings focused on Afghanistan were held in Doha, including a U.S.–Taliban meeting in August 2023 addressing unresolved issues such as lifting sanctions and unfreezing Afghan central bank assets,[114] and a UN-sponsored meeting in mid-2024 that attempted to constructively engage the Taliban and the international community in discussing economic recovery, women's rights, and sustained anti-narcotics efforts. Whilst neighbouring states offered alternative venues for Afghan-related dialogue, the protecting power agreement between the U.S. and Qatar made Doha (alongside Islamabad) one of the primary locations for international interlocutors to engage with the Taliban.[115] Similarly, the Taliban's trust in Qatar as their go-to host for negotiations with other countries was also recognized by the group's representative in Doha: 'Qatar's role during negotiations is now part and parcel of the Afghan history and a symbol of friendship between the two countries: Afghanistan and

Qatar. We hope this bond of friendship deepens with the passage of time politically, economically, socially, and culturally'.[116]

Beyond the role of Doha as a strategic meeting point, Qatar also proactively engaged with the de facto authorities in Afghanistan. This perspective was echoed in a workshop held in Doha, where it was emphasized that Qatar had played a constructive role as a messenger and facilitator between the international community and the Taliban.[117] For instance, Qatar supported a range of workshops, meetings, and other humanitarian dialogue platforms both in Doha and in Afghanistan that enabled the Taliban to deliver their concerns to the international community and provided international non-governmental organizations (NGOs) with opportunities for information sharing and coordination on the humanitarian crisis in Afghanistan.[118] As stated by a country director of an international NGO: 'Qatar workshops are crucial in fostering trust between Western humanitarian INGOs [international NGOs] and the Taliban, addressing misunderstandings, and overcoming engagement barriers. These efforts are timely, helping to mitigate the humanitarian crisis and promote meaningful dialogue'.[119]

Qatar's efforts to promote humanitarian dialogues between the Taliban and international humanitarian actors were perceived as constructive and necessary to reduce misunderstandings and gradually build trust. It also opened up strategic entry points for engaging on challenging issues such as inclusive governance, women's rights, and humanitarian space. In particular, Qatar consistently engaged on the issue of the right to education for all Afghans.[120] Whilst education remains a point of contention between the international community and the Taliban, Qatar's diplomatic positioning and open lines of communication with the de facto authorities enabled greater space for engagement on educational issues.

Finally, Qatar also continued to play a role in mediation even after 2021. The international community increasingly solicited Qatar's mediation for its established ties with the de facto authorities in Afghanistan and its proven track record. For instance, in April 2022, Qatar secured the release of two American aid workers who had been detained by the Taliban since December 2021.[121] Other achievements included mediating the release of the Austrian detainee Herbert Fritz from Afghanistan in February 2024[122] and an Argentine citizen in July 2024.[123] In early 2025, Qatari mediators facilitated the release of several American hostages from Taliban custody, beginning with Ryan Corbett and William McKenty in January,[124] followed by George Glezmann in March.[125] These high-profile releases reflect Qatar's ongoing role as a trusted intermediary. By sustaining lines of communication with the de facto authorities and responding to urgent humanitarian or consular concerns, Qatar became a key conduit for pragmatic engagement at a time when formal diplomatic channels remain limited.

7

DIPLOMACY AMIDST DEVASTATION

QATAR'S MEDIATION IN THE 7 OCTOBER WAR ON GAZA

The genocide in the Gaza Strip since 7 October 2023 stands out as an era-defining crisis that has caused immense devastation in the territory and generated mass attention globally. Throughout much of the crisis, Qatar was the lead mediator, where it has been involved in negotiating ceasefires, exchanges of captives, and attempting to broker the terms of any future post-war settlement. These efforts have undoubtedly increased the visibility of Doha's diplomatic role more than in any other previous episode of Qatari mediation. This chapter analyzes the Qatari mediation that began following the outbreak of the war on 7 October 2023 and until the collapse of the second ceasefire agreement in March 2025. To understand how this mediation came about, it is necessary to begin by contextualizing it within Qatar's long-term engagement in Gaza and more broadly in Palestine, where its multifaceted approach was notable in the provision of humanitarian and reconstruction assistance, intra-Palestinian reconciliation, and, increasingly, in preventive diplomacy and mediation.

Context of Qatar's Role in Palestine

Qatar has longstanding political, social, and cultural ties with Palestine, going back many decades. Diplomatic relations between the two countries were formally launched in 1965, with the opening of the first representative office for the Palestine Liberation Organization (PLO) in Doha, Qatar. Later, in 1988, Qatar was amongst the first countries to recognize Palestine with Jerusalem as its capital following the Palestinian declaration of independence.[1] Qatar strengthened bilateral relations with the Palestinian Authority in the post-Oslo era, opening a Qatari diplomatic office in Palestine in 1995. Shortly after, Qatar bolstered its humanitarian presence in Palestine when Qatar Charity opened offices in Gaza and the southern West Bank in 1996. This humanitarian role has increased substantially, with Qatar becoming one of the largest bilateral donors to the Gaza Strip over the past decade.

Qatar's growing diplomatic engagement with Palestine reflects a mixture of strategic calculation, soft power ambitions, and social ties. Initially aligned with broader Arab consensus, in particular the Saudi-led Arab Peace Initiative in 2002, Qatar acted distinctly throughout the 2000s as it positioned itself independently as an ambitious diplomatic force with a prominent standing in the heart of global geopolitics. The Gaza Strip was long considered within the domain of Egypt and, to a lesser extent, Jordan. As a politically charged context at the epicentre of the Middle Eastern security conundrum, the Israeli–Palestinian conflict was an apt arena for Qatar to demonstrate its growing regional leadership ambitions and showcase the utility of its foreign policy of maintaining relations with all sides, including the United States (U.S.), Hamas, the Palestinian Authority, and Israel. In this regard, Israel established a trade mission in Doha in 1996, which was closed during the Second Intifada in November 2000.

In effect, Qatar has accrued significant soft power and support within the Arab public at relatively low material cost. When, in the aftermath of the 2008–09 war, Qatar organized an emergency summit in support of Gaza, its motives were interpreted as believing that 'it will both advance its standing in Arab public opinion and be seen as a champion of it'.[2] Thus, Qatar has long positioned itself as a resolute defender of the Palestinian cause in an era of dwindling solidarity amongst Arab governments, who remain out of step with their domestic publics that strongly support Palestine. This Arab commitment to Palestine naturally extends to Qatar itself, which also helps to explain its long-term support for the Palestinian national struggle to restore their lands and rights. Qatar has longstanding social ties to Palestine through a diaspora of over 50,000 since the 1950s and decades of cultural interactions.[3]

Qatar's Growing Role in Gaza under Blockade

Qatar, as a humanitarian and diplomatic actor in the Gaza Strip, continuously developed and adapted its tactics of bilateral engagement in response to the blockade imposed on the territory since 2006 and the cycles of destruction that followed it. Gaza's history has been significantly shaped by protracted occupation, conflict, and siege. Israel's occupation of the Strip began with the outbreak of the 1967 war. In 2005, Israel unilaterally disengaged from Gaza and dismantled its settlements. Following the Hamas victory in the 2006 Palestinian legislative elections and its subsequent takeover of the Gaza Strip following a rift with the Palestinian Authority, as well as the capture of French–Israeli soldier Gilad Shalit, Israel intensified its strict land, air, and sea siege of the Strip. Since then, Gaza faced five Israeli wars of aggression between 2008 and 2023 that reversed decades of developmental progress, destroyed its infrastructure, and decimated its local economy.[4]

In response to these wars, Qatar emerged as a major actor in supporting reconstruction in the Gaza Strip. To this end, the Qatar Gaza Reconstruction Committee was established in 2012 to disburse and manage Qatari reconstruction and development projects in the Gaza Strip. Qatar provided USD 407 million for reconstruction in 2012,[5] and over USD 1 billion in 2014, emerging as one of the single largest bilateral donors to the besieged territory.[6] Despite vast obstacles of rebuilding under the blockade, Qatar's efforts proved highly effective[7] due to its ability to communicate with all parties, particularly Israel, to ensure the delivery of necessary construction materials, fuel, and electricity.[8] This experience of humanitarian diplomacy and brokering reconstruction access was an important aspect of the route through which Qatar came to act as a key mediator in the Gaza Strip.

Establishing the Hamas Office in Doha

Qatar's diplomatic engagement in Palestinian affairs was elevated greatly when, in 2012, a request was made by the U.S. for Doha to host a political office of Hamas following a rift between the group and the Syrian government.[9] This step enabled stronger, more frequent, and logistically easier forms of engagement between Hamas and various international and regional interlocutors. This, in turn, set the stage for Doha's growing importance as a diplomatic hub for international efforts towards conflict management in Palestine, and further highlighted Qatar's ability to maintain its relations with Israel (where necessary) whilst maintaining a pro-Palestinian foreign policy.

Within the context of diplomacy more specifically, the relocation of the political leadership of Hamas (then led by Khaled Meshaal and later by Ismail Haniyeh) from Syria to Qatar in 2012 led to the establishment of communication lines between the group and the Western world through Qatar. The decision was coordinated with the U.S. and Israel, with the Americans explicitly preferring Doha as a venue for engagement over alternatives such as Tehran or Abu Dhabi.[10] The Hamas political office in Doha functions similarly to an embassy, serving as a channel through which various regional and international actors can communicate with the de facto authorities in Gaza. This channel proved crucial in de-escalating tensions between Hamas and Israel on multiple occasions.[11]

The hosting of the Hamas political office was subject to controversy, often referenced as proof of Qatar's alleged support for, and legitimization of, Hamas as a political actor by those who characterize the movement as a terrorist organization.[12] However, this perspective overlooks the geopolitical complexities at play. The presence of a political office, opened in 2012 at the request of the U.S., does not imply endorsement of the policies or actions. Rather, it was a pragmatic step that facilitated open lines of communication and trust-building with the backing of the international community. Similarly, Qatar also maintained a working relationship with Israel as part of its pragmatic foreign policy.

Qatar's Mediation of Intra-Palestinian Reconciliation

Qatar's first major foray into active mediation on the Palestinian file was its attempt to broker an intra-Palestinian reconciliation in 2012. Following the 2006 fall-out between Fatah and Hamas, it had become clear that the intra-Palestinian schism was a major obstacle to achieving lasting peace and Palestinian statehood.[13] Qatar was well-positioned to approach this file in 2012, given its longstanding support for the Fatah-dominated Palestinian Authority, the relocation of the Hamas political office from Damascus to Doha, and the presence of a large Palestinian diaspora in Qatar.[14] Nonetheless, Qatar faced hostility from Egypt, which attempted to guard the Palestinian reconciliation file.[15]

Qatar's efforts led to the signing of the 2012 Doha Agreement between the Palestinian Authority, led by its president, Mahmoud Abbas (who spent his formative years in Doha)[16] and Hamas, then led by Khaled Meshaal.[17] However, the implementation stalled as divisions emerged on the interpretation of key provisions of the deal.[18] Despite the pitfalls of this agreement, there is an acknowledgement that each mediation attempt contributes incrementally towards long-term Palestinian reconciliation. Qatar's mediation laid the groundwork for later attempts pursued by other third parties, which resulted in the 2012 Fatah-Hamas Cairo Agreement and the 2014 Shati Agreement, the latter of which stipulated terms similar to the Doha Agreement.[19] Qatari efforts were recognized by various Palestinian factions.[20] For instance, Muhammad Shtayyeh, the former Palestinian Prime Minister, stated that Qatar 'contributed to the convergence of views to complete the Palestinian reconciliation' whilst also facilitating an agreement on Palestinian elections that were subsequently blocked by Israel.[21]

Across many years, numerous intra-Palestinian reconciliation attempts appeared to be doomed to fail, and the 2012 agreement might be perceived as yet another minor episode in Palestinian political history.[22] Yet in the face of low odds of reaching a successful agreement, Doha's dedication to fostering Palestinian reconciliation was broadly welcomed amongst the Palestinian public and wider Arab population.[23] For instance, Egypt and Saudi Arabia aimed to maintain the factional divisions between Palestinian political groups by strengthening the PLO for strategic and Political purposes.[24] Qatar, by contrast, invested in reconciling between Fatah and Hamas and acted as a bridge between Hamas and the West, which set it apart from other Arab states. Thus, when other leading Arab states sought to sideline or eliminate Hamas as part of the wider regional struggle to suppress political Islam at the peak of the Arab Spring, Qatar sought to maintain relations instead. This diplomatic positioning in acting as a go-between for Palestinian factions proved of immense strategic utility in the wider mediation framework that emerged to manage conflict in the Gaza Strip, involving Hamas, Israel, the U.S., the United Nations (UN), and other actors.[25]

Qatar's Growing Mediation Role

Over time, Qatar demonstrated progressively greater influence in brokering ceasefires between Hamas and Israel. In November 2012, Israel launched Operation Pillar of Defense, in which they killed over 100 Palestinian civilians. During that crisis, Egypt acted as the mediator, winning plaudits for successfully brokering the ceasefire that brought fighting to a halt in what proved to be the shortest and least destructive of the five Israeli wars on Gaza.[26] In July 2014, Israel launched a more destructive war: Operation Protective Edge. However, in that same year, Egyptian proposals for a ceasefire were developed without consulting Hamas. It is reported that 'the United States had approached Qatar after it realized that the Cairo deal was bound to fail with Hamas being kept out of the picture' and that 'Qatar is best placed to mediate with Hamas'.[27] Whilst the August ceasefire was ultimately brokered by Egypt, the leverage of the U.S. and the utility of Qatar's strategic reach were demonstrated in the nascent multi-party mediation framework.[28]

Notably, the agreement to end the 2014 war was the longest-held ceasefire in the Gaza Strip, holding effectively until the 2021 war. This period of relative stability was not an automatic outcome but was rather maintained through active conflict management through multi-party mediation and preventive diplomacy. Tensions over the Gaza Strip escalated in 2018, during the Great March of Return—a mass mobilization of Palestinians protesting the ongoing blockade and denial of refugee rights.[29] During the months of protests, Israeli forces killed over 100 unarmed civilian protestors.[30] It was feared that the crisis could see major escalation and further violence in the Gaza Strip.[31]

Qatar's humanitarian and diplomatic role was important during this period.[32] An 'aid-for-calm' formula emerged, which provided a political framework through which to channel aid to Gaza in a bid to manage conflict escalation, in particular during 2018–19.[33] This was the result of extensive multilateral mediation efforts involving the UN, Egypt, Israel, Hamas, and the Palestinian Authority. It sought to reduce tensions in Gaza by ensuring the flow of aid, maintaining the operations of key sectors such as health and education, and improving economic conditions.[34] Qatari humanitarian and development aid was central to this formula, with aid provided for payment of civil servant salaries, purchase of fuel for Gaza's only power plant, and to provide assistance to poor families.[35] Qatar also brokered Israeli approval to channel reconstruction materials into Gaza under the tight Israeli–Egyptian blockade.

Qatari diplomats frame this as a period of preventive diplomacy. One senior Qatari government mediator claimed that Qatar prevented four wars in the Gaza Strip.[36] Similarly, Ambassador Al-Emadi affirmed that Qatar's 'presence in Gaza is a safety valve to prevent war, and we have succeeded in that more than once, and in sparing Gaza a humanitarian catastrophe'.[37] The relief initiatives were appreciated by many families in Gaza who were beneficiaries of the aid packages. Nevertheless, the use of the term 'calm' caused some backlash against Qatar in the Palestinian public, including perceptions that the aid formula had the inadvertent effect of playing into Israeli strategies of keeping the lid on tensions in the Gaza Strip under deplorable conditions of blockade. Moreover, whilst Israeli voices criticized the aid as tacit support for Hamas, Qatari officials emphasized that this humanitarian and diplomatic engagement demonstrated its distance from the movement.[38]

In short, Qatar's strategic integration of humanitarian aid and diplomacy helped restore intermittent periods of calm in Gaza. However, this aid-for-calm approach proved inadequate in the face of Gaza's worsening humanitarian and political conditions. As the limits of this formula became evident, and Qatar's credibility as a mediator grew, it began to play a more direct role in ceasefire negotiations, particularly during the 2021 war, which marked a shift from conflict mitigation to active peacemaking.

Multi-Party Mediation in the 2021 War

In 2021, following months of escalating tensions over Israel's repeated incursions into the Al Aqsa Mosque compound, viewed by Palestinians as assaults on religious and national identity, Israel launched an eleven-day war on the Gaza Strip that killed over 250 people, destroyed infrastructure, and led to over USD 350 million in economic losses.[39] The war also shattered the seven years of relative stability, with the previous war on Gaza occurring in 2014.[40]

The 2021 war marked a shift towards enhanced coordination amongst mediation parties, including Qatar, the UN, the U.S., and Egypt, the latter with which Qatar had just restored formal diplomatic ties, resulting in an unconditional bilateral ceasefire after the eleven-day escalation. Notably, Qatar communicated with Hamas due to the 'No Contact Policy' followed by the U.S. This dual role as a strategic U.S. ally whilst engaging with Hamas created a valuable diplomatic channel for the conflict parties and the mediation actors. These developments have been recognized by international political actors from across the world, including French, European Union, U.S., and Israeli officials.[41]

Qatar's mediation in the Israeli–Palestinian conflict has been contentious, attracting significant scrutiny due to its interactions with Hamas. The country faced a regional blockade from 2017 to 2021, highlighting the sensitivities surrounding its diplomatic efforts. Geopolitical dynamics often position Qatar's approach as competing with those of other regional states.[42] For instance, Egypt increasingly viewed Qatar's expanding influence in Palestine with caution, since it saw 'itself as the exclusive mediator in the Palestinian issue'[43] for several years, with other countries only supporting Egypt's role. This wariness contributed to Egypt's alignment with Saudi Arabia, the United Arab Emirates (UAE), and Bahrain in their blockade of Qatar. The quartet's vision regarding the question of Palestine diverged from that of Qatar, particularly as Qatar asserted its independence and intensified its support for the Palestinian cause.[44]

Following the 2021 rapprochement with its neighbours, Qatari–Egyptian cooperation and collaboration on this file grew. Qatar's role was seen as 'a force multiplier for Egyptian mediation in the Gaza Strip'.[45] Mohammed Al-Aila, the secretary of the Hamas Office for International and Legal Affairs, highlights that Hamas positively viewed the achievements made by Egypt and Qatar in the negotiations, considering the repeated efforts to bridge the gaps despite not being the direct parties to the conflict.[46] Hamas official Husam Badran also noted that 'Qatar has never had any problem with discussions taking place in Doha, whilst events or celebrations, so to speak, are held in Cairo'.[47] This understanding between the two countries and the notable Qatari flexibility in sharing recognition for mediation achievements with Egypt have served mediation efforts. This is a direct result of Qatar's mediation in the Gaza Strip, marked by preventive diplomacy, particularly Qatar's desire to avoid the eruption of conflict or to prevent its escalation.

Qatar's Mediation after the 7 October War

On 7 October 2023, armed Palestinian groups attacked Israeli towns, settlements, and military bases surrounding the Gaza Strip. The operation—dubbed the Al Aqsa Flood—was framed by its progenitors as a response to the worsening living conditions in Gaza, the repeated violations of the sanctity of the Al Aqsa Mosque, and the deepening blockade.[48] In response, Israel launched a full-scale war that killed over 60,000 Palestinian civilians, decimated much of Gaza's infrastructure, and displaced almost its entire population. Israel's conduct of the 7 October War clearly crossed into genocidal intent and was judged to be 'plausible' genocide by the International Court of Justice.[49] The war on Gaza rapidly became a defining issue in global politics, transforming the context in which the Strip, which had long been treated as a peripheral theatre in the broader Middle East conflict, was now positioned at the centre of international diplomatic and humanitarian attention. This shift created, first, the urgency of addressing this file and, second, the visibility for Qatar's entry into one of its most high-profile mediation efforts to date.

In the aftermath of 7 October, Qatar adopted a firm and unapologetic stance on the war. It condemned Israel's conduct, maintained its longstanding ties with Hamas, and sought to preserve its ability to mediate by continuing to engage all sides. As one analysis noted, Qatar from the outset made clear its policies and worked to expand its role as mediator, despite growing international scrutiny.[50] These efforts were not without risk. Tensions with Washington grew over perceived differences in approach, and questions were raised about the future of Doha's relationship with Hamas. Yet within weeks, Qatar showed consistent maintenance of access to both parties and consolidated its position within the emerging mediation framework. By late November 2023, it had become central to the negotiation of the first ceasefire, positioning itself, once again, as an actor that could not be excluded from international attempts to de-escalate the crisis in Gaza.

Qatar's Acceptance as a Mediator in the 7 October War

To casual observers, Qatar's central role in mediating between Hamas and Israel may seem unexpected, yet it reflects years of strategic positioning and diplomatic engagement. Several reasons have been advanced to explain why the parties came to accept Doha as a trusted intermediary.

Qatar's entry as a mediator in the post-7 October era was not a given, particularly as it faced considerable political challenges. The earliest signs of official U.S. criticism towards Qatar came only a few days after the start of the war with a letter from Congress, signed by fifty Republicans and sixty-three Democrats, calling for increased pressure on Qatar and Türkiye to expel Hamas leaders from their countries.[51] This early disapproval hinted at the broader scrutiny that Qatar was to face in its role as a mediator, eventually prompting both defensive and supportive responses from countries around the world.

Qatar's mediation efforts have consistently garnered positive recognition on regional and global levels. The war in Gaza highlighted Qatar's pre-eminence as a mediator globally, solidifying its reputation as a leading middle power in the Middle East and North Africa region.[52] Described as the region's 'master mediator',[53] Qatar has been acknowledged for its important steps in this context,[54] thus making it difficult for any of the parties 'to bypass Qatar's mediation'.[55] This sentiment was echoed by a leading UN official who noted that Qatar's strategic reach entailed that the country was 'impossible to exclude' from the mediation framework.[56]

Firstly, on a logistical level, the presence of a Hamas office in Doha ensured that Qatar could facilitate communication between the Hamas leadership and the mediation structure involving Qatar itself and other third parties. The eruption of the war in October 2023 placed Qatar's relationship with Hamas in the spotlight. Nonetheless, Qatar maintained its professional and neutral stance as a mediator and pressed on with negotiations to end the war. The continued presence of the office in Doha was crucial to the ceasefire in late 2023 and the continued talks in early 2025. Such facilitation and mediation would have been incredibly challenging had the office been based in Tehran, for instance, as U.S. and Israeli delegations would not have been able to travel to Iran for talks.[57]

Secondly, there was a path-dependent effect in that mediation in the 7 October War closely resembled the mediation structure that had emerged since 2018, with Qatar, Egypt, and the U.S. cooperating on a ceasefire and negotiations over exchanges of captives. Qatar's previous engagement in mediation between Hamas and Israel thus positioned it to lead mediation efforts during the 7 October War on the Gaza Strip. This experience equipped Qatar with a 'well-trained team possessing knowledge of the parties involved and a deep understanding of the issue'.[58] Qatar also drew from its wider societal capacities, such as its Gaza Reconstruction Committee and ground presence of humanitarian and media workers in Palestine.

Thirdly, it has also been imputed that Qatar was accepted as a mediator by Israel because it believed Qatar exercised leverage over Hamas. This is largely due to the presence of a political office in Doha as well as the Qatari aid provided to the Strip over many years. To this end, Qatar's financial prowess lends it greater negotiating power. Within the context of Gaza, Qatar has clearly employed its aid and assistance levers to support its mediation. This has helped Qatar maintain its attractiveness as a mediator through long-term trust-building measures, where even a hostile Israeli government finds itself compelled to enlist the support of Qatar as a mediator.[59]

Fourthly, Qatar has proven itself to be a successful and trustworthy mediator in multiple rounds of escalation between Hamas and Israel. Additionally, Israeli officials understand that the preservation of the integrity of Qatari mediation is vital for Doha in any mediation process, especially when related to the Palestinian file, where it would also need to battle accusations of supporting Hamas. Therefore, although Israel would like to push Qatar out of the Gaza Strip, it remained aware that the country's involvement was necessary during the war and potentially in its aftermath.[60]

Collectively, these reasons entailed that, despite loud criticism of Qatar from some sections of Israeli politics and public discourse, Doha's role in the mediation process following the 7 October War came to be viewed as indispensable by the conflict parties themselves as well as other third parties.

Multi-Party Mediation Framework

Throughout the war on the Gaza Strip, mediation between Hamas and Israel was conducted by several third parties, primarily Qatar, Egypt, and the U.S. At times, mediation was strongly collaborative, with all three actors in constant coordination. Rounds of meetings involving conflict parties took place in various locations, including Doha, Cairo, and Paris. Negotiations remained indirect, with messages relayed through mediators rather than face-to-face engagement between the parties.

Qatari mediation was highly centralized, led by the Ministry of Foreign Affairs in collaboration with the Amiri Diwan and several advisors. It was conducted by several key personnel within the Ministry of Foreign Affairs, including the Prime Minister and Foreign Minister, Sheikh Mohammed bin Abdulrahman bin Jassim Al Thani; Minister of State Mohammad bin Abdulaziz Al-Khulaifi; and Lolwah Al Khater, who served as Minister of State for International Cooperation during much of 2023 and 2024. On the Egyptian side, the primary mediator was Abbas Kamel, then director of the Egyptian General Intelligence Service. Mediation efforts have also often included several U.S. officials, including William Burns, Director of the Central Intelligence Agency.

Amongst the prominent individuals on the Hamas side was Ismail Haniyeh, the former political leader of Hamas, who was assassinated during a diplomatic visit to Tehran in August 2024. Other figures also included Khalil Al Hayya, the deputy chairman of Hamas Political Bureau—dubbed its unofficial foreign minister.[61] On the Israeli side, negotiations were led by the Mossad chief, David Barnea, and included the head of the Shin Bet and various military and political advisers.[62]

Notably, negotiations did not directly involve Israeli Prime Minister Benjamin Netanyahu. Beyond Israel's longstanding refusal to formally legitimize Hamas through high-level engagement, Netanyahu was widely perceived to be undermining negotiations behind the scenes, in particular as the ceasefire process threatened to expose divisions within his coalition and constrain the military campaign.[63]

Mediating the November 2023 Ceasefire

The first major success of the multi-party mediation between Hamas and Israel was the brokering of a captive exchange agreement and a four-day ceasefire that came into effect on 24 November 2023. Under the terms of the deal, around 110 Israeli captives were released in exchange for more than 240 Palestinian captives held in Israeli jails.[64] The initial deal included a pause in fighting to facilitate the release of fifty Israeli women and children from Gaza in return for 150 Palestinian women and children held in Israeli prisons.[65]

It was reported that Qatar's 'muscular' and 'proactive' approach to mediation was crucial to the November ceasefire agreement.[66] This involved intensive talks in Doha on 22 and 23 November 2023, involving the Mossad chief, Egyptian intelligence officials, and a separate video-conferencing room where Qatari officials communicated directly with Hamas leaders present in Doha. Crucially, Qatar did not simply engage in shuttle diplomacy but rather actively pushed the sides towards a workable agreement over the course of multiple rounds of negotiations.[67]

The initial four-day ceasefire—which involved the release of fifty captives by Hamas—was followed by an extension of a further two days and finally another extension for a seventh day, with each additional day requiring Hamas to release at least ten captives. Qatar was also crucial to negotiating these extensions, with Qatari officials publicly visiting Israel for the first time to hold intensive talks to resolve the faltering ceasefire amidst mutual accusations between the two conflict parties of ceasefire violations.[68]

The reprieve from fighting enabled the delivery of crucial humanitarian aid into the Gaza Strip; however, it was not enough to meet the vast need for life-saving assistance. Throughout this truce, roughly 750 aid trucks entered the Strip through the Rafah border.[69] The United Nations Relief and Works Agency for Palestine Refugees in the Near East warned, however, that this would not be enough to alleviate the suffering of Palestinians in the Gaza Strip, where nearly 80 per cent of the population had been displaced by the war. It further noted that 200 aid trucks would need to enter Gaza every day over the course of two months to address the severe shortages faced by the population. Additionally, fuel allowed into the Strip was insufficient to ensure the continued operation of the sewage treatment and water desalination plants. Prior to the 7 October War, Gaza received an average of 500 aid trucks daily, which even then fell drastically short of the population's basic survival needs in the besieged territory, further exacerbating collective suffering. By comparison, the UN delivered just under 130,000 litres of fuel during the truce, which equates to just over 10 per cent of the daily volume received in pre-war Gaza.[70]

During the truce, both sides repeatedly accused each other of violating its terms. Israel cited rockets launched from Gaza just an hour before the pause was due to expire, whilst its own forces were reported to have opened fire on Palestinians, killing two people, two days earlier. On 30 November 2023, Israeli shelling of Gaza drew further allegations of breach, even though the ceasefire was still formally in place. Once the seven-day pause ended, hostilities resumed almost immediately. Within minutes, Israeli air raids and artillery strikes recommenced, evacuation orders were dropped via leaflets, and clashes between Israeli forces and Palestinian fighters escalated. In the first two months of the war, 60 per cent of homes in the Strip were destroyed, and more than 15,000 people were killed.[71]

Although the short-term ceasefire in November 2023 offered a rare pause in hostilities, it did not lay the groundwork for a lasting resolution. The opportunity to build towards a broader political process was not seized, and fighting quickly resumed. Nonetheless, even if achieving a sustainable truce produced diminishing returns, Qatar continued to mediate throughout 2024. Amidst a backdrop of regional escalation and diplomatic gridlock, the limits of external mediation became increasingly apparent.

Mediation amidst Regional Escalation throughout 2024

In December 2023, Qatar and Egypt jointly proposed a framework for a long-term ceasefire involving a sequence of captive releases as confidence-building measures.[72] This was to be followed by a transitional phase led by a Palestinian unity government to administer the Gaza Strip and the West Bank. Ultimately, this process was intended to lead to Palestinian elections and the recognition of Palestinian statehood. In the initial proposals, the unity government was suggested to involve Hamas and Fatah.[73]

By February 2024, the leading proposals discussed by Qatari and Egyptian mediators involved a transitional government led by the Palestinian Authority, limited to only consultation with Hamas rather than its participation.[74] Qatar reached out to various Palestinian individuals to gauge their willingness to participate in any technocratic government that would take on responsibility for the governance and reconstruction of the Gaza Strip in the event of a long-term ceasefire arrangement.[75] As such, Qatar planned to secure a ceasefire and also broker the terms of a 'Day After' or post-war political settlement acceptable to both Hamas and Israel.

In May 2024, Qatar, Egypt, and the U.S. put forward a proposal—accepted by Hamas but rejected by Israel—that laid the groundwork for the 2025 ceasefire agreement.[76] It outlined three phases. The first was to include a ceasefire, the partial suspension of reconnaissance drone flights over Gaza, the exchange of prisoners, the entry of humanitarian aid, Israeli withdrawal from certain parts of the Strip, and the gradual return of displaced Palestinians to the north. The second phase included further prisoner exchanges, a permanent ceasefire, and Israel's complete withdrawal from the Strip. The third and final phase stipulated the exchange of the deceased, the implementation of a comprehensive reconstruction plan, and the opening of border crossings.

This proposed framework for a ceasefire was, however, blocked by Netanyahu. Moreover, throughout mid-2024, the Gaza crisis escalated regionally. On 1 October 2024, Israel invaded southern Lebanon following months of attacks that degraded the capabilities of Hezbollah. Iran and Israel also traded rocket fire in April and October 2024, with many observers internationally concerned with the risk of an escalating all-out regional war.[77] Mediation efforts were thus sidelined in Israel's concerted agenda to shape a new regional order founded on the destruction of its neighbouring states and mass expulsion.

Overcoming Obstacles: Qatar's Threat to Withdraw from Mediation

In April 2024, Qatar stated that it would seek to fundamentally re-evaluate its mediation in Gaza. Qatar's Prime Minister, Sheikh Mohammed bin Abdulrahman Al Thani, said that there was 'exploitation and abuse of the Qatari role' which had been misused 'for narrow political interests', thus necessitating a complete evaluation of Qatari mediation.[78] This was, in part, due to what Qatar perceived as unjust and baseless criticisms made by officials in Israel and the U.S. towards its mediation. Such criticism of Qatar was intensified in the post-7 October War era, where Qatar's mediation in the Gaza Strip received a greater magnitude of global attention than any other case in which the country had previously mediated. With Qatar's diplomatic role in the 7 October War bringing the country under the international limelight, this inevitably invited a spectrum of reactions—from positive recognition to harsh criticism.

Repeatedly, partisan think tanks in the U.S. made unfounded attacks against the diplomatic role played by Doha over the course of many years. Most commonly, Qatar faced accusations that it provides financial, logistical, and military support for Hamas. Older claims also resurfaced alleging that Qatar's humanitarian and development assistance to Gaza prior to 2023 was tantamount to supporting terrorism.[79] These accusations placed Qatar under intense scrutiny in the form of urging a boycott of the country and its businesses, the imposition of sanctions, and petitions and smear campaigns targeting Qatar and its royal family. One striking example of this was the slanderous headline 'State visit by the blood emir' published by the German tabloid *Bild* upon the occasion of the Qatari emir's visit to Berlin in October 2023.[80]

Additionally, Qatar has been accused of disseminating propaganda supportive of Hamas through its state-owned TV network Al Jazeera, with U.S. Secretary Antony Blinken having reportedly requested that the government reduce the 'volume on Al Jazeera's coverage because it is full of anti-Israel incitement'.[81] Within this context, the Israeli cabinet unanimously voted to temporarily shut down Al Jazeera in Israel and ordered the immediate closure of its offices.[82] The decision was not supported by the U.S. and was condemned by the UN Human Rights Office, in addition to many countries globally. Israel was also accused of intentionally targeting and killing several Al Jazeera Arabic journalists in Gaza during the war.[83]

In response to Qatar's prospective exit from the mediation, various voices drew attention to Doha's valuable diplomatic input. Even Israeli officials reportedly acknowledged Qatar's crucial role, despite the politicized statements made by the embattled wartime Prime Minister Benjamin Netanyahu. Reflecting this split in Israeli opinion, the Israeli newspaper *Haaretz* ran an op-ed online with the headline 'Qatar Is Part of the Solution to Israel's War in Gaza, not the Problem'.[84] Furthermore, several major powers, including France, Germany, Italy, and the United Kingdom, issued diplomatic statements in support of Qatar's continued involvement in the negotiations between Hamas and Israel.[85]

On 9 November 2024, Majed Al-Ansari, spokesperson for the Qatari Ministry of Foreign Affairs, announced that Qatar had suspended its role as a mediator between Hamas and Israel. According to Al-Ansari, this decision was both a reaction to what he characterized as the parties' lack of seriousness and commitment to reaching a comprehensive ceasefire agreement, and a self-protection measure by Qatar against criticisms and allegations levelled against its reputation as a neutral and credible mediator.[86] Additionally, it was made clear that this does not mean the closure of Hamas office in Doha, and any decision on this matter would be announced through an official statement by the Qatari Ministry of Foreign Affairs.[87] However, key figures in the Hamas negotiating team were reported to have left Qatar, with widespread assumptions that most had relocated to Türkiye.[88]

Whilst the official Qatari statement attributed the suspension of mediation to the lack of genuine commitment from the parties, other analysts explained this decision as a compliant response to the U.S. request amidst growing pressure on Doha (particularly after the death of the American–Israeli hostage Hersh Goldberg-Polin in

September 2024) to expel the Hamas political leadership, which the U.S. accused of having repeatedly rejected a ceasefire deal with Israel.[89] This marked a shift in U.S. policy towards the movement, with the Hamas presence in Doha increasingly viewed as a point of contention. Therefore, the revision of Qatar's policy towards the continued presence of the political office was part of a risk-aversion strategy to preserve the strategic relationship with Washington.[90]

Whilst this announcement sent shockwaves amongst the public, it was unsurprising. Only days earlier, the Associated Press revealed that a diplomatic source had expressed that the Hamas political office in Qatar 'no longer serves its purpose'.[91] Moreover, early in the war, it was reported that Qatar informed the U.S. that it was willing to reconsider the presence of the Hamas office in Doha once the crisis was resolved, yet this was never officially confirmed by any Qatari source.[92] This position stemmed from Qatar's awareness of the frustration in Washington with the Hamas leadership. In strategic terms, from the perspective of the overall mediation structure, expelling Hamas would be 'a major strategic error' as the group would most likely relocate to a location far less accessible to the U.S. and Israel, thereby further complicating communication and negotiations with the group.[93] Therefore, Hamas remaining in Qatar offers a greater advantage for any long-term ceasefires or peace agreements in Palestine.[94]

Qatar's decision in November 2024 to temporarily suspend its mediation efforts came after the Hamas–Israel negotiations process stalled. This impasse was due to multiple factors. In late 2024, Israel intensified its military operations on various fronts, notably assassinating various primary negotiators and interlocutors within Hamas' senior ranks (for instance, Yahya Sinwar was killed on 16 October 2024). Despite the fact that the assassinations depleted the momentum of mediation, Hamas sources note that the performance and positions of its mediation team remained unchanged.[95] Another constraint lay in the fact that mediators increasingly viewed the two as firmly entrenched in their positions and refusing to engage constructively.[96] Hamas insisted upon a complete withdrawal of Israeli forces from Gaza as a precondition for any ceasefire, whilst Israel held the firm position that any agreement must allow it to continue its military operations and control over the Gaza Strip, which together made the goal of reaching an agreement elusive.[97]

Qatar's decision to publicly withdraw as a mediator came because of what it considered to be a lack of serious engagement with the negotiations by both sides.[98] This move served as a strategic manoeuvre to exert pressure on the parties, who thus recognized that Qatari mediation was indispensable to any possible agreement.[99] Ultimately, this move proved effective. Qatar announced on 7 December 2024 that it had resumed its mediation role. Within weeks of the announcement, talks gained momentum. As these continued, Qatar struck a more optimistic tone that an agreement could be reached, with Qatari mediator and spokesperson Dr Majed Al-Ansari stating that the major issues between the two parties had been agreed upon.[100] Anticipation grew that a ceasefire deal could be announced prior to the inauguration of President Trump in January 2025.

2025 Ceasefire Deal

On 19 January 2025, a six-week ceasefire agreement between Israel and Hamas came into effect. The agreement paved the way for a three-phase period leading from the cessation of hostilities and exchanges of captives to humanitarian aid, the withdrawal of Israeli forces, and eventually to large-scale reconstruction. The ceasefire itself was nearly identical to the text of the May 2024 draft agreement that was accepted by Hamas and brokered by Qatar, Egypt, and the U.S.,[101] and yet was still blocked by Israeli Prime Minister Netanyahu. Notably, however, it included written guarantees by the U.S., as opposed to the verbal assurances provided by the Biden administration, and did not contain a clause that would allow Israel to resume its aggression. It also included a more detailed section on the humanitarian aspect of the ceasefire, which guaranteed the entry of temporary housing, the rebuilding of critical infrastructure, the rehabilitation of hospitals, and financial aid.[102]

The timing of the agreement was significant, coming one day before the inauguration of President Trump. Much analysis points to threats issued by President Trump in early December that 'all hell would break out' if the agreement was not signed before his administration took office,[103] as a critical factor in increasing pressure on the conflict parties. This was followed by concerted and unprecedented diplomatic efforts involving officials from the outgoing Biden and incoming Trump administrations in the run-up to the deal.

Laying the groundwork for the 2025 ceasefire involved persistent actions by Qatari and Egyptian mediators, working through 'months of torturous, on-off negotiations'.[104] Throughout the days in the run-up to the ceasefire agreement, mediators worked tirelessly in Doha. It is reported that the breakthrough came after ninety-six hours of intense negotiations involving Qatari and Egyptian mediators, in addition to officials from the Biden and Trump administrations working in tandem.[105] The multi-party mediation team reportedly sat until 3 am, shuttling between the Hamas delegation on the first floor and the Israeli delegation on the second floor of the venue.[106] It marked a major turnaround for Qatar's role in the negotiations, considering that it had appeared to withdraw from multi-party mediation altogether just two months previously.

The U.S. leverage was critical to persuading Israel to agree to the ceasefire deal. At the same time, Qatar utilized its leverage over Hamas. It is reported that 'Witkoff and McGurk were pushing the Israelis. Qatar was pushing Hamas'.[107] This dynamic illustrates Qatar's comparative advantage but also the limitations of leverage compared to the U.S. Throughout the 7 October War, Qatar faced accusations that it had not utilized its apparent leverage over Hamas to reach a negotiated deal. Maintaining an office in Doha provides many opportunities for communication and influence, yet Qatar does not control the group's policies and decisions. Rather, throughout the multi-party mediation process, Qatar utilized its credibility and access, which were needed to bring Hamas to the negotiating table. Whilst this was necessary to make any kind of deal, it was not sufficient to hold the ceasefire together, with only power and leverage on the American side facing any chance of pressuring Israel to keep to its terms.

Brokering Phase Two and Three

At the outset of the six-week ceasefire, Qatar and Egypt established a communications hub to address any post-agreement implementation challenges arising between Hamas and Israel. Although the ceasefire agreement outlined a phased framework, the terms of phases two and three were not finalized at the time the truce came into effect. Instead, these were intended to be negotiated during the first phase, with talks on phase two scheduled to begin on the sixteenth day.[108] Phase two was expected to last for forty-two days and involve the release of all remaining living captives held in Gaza, the complete withdrawal of Israeli forces from the Strip, and the establishment of a permanent ceasefire.[109] The third phase stipulated the return of all remaining bodies of the dead and the reconstruction of the Gaza Strip. In early March 2025, Qatari delegations participated in the Extraordinary Arab League Summit held in Cairo and the Extraordinary Meeting of the Council of Foreign Ministers of the Organization of Islamic Cooperation in Jeddah, both dedicated to the situation in Gaza, bringing particular attention to early recovery and reconstruction matters.[110] Overall, this ceasefire agreement held greater potential for long-term peace in the Gaza Strip.

However, the ceasefire collapsed on 18 March 2025, before the start of the second phase and following Israel's decision to resume its war on the Gaza Strip, conducting bombing there and displacing hundreds of thousands of civilians.[111] In the days leading up to the collapse, Qatar and Egypt intensified their diplomatic efforts in a last-ditch attempt to preserve the agreement. Negotiations between Qatar, Egypt, the U.S., and Hamas were held in Doha, with U.S. Special Envoy to the Middle East Steve Witkoff landing in the Qatari capital on 11 March to join 'indirect talks' between Israel and Hamas.[112] On 12 March, the Qatari Prime Minister and Egyptian Foreign Minister held a bilateral meeting to coordinate the new round of negotiations on the implementation of phase two.[113] On the same day, following the meeting with Witkoff, a joint communiqué of the five-member ministerial committee on Gaza (composed of representatives of Qatar, Jordan, Saudi Arabia, Egypt, the UAE, and the PLO) was issued to reaffirm collective support for the ceasefire framework.[114] However, the efforts were ultimately unsuccessful. Already in February, Israeli officials placed the ceasefire agreement in jeopardy by delaying the release of more than 600 Palestinians and attempting to justify the delays by accusing Hamas of staging 'theatrical' handovers of captives—a narrative that appeared more concerned with domestic posturing than substantive diplomacy.[115]

The collapse of the agreement also highlighted the challenges of conflict mediation when some of the parties to the conflict actively work to sabotage the process. In reality, it was evident that key actors within the Israeli government had never intended to honour the agreement. Extremist ministers such as Itamar Ben-Gvir and Bezalel Smotrich had openly threatened to bring down the governing coalition unless fighting resumed. As a result, the ceasefire's implementation became a political liability for Prime Minister Netanyahu, whose survival depended on appeasing these factions. This domestic dynamic guided the Israeli decision to block the second phase of the deal, reflecting a broader strategy of undermining ceasefire negotiations.[116] As Qatar had repeatedly warned, any temporary truce must be followed by serious political dialogue to address the root causes of the conflict in the Gaza Strip—namely, the occupation. The collapse of the agreement thus highlighted the need for a just and sustainable peace that could prevent the outbreak of renewed violence.

Conclusion

The 7 October War on the Gaza Strip stands as the most high-profile case of mediation in Qatar's long and storied experience in peacemaking. This role, however, did not come from out of the blue. Rather, Qatar built its credentials as a mediator in Gaza through more than a decade of sustained engagement involving humanitarian and reconstruction assistance, reconciliation between Palestinian factions, and an ability to talk to all parties involved in a highly geopolitically charged context. Thus, at the outbreak of the 7 October War, Qatar was a natural go-to mediator within the multi-party mediation framework that attempted to broker peace between Israel and Hamas. Throughout the devastating war, Qatar leveraged its diplomatic channels and longstanding relationships with key actors to facilitate indirect negotiations, secure humanitarian aid, and push for temporary ceasefire. Despite facing multiple challenges, not least criticism from various international actors, Qatar remained central to back-channel diplomacy, focusing on de-escalation. Finally, addressing the Gaza crisis placed Qatar in the international spotlight to an unprecedented degree and drew attention to the increasingly global and proactive role of the country in conflict mediation, which is explored in depth in the next chapter.

8

QATARI MEDIATION AT THE HEART OF GLOBAL CRISES

In the early 2020s, Qatar emerged as one of the world's leading mediators, transforming from its status as an influential regional actor into a powerhouse for conflict mediation globally. This was an impressive turnaround given that just a few years previously, and amidst the uncertainty of the Arab Spring and the Gulf Crisis, it seemed that Qatar's influence in mediation was waning. Whilst analytical attention to Qatar's renewed engagement in mediation since then has been mostly analyzed in visible cases like Afghanistan and the Gaza Strip, there are many other lesser-noted cases in the early 2020s that warrant attention—spanning across Africa, Latin America, and Europe, and often at the heart of some of the most high-profile contemporary global crises. The following analysis traces Qatar's post-2020 mediation trajectory well beyond its traditional orbit of influence. The discussion situates this rise within the internal and external dynamics that have enabled Doha to mediate, including the evolution of an increasingly sophisticated approach tailored to mediation and the growing influence of the Gulf States in global affairs.[1]

Qatar's Re-entry into Mediation Post-2020

In February 2020, a landmark agreement signed in Doha between the United States (U.S.) and the Taliban proved to be a turning point for

Qatari mediation. The reputation that Qatar cultivated as a mediator during the 2006–10 phase was significant, yet this inevitably faded over time. The U.S.–Taliban agreement generated significant momentum and reaffirmed Qatar's commitment to resolving international disputes, defying the pre-2020 narrative that the country had downsized its diplomatic ambitions in the wake of the Arab Spring and Gulf Crisis.

The Al-Ula Summit on 5 January 2021 was another catalyst for renewed action, officially ending the blockade imposed on Qatar by its neighbours. Geopolitical constraints on Qatar's proactive diplomatic role—including regional isolation, disruption of multilateral cooperation, and media pressure—were lifted through this resolution of the Gulf Crisis. This sub-regional détente enabled Qatar to focus its efforts outwards once more, rather than on domestic self-sufficiency and resilience.[2] Thus, Qatar's rise in conflict mediation in the 2020s was further enabled by the lifting of the geopolitical constraints imposed during the Gulf Crisis 2017–21.

The end of the Gulf Crisis and the signing of the Al-Ula Declaration in 2021 did not simply lift the shackles that constrained Doha's diplomatic role, however. Rather, Qatar's engagement in conflict mediation as a central focus of its foreign policy was itself constitutive of reshaping these shifts. In particular, Qatar mediation in high-profile crises such as the U.S.–Taliban agreement and the May 2021 ceasefire in the Gaza Strip both served as a strategic message to the White House that Qatar was a responsible actor, acting as a counter to the accusations propagated by the blockading countries. This strategic rationale is not imputed but rather apparent in public statements, such as the declaration by Sheikh Tamim bin Hamad Al Thani, the Emir of Qatar, who in 2022 told the 77th United Nations (UN) General Assembly that 'mediation in the peaceful settlement of disputes' was at the centre of Qatar's foreign policy to 'solidify [its] reputation as an internationally reliable partner'.[3]

The post-2020 track record of Qatari mediation that involved diplomatic engagement in far-flung locales—ranging from Caracas to Tehran—was thus not a coincidence. By mediating in conflicts in areas far removed from what are popularly perceived to be Qatar's zones of strategic interest, the perception of its impartiality and reliability is further strengthened. This was particularly true of cases such as the Russia–Ukraine efforts and U.S.–Venezuela talks—both contexts in which many large states could be assumed to have vested interests at stake hindering their mediation. In parallel with its growing global reach, Qatari mediation in the post-2020 phase also involved engaging in conflicts and crises in Africa, where it undertook several notable initiatives in contexts such as Somalia, Chad, and Libya, as well as Rwanda and the Democratic Republic of Congo (DRC).

Mediation in Africa

By exploring this shift in mediation beyond Qatar's primary focus, the following analysis sheds light on a number of notable cases of third-party facilitation in Somalia, Chad, and Libya during 2021 and 2022.

Somali–Kenyan Bilateral Relations and the Somali Election Crisis

In May 2021, Qatar successfully mediated the restoration of diplomatic relations between Somalia and Kenya, which had been severed since December 2020.[4] The escalation of tensions was driven by accusations from Somalia that Kenya had interfered in its internal political affairs (notably, the electoral process in Jubbaland) and supported Somali federal states critical of Mogadishu's central government.[5] These frictions were compounded by longstanding tensions over the maritime boundary in the Indian Ocean, known to be an economically valuable territory rich in petroleum, marine resources, and trade routes.[6] In addition, Kenya's security concerns over Somali refugees and the threat posed by Al-Shabab prompted repeated calls to close the Dadaab and Kakuma camps that host large Somali populations.[7] Escalating tensions were further shaped by entrenched mistrust and deteriorating interpersonal relations between the Somali and Kenyan presidents, as well as between the intelligence chiefs of both states.[8]

Qatari mediation in the Kenya–Somalia crisis culminated in both parties signing a communiqué on 6 May 2021.[9] Although the two countries continued to experience intermittent diplomatic tensions and public disagreements over deeper underlying issues in the following months,[10] there was a cautious improvement in relations. Several official talks occurred in August 2021, which included meetings between Somali Prime Minister Mohamed Hussein Roble and Kenyan President Uhuru Kenyatta in Mombasa, as well as between Roble and Kenyan Foreign Minister Raychelle Omamo in Mogadishu.[11] Restoring bilateral relations and presenting the mutual benefits of reconciliation was amongst the initial steps in Qatar's mediation in this case, as the inter-governmental crisis was part of the 'group of crises' that had long afflicted Somalia.[12]

The attempt to restore the ties by de-escalating tension over the Somali political elections at that time included a Qatari delegation's intensive diplomatic tour of East Africa, headed by His Excellency Dr Mutlaq bin Majid Al-Qahtani in May 2021.[13] A series of meetings were held with members of the Farmaajo administration, as well as with opposition leaders and presidential candidates. Acting primarily as a facilitator, Qatar encouraged intra-governmental dialogue behind the scenes and supported consensus-building efforts around the September 2020 electoral agreement.[14] This agreement was reinstated as the sole electoral procedure and led to the setting of a new election date. As a result, and following further postponement of the elections until May 2022, President Hassan Sheikh Mohamud was subsequently re-elected after his 2012–17 term, bringing the contentious electoral cycle to an end.[15] The 2022 elections and the ensuing political processes have prevented the outbreak of another civil war in Somalia.

Previously framed in terms of intra-Gulf competition in the Horn of Africa vying for influence in Somali politics,[16] in particular between Qatar and the United Arab Emirates (UAE), Qatar's successful mediation efforts in 2021 garnered praise from previously sceptical Somali factions, demonstrating a shift in perceptions.[17] In May 2021, Qatar's Permanent Representative to the UN, Ambassador Sheikha Alya Ahmed bin Saif Al-Thani, highlighted Qatar's efforts in resolving the Somalia–Kenya dispute as part of its broader strategy to promote peace and stability on the continent.[18]

Chad: The 2022 Doha Agreement

Qatari mediation in Chad, resulting in the 2022 Doha Agreement, was another successful diplomatic engagement. Following the death of President Idris Déby in 2021, a political crisis erupted, which led to the formation of the Transitional Military Council led by his son, Mahamat Déby. Qatar, utilizing its diplomatic leverages, facilitated negotiations between the Chadian government and over forty rebel factions, leading to the Doha Agreement on 8 August 2022.[19]

The Qatari mediation, led initially by Qatar's Special Envoy, Dr Mutlaq bin Majid Al-Qahtani, and later by the Advisor to His Highness the Emir for National Security, Mohammed bin Ahmed Al-Misnad, involved a five-month-long mediation process that included hosting the parties in Doha, facilitating indirect negotiations, and ensuring the inclusion of key demands, such as the guarantee of amnesty for rebel leaders upon their return to Chad.[20] The resultant Doha Agreement ensured commitments to a permanent ceasefire, safe passage for rebel leaders, and the integration of armed groups into the national army, thus stabilizing the situation in Chad.

The acceptance of Qatar as a mediator, even by sceptical factions, demonstrated the trust that had developed over years of diplomatic engagement in the region. For instance, before signing the Doha Document for Peace in Darfur, Qatar maintained good relations with Chad and the armed movements there, whilst there were also personal relations between His Highness Emir Sheikh Hamad bin Khalifa Al Thani and President Idris Déby.[21] Qatar's prior experience in brokering the 2009 Doha Accord between Sudan and Chad, and its efforts to restore diplomatic ties with Chad in 2018, were important steps towards the 2022 agreement.[22]

During the post-agreement phase, Qatar's role shifted back to facilitation, with the commencement of the National Dialogue in Chad on 20 August 2022. The National Dialogue included over 1,400 participants, with delegates from the military, civil society, opposition parties, trade unions, and rebel signatories of the 2022 Doha Agreement.[23] Their presence was crucial for the implementation of the Doha Agreement's provisions and the drafting of a new constitution. Qatar's continued involvement in the process, alongside other international actors, demonstrated its commitment to ensuring the success of the transition in Chad.

The Chad mediation process represented one of the most extensive peacemaking efforts ever undertaken by Qatar, both in terms of the scale of the negotiations and the resources committed. France, the African Union (AU), the U.S. and the European Union (EU) commended Qatar's role in the deal reached between the parties, whilst the UN Secretary-General thanked Qatar for mediating the National Dialogue.[24]

De-escalating Tensions in Libya

The 2022 political crisis in Libya resulted in violent clashes between militias backed by Libya's rival governments, which killed at least thirty-two people and wounded 159.[25] The hostilities intensified after fighters who aligned with the prime minister appointed by the eastern-based House of Representatives, Fathi Bashagha, fired on a convoy in the capital, and groups affiliated with the prime minister of the Tripoli-based government, Abdul Hamid Dbeibah, stormed a military base of a Bashagha-affiliated group. In a visit to Türkiye, Libya's Parliament Speaker, Aguila Saleh, was invited by the Qatari Foreign Minister to discuss de-escalation in Libya. In September 2022, Doha facilitated meetings with key Libyan political figures, including Saleh and Belqasim Haftar, son of Khalifa Haftar.[26] This move marked the first visit of representatives from the Tobruk government to Qatar since 2014.

Historically, Qatar had been closely associated with the Tripoli-based government in western Libya, which led to a severing of diplomatic ties with the eastern Tobruk-based government. However, the changing geopolitical landscape, including the restoration of ties between Qatar and Egypt after the Gulf Crisis, made Qatar appear more acceptable as a mediator, particularly as Russia and the UAE reduced their level of involvement in Libya. Furthermore, President Sisi's visit to Doha in September 2022 bolstered Qatar's acceptance as a regional peace broker.[27]

During the mediation process, the meetings were personally hosted by the Emir of Qatar and included shuttle diplomacy between the Tobruk and Tripoli-based governments. A distinctive element of Qatar's mediation was its focus on managing spoilers within the process. For instance, Qatar's good relations with Khaled Al-Mishri, head of the High Council of State in the western government, were instrumental in securing his buy-in to counteract opposition to General Haftar's potential presidential bid.[28] Haftar's inclusion was a contentious issue due to his previous role in derailing peacebuilding efforts in 2019 by instigating the Battle of Tripoli.[29]

Qatar's diplomatic engagement averted the escalation of violence and helped to restore the faltering political process.[30] A significant outcome was the political proposal presented by Aguila Saleh to the Libyan parliament in September 2022,[31] prioritizing parliamentary elections before presidential elections, and calling for the formation of a new three-member Presidential Council led by him and including Khaled Al-Mishri. Despite ongoing tensions, the proposal gained international backing, including support from the U.S. and the UN.[32]

Finally, Qatar's mediation in Libya received strong backing, with statements released on the same day in January 2023 from the U.S. urging that there is 'no reason to delay', and the UN, which 'strongly encourage[d]' the finalization of the agreement.[33] Although the Libyan political landscape remains fragile to this day, Qatar's renewed engagement in Libya through impartial mediation and a focus on building political consensus provides a viable platform for constructive dialogue between the Libyan political actors.

Qatar's Balanced Diplomatic Engagement in the Russia–Ukraine Conflict

Throughout the history of the Russia–Ukraine conflict, Qatar maintained a balanced approach and remained in contact with the leaders of both countries through official visits and continuous dialogue on political and economic issues.[34] Following the intensification of the confrontation in early 2022, Qatar carved out a niche role as a mediator by launching the Reunion Initiative, which helped secure the reunification of Ukrainian children with their families.[35] Between the February 2022 Russian invasion and the end of 2023, up to 20,000 Ukrainian children were abducted by Russia.[36] Multiple attempts to diplomatically engage on this issue were constrained by the International Criminal Court's March 2023 arrest warrants for Vladimir Putin and the Commissioner for Children's Rights in Russia, Maria Lvova-Belova, accusing them of the 'unlawful deportation of population and that of unlawful transfer of population from occupied areas of the Ukraine to the Russian Federation'.[37]

In mid-2023, Qatar-brokered negotiations established a longer-term reunification mechanism under the special initiative. Qatar hosted the first reunification of four children, aged between two and seventeen, with their families at its mission in Moscow in October 2023, followed by a second group of six children in December 2023.[38] The return process involved family consent, identification and verification of children, coordination with humanitarian organizations, and logistical arrangements.[39] Qatari officials accompanied the children and their family members through Moscow and Minsk to the Ukrainian border, where they were received by the Ukrainian authorities.[40] Doha continued its reunification efforts throughout 2024.[41]

Beyond that, in April 2024, Qatar hosted approximately twenty Russian and Ukrainian families under a comprehensive health and recovery program. This initiative provided essential medical, psychological, and social support to address the immediate and long-term needs of these families, facilitating their rehabilitation and reintegration.[42] Additionally, Qatar pledged USD 100 million in humanitarian support for Ukraine, covering projects related to health, education infrastructure, drinking water provision, and other essential services.[43] It also allocated fifty scholarships for Ukrainian students in Qatari universities during the 2023–24 academic year.[44] Moreover, Qatar committed USD 3 million to the Office of the Ukrainian Parliament Commissioner for Human Rights to enhance monitoring and support services for families affected by the conflict.[45]

Qatar's confidence-building strategy aimed 'to identify areas where both the Ukrainian and Russian sides share common interests and use that as a foundation to build trust',[46] a move appreciated by both Russian and Ukrainian leaders. In June 2024, during a visit to Doha, Ukrainian President Volodymyr Zelenskyy thanked Qatar for its role in returning Ukrainian children.[47] Similarly, on the sidelines of the Shanghai Cooperation Organization Summit in July 2024, Russian

President Vladimir Putin extended his gratitude for Qatari efforts in resolving humanitarian issues and those arising from the Ukrainian crisis.[48] These efforts illustrate Qatar's evolving expertise in mediation 'from a regional outlier into a critical player on the world stage'.[49] The focus on humanitarian protection once more highlighted its principled approach to conflict mediation.

Qatari Mediation Involving U.S. as a Primary Party to the Negotiations

In the post-2020 period, Qatar facilitated a series of high-profile negotiations directly involving Washington. After the U.S.–Taliban agreement in 2020, Qatari diplomats went on to coordinate talks between the U.S. and Iran, as well as between the U.S. and Venezuela. This reflects both Qatar's rise as a global mediator and its emergence as a key diplomatic partner to the U.S. These strengthened bilateral ties were apparent when it was agreed that Doha would 'represent the diplomatic interests of the U.S.' in Afghanistan,[50] and in Qatar being formally designated a major non-ally of the North Atlantic Treaty Organization.[51] Under the Biden administration in particular, the two states cultivated a robust partnership grounded in shared goals, strategic dialogue, and military cooperation.[52] Furthermore, 'U.S. officials have acknowledged Qatar's role in supporting U.S. diplomatic efforts globally', including in Ukraine, Lebanon, and the DRC.[53] Qatar also engaged in multi-party mediation alongside the U.S., most notably in ceasefire negotiations between Hamas and Israel. The following analysis explores these U.S.-linked mediation efforts, starting with U.S.–Venezuela negotiations.

U.S.–Venezuela Talks

In June 2023, Qatar hosted secret talks between the U.S. and Venezuela, marking an intriguing episode in its emergence as an influential broker in an increasingly multipolar world order. These talks took place alongside various Qatari diplomatic initiatives, including a meeting between the Qatari and Venezuelan prime ministers, on the sidelines of the seventy-eighth session of the United Nations General Assembly, which laid the foundations for future dialogue.[54] This phase of concerted mediation efforts culminated in Qatar brokering a prisoner swap between the U.S. and Venezuela in December 2023.[55] Through the deal, ten American prisoners were exchanged for a Venezuelan detainee.[56]

The prisoner exchange was part of a broader strategy by Qatar to foster dialogue, address longstanding tensions between the U.S. and Venezuela,[57] and even 'normalise political life in Venezuela'.[58] This continued role was reflected in the fact that in June 2024, Doha hosted high-level talks between the president of the Venezuelan National Assembly and President Nicolás Maduro's ally Jorge Rodríguez, as well as Juan Gonzalez, an advisor to President Joe Biden.[59]

Qatar's neutrality, neither swayed by U.S. endorsements nor aligned with U.S. sanctions on Venezuela, made it a credible mediator. By mediating between the two countries, Qatar filled the diplomatic void left by regional actors, like the Union of South American Nations, which had been sidelined due to internal preoccupations and perceived bias.[60] It was also well placed to mediate the talks given Venezuela's close ties with Iran and Qatar's pragmatic relations with the U.S. and Iran. Through this engagement, Qatar managed to hedge its security bets whilst continuing to be of strategic value to Washington, converting protracted negotiation deadlocks into measurable diplomatic gains.[61]

Deserving of closer examination, the U.S.–Venezuela case aligns with the broader objective of consolidating Qatari influence in Latin America, a region where it has been actively expanding its economic and diplomatic footprint.[62] The expansion is evident, particularly through Qatar's deepening relations with Guyana, driven by shared energy interests, which potentially positions Qatar to resolve the country's border dispute[63] with Venezuela over the strategically important Essequibo region.[64] By capitalizing on its diplomatic success beyond its immediate neighbourhood, Qatar has established itself in Latin American diplomacy as a reliable mediator.

Rwanda–DRC Talks

Qatar also played a supporting role in U.S-led mediation between the DRC and Rwanda. This diplomatic role took place against the backdrop of decades of instability in eastern DRC, characterized by entrenched state fragility, regional power struggles, and repeated cross-border interventions by Rwanda.[65] The mediation efforts to resolve tensions took place in a context of crisis escalation, as the Rwanda-backed M23 armed group made rapid territorial gains, capturing the strategic city of Goma in eastern DRC in January 2025.[66] The crisis heightened complex regional tensions and prompted international concern for the wider stability of the Great Lakes region.[67]

At the request of both the DRC and Rwanda, and at the invitation of the AU, Qatar became engaged as a mediator, playing a diplomatic role as part of a multi-party mediation and facilitation process that involved the U.S., the AU, and, at a later stage, the Republic of Togo. In March 2025, Qatar hosted a trilateral summit in Doha between Rwandan President Paul Kagame and DRC President Félix Tshisekedi, aimed at de-escalating the conflict through resolving Rwanda–DRC tensions.[68] In mid- to late-April 2025, Qatar mediated negotiations between the DRC government and the M23 rebels in Doha, resulting in a ceasefire agreement, a rare joint statement by both sides (the first since 2021), and a mutual commitment to halt hostilities and refrain from hate speech.[69] In June 2025, a U.S.-brokered draft peace proposal was presented to DRC and the Rwanda-backed M23 rebels following months of mediation in Doha.[70] On 18 June, technical teams from both Rwanda and the DRC approved the final text of a peace agreement between the two countries mediated by the U.S. and observed by Qatar,[71] with the deal signed on 27 June 2025.[72]

U.S.–Iran Prisoner Exchange

In 2022, Qatar's entry into the mediation process between the U.S. and Iran was both timely and strategic, occurring amidst rising tensions following the U.S. withdrawal from the Joint Comprehensive Plan of Action (JCPOA)[73] in 2018, after which traditional diplomatic channels were largely severed. Qatar, with its longstanding policy of maintaining open lines of communication with Washington and Tehran, was well-positioned to act as a diplomatic bridge on this geostrategic issue.[74]

From March 2022, Qatar mediated prisoner exchange between the U.S. and Iran, hosting multiple rounds of talks and facilitating communication between the parties through shuttle diplomacy. Qatari officials visited Washington and Tehran, extensively engaging in both direct and indirect meetings to reach an agreement. Through trust-building, careful logistics, and management of highly sensitive information, a prisoner exchange agreement was reached in September 2023, involving five Iranians and five Americans.[75] The release of the American detainees was particularly celebrated in the U.S., ending what President Biden described as 'years of agony, uncertainty, and suffering' for the families involved.[76]

Qatar also monitored the implementation of the financial aspects of the deal. The unfreezing of USD 6 billion in Iranian funds, held in two South Korean banks since 2018 due to U.S. sanctions was a significant component of the exchange deal. Under the agreement, these funds were transferred to Qatari bank accounts, allowing Iran access only for humanitarian purposes such as food and medicine.[77]

Following the finalization of the deal, President Biden personally thanked Qatar's Emir Sheikh Tamim bin Hamad Al Thani for his 'active and constructive' efforts.[78] Iranian President Ebrahim Raisi and then Foreign Minister Hossein Amir-Abdollahian acknowledged Qatari efforts, framing the release of American detainees as a 'purely humanitarian action' that could lead to similar initiatives in the future.[79] Nevertheless, the agreement was met with scepticism by some U.S. lawmakers, who argued that the unfreezing of Iranian assets could embolden Tehran and potentially lead to further hostile actions. This prompted contradictory statements between the U.S. and Iran on the control and allocation of the unfrozen funds, with Washington insisting on strict oversight and restrictions for humanitarian use, whilst Tehran maintained that it would have full discretion over how the funds are utilized.[80] Critics also pointed to the broader geopolitical implications, especially with the perceived Iranian involvement in the Hamas–Israel war.

Whilst the deal represented only one step towards addressing the decades-long, underlying issues between the U.S. and Iran, the immediate outcomes were positive, contributing constructively towards greater political engagement between the two countries. The case highlights Qatar's capacity to mediate high-profile, geopolitically sensitive talks. Attempting to capitalize on a U.S.–Iran deal, Qatar then embarked on a more intensified exploration of the potential to broker a renewed nuclear deal between the U.S. and Iran.

U.S.–Iran Nuclear Deal

The JCPOA, signed in 2015 between Iran and the P5+1 countries (China, France, Germany, Russia, the United Kingdom, and the U.S.) and adopted by the UN Security Council through Resolution 2231, did not include any of the Gulf States, even though it significantly impacts security in the Gulf region. Following the U.S. withdrawal from the JCPOA in 2018, however, tensions escalated between Washington and Tehran. The Qatari leadership, along with its Gulf neighbours, recognized that its regional stability was intertwined with resolving the nuclear issue and thus sought to bring parties back to the negotiation table.[81] Qatar's mediation of the 2023 prisoner exchange deal had established a communication channel for future engagement, which it later utilized to encourage both sides to renew their commitment to implementing the terms of the nuclear agreement.

During the International Atomic Energy Agency's (IAEA) Board of Governors meeting in Vienna in September 2023, His Excellency Secretary-General of the Ministry of Foreign Affairs and IAEA's Governor from the State of Qatar, Dr Ahmed bin Hassan Al-Hammadi, urged Iran and the IAEA to continue cooperation on resolving outstanding issues around safeguards.[82] In March 2023, Qatar welcomed the agreement between Iran and the IAEA, urging continued dialogue to resolve nuclear programme issues and emphasizing the importance of cooperation and positive developments as a foundation for resuming the JCPOA.[83] Doha also facilitated several rounds of indirect talks between the two states by hosting high-level meetings in June 2024.[84]

Parallel to these efforts, Qatari mediators helped reduce regional tensions by engaging with other Gulf Cooperation Council members to obtain broader regional support for the negotiations. When Iran retaliated against Israel's aggression in June 2025, the U.S. Middle East envoy asked the foreign ministers of Iraq, Qatar, Saudi Arabia, and the UAE to deliver a message to Iran, urging it to seek to de-escalate tensions with Israel.[85] A prominent Gulf scholar noted that

Qatar has 'kept windows for dialogue open' through its good working relationship with Iran, whilst remaining useful to the U.S. and other Western allies, especially in de-escalating tensions or prisoner exchanges.[86] Although a renewed agreement on the JCPOA was not fully realized and the talks continued under Omani mediation in 2025, Qatar reiterated its readiness to communicate with all sides to prevent further deterioration of U.S.–Iran relations, and expressed support for broader Gulf and international efforts.

Israel–Iran Ceasefire

These years of quiet involvement in U.S.–Iran talks in support of Omani-led mediation over renewing the JCPOA or formulating a new nuclear deal meant that Qatar was well positioned to act as a key mediator during what President Trump coined as the '12-Day War' between Iran and Israel in June 2025. At the outbreak of the crisis, it was reported that Oman and Qatar, amongst other states, were in contact with both sides seeking immediate de-escalation.[87]

On 22 June 2025, the U.S. joined the Israeli war and attacked Iranian nuclear facilities in Isfahan, Fordow, and Natanz. The risk of further escalation, including damage or destruction to nuclear facilities and the possibility of radioactive leaks, posed an existential risk to the neighbouring Gulf states.

In a dramatic escalation, Qatar itself came under attack on 23 June 2025, when Iran launched nineteen missiles at the Al Udeid Air Base, near Doha, with eighteen missiles intercepted.[88] Rather than respond punitively to what it considered as a 'flagrant violation' of its sovereignty, Qatar used the momentum and proceeded with a diplomatic push to resolve the wider war between Iran and Israel.[89] Only a few hours later, on 24 June, a Qatari-brokered ceasefire was announced. This diplomatic success led to positive appraisals from both Iran[90] and the U.S.,[91] along with the wider diplomatic community.

The events of 23 and 24 June, along with Doha's de-escalatory approach, are a poignant display of Qatar's conviction that dialogue and mediation are the pathway to regional peace. Whether mediating in African contexts, facilitating humanitarian negotiations in the Ukraine conflict, coordinating prisoner exchanges, supporting nuclear deal negotiations, or de-escalating fundamental tensions between geopolitical rivals in the immediate aftermath of missile strikes on its own soil, Qatar maintained a consistent commitment to conflict mediation, often in the heart of global crises.

9

PILLARS OF QATARI MEDIATION

Qatar is not wholly unique in every aspect of its profile as a global actor in conflict mediation. However, the constellation of diverse characteristic features that Qatar brings to the table distinguishes it from other mediators. The combination of impartiality, its wide diplomatic reach, as well as its long-term commitment and whole-of-government approach in dealing with international conflicts, makes Qatar a distinct player in the world of mediation. This chapter aims to summarize these distinct features, which constitute the key pillars of Qatari mediation. It draws upon the comparative findings of the case studies presented in this book, as well as insights from the database of interviews conducted with leading Qatari mediators and conflict parties from contexts in which Qatar has mediated.

Constitutional Commitment to Mediation and Peacemaking

Qatar's role in mediation and peacemaking is enshrined in its constitution, highlighting the goal of 'strengthening international peace and security by means of encouraging peaceful resolution of international disputes'.[1] The depth of this foundational national commitment to peacemaking is rare amongst the international community of states.

Qatari officials often express a self-understanding that engagement in mediation is driven by ethical, civic, and religious duties.[2] Sheikh

Jassim bin Mohammed Al Thani, the founder of the State of Qatar, referred to Qatar as the 'Kaaba of the Oppressed'.[3] Just as the Kaaba serves as a unifying focal point for Muslims worldwide, Qatar has positioned itself as a beacon of hope and support for those facing hardships, as well as ostracized political figures, regardless of their origin. The country has consistently demonstrated this commitment through its humanitarian initiatives, diplomacy, and mediation efforts.[4]

As the analysis of multiple interviews and secondary data in this book suggests, ethical values are often reported by Qatari mediators as a primary driver behind Qatar's conflict mediation efforts, commonly invoking Qatar's role in peacemaking as grounded in humanitarian imperatives rather than purely strategic interests. The emphasis on humanitarian diplomacy implies a proactive stance towards regional challenges that positions the approach as a principled response to geopolitical tensions.[5]

Additionally, mediation as a practice is rooted in Arab culture that goes back millennia, and is related to both Islamic teachings and tribal customs like *sulh* and *majlis*. One Qatari diplomat clearly illustrates this point: 'Qatar is a Muslim country, and the Quranic verses, Prophetic traditions, and Islamic jurisprudence all promote mediation, reconciliation, and the preservation of life. As Allah says: "*And whoever saves one life, it is as if he has saved all of humanity*"'.[6]

These cultural and normative roots of Qatari mediation are, however, frequently overlooked in much Western analysis that is clouded by a variant of Orientalism and dismisses the ethical dimensions of the Gulf States in peacemaking.[7] Thus, Qatar's constitutional framework enshrines mediation and peacemaking as core principles and serves as a foundational pillar for its proactive diplomatic engagements, reflecting a deep-rooted commitment to fostering regional and global stability through peaceful conflict resolution mechanisms.

Impartiality and Trust-Building

Building trust with conflicting parties is a fundamental step towards successful mediation. In the words of one Qatari mediator: 'Qatar insists on being a fair and impartial mediator for both sides'.[8] Qatar's willingness to engage with diverse and often opposing factions has enabled it to act as a facilitator in entrenched geopolitical disputes, establishing trust through longstanding relationships and proactive engagement with all parties. Furthermore, Qatar has utilized shuttle diplomacy and the personal engagement of its top leadership to maintain its position as a trusted and respected mediator.

Reflecting on years of experience in Qatari mediation, one diplomat noted that 'the most important lesson is that the state should maintain good relations with everyone. You must have distinguished relationships with all parties'.[9] The case of the Gaza Strip was notable in this regard, where Qatar built strong relationships with various Palestinian factions and Israel, which allowed it to mediate in intra-Palestinian reconciliation and multiple wars, including the 7 October War on Gaza. During that war, Qatar became a driving force behind the talks for a ceasefire agreement in November 2023, as well as bringing emergency relief to the Gaza Strip. Qatar's ability to maintain impartiality whilst building strong connections and trust with conflicting parties was crucial in defusing political crises and achieving ceasefire agreements. Qatar's leading diplomat on the Palestine file explains that 'in any mediation, everything you need is relationships. When you have good relationships with all parties, it qualifies you to mediate simply'.[10]

Thus, Qatar's longstanding relationships and consistent engagement with all relevant parties to various conflicts allowed it to gain trust and, with it, influence. This trust, combined with a commitment to impartiality, peaceful constructive dialogue, and cooperation, earned Qatar its reputation as a credible party. His Excellency Ambassador Ali bin Hassan Al-Hammadi, former Qatari Ambassador to Sudan, further emphasizes this aspect of Qatari mediation: 'Qatar strives to maintain an equal distance from all parties without bias towards one side or the other in order to provide the appropriate climate for successful mediation'.[11]

Evidently, Qatar's mediation efforts since the 2000s have been characterized by impartiality, as seen with the various case studies analyzed in this book. Importantly, the consensus-driven peace agreements resulting from these processes were primarily steered by the conflict parties and local stakeholders, with Qatar playing a crucial but non-intrusive role. This approach has proven effective in various conflicts, including those in Afghanistan, Darfur, Gaza, Lebanon, and, more recently, in the mediation efforts between Russia and Ukraine, Latin America, and the United States (U.S.) and Iran, Libya, and Chad.

Qatar's Diplomatic Reach

Qatar's mediation over the past few decades has been highly varied, ranging from low-profile to high-profile interventions, and involving multiple types of conflicts and crises. Qatar has been engaging with a diverse array of actors, including national governments, non-state armed groups, national liberation movements, regional and international states, and international organizations. This is a testament to Qatar's expansive diplomatic reach, which has been instrumental in its mediation and facilitation across challenging conflict contexts.

During the 2000s, Qatar's emergence as a major mediator was largely enabled by its widely perceived impartiality, during a period in which it had cultivated an unusually independent foreign policy. The seemingly contradictory presence of a U.S. military base, an Israeli trade office, and later the Taliban political office and Hamas leadership in Doha are all testament to Qatar's insistence on maintaining open channels of communication with diverse and often opposing parties. This has allowed them to create an environment conducive to fostering dialogue between conflicting sides for effective conflict resolution. This physical hosting not only facilitates direct negotiations but also nurtures networks with far-reaching influence. Often, Qatar has maintained communication channels with all parties to conflicts, including non-state armed groups ostracized by Western powers or subject to formal terrorist proscription regimes, such as the Taliban, Hamas, and Hezbollah, enabling it to mediate conflicts wherein third-party involvement was largely unwelcome.

The cases of the Gaza Strip and Afghanistan are the most illustrative examples of how the extent of Qatar's diplomatic reach made its mediation indispensable. In the 7 October War on Gaza, 'the conflict parties and their backers had no choice but to turn to Qatar to play a mediation role'.[12] This claim is corroborated by a leading United Nations (UN) official involved in those talks, who noted that the notion of excluding Qatar from the mediation structure was out of the question because 'no mediator can compete with Qatar's reach'.[13]

Another aspect of Qatar's strategic reach is its willingness to mediate conflicts and disputes as a lone actor in some cases and engaging in cooperative partnerships with other parties elsewhere.[14] These parties include states and international organizations, such as Egypt, the UN, and the African Union. In so doing, 'Qatar engages with international actors by earning their trust in its ability to achieve tangible results that help resolve conflicts peacefully'.[15] In addition to multi-party mediation, Qatar also brokered several agreements independently, including between the Houthis and the Yemeni government in 2007, the 2008 Doha Agreement for Lebanon, and the 2020 U.S.–Taliban agreement.

Fostering strong relationships with conflict parties and maintaining consistent channels of communication reflects Qatar's broader foreign policy strategy of engagement through dialogue rather than confrontation. Ultimately, these factors promoted Qatar's reputation and made it a sought-after mediator at the global level.

Long-Term Commitment

A notable feature of Qatari mediation is the long-term commitment towards the conflict-affected contexts in which it has engaged as a third party. Early research often failed to recognize this, characterizing Qatari mediation as highly transactional, focused on short-term peace deals, and lacking capacities for long-term conflict prevention and peacebuilding. This portrayal is clear from claims that 'when the tension is reduced, Doha finishes its job'.[16] Similarly, it is argued that once a peace deal is signed, Qatar has little capacity to ensure compliance with its provisions.[17] However, this observation no longer reflects the reality of Qatari mediation as it overlooks the speed at which the country has expanded its tools and approaches in mediation, facilitation, and post-agreement monitoring.

Qatar's institutionalized focus on Afghanistan, Darfur, and Gaza demonstrates that it has remained deeply involved in the monitoring and implementation of agreements it once helped broker and, wherever necessary, was involved in further mediation to overcome challenges on the pathway to peace. This is also reflected in a flexible and pragmatic approach, with Qatar adapting its mediation style over the course of long-term engagement. Across many conflict contexts, Qatar has assumed diverse roles during mediation processes, moving from a facilitator to a more directive mediator, making proposals when necessary based on the shifting demand of the conflict context.[18] For example, in Lebanon and Yemen, Qatar took on a directive mediator role. However, in the U.S.–Taliban negotiations and the Darfur conflict, Qatar initially served as a facilitator, providing support for the mediation process.

Qatar's strategic patience in laying the groundwork for future mediation initiatives, often many years in advance, such as in the cases of Afghanistan and the Gaza Strip, shows its long-term thinking. Despite facing a turbulent geopolitical environment in the 2010s, Qatar laid the groundwork for its later successes as a mediator through consistent and long-term diplomatic efforts. The hosting of the Taliban office from 2013 initiated Qatar's entry into the nascent Afghan peace process, which culminated in the U.S.–Taliban agreement seven years later. Likewise, the entry of Qatar into the multiparty mediation structure to manage tensions in the Gaza Strip in 2014 effectively sowed the seeds of Qatar's role as the go-to mediator in the 7 October War. Furthermore, Qatar's re-entry as a mediator in Lebanon in the early 2020s, coming fifteen years after its lauded mediation of the 2008 crisis, was a testament to the consistency of its diplomatic engagement.

In many cases, Qatar remains committed over the long term through its provision of humanitarian and development assistance to the crisis-affected societies in which it has been involved as a mediator. This is well captured by a Qatari diplomat who notes that: 'Qatar is present before the mediation, during the mediation, and after the mediation. The state places serious emphasis on the post-mediation phase, sometimes even more than the mediation itself'.[19]

Over the course of several decades, Qatar has emerged as one of the leading so-called 'non-traditional donors' in the Global South, providing high levels of foreign aid.[20] Qatar's humanitarian and development assistance has been strategically utilized in various ways in relation to mediation efforts, including fostering acceptance of Qatari mediation, building goodwill amongst conflict parties in order to create a conducive environment for talks, and in fulfilment of commitments made by Qatari mediators as part of negotiated agreements.

Multifaceted Conflict Response

A highly distinct feature of Qatari mediation is its use of diverse conflict-resolution tools. Qatar has adopted a comprehensive approach to conflict resolution, integrating preventive diplomacy, mediation, and backing multilateral efforts for conflict prevention and peacebuilding. This defies reductive narratives that Qatar simply engages in financially driven leverage to reach deals. The role of financial incentives in Qatari mediation is not static and varies highly across contexts. In some cases, Qatar has strategically linked its humanitarian and developmental aid to the signing and implementation of ceasefires and peace agreements, such as in Darfur and Gaza. In these key cases, Qatar has most recently demonstrated a long-term commitment, fully challenging the characterization of Qatari mediation as driven by short-term transactionalism.

In other words, reducing Qatar's role to its financial capacity fails to capture the country's comprehensive and multifaceted engagement in conflict-affected contexts. There is a need to recognize Qatar's shift from reactive engagement to a state actor with a distinct model of conflict mediation.[21] This model encompasses the skilful application of sophisticated strategies and diverse diplomatic tools such as humanitarian diplomacy and aid, dialogue, and advocacy, amongst others. The case studies of Lebanon, Darfur, and Afghanistan analyzed in this book provide prime examples and offer key insights into Qatar's mediation style and how it strategically interweaves mediation with other diplomatic and aid mechanisms.

This comprehensive strategy highlights Qatar's evolving role in international diplomacy, and demonstrates its commitment to sustainable peacemaking through a blend of various diplomatic tools, particularly the ability to leverage its resources, strategic alliances, and solid diplomatic connections in the Global North and Global South. Additionally, by combining diplomatic efforts with humanitarian and developmental initiatives, Qatar has crafted a comprehensive approach to conflict response—one that addresses immediate political issues and extends to resolving the root causes of conflicts. This includes strategic investments in key components of the sustainable development goals, such as education, health and well-being, and economic growth. Through a network of well-coordinated national-level institutions, such as think tanks, humanitarian organizations, financial institutions, and ministerial agencies, Qatar is able to facilitate conflict resolution and sustain long-term engagement in various conflict contexts.[22]

Whole-of-Government Approach

Qatar is notable amongst mediators globally for the high level of political representation actively involved in conflict mediation efforts. This has frequently entailed the personal involvement of leading individuals such as the Prime Minister and Foreign Minister, various other ministers, ambassadors, and even the Emir himself. For instance, one Qatari ambassador underscored the consistency of leadership at the highest level, noting that successive Emirs and the Prime Minister 'played major roles in the success of the mediation efforts'.[23] This responsiveness and resolve are apparent in the fact that 'the leadership in Qatar has the courage to play mediation roles even if Qatar bears a political cost as a result'.[24] Their strategic vision and willingness to commit significant resources in pursuit of peace have been instrumental in building Qatar's reputation as a mediator on the global stage.

In the 2000s, during the initial period of Qatar's high-profile mediation, a select few individuals held the authority to lead mediation portfolios, such as the former Prime Minister and Foreign Minister, Sheikh Hamad bin Jassim Al Thani, and former Minister of State for Foreign Affairs, His Excellency Ahmed bin Abdullah Al Mahmoud. In that era, Qatari mediation faced hurdles due to 'limited capabilities to affect long-term changes to the preferences of the disputants through power projection abilities, in-depth administrative and on-the-ground resources, and apparent underestimations of the complexities of the deep-rooted conflicts at hand'.[25] Capacity limitations also hindered post-agreement monitoring and the application of best practice in the design of mediation processes. Moreover, with so few individuals fully engaged in mediation, Qatar could not accept all offers to mediate.[26]

These constraints spurred a gradual shift from more ad hoc and informal practices shaped by personal relationships and elite diplomacy towards a more institutionalized and professionalized mediation apparatus. A key milestone came in 2016 with the establishment of the Office of the Special Envoy for Counterterrorism and Mediation in Conflict Resolution within the Ministry of Foreign Affairs, which possessed a mandate to facilitate talks or mediate peace negotiations at the local or global level. This reflected a move towards a more coordinated and institutionalized mediation apparatus whilst preserving Qatar's personalized diplomatic approach. The post-2020 engagement—namely, its scale, frequency, and complexity—further necessitated a more structured, institutional approach.[27]

As such, Qatar's mediation architecture evolved from a small and dedicated team to a whole-of-government approach, working in tandem to respond to crises. This involved coordination and collaboration between various institutions, including the Ministry of Foreign Affairs, the Qatar Emiri Air Force, and the Qatar Fund for Development, as well as non-governmental organizations such as Qatar Charity and the Qatar Red Crescent Society. Another key development was the appointment of His Excellency Sheikh Mohammed bin Abdulrahman Al Thani as Prime Minister in March 2023 whilst continuing as Minister of Foreign Affairs—with the simultaneous holding of those two portfolios indicating the greater emphasis on mediation and foreign policy more generally in Qatar's national priorities in the 2020s.

In the 2020s, Qatar's mediation efforts diversified significantly, reflecting a new orientation towards a whole-of-government approach that mobilized multiple institutions and individuals. Several appointments were also made, including that of His Excellency Dr Mohammed bin Abdulaziz Al-Khulaifi as State Minister with a mandate for conflict mediation, in addition to a wider team of special envoys and high-level officials dedicated to mediation. In each mediation portfolio, a team is mobilized and tailored to the nature of the conflict that Qatar is mediating. It is explained that 'we begin by conducting a thorough analysis to understand all its dimensions. Based on this, we assemble a specialized team equipped to handle the political, security, and other relevant aspects'.[28] This model was tested in highly sensitive operating environments such as Afghanistan, the Gaza Strip, and Chad, in which Qatar's ability to mobilize multi-institutional teams proved critical. Reflecting on the experience in mediating the Chad talks, a leading Qatari mediator noted that 'success belongs to the entire team. You can't credit one party alone. It was a collective effort under wise leadership'.[29]

In short, Qatar's mediation stands out for its whole-of-government approach, as the country dedicates substantial resources to conflict resolution. The Prime Minister, Foreign Minister, and multiple other state and non-state institutions work simultaneously on various aspects of the mediation process, a level of commitment rarely seen in other states. Institutionalization thus enabled Qatar to actualize its diplomatic ambitions into a robust and sustainable architecture of mediation.

Doha as a Diplomatic Hub

Qatar's role in conflict mediation is also strongly supported by the emergence of Doha as a major diplomatic hub. Doha's strategic location and state-of-the-art facilities have made it an ideal platform for high-level meetings and conferences, attracting diplomats and negotiators from around the world, becoming a go-to venue for international negotiations, hosting talks between various parties, and providing logistical support for diplomatic efforts. Zalmay Khalilzad, who led U.S. efforts to reach a deal with the Taliban, visited Doha for countless diplomatic engagements over the course of many years. He underlined the role of Doha's infrastructure, including hotels, restaurants, museums, mosques, and other facets of social life, all located within close proximity of one another, as providing a conducive environment that supported the facilitation of negotiations.[30]

Doha's emergence as a diplomatic hub was catalyzed by Qatar's facilitation of talks with the Taliban. The establishment of the Taliban political office in 2013 marked a significant milestone, transforming Doha into a meeting point for international delegations seeking to engage with the movement. Almost a decade later, during the Taliban's takeover of Kabul, Doha served as a spatial centre for crisis management. Qatar's ability to charter planes for evacuations and serve as a transit point for over 40 per cent of those fleeing Afghanistan demonstrated its logistical capabilities during the crisis.[31] Additionally, Qatar's move to host the Afghanistan embassies for multiple countries following the withdrawal of their Kabul missions further cemented its diplomatic importance.

Doha has increasingly served as a regional and global hub for humanitarian coordination, negotiation, and diplomacy. This was evident in the establishment of a UN house in Qatar in 2023, which coordinates regional functions of around twelve UN agencies, and the growing presence of international organizations based in the country, including the headquarter agreement with the International Committee of the Red Cross signed in the same year. Qatar also organizes multiple annual Doha-based events, such as the Doha Forum, Qatar Mediation Forum, Al Jazeera Forum, or Annual Palestine Forum, which strengthened its convening capacity and brought many leading individuals and institutions engaged in peace-making to Doha each year.

Qatar has also fostered an emerging research and knowledge ecosystem, with research centres and think tanks such as the Middle East Council on Global Affairs, the Center for International Policy Research, and the Center for Conflict and Humanitarian Studies actively contributing to mediation and peacemaking efforts. As part of its expanding peacemaking role, Qatar has supported a range of Track 1.5. and 2.0. initiatives, often working in tandem with research institutes and think tanks in Doha and internationally. By strategically cultivating these capacities, Qatar has enhanced its influence on the global stage and its reputation as a leading actor in conflict mediation.[32]

The synergy between Qatar's diplomatic reach and its establishment of Doha as a diplomatic hub has created a flourishing ecosystem that facilitates formal and informal peace processes. This environment allows Qatar to seamlessly blend different diplomatic tracks, addressing high-level political issues whilst simultaneously engaging with grassroots actors. The whole-of-government approach adopted by Qatar ensures that this comprehensive strategy is consistently applied across all its mediation initiatives, with key institutions working together to leverage the country's diplomatic assets. At the core of this approach lies Qatar's commitment to impartiality and trust-building, based on a constitutional mandate for peaceful conflict resolution. This foundational principle permeates all aspects of Qatar's mediation efforts.

10

CONCLUSION

Over several decades, Qatar has advanced from the periphery to the centre of international conflict mediation. This path from the Gulf to the global has been shaped by moments of high-stakes success, and also by the challenges that were demanded from the country's leadership through reflection, adaptation, and growth. Each experience, whether celebrated or contested, has informed a more confident and refined approach to mediation. In this process, Qatar has created a distinct profile within the increasingly diverse global landscape of peacemaking. Through in-depth empirical research and comparative analysis, this book narrates the evolution of the Qatari mediation practice from its origins in Gulf sub-regional dispute resolution to the global stage of contemporary conflict response. In so doing, it provides novel insight into the rise of Qatar as a mediator.

The comparative case study design includes contexts from various regions and time periods, offering a longitudinal perspective on Qatari mediation style and strategies. Through the case studies of Lebanon, Darfur, Afghanistan, the Gaza Strip, and multiple other post-2020 crises, the book offers the most systematic analysis of Qatari mediation to date.

The book first explores the structural, sociopolitical, and economic factors that shaped the country's development trajectory since its independence in 1971. Economically, the hydrocarbon sector represented the driving force of the country's significant domestic transformation, which was marked by rapid urban development and modernization, with substantive investment in vital sectors, such as infrastructure, healthcare, and education. These large-scale investments, in addition to sociopolitical reforms, earned Qatar a reputation for commitment to progressive change. This interplay of economic affluence and sociopolitical stability has been a cornerstone of Qatar's steady advancement in conflict mediation efforts since the 1990s.

Notably, vast natural resources and progressive socioeconomic reforms were amongst the major drivers of the country's modernization and transformation in the 2000s. However, it was the strategic decision by Qatar's leadership to adopt an independent foreign policy, deliberately positioning the nation outside the Saudi–Iranian rivalry that has long dominated the Gulf region, that created the space for its diplomatic distinctiveness to take shape. In this context, the analysis examined the tools employed by Qatar to structure its diplomatic identity, including place branding, the strategic use of its financial leverage, and soft power, whilst also exploring the guiding principles of non-interference and neutrality that have consistently defined its approach to international relations.

When it comes to conceptual frameworks, this book diverges from the prevailing perspectives and analyses of international relations and the widely held assumptions that have often interpreted Qatar's mediation as a necessary strategy to position itself internationally, given its small size and lack of politico-military clout. This book also appraised the constructivist framing of Qatari mediation as being merely motivated by cultural and religious norms and a commitment to alleviate the suffering of those affected by conflict. The reductionist 'chequebook diplomacy' perspective, attributing Qatar's success in conflict mediation solely to its financial leverage, has been challenged by demonstrating how Qatar's financial resources were used strategically and skilfully to encourage dialogue and participation, rather than to impose solutions.

This book presents innovative conceptual perspectives on the Qatari mediation model, analyzing it through various lenses, such as the dynamics of big- versus small-state mediation, the emergence of the Global South as alternative actors in the international aid and development system, and the role of Gulf States in peacemaking and humanitarian aid. It further examines Qatari mediation through the analytical prism of strategically linking mediation with other forms of conflict response, such as humanitarian aid and peacebuilding at large. Qatar has adopted an integrated conflict response, as seen in the case of Afghanistan and Darfur, where its engagement extends beyond the negotiation phase. This shift towards supporting the implementation of peace agreement provisions marks a departure from earlier patterns in the Qatari model, one that previous narratives have failed to capture and demonstrate.

Against this background, the book analyzes Qatar's different roles in conflict mediation across different phases. The period between 2006 and 2010 was characterized by ad hoc mediation efforts, often initiated and led by the country's senior leadership. This phase proved instrumental in shaping Qatar's mediation approach and forging its diplomatic identity. Qatar's success extended beyond merely facilitating negotiations and brokering ceasefire agreements—it also encompassed defusing political tensions in regions such as Darfur and Lebanon. These accomplishments bolstered Qatar's reputation as an impartial and influential political actor in conflict resolution, enhancing its credibility in the region. Consequently, these initial forays into mediation during the 2000s laid a solid foundation for Qatar's diplomatic rise, allowing the country to assume more substantial roles in fostering global stability and peacebuilding efforts in the years that followed.

The book examines the evolution of Qatar's mediation strategies, highlighting a significant shift in its approach during the Arab Spring compared to earlier periods. Regional events and developments forced Qatar to make structural reforms and reconsider its approach to conflict mediation. Accordingly, a process of professionalization was initiated, leading to the establishment of specialized offices in the Ministry of Foreign Affairs and several think tanks to conduct evidence-based policy research. By analyzing these developments, the book provides insights into how Qatar's foreign policy evolved to respond to regional political events.

After contextualizing Qatar's ascent to a global mediator status, this book systematically analyzes its experiences in Lebanon, Darfur, Afghanistan, Gaza, and post-2020 crises. In Lebanon and Darfur,

Qatar mediated to resolve political deadlock, where it brokered agreements to end civil conflict. Similarly, the facilitation of the negotiations between the United States and the Taliban and intra-Afghan talks in Doha were examples of advanced transitional efforts in Afghanistan, resulting in the historic 2020 agreement between previously intransigent parties. In several episodes of conflict escalation between Hamas and Israel, Qatar mediated ceasefires between the two parties, facilitated dialogue, and secured humanitarian aid access to alleviate civilian suffering, which persistently showcased its diplomatic weight in regional diplomacy. Elsewhere, Qatar's involvement in Chad, Libya, Somalia, Venezuela, and Ukraine further illustrated its growing influence in Africa, South America, and Eastern Europe, where it continued to mediate between conflicting parties to foster national reconciliation and resolve protracted political crises beyond its immediate periphery. These cases proved Qatar's willingness to engage in dialogue, explore avenues for mediation, and maintain its broader commitment to global peace.

This book has comprehensively provided a stylized account of the pillars of the Qatari mediation model, including impartiality and trust-building, diplomatic reach, long-term commitment, multifaceted conflict response, a constitutional commitment to peacemaking, a whole-of-government approach, and Doha being a global diplomatic hub. This detailed exploration offers valuable insights for policymakers and scholars interested in understanding the nuances of Qatar's mediation and peacemaking strategies. The book offers a new conceptual framework for understanding small-state mediation based on the comprehensive analysis of Qatar's distinct role and its unconventional model of mediation.

In the final analysis, conflict mediation is an inherent and key aspect of Qatari foreign policy, characterized by a commitment to dialogue and peaceful resolution of conflicts in the Middle East and beyond. By building upon its continuous engagement in international diplomacy, Qatar has taken on a more significant role as a global mediator in fostering broader peace and stability within the international system. As global crises grow more fragmented and polarized, Qatar's credibility, resourcefulness, and consistent investment in dialogue will likely ensure its continued relevance as a distinctive and effective actor within the evolving international architecture of conflict mediation.

NOTES

1. INTRODUCTION

1. Institute for Economics & Peace, *Global Peace Index 2024: Measuring Peace in a Complex World* (Sydney: Institute for Economics & Peace, 2024), https://www.economicsandpeace.org/wp-content/uploads/2024/06/GPI-2024-web.pdf
2. Jacqui Cho and Dana M. Landau, 'In Search of the Golden Formula: Trends in Peace Mediation Research and Practice', *Civil Wars* 25, no. 2–3 (15 December 2023), pp. 317–40, https://doi.org/10.1080/13698249.2023.2249326
3. Mehran Kamrava, 'Mediation and Qatari Foreign Policy', *The Middle East Journal* 65, no. 4 (1 September 2011), pp. 539–56, https://doi.org/10.3751/65.4.11; Kristian Coates Ulrichsen, *Qatar and the Arab Spring* (Oxford: Oxford University Press, 2014); Sultan Barakat, 'The Qatari Spring: Qatar's Emerging Role in Peacemaking', Kuwait Programme on Development, Governance and Globalisation in the Gulf States, July 2012, https://www.brookings.edu/wp-content/uploads/2016/06/qatar-role-peacekeeping-barakat.pdf; David B. Roberts, 'Understanding Qatar's Foreign Policy Objectives', *Mediterranean Politics* 17, no. 2 (18 July 2012), pp. 233–39, https://doi.org/10.1080/13629395.2012.695123
4. Ulrichsen, *Qatar and the Arab Spring*.
5. Kamrava, 'Mediation and Qatari Foreign Policy'; Barakat, 'The Qatari Spring'.
6. Anne Holper and Lars Kirchhoff, 'Rethinking the Professionalization of Peace Mediation', *Rethinking Peace Mediation*, 11 January 2021, pp. 355–72, https://doi.org/10.51952/9781529208207.ch017
7. Philipp Kastner, 'Glocal Peace Mediators as Norm Translators', *Swiss Political Science Review* 26, no. 4 (22 November 2020), pp. 364–83, https://doi.org/10.1111/spsr.12423; United Nations, 'United Nations Guidance for Effective Mediation', United Nations, September 2012, https://unrcca.unmissions.org/sites/default/files/dpa_msu_guidance_english_web.pdf (accessed 26 December 2024).
8. Cho and Landau, 'In Search of the Golden Formula'.

2. THE RISE OF QATAR AS A MEDIATOR

1. The Amiri Diwan, 'Sheikh Ahmad Bin Ali Al Thani', The Amiri Diwan, https://www.diwan.gov.qa/about-qatar/qatars-rulers/sheikh-ahmad-bin-ali-al-thani (accessed 18 February 2025).
2. Planning & Statistics Authority in Qatar, *Sustainable Development Goals in the State of Qatar 2022*, March 2023, https://www.npc.qa/en/media/Doc/Sustainable/SDG_Report_2022.pdf (accessed 15 June 2025).
3. Karen E. Young, 'Sovereign Risk: Gulf Sovereign Wealth Funds as Engines of Growth and Political Resource', *British Journal of Middle Eastern Studies* 47, no. 1 (2020), pp. 96–116, https://doi.org/10.1080/13530194.2020.1714866
4. Matthew Gray, 'A Theory of "Late Rentierism" in the Arab States of the Gulf', *CIRS Occasional Papers*, 18 August 2011, http://dx.doi.org/10.2139/ssrn.2825905; Justin J. Gengler, Bethany Shockley, and Michael C. Ewers, 'Refinancing the Rentier State: Welfare, Inequality, and Citizen Preferences toward Fiscal Reform in the Gulf Oil Monarchies', *Comparative Politics* 53, no. 2 (1 January 2021), pp. 283–317, https://doi.org/10.5129/001041521x15903211136400
5. Mehran Kamrava, *Qatar: Small State, Big Politics* (Ithaca, NY: Cornell University Press, 2013); Kristian Coates Ulrichsen, *Qatar and the Arab Spring* (Oxford: Oxford University Press, 2014).
6. Allen James Fromherz, *Qatar: Rise to Power and Influence* (London: Bloomsbury, 2012); World Bank, 'Population, Total—Qatar', World Bank, https://data.worldbank.org/indicator/SP.POP.TOTL?locations=QA (accessed 18 February 2025).
7. Emile A. Nakhleh, 'Labor Markets and Citizenship in Bahrayn and Qatar', *Middle East Journal* 31, no. 2 (1977), pp. 143–56.
8. Ulrichsen, *Qatar and the Arab Spring*.
9. Kristian Coates Ulrichsen, 'Qatar's Mediation Initiatives', The Norwegian Peacebuilding Resource Centre (NOREF), February 2013, https://www.files.ethz.ch/isn/160109/da1df25567ebd34af26d634892934b03.pdf
10. Hira Amin, Khoulood Sakbani, and Evren Tok, 'State Aspirations for Social and Cultural Transformations in Qatar', *Social Sciences* 13, no. 7 (5 July 2024), https://doi.org/10.3390/socsci13070359
11. Ahmed Ibrahim Abushouk, 'Qatar: From a Tribal Confederacy to a Modern State', in Mahjoob Zweiri and Farah Al Qawasmi (eds), *Contemporary Qatar: Examining State and Society*, 1st edn (Singapore: Springer, 2021), p. 9.
12. Kamrava, *Qatar: Small State, Big Politics*; Esra Cavusoglu, 'From Rise to Crisis: The Qatari Leadership', *Türkiye Ortadoğu Çalışmaları Dergisi* 7, no. 1 (30 June 2020), pp. 81–110, https://doi.org/10.26513/tocd.624334; Kristian Coates Ulrichsen, *Qatar and the Gulf Crisis* (New York: Oxford University Press, 2020).
13. General Secretariat for Development Planning—Qatar, *Qatar National Vision 2030* (Doha: General Secretariat for Development Planning—Qatar, July 2008), https://www.npc.qa/en/QNV/Documents/QNV2030_English_v2.pdf

14. Yagoub Ali Gangi and Alfadil Timan Idris, 'Qatar's Path to a Knowledge-Based Economy: A Content Analysis of Entrepreneurship Training Initiatives', *Business and Economic Research* 13, no. 4 (14 October 2023), https://doi.org/10.5296/ber.v13i4.21256
15. Xavier Ginesta and Jordi San Eugenio, 'The Use of Football as a Country Branding Strategy: Case Study', *Communication & Sport* 2, no. 3 (25 April 2013), pp. 225–41, https://doi.org/10.1177/2167479513486886; André Richelieu, Yen-Chun Lin, and Ho Keat Leng, 'A Typology of Countries Using Place Branding through Sport', *Journal of Global Sport Management*, 19 September 2021, pp. 1–19, https://doi.org/10.1080/24704067.2021.1972431
16. Kristian Coates Ulrichsen, 'Qatar and the 2022 FIFA World Cup: Soft Power, State Branding, or Nation Building?' in Simon Chadwick, Paul Widdop, and Michael M. Goldman (eds), *The Geopolitical Economy of Sport: Power, Politics, Money, and the State*, 1st edn (London: Routledge, 2023), pp. 127–33.
17. Rabi H. Mohtar, 'Opportunities and Challenges for Innovations in Qatar', *The Muslim World* 105, no. 1 (19 December 2014), pp. 46–57, https://doi.org/10.1111/muwo.12079; Abushouk, 'Qatar: From a Tribal Confederacy'.
18. Aidyn Bibolov, Tongfang Yuan, Sidra Rehman, and Ken Miyajima, '2022 FIFA World Cup', *Selected Issues Papers* 2024, no. 011 (February 2024), https://doi.org/10.5089/9798400267864.018
19. Jonathan Grix and Paul Michael Brannagan, 'Sports Mega-Events as Foreign Policy: Sport Diplomacy, "Soft Power", and "Sportswashing"', *American Behavioral Scientist*, 23 July 2024, https://doi.org/10.1177/00027642241262042; Wadih Ishac, 'Examining Sport Tourism Role in Fostering Social Sustainability: Qatar Youth Perceptions', *Frontiers in Sports and Active Living* 6 (31 May 2024), https://doi.org/10.3389/fspor.2024.1388123
20. Ali A. Alraouf, 'Museums as a Catalyst for a New Urban and Cultural Identity in Qatar: Interrogating the Case of the Museum of Islamic Art', in Karen Exell and Sarina Wakefield (eds), *Museums in Arabia* (London: Routledge, 2016), pp. 151–66.
21. Fromherz, *Qatar: Rise to Power and Influence*; Gertjan Hoetjes, 'Stepping Out of the Shade: Qatari-Saudi Relations Amid the Rise of Cosmopolitan Qatar', in Thomas R. Klassen, Nara Park, and Ian Roberge (eds), *Asymmetric Neighbors and International Relations: Living in the Shadow of Elephants* (London: Routledge, 2023), pp. 175–88.
22. Ahmad S. Nufal, 'The Gulf States and the Crisis over Kuwait', *Arab Studies Quarterly* 13, no. 1/2 (1 January 1991), pp. 37–51, http://www.jstor.org/stable/10.2307/41858950?refreqid=fastly-default; Sanam Vakil, 'Understanding the GCC Collective Security Mindset', Chatham House, 30 November 2022, https://kalam.chathamhouse.org/articles/understanding-the-gcc-collective-security-mindset/
23. Omar Al Hassan, 'The GCC's Formation: The Official Version', Al Jazeera Centre for Studies, 30 March 2015, https://studies.aljazeera.net/en/dossiers/2015/03/201533011258831763.html
24. Abdulkhaleq Abdullah, 'The Gulf Cooperation Council: Nature, Origin, and

Process', in Michael Hudson (ed.), *Middle East Dilemma: The Politics and Economics of Arab Integration* (New York: Columbia University Press, 1999), pp. 150–70.

25. Nufal, 'The Gulf States and the Crisis over Kuwait'; Gerd Nonneman, 'The Gulf States and the Iran–Iraq War: Pattern Shifts and Continuities', in Lawrence G. Potter and Gary G. Sick (eds), *Iran, Iraq, and the Legacies of War* (New York: Palgrave Macmillan, 2004), pp. 167–92; Kristian Coates Ulrichsen, 'The Gulf States and the Iran–Iraq War: Cooperation and Confusion', in Nigel Ashton and Bryan Gibson (eds), *The Iran–Iraq War: New International Perspectives* (London: Routledge, 2012).
26. Vakil, 'Understanding the GCC Collective Security Mindset'.
27. Mehran Kamrava, 'Iran-Qatar Relations', in Anoushiravan Ehteshami, Neil Quilliam, and Gawdat Bahgat (eds), *Security and Bilateral Issues between Iran and Its Arab Neighbours* (Cham: Palgrave Macmillan, 2017), pp. 167–87.
28. Leah Bower, 'Gulf Could Gain from Thaw in Saudi-Qatar Relations', Gulf News, 8 July 2008, https://gulfnews.com/business/analysis/gulf-could-gain-from-thaw-in-saudi-qatar-relations-1.117086; Andrew R. Goetz and Lucy Budd, *The Geographies of Air Transport* (London: Routledge, 2016).
29. Nonneman, 'The Gulf States and the Iran-Iraq War', p. 178.
30. Justin Dargin, 'Qatar's Natural Gas: The Foreign-Policy Driver', *Middle East Policy* 14, no. 3 (2007), pp. 136–42; Sultan Barakat and Sansom Milton, 'Qatar's Role in Conflict and Peace: An Assessment of Motivations and Influence', *Saferworld*, 20 September 2011.
31. Mehran Kamrava, 'Iran-Qatar Relations'; David B. Roberts, *Reflecting on the GCC Crisis: Qatar and its Neighbours*, 1st edn (London: Routledge, 2022); Hoetjes, 'Stepping Out of the Shade'.
32. Kenneth Katzman, *Qatar: Governance, Security, and U.S. Policy* (Washington, DC: Congressional Research Service, 2018).
33. Christopher M. Blanchard, *Qatar: Background and US Relations* (Washington, DC: Congressional Research Service, 2010); Jill Crystal, 'US Relations with Qatar', in Robert Looney (ed.), *Handbook of US-Middle East Relations*, 1st edn (London: Routledge, 2014), pp. 391–402; Brahim Saidy, 'Qatari-US Military Relations: Context, Evolution and Prospects', *Contemporary Arab Affairs* 10, no. 2 (1 April 2017), pp. 286–99, https://doi.org/10.1080/17550912.2016.1244902
34. Crystal, 'US Relations with Qatar'.
35. Shadi Hamid, 'From the Arab Spring Comes a More Unified Gulf Cooperation Council', Brookings, 15 April 2011, https://www.brookings.edu/articles/from-the-arab-spring-comes-a-more-unified-gulf-cooperation-council/; Kamrava, 'Iran-Qatar Relations'.
36. Bill Law, 'Egypt Crisis: Fall of Morsi Challenges Qatar's New Emir', BBC News, 5 July 2013, https://www.bbc.com/news/world-middle-east-23185441; Al Jazeera, 'Analysts: Qatar Supports Gaza Not Hamas', Al Jazeera, 7 June 2017, https://www.aljazeera.com/features/2017/6/7/analysts-qatar-supports-gaza-not-hamas; Al Jazeera, 'Profile: Abdul Ghani Baradar, Taliban's

Political Head in Qatar', Al Jazeera, 25 January 2019, https://www.aljazeera.com/news/2019/1/25/profile-abdul-ghani-baradar-talibans-political-head-in-qatar; Usaama Al-Azami, 'Yusuf Al-Qaradawi, the Muslim Scholar Who Influenced Millions', Al Jazeera, 27 September 2022, https://www.aljazeera.com/news/2022/9/27/yusuf-al-qaradawi-the-muslim-scholar-who-influenced-millions; Al Jazeera, 'Photos: Mourners Pay Tributes at Ismail Haniyeh's Funeral in Qatar', Al Jazeera, 2 August 2024, https://www.aljazeera.com/gallery/2024/8/2/anger-calls-for-resistance-at-hamas-chief-haniyehs-funeral-in-qatar

37. David B. Roberts, 'Qatar and the UAE: Exploring Divergent Responses to the Arab Spring', *The Middle East Journal* 71, no. 4 (1 September 2017), pp. 544–62, https://doi.org/10.3751/71.4.12; Ulrichsen, *Qatar and the Gulf Crisis*; Kamrava, *Qatar: Small State, Big Politics*.
38. Kamrava, 'Iran-Qatar Relations'.
39. Ulrichsen, *Qatar and the Arab Spring*.
40. Thomas Fischer, 'Switzerland's Good Offices: A Changing Concept, 1945–2002', *Eidgenössische Technische Hochschule (ETH Zürich)* 37 (2002), https://doi.org/10.3929/ethz-a-004445304
41. Ruslan Minich, 'Conflict Mediation: The Qatari Experience', *Historia i Polityka* 14, no. 21 (24 November 2015), pp. 121–33, https://doi.org/10.12775/hip.2015.026
42. Jeffrey A. Lefebvre, 'Red Sea Security and the Geopolitical-Economy of the Hanish Islands Dispute', *Middle East Journal* 52, no. 3 (1998), pp. 367–85.
43. United Press International, 'Qatar Mediates Yemen, Eritrea Dispute', United Press International, 20 December 1995, https://www.upi.com/Archives/1995/12/20/Qatar-mediates-Yemen-Eritrea-dispute/6433819435600/
44. United Nations, 'Eritrea v. Yemen (Award of the Arbitral Tribunal in the First Stage of the Proceedings between Eritrea and Yemen (Territorial Sovereignty and Scope of the Dispute))', in *Reports of International Arbitral Awards* (New York: United Nations, 1998), pp. 209–332, https://legal.un.org/riaa/cases/vol_xxii/209–332.pdf
45. Interview with H.E. Dr Abdulaziz bin Mohamed Al-Horr, Director of the Diplomatic Institute, Ministry of Foreign Affairs of the State of Qatar, Doha, Qatar, October 2024.
46. Minich, 'Conflict Mediation'.
47. Gareth R.V. Stansfield, 'The 1995–96 Yemen-Eritrea Conflict over the Islands of Hanish and Jabal Zuqar: A Geopolitical Analysis', *Durham Middle East Papers* 66 (February 2001), https://durham-repository.worktribe.com/output/1699302
48. The New Humanitarian, 'SUDAN-ERITREA: Reconciliation Agreement Signed', The New Humanitarian, 1 May 1999, https://www.thenewhumanitarian.org/news/1999/05/01/sudan-eritrea-reconciliation-agreement-signed
49. Berouk Mesfin, 'Qatar's Diplomatic Incursions into the Horn of Africa', Institute for Security Studies, November 2016, https://issafrica.s3.amazonaws.com/site/uploads/ear8.pdf

50. African Studies Centre, 'Eritrea-Sudan: Text of Agreement Signed in Qatar, 5/4/99', University of Pennsylvania—African Studies Center, 3 May 1999, https://www.africa.upenn.edu/Hornet/irin_5499.html
51. Michael J. Greig and Paul Diehl, *International Mediation* (Cambridge: Polity Press, 2012).
52. Ibid.
53. Ulrichsen, 'Qatar's Mediation Initiatives'.
54. Ibid., p. 2.
55. Barakat and Milton, *Qatar's Role in Conflict and Peace*.
56. Robert F. Worth, 'Qatar, Playing All Sides, Is a Nonstop Mediator', *The New York Times*, 9 July 2008, https://www.nytimes.com/2008/07/09/world/middleeast/09qatar.html
57. Gertjan Hoetjes, 'The Gulf Cooperation Council and the Failure of Peacebuilding in Yemen', *The International Spectator* 56, no. 4 (15 November 2021), pp. 151–66, https://doi.org/10.1080/03932729.2021.1987034
58. Barak Salmoni, Bryce Loidolt, and Madeleine Wells, 'Regime and Periphery in Northern Yemen: The Huthi Phenomenon', RAND Corporation, 14 April 2010, pp. 315–16, https://www.rand.org/pubs/monographs/MG962.html
59. Ulrichsen, 'Qatar's Mediation Initiatives'.
60. Minich, 'Conflict Mediation'.
61. Barakat and Milton, *Qatar's Role in Conflict and Peace*.
62. Sultan Barakat and Sansom Milton, '8 Qatar: Conflict Mediation and Regional Objectives', in Agnieszka Paczyńska (ed.), *The New Politics of Aid: Emerging Donors and Conflict-Affected States* (Boulder, CO: Lynne Rienner Publishers, 2019), pp. 141–60, https://doi.org/10.1515/9781626378407-009
63. Ulrichsen, *Qatar and the Arab Spring*, p. 1.
64. Müjge Küçükkeleş, *Arab League's Syrian Policy* (Ankara: The SETA Foundation, 2012).
65. Barakat and Milton, '8 Qatar: Conflict Mediation', p. 154.
66. Alan J. Kuperman, 'A Model Humanitarian Intervention? Reassessing NATO's Libya Campaign', *International Security* 38, no. 1 (July 2013), pp. 105–36, https://doi.org/10.1162/isec_a_00126
67. Ulrichsen, *Qatar and the Arab Spring*.
68. Ibid.
69. Barakat and Milton, '8 Qatar: Conflict Mediation'.
70. Ulrichsen, *Qatar and the Arab Spring*; Doha News, 'It's Official: Qatar Has Sent Troops to Bahrain', *Doha News*, 19 March 2011, https://dohanews.co/its-official-qatar-has-sent-troops-to-bahrain/
71. Mohammed Nuruzzaman, 'Qatar and the Arab Spring: Down the Foreign Policy Slope', *Contemporary Arab Affairs* 8, no. 2 (27 April 2015), pp. 226–38, https://doi.org/10.1080/17550912.2015.1024034
72. Jane Kinninmont, 'The Gulf Divided: The Impact of the Qatar Crisis', Chatham House, May 2019, https://www.chathamhouse.org/sites/default/files/publications/research/2019-05-30-Gulf Crisis_0.pdf
73. Abdullah Baabood, 'Gulf Countries and Arab Transitions: Role Support and

Effects', The European Institute of the Mediterranean (IEMed), 2014, https://www.iemed.org/publication/gulf-countries-and-arab-transitions-role-support-and-effects/

74. Ian Black, 'Arab States Withdraw Ambassadors from Qatar in Protest at "Interference"', *The Guardian*, 5 March 2014, https://www.theguardian.com/world/2014/mar/05/arab-states-qatar-withdraw-ambassadors-protest; Alexis Antoniades, Rafia Al-Jassim, and Khalique Gharatkar, 'The Blockade against Qatar: A Blessing in Disguise?' *Journal of Arabian Studies* 11, no. 1 (2 September 2021), pp. 81–99, https://doi.org/10.1080/21534764.2021.1954354; Anna Jacobs, 'Gulf Arab Reconciliation Hides Simmering Tensions', International Crisis Group, 12 July 2023, https://www.crisisgroup.org/middle-east-north-africa/gulf-and-arabian-peninsula/qatar-saudi-arabia-united-arab-emirates/gulf-arab-reconciliation-hides-simmering-tensions
75. Ulrichsen, *Qatar and the Gulf Crisis*.
76. Middle East Eye, 'Qatar Blockade: Top UN Court Rules in Favour of Doha in Airspace Case', Middle East Eye, 14 July 2020, https://www.middleeasteye.net/news/qatar-blockade-un-icj-rules-favour-aviation-saudi-uae
77. Ulrichsen, *Qatar and the Gulf Crisis*.
78. Ali Bakir, 'The Evolution of Turkey—Qatar Relations amid a Growing Gulf Divide', in Andreas Krieg (ed.), *Divided Gulf: Anatomy of a Crisis* (Singapore: Palgrave Macmillan, 2019), pp. 197–215, https://doi.org/10.1007/978-981-13-6314-6_12
79. Gengler, 'Society and State in Post-Blockade Qatar', p. 238; Ulrichsen, *Qatar and the Gulf Crisis*.
80. Sultan Barakat, 'Qatari Mediation: Between Ambition and Achievement', Brookings Doha Center, November 2014, p. 5, https://www.brookings.edu/wp-content/uploads/2016/06/Final-PDF-English.pdf
81. Ibrahim Fraihat, 'Superpower and Small-State Mediation in the Qatar Gulf Crisis', *The International Spectator* 55, no. 2 (2020), pp. 79–91, https://doi.org/10.1080/03932729.2020.1741268
82. Kristian Coates Ulrichsen, 'Qatar and the Arab Spring: Policy Drivers and Regional Implications', Carnegie Endowment for International Peace, 24 September 2014, https://carnegieendowment.org/research/2014/09/qatar-and-the-arab-spring-policy-drivers-and-regional-implications?lang=en
83. Middle East Eye, 'Rival Libyan Tribes Sign Peace Deal in Qatar', Middle East Eye, 25 November 2015, https://www.middleeasteye.net/news/rival-libyan-tribes-sign-peace-deal-qatar
84. France 24, 'Thousands of Syrians Evacuated under Qatar-Iran Deal', France 24, 14 April 2017, https://www.france24.com/en/20170414-syria-four-towns-begin-evacuating-30000-qatar-iran-deal-madaya-zabadani
85. MOFA, 'HE the Foreign Minister Participates in Ministerial Meeting on Syria', Ministry of Foreign Affairs in the State of Qatar, 15 October 2016, https://mofa.gov.qa/en/qatar/latest-articles/latest-news/details/2016/10/15/he-the-foreign-minister-participates-in-ministerial-meeting-on-syria; MOFA, 'Qatar, Turkey and Russia Affirm the Need to Preserve Sovereignty and

Territorial Integrity of Syria', Ministry of Foreign Affairs in the State of Qatar, 11 March 2021, https://mofa.gov.qa/en/qatar/latest-articles/latest-news/details/1442/07/27/qatar-turkey-and-russia-affirm-the-need-to-preserve-sovereignty-and-territorial-integrity-of-syria

86. Guido Steinberg, *Qatar's Foreign Policy: Decision-Making Processes, Baselines, and Strategies* (Berlin: Stiftung Wissenschaft und Politik, 2023).
87. Qatar Embassy in Dushanbe—Republic of Tajikistan, 'Qatari Mediation Succeeds in Releasing Four Tajikistani Soldiers', Qatar Embassy in Dushanbe—Republic of Tajikistan, Ministry of Foreign Affairs, 13 June 2015, https://dushanbe.embassy.qa/en/media/news/detail/2016/12/06/qatari-mediation-succeeds-in-releasing-four-tajikistani-soldiers
88. Interview with H.E. Mirdef Alqashouti, Chargé d'Affaires of Qatar for Afghanistan, Doha, Qatar, August 2023.
89. Mirdef Alqashouti, 'Qatar Mediation: From Soft Diplomacy to Foreign Policy', in Mahjoob Zweiri and Farah Qawasmi (eds), *Contemporary Qatar: Examining State and Society*, vol. 4 (Singapore: Springer, 2021), pp. 73–92, https://doi.org/10.1007/978-981-16-1391-3_6
90. Parisa Hafezi and Andrew Mills, 'Iran, US on Verge of Prisoner Swap under Qatar-Mediated Deal', Reuters, 11 September 2023, https://www.reuters.com/world/iran-us-verge-prisoner-swap-under-qatar-mediated-deal-2023-09-10/; Al Jazeera, 'Russia Returns Six Children to Ukraine in Qatar-Brokered Deal: State Media', Al Jazeera, 22 May 2024, https://www.aljazeera.com/news/2024/5/22/russia-returns-six-children-to-ukraine-in-qatar-brokered-deal-state-media
91. Hafezi and Mills, 'Iran, US on Verge of Prisoner Swap'.
92. Tanner Manley and Leily Rossi, 'Mediating Multipolarity: Qatar's Role in U.S.-Venezuela Negotiations', Carnegie Endowment for International Peace, 5 September 2023, https://carnegieendowment.org/sada/2023/09/mediating-multipolarity-qatars-role-in-us-venezuela-negotiations?lang=en
93. Jacob Wirtschafter, 'Qatar's Balancing Act in Middle East Is Mediation amid Crisis', Voice of America, 2 October 2024, https://www.voanews.com/a/qatar-s-balancing-act-in-middle-east-is-mediation-amid-crisis/7807833.html

3. CONCEPTUALIZING QATARI MEDIATION

1. Abdelraouf Mostafa Galal, 'External Behavior of Small States in Light of Theories of International Relations', *Review of Economics and Political Science* 5, no. 1 (20 January 2020), pp. 38–56, https://doi.org/10.1108/reps-11–2018–0028
2. William I. Zartman and Saadia Touval, 'International Mediation: Conflict Resolution and Power Politics', *Journal of Social Issues* 41, no. 2 (1985), pp. 27–45, https://doi.org/10.1111/j.1540-4560.1985.tb00853.x; Jacob Bercovitch and Richard Dean Wells Jackson, *Conflict Resolution in the Twenty-First Century: Principles, Methods, and Approaches* (Ann Arbor, MI: University of Michigan Press, 2009), https://doi.org/10.3998/mpub.106467; Luke Heemsbergen and Asaf Siniver, 'New Routes to Power: Towards a Typology

of Power Mediation', *Review of International Studies* 37, no. 3 (2011), pp. 1169–90, https://doi.org/10.1017/S0260210510001002

3. Deiniol Lloyd Jones, 'Mediation, Conflict Resolution and Critical Theory', *Review of International Studies* 26, no. 4 (2000), pp. 647–62, https://doi.org/10.1017/S0260210500006471; Bercovitch and Jackson, *Conflict Resolution in the Twenty-First Century*.
4. Charles T. Call, 'Interests or Ideas? Explaining Brazil's Surge in Peacekeeping and Peacebuilding', in Emel Parlar Dal (ed.), *Rising Powers in International Conflict Management: Converging and Contesting Approaches* (London: Routledge, 2020), pp. 66–84; William Ira Zartman, 'Structuring in a Vacuum: Negotiating in the Current World Disorder', *International Negotiation* 25, no. 1 (2020), pp. 5–17, https://doi.org/10.1163/15718069-25131236; Ido Gadi Raz, 'China's New Mediating Role and the Palestinian-Israeli Conflict', *Israel Affairs* 30, no. 5 (2024), pp. 1090–112, https://doi.org/10.1080/13537121.2024.2394320
5. Øystein Haga Skånland, '"Norway Is a Peace Nation": A Discourse Analytic Reading of the Norwegian Peace Engagement', *Cooperation and Conflict* 45, no. 1 (2010), pp. 34–54, https://doi.org/10.1177/0010836709347212; James Larry Taulbee, Ann Kelleher, and Peter C. Grosvenor, 'The Peace Engagement of a Peace Culture: Observations on the National Identity Foundations of Norwegian Foreign Policy', in *Norway's Peace Policy* (New York: Palgrave Macmillan, 2014), pp. 23–47, https://doi.org/10.1057/9781137429193_2
6. Annika Björkdahl, 'Ideas and Norms in Swedish Peace Policy', *Swiss Political Science Review* 19, no. 3 (2013), pp. 322–37, https://doi.org/10.1111/spsr.12046
7. Mikael Eriksson and Roland Kostić (eds), *Mediation and Liberal Peacebuilding: Peace from the Ashes of War?* (Abingdon: Routledge, 2013).
8. Anders Gulbrandsen, 'Bridging the Gulf: Qatari Business Diplomacy and Conflict Mediation', Master's thesis, Georgetown University, Washington, DC, USA 2010, https://repository.library.georgetown.edu/bitstream/handle/10822/552827/gulbrandsenAnders.pdf
9. Diana Galeeva, *Qatar: The Practice of Rented Power* (Abingdon: Routledge, 2022).
10. Mirdef Alqashouti, 'Qatar Mediation: From Soft Diplomacy to Foreign Policy', in Mahjoob Zweiri and Farah Qawasmi (eds), *Contemporary Qatar: Examining State and Society*, vol. 4 (Singapore: Springer, 2021), pp. 73–92, https://doi.org/10.1007/978-981-16-1391-3_6
11. Joseph Nye, *Soft Power: The Means to Success in World Politics* (New York: Public Affairs, 2004).
12. Andrew F. Cooper and Bessma Momani, 'Qatar and Expanded Contours of Small State Diplomacy', *The International Spectator* 46, no. 3 (September 2011), pp. 113–28, https://doi.org/10.1080/03932729.2011.576181
13. Ignacio Álvarez-Ossorio and Leticia Rodríguez García, 'The Foreign Policy of Qatar: From a Mediating Role to an Active One', *Revista Española de Ciencia Política* 56 (24 July 2021), p. 105, https://doi.org/10.21308/recp.56.04

14. Mutlaq Majed Al Qahtani and Dana Mansour Al-Thani, 'Qatar's Policy and Experience in Mediation and Dispute Settlement', *Siyasat Arabiya* 9, no. 51 (1 July 2021), pp. 7–22, https://doi.org/10.31430/muib3023
15. Larbi Sadiki and Layla Saleh, '"Writing" Small States: Contextualizing the Construct in the Arab Gulf', *International Politics* 60, no. 2 (27 July 2021), pp. 371–89, https://doi.org/10.1057/s41311-021-00335-y
16. Alqashouti, 'Qatar Mediation'.
17. Nickolay Mladenov, 'The Arab Approach to Mediation: Reshaping Diplomacy in a Multipolar World', The Washington Institute, Spring 2024, https://www.washingtoninstitute.org/policy-analysis/arab-approach-mediation-reshaping-diplomacy-multipolar-world
18. The Peninsula, 'Full Speech of Amir at the Opening Session of 77th UN General Assembly', *The Peninsula*, 20 September 2022, https://thepeninsulaqatar.com/article/20/09/2022/full-speech-of-amir-at-the-opening-session-of-77th-un-general-assembly
19. Sir Graham Boyce, 'Qatar's Foreign Policy', *Asian Affairs* 44, no. 3 (28 October 2013), pp. 365–77, https://doi.org/10.1080/03068374.2013.826003
20. Jacob Bercovitch and Su-Mi Lee, 'Mediating International Conflicts: Examining the Effectiveness of Directive Strategies', *International Journal of Peace Studies* 8, no. 1 (2003), pp. 1–17, http://www.jstor.org/stable/41852891
21. Saadia Touval and Jeffery Z. Rubin, 'The Superpowers as Mediators', in Jacob Bercovitch and Jeffery Z. Rubin (eds), *Mediation in International Relations: Multiple Approaches to Conflict Management* (London: Palgrave Macmillan, 1992), pp. 232–48.
22. Kenneth Schultz, *Great Power Mediation: Opportunities and Challenges for China* (Washington, DC: The Stimson Center, 2019), https://bit.ly/42NWn4e
23. Leon Hartwell, 'Conflict Resolution: Lessons from the Dayton Peace Process', *Negotiation Journal* 35, no. 4 (October 2019), pp. 443–69, https://doi.org/10.1111/nejo.12300
24. Cecily Brewer, *More States Are Vying to Mediate Conflict—What Does It Mean for Global Peace?* (Washington, DC: United States Institute of Peace, 2024), https://www.usip.org/publications/2024/10/more-states-are-vying-mediate-conflict-what-does-it-mean-global-peace
25. Matt Waldman, *Peacemaking in Trouble: Expert Perspectives on Flaws, Deficiencies and Potential in the Field of International Mediation* (Cambridge: Belfer Center for Science and International Affairs, Harvard Kennedy School, 2024); Teresa Whitfield (ed), *Still Time to Talk: Adaptation and Innovation in Peace Mediation* (London: Conciliation Resources, 2024).
26. Martin Griffiths, remarks made at the inaugural Qatar Mediation Forum, Doha, Qatar, 9 December 2024.
27. Deiniol Lloyd Jones, *Cosmopolitan Mediation? Conflict Resolution and the Oslo Accords* (Manchester: University of Manchester Press, 1999), p. 112.
28. Ksenia Efremova, 'Small States in Great Power Politics: Understanding the "Buffer Effect"', *Central European Journal of International and Security Studies* 13, no. 1 (22 March 2019), pp. 100–21, https://doi.org/10.51870/cejiss.a130102

29. Randa M. Slim, 'Small-State Mediation in International Relations: The Algerian Mediation of the Iranian Hostage Crisis', in Jacob Bercovitch and Jeffery Z. Rubin (eds), *Mediation in International Relations: Multiple Approaches to Conflict Management* (London: Palgrave Macmillan, 1992), p. 207.
30. Jonas Baumann and Govinda Daniel Clayton, 'Mediation in Violent Conflict', *CSS Analyses in Security Policy* 211 (June 2017), pp. 1–2, https://doi.org/10.3929/ethz-b-000169653
31. Baumann and Clayton, 'Mediation in Violent Conflict'.
32. Kyle C. Beardsley et al., 'Mediation Style and Crisis Outcomes', *Journal of Conflict Resolution* 50, no. 1 (February 2006), p. 82, https://doi.org/10.1177/0022002705282862
33. Bercovitch and Jackson, *Conflict Resolution in the Twenty-First Century*.
34. Uzi Rabi, 'Qatar's Relations with Israel: Challenging Arab and Gulf Norms', *Middle East Journal* 63, no. 3 (2009), pp. 443–59; Taylor Luck, 'Checkbook Diplomacy? How Qatar's Renewed US Ties Reshape the Gulf', The Christian Science Monitor, 12 August 2019, https://www.csmonitor.com/World/Middle-East/2019/0807/Checkbook-diplomacy-How-Qatar-s-renewed-US-ties-reshape-the-Gulf
35. Gulbrandsen, 'Bridging the Gulf'; Mehran Kamrava, 'Mediation and Qatari Foreign Policy', *The Middle East Journal* 65, no. 4 (1 September 2011), p. 554, https://doi.org/10.3751/65.4.11; Ruslan Minich, 'Conflict Mediation: The Qatari Experience', *Historia i Polityka* 14, no. 21 (24 November 2015), p. 122, https://doi.org/10.12775/hip.2015.026
36. Sultan Barakat and Sansom Milton, '8 Qatar: Conflict Mediation and Regional Objectives', in Agnieszka Paczyńska (ed.), *The New Politics of Aid: Emerging Donors and Conflict-Affected States* (Boulder, CO: Lynne Rienner Publishers, 2019), pp. 141–60, https://doi.org/10.1515/9781626378407-009
37. Mehran Kamrava, 'Mediation and Qatari Foreign Policy'; Sultan Barakat, 'Qatari Mediation: Between Ambition and Achievement', Brookings Doha Center, November 2014, https://www.brookings.edu/wp-content/uploads/2016/06/Final-PDF-English.pdf
38. Matthew Gray, *Qatar: Politics and the Challenges of Development* (Boulder, CO: Lynne Rienner Publishers, 2013), https://doi.org/10.1515/9781626370784
39. Galeeva, *Qatar: The Practice of Rented Power*, p. xiii.
40. Ibid., p. 51.
41. Ghassan Elkahlout and Sansom Milton, 'The Evolution of the Gulf States as Humanitarian Donors', *Third World Quarterly* 45, no. 15–16 (10 July 2023), pp. 2246–65, https://doi.org/10.1080/01436597.2023.2229742; Bulent Aras, Burcu Fazlioglu, and Majed Al Ansari, 'Interest, Need, or Reputation? Determinants of Qatar's Foreign Aid', *Foreign Policy Analysis* 20, no. 4 (4 October 2024), p. orae027, https://doi.org/10.1093/fpa/orae027
42. Sansom Milton and Ghassan Elkahlout, 'Qatar's Multifaceted Humanitarian Role in Afghanistan since August 2021', *Development Policy Review* 43, no. 1 (8 July 2024), pp. 1–21, https://doi.org/10.1111/dpr.12793
43. Wadee Alarabeed, 'Qatar's Approach across the Triple Nexus in Conflict-

Affected Contexts: The Case of Darfur', *Third World Quarterly* 45, no. 1 (2023), pp. 6–23, https://doi.org/10.1080/01436597.2023.2215724; Altea Pericoli and Federico Donelli, 'Qatar's Foreign Aid and Political Strategies in the Horn of Africa: The Case of Somalia', *Global Policy* 15, no. 1 (26 October 2023), pp. 53–65, https://doi.org/10.1111/1758-5899.13294; Abdulfatah Mohamed, 'Qatari Peace Mediation and Humanitarian Aid in Sudan: Lessons from the War in Darfur 2003–2022', *Journal of Peacebuilding & Development* 20, no. 1 (2025), https://doi.org/10.1177/15423166241312874

44. Jesse Marks, 'China's Strategic Facilitation in the Persian Gulf Security Crisis', in *China and Conflict Mediation Series* (Washington, DC: Stimson Center, 2024), https://www.stimson.org/2024/chinas-strategic-facilitation-in-the-persian-gulf-security-crisis/; Ahmed Aboudouh, 'The Fatah–Hamas Agreement Increases Chinese Influence in Palestinian Affairs. But the Road to Unity Is Rocky', Chatham House, 24 July 2024, https://www.chathamhouse.org/2024/07/fatah-hamas-agreement-increases-chinese-influence-palestinian-affairs-road-unity-rocky
45. Benjamin De Carvalho and Cedric De Coning, 'Rising Powers and the Future of Peacekeeping and Peacebuilding', Norwegian Peacebuilding Resource Centre (NOREF), November 2013, p. 5, https://www.files.ethz.ch/isn/175234/f194e6326ee12f80c3705117b151ef78.pdf; Jakub Wódka, 'Turkey's Middlepowermanship, Foreign Policy Transformation and Mediation Efforts in the Russia-Ukraine War', *Studia Europejskie—Studies in European Affairs* 2023, no. 4 (15 December 2023), pp. 215–33, https://doi.org/10.33067/se.4.2023.12
46. Saban Kardaş and Bulent Aras, 'What Drove Syria Back into the Arab Fold?' *Middle East Policy* 30, no. 3 (7 August 2023), pp. 70–80, https://doi.org/10.1111/mepo.12704
47. Agnieszka Paczyńska, '"New" State Actors and Conflict-Affected States: Confronting Violence, Shifting Ambitions, and Adjusting Principles', *Frontiers in Political Science* 3 (7 May 2021), p. 1, https://doi.org/10.3389/fpos.2021.663432
48. Kevin Gray and Barry K. Gills, 'South–South Cooperation and the Rise of the Global South', *Third World Quarterly* 37, no. 4 (24 March 2016), pp. 557–74, https://doi.org/10.1080/01436597.2015.1128817
49. Emma Mawdsley, *Recipients to Donors: Emerging Powers and the Changing Development Landscape* (London: Zed Books, 2012); Fahimul Quadir, 'Rising Donors and the New Narrative of "South–South" Cooperation: What Prospects for Changing the Landscape of Development Assistance Programmes?' *Third World Quarterly* 34, no. 2 (March 2013), pp. 321–38, https://doi.org/10.1080/01436597.2013.775788
50. Niall Duggan et al., 'Introduction: "The BRICS, Global Governance, and Challenges for South–South Cooperation in a Post-Western World"', *International Political Science Review* 43, no. 4 (2022), pp. 469–80, https://doi.org/10.1177/01925121211052211
51. Mateja Peter and Haley Rice, *Non-Western Approaches to Peacemaking and*

Peacebuilding: State-of-the-Art and an Agenda for Research (Edinburgh: PeaceRep: The Peace and Conflict Resolution Evidence Platform, 2022), https://peacerep.org/wp-content/uploads/2022/04/State-of-the-Art-Report-Digital-1.pdf
52. Pierre Hazan, *Negotiating with the Devil: Inside the World of Armed Conflict Mediation* (London: Hurst & Company, 2024), p. 13.
53. Mladenov, 'The Arab Approach to Mediation'.
54. James Worrall, '"Switzerland of Arabia": Omani Foreign Policy and Mediation Efforts in the Middle East', *The International Spectator* 56, no. 4 (8 December 2021), pp. 134–50, https://doi.org/10.1080/03932729.2021.1996004
55. The New Arab, 'Exclusive: How Iran, US Quietly Agreed to Negotiate in Oman', *The New Arab*, 8 April 2025, https://www.newarab.com/news/exclusive-how-iran-us-quietly-agreed-negotiate-oman
56. Ibrahim Fraihat, 'Superpower and Small-State Mediation in the Qatar Gulf Crisis', *The International Spectator* 55, no. 2 (2020), pp. 79–91, https://doi.org/10.1080/03932729.2020.1741268; Huzeyfe Altiok, 'Kuwait's Mediation in the Gulf Crisis: Dynamics of Kuwait's Foreign Policy Approaches', in Md Mizanur Rahman and Amr Al-Azm (eds), *Social Change in the Gulf Region: Gulf Studies*, vol. 8 (Singapore: Springer, 2023), pp. 597–618, https://doi.org/10.1007/978-981-19-7796-1_35
57. Kristian Coates Ulrichsen, 'Kuwait as a Mediator in Regional Affairs: The Gulf Crises of 2014 and 2017', *The International Spectator* 56, no. 4 (2021), p. 130, https://doi.org/10.1080/03932729.2021.1982293
58. Courtney Freer, *Interrogating Different Modes of GCC Conflict Mediation* (Edinburgh: PeaceRep: The Peace and Conflict Resolution Evidence Platform, 2022), https://peacerep.org/wp-content/uploads/2023/05/Freer-2023-Interrogating-Different-Modes-of-GCC-Conflict-Mediation-GT.pdf
59. Mladenov, 'The Arab Approach to Mediation'.
60. Aleksi Ylönen, 'Is the Horn of Africa's "Cold War" Over? Abiy Ahmed's Early Reforms and the Rapprochement between Ethiopia and Eritrea', *African Security Review* 27, no. 3–4 (25 January 2019), pp. 245–52, https://doi.org/10.1080/10246029.2019.1569079; Jonathan Fenton-Harvey, 'Interests First: The UAE's India-Pakistan Imbalance', Gulf International Forum, 2 February 2023, https://gulfif.org/interests-first-the-uaes-india-pakistan-imbalance/
61. Mohamed Elshabik, 'Sudan: Learning Lessons from the Past in Search of Peace', World Economic Forum, 9 August 2024, https://www.weforum.org/agenda/2024/08/sudan-upcoming-geneva-talks-negotiators-peace/
62. Ginny Hill, *Yemen Endures: Civil War, Saudi Adventurism and the Future of Arabia* (New York: Oxford University Press, 2017).
63. Africa Defense Forum, 'UAE Role in Sudan's Civil War Draws Criticism', *Africa Defense Forum*, 30 January 2024, https://adf-magazine.com/2024/01/uae-role-in-sudans-civil-war-draws-criticism/
64. Estifanos Balew Liyew, 'Shattering Impact of the Sudan Conflict on Regional Stability', *African Identities*, 5 March 2025, pp. 1–16, https://doi.org/10.1080/14725843.2025.2473989
65. Kristian Coates Ulrichsen, 'The Rationale and Implications of Qatar's

Intervention in Libya', in Dag Henriksen and Ann Karin Larssen (eds), *Political Rationale and International Consequences of the War in Libya* (Oxford: Oxford University Press, 2016), pp. 118–33, https://doi.org/10.1093/acprof:oso/9780198767480.003.0007

66. Gertjan Hoetjes, 'The Gulf Cooperation Council and the Failure of Peacebuilding in Yemen', *The International Spectator* 56, no. 4 (15 November 2021), pp. 151–66, https://doi.org/10.1080/03932729.2021.1987034; Courtney Freer, 'Qatar and the UAE in Peacemaking and Peacebuilding', *LSE Middle East Centre Paper Series* 60 (March 2022), https://eprints.lse.ac.uk/114561/3/Qatar_and_UAE_in_Peacemaking_and_Peacebuilding_1_.pdf; Freer, 'Interrogating Different Modes'.
67. Mohamed Evren Tok, 'Gulf Donors and the 2030 Agenda: Towards a Khaleeji Mode of Development Cooperation', Centre for Policy Research (United Nations University), 2015; Logan Cochrane, 'The United Arab Emirates as a Global Donor: What a Decade of Foreign Aid Data Transparency Reveals', *Development Studies Research* 8, no. 1 (2021), pp. 49–62, https://doi.org/10.1080/21665095.2021.1883453; Assem Dandashly and Christos Kourtelis, 'The Provision of Arab Gulf Aid: The Emergence of New Donors', *International Politics* 60, no. 2 (2023), pp. 406–27, https://doi.org/10.1057/s41311-022-00418-4; Ghassan Elkahlout and Sansom Milton, 'The Evolution of the Gulf States as Humanitarian Donors', *Third World Quarterly* 45, no. 15–16 (10 July 2023), pp. 2246–65, https://doi.org/10.1080/01436597.2023.2229742; Moosa Elayah and Hasan Al-Awami, 'Exploring the Preference for Bilateral Aid: Gulf Oil States' Aid to Yemen', *Third World Quarterly* 45, no. 15–16 (2024), pp. 2266–86, https://doi.org/10.1080/01436597.2024.2327451
68. Mohammed Abu-Nimer, 'Conflict Resolution Approaches', *The American Journal of Economics and Sociology* 55, no. 1 (January 1996), pp. 35–52, https://doi.org/10.1111/j.1536-7150.1996.tb02706.x; Mohammed Abu-Nimer, *Nonviolence and Peace Building in Islam: Theory and Practice* (Gainesville, FL: University Press of Florida, 2003); Mohammed Abu-Nimer and Timothy Seidel, 'Culture, Religion and Politics in International Mediation', in Alexia Georgakopoulos (ed.), *The Mediation Handbook: Research, Theory, and Practice* (New York: Routledge, 2017), pp. 324–33, https://doi.org/10.4324/9781315648330
69. UNESCO, 'UNESCO—Majlis, a Cultural and Social Space', United Nations Educational, Scientific and Cultural Organization, 2015, https://ich.unesco.org/en/RL/majlis-a-cultural-and-social-space-01076
70. Mladenov, 'The Arab Approach to Mediation'.
71. Freer, 'Interrogating Different Modes'.
72. Freer, 'Qatar and the UAE in Peacemaking'.

4. STEPPING BACK FROM THE BRINK: LEBANON'S 2008 DOHA AGREEMENT

1. Marwan George Rowayheb, 'Political Change and the Outbreak of Civil War:

The Case of Lebanon', *Civil Wars* 13, no. 4 (December 2011), pp. 414–36, https://doi.org/10.1080/13698249.2011.629871

2. Engin Deniz Akarli, *The Long Peace: Ottoman Lebanon, 1861–1920* (Oakland, CA: University of California Press, 1993); Max Weiss, 'The Historiography of Sectarianism in Lebanon', *History Compass* 7, no. 1 (January 2009), pp. 141–54, https://doi.org/10.1111/j.1478-0542.2008.00570.x
3. Lebanese Parliament, *The Lebanese Constitution Promulgated 23 May 1926 with Its Amendments, 23 May 1926 (with 1995 amendments)* (Beirut: Lebanese Parliament, 1926), https://lp.gov.lb/backoffice/uploads/files/Lebanese%20%20Constitution-%20En.pdf
4. Farid El-Khazen, *The Communal Pact of National Identities: The Making and Politics of the 1943 National Pact* (Oxford: Centre for Lebanese Studies, 1991).
5. United Nations, *The Taif Agreement*, negotiated in Ta'if, Saudi Arabia, September 1989, and approved by the Lebanese Parliament on 4 November 1989, https://www.un.int/lebanon/sites/www.un.int/files/Lebanon/the_taif_agreement_english_version_.pdf
6. Farah Dakhlallah, 'The Arab League in Lebanon: 2005–2008', *Cambridge Review of International Affairs* 25, no. 1 (2012), pp. 53–74, https://doi.org/10.1080/09557571.2011.646241
7. Athanasiadis, 'Re-Visioning "Lebanon": Power-Sharing during the Postwar Era (1990–2015)', PhD dissertation, Luiss University, Rome, Italy, 2017; Özlem Tür, 'The Lebanese War of 2006: Reasons and Consequences', *Perceptions*, Spring 2007, pp. 109–22.
8. Jonathan Spyer, 'Lebanon 2006: Unfinished War', *Middle East Review of International Affairs* 12, no. 1 (13 March 2008).
9. Tür, 'The Lebanese War of 2006'; Jonathan Spyer, 'Lebanon 2006: Unfinished War'.
10. Mehran Kamrava, 'Mediation and Qatari Foreign Policy', *The Middle East Journal* 65, no. 4 (1 September 2011), pp. 539–56, https://doi.org/10.3751/65.4.11; Dakhlallah, 'The Arab League in Lebanon'; Ohannes Geukjian, 'Political Instability and Conflict after the Syrian Withdrawal from Lebanon', *The Middle East Journal* 68, no. 4 (1 September 2014), pp. 521–45, https://doi.org/10.3751/68.4.12
11. Mona Yacoubian, *Facing the Abyss: Lebanon's Deadly Political Stalemate* (Washington, DC: United States Institute of Peace, 2008), https://www.usip.org/publications/2008/02/facing-abyss-lebanons-deadly-political-stalemate
12. Jeffrey Feltman, 'Hezbollah: Revolutionary Iran's Most Successful Export', Brookings, 17 January 2019, https://www.brookings.edu/articles/hezbollah-revolutionary-irans-most-successful-export/
13. International Crisis Group, 'Hizbollah and the Lebanese Crisis', International Crisis Group, October 2007, https://www.crisisgroup.org/middle-east-north-africa/eastern-mediterranean/lebanon/hizbollah-and-lebanese-crisis
14. Interview with Wael Abou Faour, Member of Parliament, Progressive Socialist Party, Minister of Social Affairs (2011–14), Minister of Public Health (2014–16), Minister of Industry (2019–20), Lebanon, 23 September 2024.

15. Almula Türedi, 'Lebanon: At the Edge of Another Civil War', *Perceptions* 13, no. 1 (2008), pp. 21–36; CBS News, 'Lebanon Factions Reach Deal to End the Crisis', CBS News, 21 May 2008, https://www.cbsnews.com/news/lebanese-factions-reach-deal-to-end-crisis
16. Andrew Arsan, *Lebanon: A Country in Fragments* (London: Hurst & Company, 2018).
17. Al Jazeera English, 'Nasrallah Addresses Lebanon—08 May 08', YouTube, 9 May 2008, https://www.youtube.com/watch?v=YrfxnCoPViI
18. Kamrava, 'Mediation and Qatari Foreign Policy'; Dakhlallah, 'The Arab League in Lebanon'; Geukjian, 'Political Instability and Conflict'.
19. Interview with Mustapha Allouch, former Member of Parliament, Future Movement (2005–22), Lebanon, 17 September 2024.
20. Interview with Jamal Jarrah, Member of Parliament for West Bekaa–Rashaya District, Future Movement (2005–present), Lebanon, 20 September 2024.
21. Interview with Ashraf Rifi, Member of Parliament, Minister of Justice (2014–16), General Director of the Lebanese Internal Security Forces (2005–13), Lebanon, 20 September 2024.
22. Interview with Gebran Bassil, Member of Parliament, Leader of the Free Patriotic Movement (2015–present), Leader of the Strong Lebanon Bloc in Parliament (2018–present), Lebanon, 24 September 2024; Interview with Michel Moussa, Member of Parliament, Minister of Labor and Social Affairs (1998–2000), Minister of Environment (2000–03), Minister of State (2003–04, 2016–20), Member of the Amal Movement, and Head of the Parliamentary Human Rights Committee, Lebanon, 21 September 2024; Interview with Cesar Abi Khalil, Member of Parliament, Free Patriotic Movement, Lebanon, 19 September 2024.
23. Interview with Bassel Salloukh, Associate Dean of the School of Social Sciences and Humanities, and Professor of Political Science at the Doha Institute for Graduate Studies; Associate Professor of Political Science (Social Sciences) at the Lebanese American University in Beirut (2006–21), Lebanon, January 2025.
24. Samir Makdisi and Marcus Marktanner, 'Trapped by Consociationalism: The Case of Lebanon', *Topics in Middle Eastern and North African Economies* 4, no. 3 (2009), pp. 1–33.
25. Interview with Alain Aoun, Member of Parliament, Member of the Free Patriotic Movement (until 2024), Lebanon, 24 September 2024.
26. Interview with Jamal Jarrah.
27. Interview with Wael Abou Faour.
28. Kamrava, 'Mediation and Qatari Foreign Policy'.
29. Interview with Bechara Khairallah, Legal Advisor to former President Michel Suleiman (elected in 2008–14), Lebanon, 26 September 2024.
30. Interview with Ashraf Rifi.
31. Kamrava, 'Mediation and Qatari Foreign Policy'.
32. Interview with Gebran Bassil.
33. Interview with Mustapha Allouch.

34. Interview with Bechara Khairallah.
35. Ibid.
36. Interview with Alain Aoun.
37. Interview with Wael Abou Faour.
38. Interview with Pierre Bou Assi, Member of Parliament, Lebanese Forces Party, Minister of Social Affairs (2016–19), Lebanon, 24 September 2024.
39. Christine Sylva Hamieh and Roger Mac Ginty, 'A Very Political Reconstruction: Governance and Reconstruction in Lebanon after the 2006 War', *Disasters* 34 (30 November 2009), pp. S103–23, https://doi.org/10.1111/j.1467-7717.2009.01101.x
40. Republic of Lebanon—Ministry of Finance, *International Conference for Support to Lebanon—Paris III: First Progress Report* (Beirut: Republic of Lebanon—Ministry of Finance, 2007), https://www.finance.gov.lb/en-us/Finance/DC/AC/Documents/Paris%20III%20First%20Progress%20Report.pdf
41. Al Jazeera, 'Qatar Pledges Support to Lebanon', Al Jazeera, 22 August 2006, https://www.aljazeera.com/news/2006/8/22/qatar-pledges-support-to-lebanon
42. Interview with Jamal Jarrah.
43. Interview with Alain Aoun.
44. Interview with Gebran Bassil.
45. Interview with Ashraf Rifi.
46. Interview with Michel Pharaon, former Member of Parliament, Minister of State for Parliamentary Affairs (2000–03, 2005–08), Lebanon, 23 September 2024.
47. WikiLeaks, 'Reported Qatari Mediation in Formation of Lebanese Cabinet', WikiLeaks, 9 November 2009, https://wikileaks.org/plusd/cables/09DOHA664_a.html
48. Interview with Pierre Bou Assi.
49. Interview with Faisal Karami, Member of Parliament, Minister of Youth and Sports (2011–14), Head of the Dignity Movement (formerly known as the Arab Liberation Party), Lebanon, 25 September 2024.
50. Dakhlallah, 'The Arab League in Lebanon'; Al-Kuwari, 'An Appraisal of Qatar Foreign Aid Effectiveness'.
51. Dakhlallah, 'The Arab League in Lebanon'.
52. Interview with Alain Aoun.
53. Dakhlallah, 'The Arab League in Lebanon'.
54. Nicholas Blanford, 'Qatari Deal Defuses Lebanese Crisis', The Christian Science Monitor, 22 May 2008, https://www.csmonitor.com/World/Middle-East/2008/0522/p01s05-wome.html; Kamrava, 'Mediation and Qatari Foreign Policy'; Dakhlallah, 'The Arab League in Lebanon'; Al-Kuwari, 'An Appraisal of Qatar Foreign Aid Effectiveness'.
55. Dakhlallah, 'The Arab League in Lebanon'; Martin Wählisch, 'The Lebanese National Dialogue: Past and Present Experience of Consensus-Building', in *National Dialogue Handbook* (Berlin: Berghof Foundation, 2017).
56. United Nations Peacemaker, 'Doha Agreement on the Results of the Lebanese

National Dialogue Conference', UN Peacemaker: Mediation Support Unit, 21 May 2008, https://peacemaker.un.org/sites/default/files/document/files/2024/05/lebanondohaagreement2008engl.pdf
57. United Nations Peacemaker, 'Doha Agreement on the Results of the Lebanese National Dialogue Conference'; Blanford, 'Qatari Deal Defuses Lebanese Crisis'; United Nations Security Council, *Letter Dated 22 May 2008 from the Permanent Observer of the League of Arab States to the United Nations Addressed to the President of the Security Council (S/2008/392)* (New York: United Nations Security Council, 2008), https://digitallibrary.un.org/record/632576
58. Blanford, 'Qatari Deal Defuses Lebanese Crisis'; Kamrava, 'Mediation and Qatari Foreign Policy'; Geukjian, 'Political Instability and Conflict'; Wählisch, 'The Lebanese National Dialogue'.
59. Dakhlallah, 'The Arab League in Lebanon'.
60. Athanasiadis, 'Re-Visioning "Lebanon"'.
61. Interview with Hassan Mrad, Member of Parliament, State Minister for Foreign Trade Affairs (2016–20), Vice-President of the Lebanese International University for Public Relations (2005–19), Lebanon, 23 September 2024.
62. Athanasiadis, 'Re-Visioning "Lebanon"'.
63. Imad Salamey, *The Government and Politics of Lebanon* (London: Routledge, 2013).
64. Blanford, 'Qatari Deal Defuses Lebanese Crisis'; Kamrava, 'Mediation and Qatari Foreign Policy'; Dakhlallah, 'The Arab League in Lebanon'.
65. Interview with Bassel Salloukh.
66. United Nations Peacemaker, 'Doha Agreement on the Results of the Lebanese National Dialogue Conference'.
67. Nassif Hitti, *The Foreign Policy of Lebanon: Lessons and Prospects for the Forgotten Dimension* (Oxford: Centre for Lebanese Studies, 1989); Marco Pinfari, 'Nothing but Failure? The Arab League and the Gulf Cooperation Council as Mediators in Middle Eastern Conflicts', *LSE Crisis States Research Centre Working Papers* 45 (2009), https://www.files.ethz.ch/isn/98212/WP45.2.pdf; Dakhlallah, 'The Arab League in Lebanon'.
68. Interview with Paula Yacoubian, Member of Parliament, Forces of Change Parliamentary Bloc (2022–present), former journalist (1995–2018), Lebanon, 23 August 2024.
69. Interview with Hassan Mrad.
70. Interview with Michel Pharaon.
71. Interview with Ashraf Rifi.
72. Interview with Salim Jreissati, former Member of Parliament, Minister of Labor (2012–14), Minister of Justice (2016–19), Free Patriotic Movement Leader since the early 2010s, Member of the Lebanese Constitutional Council (1977–2009), Lebanon, 18 September 2024.
73. Basma Mahmoud ElEtreby, 'Qatari Foreign Policy and the Arab Spring: From Mediation to Intervention', Master's thesis, American University in Cairo, Cairo, Egypt, 2014.
74. Interview with Wael Abou Faour.

75. Interview with Michel Moussa.
76. Kamrava, 'Mediation and Qatari Foreign Policy'.
77. Reuters, 'Qatar Pulls off Mediation Coup in Lebanon Crisis', Reuters, 22 May 2008, https://www.reuters.com/article/world/qatar-pulls-off-mediation-coup-in-lebanon-crisis-idUSL22740435/; Mohammed Nuruzzaman, 'Gulf Cooperation Council (GCC), Qatar and Dispute Mediations: A Critical Investigation', *Contemporary Arab Affairs* 8, no. 4 (27 October 2015), pp. 535–52, https://doi.org/10.1080/17550912.2015.1078073
78. Nuruzzaman, 'GCC, Qatar and Dispute Mediations'.
79. WikiLeaks, 'Reported Qatari Mediation'.
80. Kamrava, 'Mediation and Qatari Foreign Policy'.
81. Ibid.
82. Kresna Kusumawijaya and Yon Machmudi, 'Qatar Foreign Policy in Middle East Conflict Mediation', *Journal of Middle East and Islamic Studies* 9, no. 2 (1 December 2022), https://doi.org/10.7454/meis.v9i2.149
83. Simon Haddad, 'Lebanon: From Consociationalism to Conciliation', *Nationalism and Ethnic Politics* 15, no. 3–4 (11 December 2009), pp. 398–416, https://doi.org/10.1080/13537110903346684; Sami G. Hajjar, 'The Convoluted and Diminished Lebanese Democracy', *Democracy and Security* 5, no. 3 (1 December 2009), pp. 261–76, https://doi.org/10.1080/17419160903304864
84. Interview with Joseph Jbeily, Head of International Relations Office, Lebanese Forces Party, Lebanon, 24 September 2024.
85. Simon Haddad, 'Lebanon: From Consociationalism to Conciliation'; Sami G. Hajjar, 'The Convoluted and Diminished Lebanese Democracy'.
86. Interview with Faisal Karami.
87. Alexander Langlois, 'The Gulf's Role in Lebanon's Political and Economic Crisis', Gulf International Forum, 16 August 2023, https://gulfif.org/the-gulfs-role-in-lebanons-political-and-economic-crisis/
88. ElEtreby, 'Qatari Foreign Policy and the Arab Spring'.
89. Uzi Rabi, 'Qatar's Relations with Israel: Challenging Arab and Gulf Norms', *The Middle East Journal* 63, no. 3 (1 June 2009), p. 457, https://doi.org/10.3751/63.3.15
90. Sultan Barakat, 'The Qatari Spring: Qatar's Emerging Role in Peacemaking', Kuwait Programme on Development, Governance and Globalisation in the Gulf States, July 2012, p. 19, https://www.brookings.edu/wp-content/uploads/2016/06/qatar-role-peacekeeping-barakat.pdf
91. WikiLeaks, 'Qatar Will Consider Deposit in Lebanon's Central Bank, Mediation Role', WikiLeaks, 13 December 2006, https://wikileaks.org/plusd/cables/06DOHA1737_a.html; WikiLeaks, 'Qatar Outlines Darfur Strategy to SE Williamson', WikiLeaks, 14 December 2008, https://wikileaks.org/plusd/cables/08DOHA854_a.html; WikiLeaks, 'Scenesetter for Special Envoy Williamson's Visit to Qatar', WikiLeaks, 20 November 2008, https://wikileaks.org/plusd/cables/08DOHA817_a.html
92. Interview with Bechara Khairallah.

93. Al-Kuwari, 'An Appraisal of Qatar Foreign Aid Effectiveness'.
94. Interview with Faisal Karami.
95. Interview with Joseph Jbeily.
96. Interview with Faisal Karami.
97. Interview with Mustapha Allouch.
98. Interview with Michel Moussa.
99. Interview with Gebran Bassil.
100. Interview with Salim Jreissati.
101. Alistair Harris, *Half Full or Half Empty: Assessing Prospects for Peace in Lebanon* (Washington, DC: United States Institute of Peace, 2008); Wählisch, 'The Lebanese National Dialogue'.
102. Rabi, 'Qatar's Relations with Israel'.
103. Courtney Freer, 'Qatar and the UAE in Peacemaking and Peacebuilding', *LSE Middle East Centre Paper Series* 60 (March 2022), https://eprints.lse.ac.uk/114561/3/Qatar_and_UAE_in_Peacemaking_and_Peacebuilding_1_.pdf; Guido Steinberg, *Qatar's Foreign Policy: Decision-Making Processes, Baselines, and Strategies* (Berlin: Stiftung Wissenschaft und Politik, 2023).
104. Nuruzzaman, 'GCC, Qatar and Dispute Mediations'.
105. Al-Kuwari, 'An Appraisal of Qatar Foreign Aid Effectiveness'.
106. Robert Worth and Nada Bakri, 'Deal for Lebanese Factions Leaves Hezbollah Stronger', *The New York Times*, 22 May 2008, http://www.nytimes.com/2008/05/22/world/middleeast/22lebanon.html?_r=1&
107. Sultan Barakat, 'Qatari Mediation: Between Ambition and Achievement', Brookings Doha Center, November 2014, https://www.brookings.edu/wp-content/uploads/2016/06/Final-PDF-English.pdf
108. Samir Makdisi, Fadia Kiwan, and Marcus Marktanner, 'Lebanon: The Constrained Democracy and Its National Impact', in Ibrahim Elbadawi and Samir Makdisi (eds), *Democracy in the Arab World: Explaining the Deficit*, 1st edn (London: Routledge, 2011), pp. 115–41; Al-Kuwari, 'An Appraisal of Qatar Foreign Aid Effectiveness'.
109. Interview with Paula Yacoubian.
110. Interview with Najat Aoun Saliba, Member of Parliament, Forces of Change Parliamentary Bloc (2022–present), Lebanon, 28 August 2024.
111. Barakat, 'The Qatari Spring'.
112. Makdisi, Kiwan, and Marktanner, 'Lebanon: The Constrained Democracy'.
113. Kamrava, 'Mediation and Qatari Foreign Policy'.
114. Barakat, 'The Qatari Spring'.
115. Interview with Jamal Jarrah.
116. Nuruzzaman, 'GCC, Qatar and Dispute Mediations'.
117. Interview with Paula Yacoubian.
118. Jonathan Masters and Mohammed Aly Sergie, 'The Arab League', Council on Foreign Relations, 25 May 2023, https://www.cfr.org/backgrounder/arab-league#chapter-title-0-4
119. Stacey Philbrick Yadav, 'Lebanon's Post-Doha Political Theater', *Middle East Report*, 23 July 2008, https://merip.org/2008/07/lebanons-post-doha-political-theater

5. BROKERING PEACE IN DARFUR: THE DOHA DOCUMENT AND ITS LEGACY

1. Alex De Waal, 'Who Are the Darfurians? Arab and African Identities, Violence and External Engagement', *African Affairs* 104, no. 415 (1 April 2005), pp. 181–205, https://doi.org/10.1093/afraf/adi035
2. Yousif Hassan, 'The Evolution of the Sudanese Authoritarian State: The December Uprising and the Unravelling of a "Persistent" Autocracy', in Ozgun Topak, Merouan Mekouar, and Francesco Cavatorta (eds), *New Authoritarian Practices in the Middle East and North Africa* (Edinburgh: Edinburgh University Press, 2022), pp. 252–75.
3. Assad Mehmood Khan, Nazim Rahim, and Muhammad Javed, 'Socio-Political and Socio-Economic Perspectives of Sudan with Special Reference to Darfur Conflict', *Global Social Sciences Review* 4, no. 4 (30 December 2019), pp. 451–59, https://www.humapub.com/admin/alljournals/gssr/papers/GB5D98qzsn.pdf
4. Joyce Apsel, 'The Complexity of Destruction in Darfur: Historical Processes and Regional Dynamics', *Human Rights Review* 10, no. 2 (6 September 2008), pp. 239–59, https://doi.org/10.1007/s12142-008-0099-6
5. Ola Olsson and Eyerusalem Siba, 'Ethnic Cleansing or Resource Struggle in Darfur? An Empirical Analysis', *Journal of Development Economics* 103 (July 2013), pp. 299–312, https://doi.org/10.1016/j.jdeveco.2013.02.004
6. Mahmood Mamdani, *Saviors and Survivors: Darfur, Politics, and the War on Terror* (Dakar: Council for the Development of Social Science Research in Africa, 2010).
7. United Nations, 'At Five-Year Mark, Darfur Crisis Is Only Worsening—UN Aid Chief', United Nations, 22 April 2008, https://news.un.org/en/story/2008/04/256942
8. United Nations Office for the Coordination of Humanitarian Affairs, 'Humanitarian News from Sudan: Monthly Digest—Jul 2007', United Nations Office for the Coordination of Humanitarian Affairs, 31 July 2007, https://www.unocha.org/publications/report/chad/humanitarian-news-sudan-monthly-digest-jul-2007
9. African Development Bank Group, 'Sudan Poverty Profile: Summary Results of the 2014–2015 National Baseline Household Budget Survey', African Development Bank Group, 2018, https://www.afdb.org/fileadmin/uploads/afdb/Documents/Publications/Brief-Sudan_Poverty_Profile_2014-2015_-_Key_Findings.pdf
10. African Development Bank Group, 'Sudan—Update of the Country Brief 2017–2019 to December 2021', African Development Bank Group, 1 December 2021, https://www.afdb.org/en/documents/sudan-update-country-brief-2017–2019-december-2021
11. Mark Simmons and Peter Dixon (eds), *Peace by Piece: Addressing Sudan's Conflicts* (London: Conciliation Resources, 2006), pp. 78–80.
12. UNAMID, 'Darfur Peace Agreements: Challenges and Opportunities', United

Nations–African Union Mission in Darfur, 1 July 2012, https://unamid.unmissions.org/peace-process-0

13. Jonathan Loeb, *Talking to the Other Side: Humanitarian Engagement with Armed Non-State Actors in Darfur, Sudan, 2003–2012* (London: Overseas Development Institute, 2013), p. 4.
14. International Crisis Group, 'Darfur Rising: Sudan's New Crisis', International Crisis Group, 25 March 2004, p. 2, https://www.crisisgroup.org/africa/horn-africa/sudan/darfur-rising-sudans-new-crisis
15. Annette Weber, 'Bridging the Gap between Narrative and Practice: The Role of the Arab League in Darfur', Fundación Para Las Relaciones Internacionales y El Diálogo Exterior (FRIDE), 2010, https://www.swp-berlin.org/publications/products/fachpublikationen/03._Arab_League_Weber1_ks.pdf
16. United Nations Peacemaker, 'Humanitarian Ceasefire Agreement on the Conflict in Darfur', UN Peacemaker: Mediation Support Unit, 2 April 2004, https://peacemaker.un.org/node/9516
17. Human Rights Watch, 'Sudan: Imperatives for Immediate Change: The African Union Mission in Sudan', Human Rights Watch, 19 January 2006, https://www.hrw.org/reports/2006/sudan0106/sudan0106web.pdf
18. Ibid.
19. Refugees International, 'Sudan: Saving the Darfur Peace Agreement', *Refugees International Bulletin*, 21 August 2006, https://www.refworld.org/reference/countryrep/ri/2006/en/49658
20. Interview with Ahmed Tugud Lisan, JEM's Chief Negotiator at the Doha Platform for Peace in Darfur, Doha, Qatar, 14 September 2023.
21. Jan Pronk, 'Darfur Agreement Is Severely Paralysed', *Sudan Tribune*, 28 June 2006, https://sudantribune.com/?p=16982&lang=en
22. David Lanz, 'Sudan/Darfur, Abuja Negotiations and the DPA', in *Unpacking the Mystery of Mediation in African Peace Processes* (Zurich: Mediation Support Project, Center for Security Studies, Swisspeace, 2008), pp. 78–84.
23. United Nations, 'United Nations, African Union Agree to Convene Renewed Peace Negotiations for Darfur in Tripoli, 27 October', United Nations, 10 September 2007, https://press.un.org/en/2007/sgsm11149.doc.htm
24. Ralph Mamiya and Wibke Hansen, *Assessing the Effectiveness of the United Nations-African Union Hybrid Operation in Darfur (UNAMID)* (Oslo: Norwegian Institute of International Affairs, 2020), https://bitly.cx/vIQG
25. Sudan Tribune, 'Qatar Proposed as Host to International Summit on Darfur', *Sudan Tribune*, 4 September 2008, https://sudantribune.com/?p=28463&lang=en; Andrew S. Natsios, *Sudan, South Sudan, and Darfur: What Everyone Needs to Know* (New York: Oxford University Press, 2012).
26. Sudan Tribune, 'France Supports Qatari Efforts', *Sudan Tribune*, 12 September 2008, https://sudantribune.com/?p=28554&lang=en
27. Sudan Tribune, 'Sudan Acknowledges Obstacles with Qatari Mediation, Blast France', *Sudan Tribune*, 1 January 2009, https://sudantribune.com/?p=29633&lang=en
28. Quoted in Anders Gulbrandsen, 'Bridging the Gulf: Qatari Business Diplomacy

and Conflict Mediation', Master's thesis, Georgetown University, Washington, DC, USA, 2010, pp. 68–69, https://repository.library.georgetown.edu/bitstream/handle/10822/552827/gulbrandsenAnders.pdf
29. Rosalind Marsden, 'Peacemaking in Darfur and the Doha Process: The Role of International Actors', in Sarah M. H. Nouwen, Laura M. James, and Sharath Srinivasan (eds), *Making and Breaking Peace in Sudan and South Sudan: The Comprehensive Peace Agreement and Beyond* (London: British Academy Scholarship Online, 2020), p. 240.
30. Gulbrandsen, 'Bridging the Gulf', p. 69.
31. Interview with H.E. Ambassador Yasser Khidr Khalafallah, Sudanese Ambassador to the State of Qatar, Doha, Qatar, 16 November 2023.
32. Ibid.
33. Interview with Ahmed Tugud Lisan.
34. R. Green, 'Solving the Darfur Crisis: The U.S. Prefers Qatar to Egypt as Mediator', Middle East Media Research Institute (MEMRI), 31 August 2009, https://www.memri.org/reports/solving-darfur-crisis-us-prefers-qatar-egypt-mediator
35. Interview with Dr Amin Hassan Omar, Head of the Darfur Peace Follow-up Office, Doha, Qatar, 30 November 2023.
36. Mehran Kamrava, 'Mediation and Qatari Foreign Policy', *The Middle East Journal* 65, no. 4 (1 September 2011), p. 545, https://doi.org/10.3751/65.4.11
37. Karamalla Gaiballa Nagmeldin, 'The Qatari Efforts to Resolve the Armed Conflict in Darfur—The Challenges and Obstacles', *International Journal of Sudan Research* 7, no. 1 (15 January 2017), pp. 57–65, https://doi.org/10.47556/j.ijsr.7.1.2017.5
38. Interview with Dr Amin Hassan Omar.
39. Interview with H.E. Ambassador Ali bin Hassan Al-Hammadi, former Qatari Ambassador to Sudan and former Secretary-General of the Qatar Red Crescent, Doha, Qatar, 14 August 2023.
40. Interview with H.E. Minister Ahmed bin Abdullah bin Zaid Al Mahmoud, former Deputy Prime Minister and Minister of State for Cabinet Affairs (2011–17), and who was in charge of the file on Qatar Mediation to settle Darfur Dispute (November 2009–17), Doha, Qatar, 2024.
41. Mirdef Alqashouti, 'Qatar Mediation: From Soft Diplomacy to Foreign Policy', in Mahjoob Zweiri and Farah Qawasmi (eds), *Contemporary Qatar: Examining State and Society*, vol. 4 (Singapore: Springer, 2021), pp. 73–92, https://doi.org/10.1007/978-981-16-1391-3_6
42. Interview with H.E. Ambassador Zayed bin Rashid Al-Nuaimi, Doha, Qatar, 28 October 2023.
43. Jérôme Tubiana, Victor Tanner, and Musa Adam Abdul-Jalil, 'Traditional Authorities' Peacemaking Role in Darfur', United States Institute of Peace, 8 November 2012, https://www.usip.org/publications/2012/11/traditional-authorities-peacemaking-role-darfur
44. Marsden, 'Peacemaking in Darfur and the Doha Process'.
45. UNAMID, 'Doha Document for Peace in Darfur', United Nations–African

Union Mission in Darfur, 2011, https://unamid.unmissions.org/doha-document-peace-darfur
46. Interview with H.E. Ambassador Zayed bin Rashid Al-Nuaimi; Interview with H.E. Ambassador Ali bin Hassan Al-Hammadi.
47. Interview with H.E. Ambassador Ali bin Hassan Al-Hammadi.
48. Kamrava, 'Mediation and Qatari Foreign Policy'.
49. Ibid.
50. Interview with H.E. Minister Ahmed bin Abdullah bin Zaid Al Mahmoud.
51. Interview with H.E. Ambassador Zayed bin Rashid Al-Nuaimi.
52. Interview with Ahmed Tugud Lisan; Interview with H.E. Ambassador Ahmed Mohamed Al-Shafei, former Sudanese diplomat, Doha, Qatar, 6 September 2023.
53. Sean Brooks, 'Enforcing a Turning Point and Imposing a Deal: An Analysis of the Darfur Abuja Negotiations of 2006', *International Negotiation* 13, no. 3 (2008), pp. 413–40, https://doi.org/10.1163/157180608x365262
54. Interview with Tijani Sese, Former President of Liberation and Justice Movement, Doha, Qatar, 6 August 2024.
55. Sudan Tribune, 'JEM Holds Talks with Qataris over Darfur Peace Process', *Sudan Tribune*, 2 December 2008, https://sudantribune.com/?p=29369&lang=en
56. The Enough Project, 'First Days at Doha', The Enough Project, 13 February 2009, https://enoughproject.org/blog/first-days-doha
57. United Nations Peacemaker, 'Agreement of Good Will and Confidence-Building for the Settlement of the Problem in Darfur, Signed on 17 February 2009', UN Peacemaker: Mediation Support Unit, 5 July 2024, https://bitly.cx/5mrL
58. United Nations Peacemaker, 'Framework Agreement to Resolve the Conflict in Darfur between the Government of Sudan (GOS) and the Justice and Equality Movement Sudan (JEM), Signed on 23 February 2010', UN Peacemaker: Mediation Support Unit, 5 July 2024, https://bitly.cx/sKEk; United Nations Peacemaker, 'Framework Agreement to Resolve the Conflict in Darfur between the Government of Sudan (GOS) and Liberation and Justice Movement (LJM), Signed on 18 March 2010', UN Peacemaker: Mediation Support Unit, 5 July 2024, https://bitly.cx/vmFA
59. Interview with H.E. Minister Ahmed bin Abdullah bin Zaid Al Mahmoud.
60. Ibid.
61. Ibid.
62. UNAMID, 'Five Hundred Attend Darfur Stakeholders Conference', United Nations–African Union Mission in Darfur, 27 May 2011, https://unamid.unmissions.org/27-may-11-five-hundred-attend-darfur-stakeholders-conference
63. Interview with Djibril Yipènè Bassolé, Joint African Union–United Nations Chief Mediator for Darfur from 2008 to 2011, Doha, Qatar, 22 November 2023.
64. Interview with H.E. Ambassador Yasser Khidr Khalafallah.
65. Sudan Tribune, 'Qatar Says Ready to Participate Actively in Darfur Economic

Development', *Sudan Tribune*, 5 June 2011, https://sudantribune.com/?p=38691&lang=en
66. UNAMID, 'Final Communiqué International Donor Conference for Reconstruction and Development in Darfur', United Nations–African Union Mission in Darfur, 14 April 2013, https://unamid.unmissions.org/final-communiqu%C3%A9-international-donor-conference-reconstruction-and-developmentin-darfur-0
67. Sultan Barakat and Sansom Milton, '8 Qatar: Conflict Mediation and Regional Objectives', in Agnieszka Paczyńska (ed.), *The New Politics of Aid: Emerging Donors and Conflict-Affected States* (Boulder, CO: Lynne Rienner Publishers, 2020), pp. 141–60, https://doi.org/10.1515/9781626378407-009
68. Alex De Waal, *The Real Politics of the Horn of Africa: Money, War and the Business of Power* (Cambridge: Polity Press, 2015).
69. Sultan Barakat, 'Qatari Mediation: Between Ambition and Achievement', Brookings Doha Center, November 2014, https://www.brookings.edu/wp-content/uploads/2016/06/Final-PDF-English.pdf
70. Kristian Coates Ulrichsen, *Qatar and the Arab Spring* (Oxford: Oxford University Press, 2014).
71. Interview with H.E. Ambassador Zayed bin Rashid Al-Nuaimi.
72. Interview with Dr Amin Hassan Omar.
73. Interview with Djibril Yipènè Bassolé.
74. WikiLeaks, 'Qatari Minstate Al-Mahmoud Looks to Next Steps on Darfur Mediation, Says Qatar Wants No Part of ICC Postponement (Canonical ID:09DOHA100_a)', WikiLeaks, 9 February 2009, https://wikileaks.org/plusd/cables/09DOHA100_a.html
75. WikiLeaks, 'SUDAN/QATAR/BURKINA FASO—Qatari Minister Denies Exerting Pressure on Darfur Rebel Movements', WikiLeaks, 11 March 2013, https://wikileaks.org/gifiles/docs/67/672191_sudan-qatar-burkina-faso-qatari-minister-denies-exerting.html
76. De Waal, *The Real Politics of the Horn of Africa*.
77. Interview with H.E. Ambassador Zayed bin Rashid Al-Nuaimi.
78. Interview with H.E. Ambassador Ali bin Hassan Al-Hammadi.
79. Interview with H.E. Ambassador Yasser Khidr Khalafallah.
80. Ibid.
81. Interview with H.E. Ambassador Ahmed Mohamed Al-Shafei.
82. Interview with H.E. Ambassador Yasser Khidr Khalafallah.
83. Interview with Ali Suleiman Al-Burjo, participant in the Doha Peace Forum for Darfur, Doha, Qatar, 3 September 2023.
84. Interview with H.E. Ambassador Zayed bin Rashid Al-Nuaimi.
85. The Enough Project, 'The Darfur Peace Process: Recipe for a Bad Deal?' The Enough Project, 6 April 2010, https://enoughproject.org/reports/update-doha
86. Interview with H.E. Ambassador Zayed bin Rashid Al-Nuaimi.
87. Interview with H.E. Ahmed bin Abdullah Al Mahmoud.
88. Ibid.

89. Interview with H.E. Ambassador Yasser Khidr Khalafallah.
90. Interview with H.E. Ambassador Ali bin Hassan Al-Hammadi.
91. Abdelwahab El-Affendi, *Azmat Darfur: Nazra fi'l-Judhur wa'l-Hulul al-Mumkina* [in Arabic] (Abu Dhabi: The Emirates Centre for Strategic Studies and Research, 2009), p. 91.
92. Interview with Ahmed Tugud Lisan.
93. Ibid.
94. Interview with H.E. Ahmed bin Abdullah Al Mahmoud.
95. Ibid.
96. Interview with H.E. Ambassador Yasser Khidr Khalafallah.
97. Interview with H.E. Ahmed bin Abdullah Al Mahmoud.
98. Ibid.
99. Ulrichsen, *Qatar and the Arab Spring*; Kristian Coates Ulrichsen, *Qatar and the Gulf Crisis* (London: Hurst & Company, 2020).
100. UNAMID, '15 Oct 12—Communiqué of the Second Meeting of the Joint Commission of the Doha Document for Peace', United Nations–African Union Mission in Darfur, 16 October 2012, https://unamid.unmissions.org/15-oct-12-communiqu%C3%A9-second-meeting-joint-commission-doha-document-peace
101. Marsden, 'Peacemaking in Darfur and the Doha Process'.
102. United Nations Multi-Partner Trust Fund Office, 'Qatar Contributes 88.5 Million USD to UN Fund for Darfur', United Nations Multi-Partner Trust Fund Office, 23 September 2014, https://mptf.undp.org/news/qatar-contributes-88–5-million-usd-un-fund-darfur
103. Interview with Tijani Sese; Interview with H.E. Ambassador Zayed bin Rashid Al-Nuaimi; Interview with H.E. Ambassador Mutlaq bin Majid Al-Qahtani, Doha, Qatar, 2 August 2023.
104. Interview with Tijani Sese.
105. CMI, 'Developing Darfur: A Recovery & Reconstruction Strategy', Chr. Michelsen Institute, 2013, https://www.cmi.no/file/2320-Darfur-Development-Strategy-6–3–13.pdf
106. Qatar Fund for Development, 'Qatar Fund for Development Annual Report 2016', Qatar Fund for Development, 2017, https://exsjwzu9tz6.exactdn.com/wp-content/uploads/2021/01/QFFD-Report-English.pdf
107. Interview with H.E. Ambassador Mutlaq bin Majid Al-Qahtani.
108. Qatar Red Crescent Society, 'QRCS Commences Construction Works at QFFD-Funded Development Project in West Darfur', ReliefWeb, 19 January 2021, https://reliefweb.int/report/sudan/qrcs-commences-construction-works-qffd-funded-development-project-west-darfur-enar
109. Qatar Charity, 'Qatar Charity Opens Taiba Education City for Orphans in Sudan', Qatar Charity, 29 June 2021, https://www.qcharity.org/en/global/news/detailsinternational/19378-qatar-charity-opens-taiba
110. Zurab Elzarov, 'Community Stabilization and Violence Reduction: Lessons from Darfur', *Stability: International Journal of Security & Development* 4, no. 1 (23 February 2015), https://doi.org/10.5334/sta.ex

111. Dabanga Radio TV Online, '"31,000 Ex-Rebel Combatants Demobilised so Far": Darfur DDR Commission', Dabanga Radio TV Online, 20 July 2015, https://www.dabangasudan.org/en/all-news/article/31–000-ex-rebel-combatants-demobilised-so-far-darfur-ddr-commission
112. Marsden, 'Peacemaking in Darfur and the Doha Process', p. 247.
113. Tubiana, Tanner, and Abdul-Jalil, 'Traditional Authorities' Peacemaking Role'.
114. Ibid.
115. Interview with Magdi Khalafalla, Head of the Darfur Peace Follow-up Office, Doha, Qatar, 13 August 2023.
116. Eric Reeves, 'UN Displacement Figures for Darfur: Assessment, Confused Guesses, or Dissimulation?' *Sudan Tribune*, 21 December 2015, https://sudantribune.com/?p=55817&lang=en
117. Amnesty International, *Sudan: Scorched Earth, Poisoned Air: Sudanese Government Forces Ravage Jebel Marra, Darfur* (London: Amnesty International, 2016), https://www.amnesty.org/en/documents/afr54/4877/2016/en/
118. Marsden, 'Peacemaking in Darfur and the Doha Process'.
119. Interview with Ahmed Tugud Lisan.
120. Alex De Waal, 'Sudan: A Turbulent Political Marketplace', in Mehran Kamrava (ed.), *Fragile Politics: Weak States in the Greater Middle East* (New York: Oxford University Press, 2016), p. 187, https://doi.org/10.1093/acprof:oso/9780190246211.003.0008
121. De Waal, *The Real Politics of the Horn of Africa*, p. 66.
122. Jon Harald Lie, 'The Humanitarian-Development Nexus: Humanitarian Principles, Practice, and Pragmatics', *Journal of International Humanitarian Action* 5, no. 18 (December 2020), pp. 1–13, https://doi.org/10.1186/s41018-020-00086-0
123. Interview with Prof. Alex de Waal, Executive Director of the World Peace, online via Zoom, 18 November 2024.
124. African Union, 'Report of the African Union High-Level Panel on Darfur (AUPD)', African Union, 29 October 2009, p. 9, https://archives.au.int/handle/123456789/8263
125. Alex De Waal and Abdul Mohammed, *Defining the Crisis in the Sudans: Lessons from the African Union High-Level Panels for Sudan and South Sudan* (Johannesburg: Thabo Mbeki Foundation, 2024), https://mbeki.org/wp-content/uploads/2024/10/TMF-Crisis-in-The-Sudans-Report-Digital.pdf
126. United Nations, 'Resolution 2148 (2014) / Adopted by the Security Council at Its 7152nd Meeting, on 3 April 2014', United Nations, 3 April 2014, https://digitallibrary.un.org/record/768033?ln=en&v=pdf
127. Marsden, 'Peacemaking in Darfur and the Doha Process', p. 240.
128. Ibid., p. 241.
129. Interview with Prof. Alex de Waal.
130. Sami Saeed, 'Darfur Dialogue: From War to Peace, Coexistence and Stability', *Idea International Journal*, 6 December 2023, p. 15, https://doi.org/10.31752/idea.2023.91

131. Marsden, 'Peacemaking in Darfur and the Doha Process'.
132. Andrew S. Natsios, 'Darfur: A "Plan B" to Stop Genocide', U.S. Department of State Archive, 11 April 2007, https://2001-2009.state.gov/p/af/rls/rm/82941.htm
133. De Waal and Mohammed, *Defining the Crisis in the Sudans*, p. 18.
134. Natsios, *Sudan, South Sudan, and Darfur*, p. 191.
135. Ibid.
136. Adam Day, 'Peacekeeping Without a Partner: A Review of UNAMID's Political Strategy in Darfur', in Adam Day, Aditi Gorur, Victoria K. Holt, and Charles T. Hunt (eds), *The Political Practice of Peacekeeping: How Strategies for Peace Operations Are Developed and Implemented* (New York: United Nations University, 2020), p. 50.
137. Paul R. Williams and Matthew T. Simpson, 'Drafting in Doha: An Assessment of the Darfur Peace Process and Ceasefire Agreements', in Melanne A. Civic and Michael Miklaucic (eds), *Monopoly of Force: The Nexus of DDR and SSR* (Washington, DC: National Defense University Press, 2011), pp. 41–58.
138. Interview with H.E. Ambassador Mutlaq bin Majid Al-Qahtani.
139. Ibid.
140. ReliefWeb, 'Sudan, Armed Groups Agree to Resume Talks for Peace in Darfur', ReliefWeb, 7 December 2018, https://reliefweb.int/report/sudan/sudan-armed-groups-agree-resume-talks-peace-darfur
141. Gerrit Kurtz, 'Power Relations in Sudan after the Fall of Bashir: From Revolution to War', *SWP Research Paper*, no. 5/2024 (Berlin: Stiftung Wissenschaft und Politik, May 2014), https://doi.org/10.18449/2024RP05
142. De Waal, *The Real Politics of the Horn of Africa*, p. 67.
143. Doha Roots, 'Darfur Ruler Confirms That Qatar Has Provided Clear Support in Doha Document for the Peace of the Region', *Doha Roots*, 9 August 2021, https://doharoots.com/darfur-ruler-confirms-that-qatar-has-provided-clear-support-in-doha-document-for-the-peace-of-the-region
144. International Crisis Group, 'The Rebels Come to Khartoum: How to Implement Sudan's New Peace Agreement', International Crisis Group, 23 February 2021, https://www.crisisgroup.org/africa/horn-africa/sudan/b168-rebels-come-khartoum-how-implement-sudans-new-peace-agreement

6. AFGHANISTAN AT A CROSSROADS: THE 2020 U.S.–TALIBAN AGREEMENT AND BEYOND

1. Romain Malejacq, *Warlord Survival: The Delusion of State Building in Afghanistan* (Ithaca, NY: Cornell University Press, 2020).
2. Astri Suhrke, *When More Is Less: The International Project in Afghanistan* (New York: Columbia University Press, 2011).
3. Mary Sack and Cyrus Samii, 'An Interview with Lakhdar Brahimi', *Journal of International Affairs* 58, no. 1 (Fall 2004), pp. 239–47, https://di.idm.oclc.org/login?url=https://www.proquest.com/scholarly-journals/interview-with-lakhdar-brahimi/docview/220720597/se-2

4. Suhrke, *When More Is Less*.
5. Shehzad H. Qazi, 'The "Neo-Taliban" and Counterinsurgency in Afghanistan', *Third World Quarterly* 31, no. 3 (2010), pp. 485–99, https://doi.org/10.1080/01436597.2010.488484
6. Thomas H. Johnson and M. Chris Mason, 'Understanding the Taliban and Insurgency in Afghanistan', *World Affairs* 51, no. 1 (2007), pp. 71–89, https://doi.org/10.1016/j.orbis.2006.10.006; Thomas Ruttig, 'How Tribal Are the Taliban?' in Shahzad Bashir and Robert Crews (eds), *Under the Drones: Modern Lives in the Afghanistan-Pakistan Borderlands* (Cambridge, MA: Harvard University Press, 2012), pp. 102–35; Lindsay Maizland, 'The Taliban in Afghanistan', Council on Foreign Relations, 19 January 2023, https://www.cfr.org/backgrounder/taliban-afghanistan#chapter-title-0-8
7. Qazi, 'The "Neo-Taliban" and Counterinsurgency'; Antonio Giustozzi, 'The Taliban Beyond the Pashtuns', The Centre for International Governance Innovation, July 2010, https://www.files.ethz.ch/isn/121069/Afghanistan_Paper_5.pdf
8. Christopher D. Kolenda, 'Slow Failure: Understanding America's Quagmire in Afghanistan', *Journal of Strategic Studies* 42, no. 7 (2019), pp. 992–1014, https://doi.org/10.1080/01402390.2019.1663179
9. Bill Roggio, 'Taliban Calls Afghan Government "Impotent," Says Negotiating with It Is "a Waste of Time"', *Long War Journal*, 28 November 2018, https://www.longwarjournal.org/archives/2018/11/taliban-calls-afghan-government-impotent-says-negotiating-with-it-is-a-waste-of-time.php
10. Steve Brooking, 'Why Was a Negotiated Peace Always Out of Reach in Afghanistan? Opportunities and Obstacles, 2001–21', United States Institute of Peace, August 2022, https://www.usip.org/sites/default/files/2022-08/pw-184-why-negotiated-peace-always-out-of-reach-afghanistan.pdf
11. Nils Wörmer, *Exploratory Talks and Peace Initiatives in Afghanistan: Actors, Demands, Germany's Role as Mediator* (Berlin: Stiftung Wissenschaft und Politik, 2012), https://www.swp-berlin.org/en/publication/afghanistan-peace-initiatives/
12. Wörmer, *Exploratory Talks and Peace Initiatives*.
13. Greg Bruno, 'Saudi Arabia and the Future of Afghanistan', Council on Foreign Relations, 10 December 2008, https://www.cfr.org/backgrounder/taliban-afghanistan#chapter-title-0-4
14. Ibid.
15. Andrew Hammond, 'Saudi Arabia Hosts Taliban Talks to Bolster Pakistan', Reuters, 15 October 2008, https://www.reuters.com/article/idUSLF59145
16. Mona Sheikh and Maja Greenwood, *Taliban Talks: Past, Present and Prospects for The US, Afghanistan and Pakistan* (Copenhagen: Danish Institute for International Studies, 2013), https://www.diis.dk/files/media/publications/import/extra/rp2013-06-taliban-talks_web.jpg.pdf
17. Bjørn Tore Godal, *A Good Ally: Norway in Afghanistan 2001–2014* (Oslo: Norwegian Ministry of Foreign Affairs and Ministry of Defence, 2016), https://www.regjeringen.no/en/dokumenter/nou-2016–8/id2503028/

18. Ibid.
19. Sheikh and Greenwood, *Taliban Talks*.
20. Wörmer, *Exploratory Talks and Peace Initiatives*.
21. Ibid.
22. Henry McDonald, 'We Can Persuade Taliban to Be Peaceful—Expelled EU Man', *The Guardian*, 16 February 2008, https://www.theguardian.com/world/2008/feb/16/afghanistan.terrorism
23. McDonald, 'We Can Persuade Taliban to Be Peaceful'; Mark Tran, 'Senior Afghan Taliban Leaders Arrested in Pakistan', *The Guardian*, 18 February 2010, https://www.theguardian.com/world/2010/feb/18/pakistan-market-bombing-orakzai
24. Godal, *A Good Ally*.
25. Muhammad Riaz Shad and Sajid Iqbal, 'From Intervention to Exit: An Analysis of Post-9/11 US Strategies in Afghanistan', *Margalla Papers* 25, no. 2 (31 December 2021), pp. 23–34, https://doi.org/10.54690/margallapapers.25.2.70
26. Congressional Research Service, 'Qatar: Background and U.S. Relations', Congressional Research Service, 2014, https://www.everycrsreport.com/reports/RL31718.html#fn25
27. Interview with former member of the Taliban Political Office, Doha, Qatar, March 2022.
28. Congressional Research Service, 'Qatar: Background and U.S. Relations'.
29. Interview with Technical Staff Member, Islamic Republic of Afghanistan's negotiating team, Doha, Qatar, November 2021.
30. Interview with Muhammad Suhail Shaheen, Head of the Taliban's Political Office in Doha, Doha, Qatar, December 2024.
31. Interview with Zalmay Mamozy Khalilzad, former U.S. Special Representative for Afghanistan Reconciliation , Doha, Qatar, October 2024.
32. Peter Henne, 'The United Arab Emirates', in *Islamic Politics, Muslim States, and Counterterrorism Tensions* (Cambridge: Cambridge University Press, 2017), pp. 119–46, https://doi.org/10.1017/9781316534328.006; Leonardo Jacopo Maria Mazzucco and Kristian P. Alexander, 'Saudi Arabia and Qatar Are Cooperating with the Taliban. But Their Approaches to Afghanistan Are Different', Atlantic Council, 12 January 2023, https://www.atlanticcouncil.org/blogs/menasource/saudi-arabia-and-qatar-are-cooperating-with-the-taliban-but-their-approaches-to-afghanistan-are-different/
33. Jonathan Fenton-Harvey, 'The UAE's Adaptive Relationship with the Taliban', *The New Arab*, 30 November 2021, https://www.newarab.com/analysis/uaes-adaptive-relationship-taliban
34. Interview with Muhammad Suhail Shaheen.
35. Dania Akkad, 'How Qatar Became the US-Taliban Mediator—and What Happens Next', Middle East Eye, 13 September 2021, https://www.middleeasteye.net/news/qatar-us-taliban-how-became-mediator-talks
36. Interview with H.E. Mohamed bin Ahmad bin Abdullah Al-Misnad, National Security Advisor to the Emir of Qatar, Doha, Qatar, December 2024.

37. Interview with an INGO Managing Director, online via Microsoft Teams, 6 August 2024.
38. Interview with H.E. Ambassador Dr Mutlaq Al-Qahtani, Special Envoy of the Foreign Minister of the State of Qatar for Counterterrorism and Mediation of Conflict Resolution, Doha, Qatar, March 2023.
39. Interview with H.E. Hamad Mohammed Hussein Al-Muftah, Deputy Chief of Mission of the State of Qatar to the United States, Doha, Qatar, August 2024.
40. Observation of the lead author in his capacity as research manager responsible for producing conflict and context analysis reports on behalf of Qatar's Ministry of Foreign Affairs.
41. Interview with INGO Managing Director.
42. International Crisis Group, 'Afghanistan Peace Talks Since 2018: A Timeline', International Crisis Group, 11 August 2020, https://www.crisisgroup.org/asia/south-asia/afghanistan/afghanistan-between-february-2018-and-august-2020-timeline
43. Interview with H.E. Mirdef Alqashouti, Chargé d'Affaires of Qatar for Afghanistan, Doha, Qatar, August 2023.
44. Author observation from working as technical support to the Qatari mediation team and being present throughout much of the sixteen-day negotiations.
45. Interview with Muhammad Suhail Shaheen.
46. Interview with H.E. Mohamed bin Ahmad bin Abdullah Al-Misnad.
47. Interview with H.E. Mirdef Alqashouti.
48. The Economist Intelligence Unit, 'Qatari Mediation Still Needed for US-Taliban Deal', *The Economist Intelligence Unit*, 19 September 2019, https://country.eiu.com/article.aspx?articleid=1288456512&Country=Qatar&topic=Politics&subtopic=Forecast&subsubtopic=International+relations&oid=1858473769
49. France 24, 'Taliban Release Western Hostages in Prisoner Swap', France 24, 19 November 2019, https://www.france24.com/en/20191119-taliban-afghanistan-prisoner-haqqani-usa-king-weeks-australia-professor-khan
50. Interview with H.E. Ambassador Dr Mutlaq Al-Qahtani.
51. Leonardo Jacopo Maria Mazzucco, 'The Gulf States Weigh Trade-Offs of Engaging with the Taliban', Gulf International Forum, 24 November 2022, https://gulfif.org/the-gulf-states-weigh-trade-offs-of-engaging-with-the-taliban/
52. Interview with H.E. Ambassador Dr Mutlaq Al-Qahtani.
53. Ibid.
54. Ibid.
55. Ibid.
56. Al Arabiya, 'Khalid Bin Salman: We Will Continue to Work with Allies to Reach Afghanistan Peace', Al Arabiya, 20 December 2018, https://english.alarabiya.net/News/gulf/2018/12/20/Khalid-bin-Salman-We-will-continue-to-work-with-allies-to-reach-Afghanistan-peace
57. Interview with H.E. Mirdef Alqashouti.
58. Interview with H.E. Ambassador Dr Mutlaq Al-Qahtani.
59. Aamir Latif, 'Taliban Reluctant to Meet US Officials in Pakistan', Anadolu

Agency, 18 January 2019, https://www.aa.com.tr/en/asia-pacific/taliban-reluctant-to-meet-us-officials-in-pakistan/1368622#

60. Latif, 'Taliban Reluctant to Meet US Officials'.
61. Ibid.
62. Interview with H.E. Ambassador Dr Mutlaq Al-Qahtani.
63. Husain Haqqani, 'Pakistan Reaps What It Sowed: How the Country's Support for the Taliban Backfired', *Foreign Affairs*, 23 May 2022, https://www.foreignaffairs.com/articles/afghanistan/2022-05-23/pakistan-reaps-what-it-sowed
64. Ibid.
65. Yelena Biberman and Jared Schwartz, 'Pakistan Is Ready for Stability in Afghanistan', East Asia Forum, 29 March 2019, https://eastasiaforum.org/2019/03/29/pakistan-is-ready-for-stability-in-afghanistan
66. Interview with H.E. Ambassador Dr Mutlaq Al-Qahtani.
67. Ibid.
68. U.S. Department of Defense, *Semiannual Report: Enhancing Security and Stability in Afghanistan ('1225 Report')*, U.S. Department of Defense, 2020, https://media.defense.gov/2021/Apr/23/2002626546/-1/-1/0/ENHANCING-SECURITY-AND-STABILITY-IN-AFGHANISTAN.PDF
69. Hamid Shalizi, Abdul Qadir Sediqi, and Rupam Jain, 'Taliban Step up Attacks on Afghan Forces since Signing U.S. Deal—Data', Reuters, 1 May 2020, https://www.reuters.com/article/us-health-coronavirus-afghanistan-taliba/taliban-step-up-attacks-on-afghan-forces-since-signing-u-s-deal-data-idUSKBN22D5S7
70. Eleonora Ardemagni, 'Still a Mediator: Qatar's Afghan Shot on the International Stage', Institute for International Political Studies, 3 September 2021, https://www.ispionline.it/en/publication/still-mediator-qatars-afghan-shot-international-stage-31542
71. MOFA, 'Security Council Hails Qatar's Role in US-Taliban Negotiations', Ministry of Foreign Affairs in the State of Qatar, 11 March 2020, https://ny.mission.qa/en/media/news/detail/1442/04/16/security-council-hails-qatar's-role-in-us-taliban-negotiations
72. William Maley and Ahmad Shuja Jamal, 'Diplomacy of Disaster: The Afghanistan "Peace Process" and the Taliban Occupation of Kabul', *The Hague Journal of Diplomacy* 17, no. 1 (2022), pp. 32–63, https://doi.org/10.1163/1871191x-bja10089
73. Ibid.
74. David Petraeus, 'Afghanistan Did Not Have to Turn out This Way', *The Atlantic*, 8 August 2022, https://www.theatlantic.com/international/archive/2022/08/us-withdrawal-afghanistan-strategy-shortcomings/670980/
75. John Sopko and David Young, 'The Factors Leading to the Collapse of the Afghan Government and Its Security Forces', Special Inspector General for Afghanistan Reconstruction, 2 March 2023, https://www.sigar.mil/Portals/147/Files/News/Speeches/SIGAR_John_Sopko_David_Young_Berlin_Speech_2023-03-02.pdf

76. International Crisis Group, 'Taking Stock of the Taliban's Perspectives on Peace', International Crisis Group, 11 August 2020, https://www.crisisgroup.org/asia/south-asia/afghanistan/311-taking-stock-talibans-perspectives-peace
77. Scott Worden, 'Breaking the Stalemate: Biden Can Use the U.S.-Taliban Deal to Bring Peace', United States Institute of Peace, 2021, https://www.usip.org/publications/2021/02/breaking-stalemate-biden-can-use-us-taliban-deal-bring-peace
78. Maley and Jamal, 'Diplomacy of Disaster'.
79. Ibid.
80. Baryalai Helali, *An Insider's View: Lessons from the Afghan Peace Process, 2001–2021* (Stockholm: Folke Bernadotte Academy, 2024), https://doi.org/10.61880/JNPH7128
81. Interview with Zalmay Mamozy Khalilzad.
82. Mujib Mashal and Fatima Faizi, 'Afghanistan to Release Last Taliban Prisoners, Removing Final Hurdle to Talks', *The New York Times*, 9 August 2020, https://www.nytimes.com/2020/08/09/world/asia/afghanistan-taliban-prisoners-peace-talks.html
83. Helali, *An Insider's View*, p. 12.
84. Ibid.
85. Ibid.
86. Sansom Milton, Ghassan Elkahlout, and Sana Tariq, 'Qatar's Evolving Role in Conflict Mediation', *Mediterranean Politics* 30, no. 1 (16 October 2023), pp. 53–77, https://doi.org/10.1080/13629395.2023.2266665
87. Ibid.
88. Helali, *An Insider's View*.
89. Milton, Elkahlout, and Tariq, 'Qatar's Evolving Role in Conflict Mediation'.
90. Yaqub Ibrahimi, 'False Negotiations and the Fall of Afghanistan to the Taliban', *International Journal: Canada's Journal of Global Policy Analysis* 77, no. 2 (2022), pp. 168–87, https://doi.org/10.1177/00207020221135299
91. Helali, *An Insider's View*, pp. 13–16.
92. Helali, *An Insider's View*.
93. Ibid., pp. 7–8.
94. Ibid.
95. Ibid., p. 22.
96. Ibid., p. 23.
97. Interview with Muhammad Suhail Shaheen.
98. Shamil Shams and Masood Saifullah, 'Ghani's Last-Ditch Effort to Stop Taliban Gains', Deutsche Welle, 24 June 2021, https://www.dw.com/en/biden-ghani-meeting-afghan-president-makes-last-ditch-effort-to-stop-taliban-gains/a-58034686
99. Helali, *An Insider's View*.
100. Maley and Jamal, 'Diplomacy of Disaster'.
101. Interview with H.E. Ambassador Dr Mutlaq Al-Qahtani.
102. Qatar-Afghanistan Mediation Archive, 'The Qatari Role in Operating Kabul

Airport: A World Perspective', Qatar-Afghanistan Mediation Archive, 28 September 2024, https://qama.qa/2024/09/28/the-qatari-role-in-operating-kabul-airport-a-world-perspective/

103. MOFA, 'Le Monde: Qatar Gave the Afghan Refugees Park View Facilities before the World Cup Fans', Ministry of Foreign Affairs in the State of Qatar, 18 October 2021, https://ny.consulate.qa/en/media/news/detail/1443/03/12/le-monde-qatar-gave-the-afghan-refugees-park-view-facilities-before-the-world-cup-fans; Qatar Foundation, 'Qatar Has Been the Gateway to a Better Life for Us, Says Captain of Afghan Robotics Team', Qatar Foundation, 1 August 2022, https://www.qf.org.qa/stories/qatar-has-been-the-gateway-to-a-better-life-for-us-says-captain-of-afghan
104. Al Jazeera, 'Qatar Lauded for Its Role in Afghanistan Evacuations', Al Jazeera, 30 August 2021, https://www.aljazeera.com/news/2021/8/30/qatar-emerges-as-key-player-in-afghanistan-after-us-pullout
105. Asmahan Qarjouli, 'Exclusive: Mass Evacuation of Afghans "Draining Afghanistan of Its Brains", Qatar's Lolwah Al Khater Says', *Doha News*, 29 August 2021, https://dohanews.co/exclusive-mass-evacuation-of-afghans-draining-afghanistan-of-its-brains-qatars-lolwah-al-khater-says/; Qatar Foundation, 'QF Volunteers Support Afghan Refugees in Qatar', Qatar Foundation, 13 September 2021, https://www.qf.org.qa/stories/qf-volunteers-support-afghan-refugees-in-qatar
106. Al Jazeera, 'Qatar Lauded for Its Role in Afghanistan Evacuations'.
107. UN Office for the Coordination of Humanitarian Affairs, 'High-Level Pledging Event on Supporting the Humanitarian Response in Afghanistan 2022', United Nations Office for the Coordination of Humanitarian Affairs, 31 March 2022, https://www.unocha.org/events/high-level-pledging-event-supporting-humanitarian-response-afghanistan-2022
108. Qatar Red Crescent Society, 'QRCS, KRCS Relieve Affected Population in Afghanistan', Qatar Red Crescent Society, 19 July 2022, https://www.qrcs.org.qa/en/News/Pages/QRCS,-KRCS-relieve-affected-population-in-Afghanistan.aspx?NewsId=51O5pbICUEM; Qatar Red Crescent Society, 'QRCS Online Reporting for Projects in Afghanistan', Qatar Red Crescent Society, https://www.qrcs.org.qa/en/Pages/CountryDetails.aspx?CountryId=/5cV605IEqY=# (accessed 30 April 2025).
109. Fatemeh Salari, 'Qatar Charity Partners with UN to Help Afghan Refugees', *Doha News*, 30 January 2022, https://dohanews.co/qatar-charity-partners-with-un-to-help-afghan-refugees/
110. Asmahan Qarjouli, 'Qatar Supports Students in Afghanistan with 60 Tonnes of Educational Material', *Doha News*, 19 April 2023, https://dohanews.co/qatar-supports-students-in-afghanistan-with-60-tonnes-of-educational-material/
111. Sansom Milton and Ghassan Elkahlout, 'Qatar's Multifaceted Humanitarian Role in Afghanistan since August 2021', *Development Policy Review* 43, no. 1 (8 July 2024), pp. 1–21, https://doi.org/10.1111/dpr.12793
112. The Peninsula, 'QFFD Signs Deal to Support 30,000 Afghan Students', *The*

Peninsula, 22 March 2023, https://thepeninsulaqatar.com/article/22/03/2023/qffd-signs-deal-to-support-30000-afghan-students

113. Oxford Analytica, 'Qatar's Rewarding Afghan Role Carries Future Risks', *Expert Briefings*, 23 September 2021, https://doi.org/10.1108/OXAN-DB264285
114. U.S. Department of State, 'Meeting of U.S. Officials with Taliban Representatives', U.S. Department of State, 31 July 2023, https://2021–2025.state.gov/meeting-of-u-s-officials-with-taliban-representatives/
115. Milton and Elkahlout, 'Qatar's Multifaceted Humanitarian Role'.
116. Interview with Muhammad Suhail Shaheen.
117. Author observation during a closed round table 'Unprecedented Terrains: Deliberating U.S. Policy on Afghanistan under the New Trump Administration and considering Evolving regional Dynamics', Center for Conflict and Humanitarian Studies, Doha, Qatar, 19 February 2025, https://chs-doha.org/en/Events/Pages/Unprecedented-Terrains-Deliberating-US-Policy-on-Afghanistan-under-the-new-Trump-Administration-and-Considering-Evolving-Re.aspx
118. Interview with Country Director 2 of an international humanitarian NGO, online via Microsoft Teams, 6 August 2024.
119. Interview with Country Director 1 of an international humanitarian NGO, online via Microsoft Teams, 5 August 2024.
120. Milton and Elkahlout, 'Qatar's Multifaceted Humanitarian Role'.
121. Asmahan Qarjouli, 'Qatar Helps Facilitate Release of US Aid Worker from Taliban Custody', *Doha News*, 3 April 2022, https://dohanews.co/qatar-helps-facilitate-release-of-us-aid-worker-from-taliban-custody/
122. Al Jazeera, 'Taliban Releases Austrian Far-Right Activist Held in Afghanistan', Al Jazeera, 25 February 2024, https://www.aljazeera.com/news/2024/2/25/taliban-releases-austrian-far-right-activist-held-in-afghanistan
123. Gale, 'The Argentine Who Was Kidnapped for Eight Months in Afghanistan Speaks: "I'm Fine, Back with My Family"', Gale, 4 August 2024, https://link.gale.com/apps/doc/A803949626/IFME?u=anon~f0117489&sid=sitemap&xid=f3277512
124. Jennifer Jett, Abigail Williams, and Mushtaq Yusufzai, 'Two Americans Released from Afghanistan in Deal Struck in Biden's Final Hours in Office', NBC News, 21 January 2025, https://www.nbcnews.com/news/world/american-held-afghanistan-released-final-hours-biden-administration-rcna188496
125. The Peninsula, 'Rubio Praises Qatar's "Reliable" Mediation in American Hostage Release', *The Peninsula*, 21 March 2025, https://s.thepeninsula.qa/nbkvsl

7. DIPLOMACY AMIDST DEVASTATION: QATAR'S MEDIATION IN THE 7 OCTOBER WAR ON GAZA

1. United Nations, *UNGA Resolution 43/177 (A/RES/43/177)* (New York: United Nations, 1988), https://www.un.org/unispal/document/auto-insert-184706/

2. WikiLeaks, 'Doha's Gaza Summit—Qatar Lurches Toward the Radical Camp', WikiLeaks, 19 January 2009, https://wikileaks.jcvignoli.com/cable_09DOHA42
3. Youssef Courbage and Hala Naufal, *Palestinian Worldwide: A Demographic Study* (Doha/Beirut: Arab Center for Research and Policy Studies, 2020), p. 190; Qatar News Agency, 'Qatar's Support for Palestinian Cause… Firm Principles, Noble Humanitarian Values', Qatar News Agency, 21 October 2023, https://www.qna.org.qa/en/News-Area/News/202310/21/0009-qatars-support-for-palestinian-cause-firm-principles,-noble-humanitarian-values
4. Sansom Milton, Ghassan Elkahlout, and Saba Attallah, 'Shrinking Reconstruction Space in the Gaza Strip: Rebuilding after the 2021 and 2022 Wars', *Conflict, Security & Development* 24, no. 1 (4 March 2024), pp. 49–78, https://doi.org/10.1080/14678802.2024.2314034
5. MOFA, 'Qatar Committee for Reconstruction of Gaza Affirms Qatar's Continuous Support for Palestinians', Ministry of Foreign Affairs in the State of Qatar, 4 February 2025, https://mofa.gov.qa/en/qatar/latest-articles/latest-news/details/1442/06/22/qatar-committee-for-reconstruction-of-gaza-affirms-qatar's-continuous-support-for-palestinians
6. World Bank, *Economic Monitoring Report to the Ad Hoc Liaison Committee* (Washington, DC: World Bank, 2016), p. 33, https://documents1.worldbank.org/curated/en/474311473682340785/pdf/108205-V2-WP-PUBLIC-SEPT-14–2PM-September–2016-AHLC-World-Bank-Report.pdf
7. Elia Zureik, 'Qatar's Humanitarian Aid to Palestine', *Third World Quarterly* 39, no. 4 (6 November 2017), pp. 786–98, https://doi.org/10.1080/01436597.2017.1392087; Ghassan Elkahlout, '"Hearts and Minds": Examining the Kuwaiti Humanitarian Model as an Emerging Arab Donor', *Asian Journal of Middle Eastern and Islamic Studies* 14, no. 1 (2 March 2020), pp. 141–57, https://doi.org/10.1080/25765949.2020.1728975; Milton, Elkahlout, and Attallah, 'Shrinking Reconstruction Space'.
8. Interview with H.E. Ambassador Mohammad Al-Emadi, Qatari Envoy to the Gaza Strip and the Chairman of Qatar's Gaza Reconstruction Committee, Doha, Qatar, 3 January 2024; Interview with Mukhaimer Abu Sada, Professor of Political Science at Al-Azhar University in Gaza, Doha, Qatar, 20 August 2024.
9. Bülent Aras and Majed Al Ansari, 'Standing Tall like Caesar? Qatar's Unwavering Voice for Palestine at the United Nations', *Third World Quarterly* 45, no. 9 (10 May 2024), pp. 1458–75, https://doi.org/10.1080/01436597.2024.2346214
10. Kristian Coates Ulrichsen, *Qatar and the Gulf Crisis* (New York: Oxford University Press, 2020).
11. Middle East Monitor, 'Qatar: Hamas Office in Doha Cannot Be Closed Due to Its Importance in Ending the Conflict', Middle East Monitor, 30 October 2023, https://www.middleeastmonitor.com/20231030-qatar-hamas-office-in-doha-cannot-be-closed-due-to-its-importance-in-ending-the-conflict
12. Yousef M. Aljamal, 'Hamas: A Terrorist Organization or Liberation Movement?'

Politics and Religion Journal 8, no. 1 (1 June 2014), pp. 39–58, https://doi.org/10.54561/prj0801039a
13. Tamer Qarmout, 'How the International System Failed', Middle East Eye, 2 February 2024, https://www.middleeasteye.net/opinion/israel-war-gaza-upended-region-what-comes-next
14. Adnan Abu Amer, 'Hamas Ties to Qatar Have Cost', Al-Monitor, 22 April 2013, https://www.al-monitor.com/originals/2013/04/hamas-qatar-relationship-independence.html
15. Interview with Mouin Rabbani, Non-Resident Fellow, Center for Conflict and Humanitarian Studies, Doha, Qatar, May 2025.
16. Mouin Rabbani, 'Qatar and the Palestinians', Jadaliyya, 1 December 2012, https://www.jadaliyya.com/Details/27510
17. Ali Sawafta, 'Palestinian Rivals Agree to Form Unity Government', Reuters, 6 February 2012, https://www.reuters.com/article/world/palestinian-rivals-agree-to-form-unity-government-idUSTRE8150KX
18. Institute for Palestinian Studies (IPS), 'Prospects of Reconciliation after the "Doha Declaration"', Masarat Center, 2 June 2012, https://store.palestine-studies.org/en/node/1635965
19. MOFA, 'Qatar Calls on the International Community to Support Palestinian Reconciliation', Ministry of Foreign Affairs in the State of Qatar, 30 April 2014, https://mofa.gov.qa/en/qatar/latest-articles/latest-news/details/2014/04/30/qatar-calls-on-the-international-community-to-support-palestinian-reconciliation
20. Interview with Mohsen Abu Ramadan, Director of the Dr Haidar Abdel Shafi Center for Culture and Development in Gaza and former Director of the Palestinian Non-Governmental Organization Network, Online, 19 August 2024.
21. Qatar News Agency, 'Palestinian PM to QNA: Qatar Provides Fundamental Political, Moral, Financial Support for Palestinian Cause', Qatar News Agency, 7 June 2021, https://qna.org.qa/en/news/news-details?id=0043-palestinian-pm-to-qna-qatar-provides-fundamental-political,-moral,-financial-support-for-palestinian-cause&date=7/06/2021
22. Tamer Qarmout, 'Predictable in Their Failure: An Analysis of Mediation Efforts to End the Palestinian Split', *International Peacekeeping* 31, no. 4 (15 April 2024), pp. 283–308, https://doi.org/10.1080/13533312.2024.2338410
23. Khalil E. Jahshan, 'The Persistent Illusion of Palestinian Reconciliation', Arab Center Washington DC, 7 August 2023, https://arabcenterdc.org/resource/the-persistent-illusion-of-palestinian-reconciliation/
24. Aras and Al Ansari, 'Standing Tall like Caesar?'
25. Interview with Mouin Rabbani, Non-Resident Fellow, Center for Conflict and Humanitarian Studies, Doha, Qatar, May 2025.
26. Kersten Knipp, 'Gaza Cease-fire', Deutsche Welle, 21 November 2012, https://www.dw.com/en/cairo-mediators-achieve-breakthrough-cease-fire/a-16397749
27. Amena Bakr, 'Qatar Seeks Role as Gaza Mediator, Israel Wary', Reuters,

17 July 2014, https://www.reuters.com/article/world/qatar-seeks-role-as-gaza-mediator-israel-wary-idUSKBN0FM2GD/

28. Amr Hamzawy, 'The Political Impact of the Israel-Hamas Ceasefire', Carnegie Endowment for International Peace, 6 December 2023, https://carnegieendowment.org/posts/2023/12/the-political-impact-of-the-israel-hamas-ceasefire?lang=en
29. Jehad Abusalim, 'The Great March of Return: An Organizer's Perspective', *Journal of Palestine Studies* 47, no. 4 (21 December 2020), pp. 90–100, https://doi.org/10.1525/jps.2018.47.4.90
30. Tariq Dana, 'A Cruel Innovation: Israeli Experiments on Gaza's Great March of Return', *Sociology of Islam* 8, no. 2 (2020), pp. 175–98, https://doi.org/10.1163/22131418-00802003
31. Maram Humaid, 'Fears of More Violence as Palestinians Protest in Gaza', Al Jazeera, 6 April 2018, https://www.aljazeera.com/news/2018/4/6/fears-of-more-violence-as-palestinians-protest-in-gaza
32. Aras and Al Ansari, 'Standing Tall like Caesar?'
33. Amira Schiff, 'The Boy Who Plugs a Dike with His Finger: UN Mediation in the Gaza-Israel Crisis, 2018–2019', *International Negotiation* 27, no. 3 (2022), pp. 386–417, https://doi.org/10.1163/15718069-bja10051
34. Interview with Salah Taha, Director at RAI Consulting, online, October 2022.
35. Q-GRC, 'Grant of HH the Emir of the State of Qatar for the Relief of the Gaza Strip 2018' [in Arabic], Qatar's Gaza Reconstruction Committee, https://q-grc.ps/grants (accessed 5 November 2024).
36. Public lecture delivered by Dr Mutlaq Al-Qahtani, Qatar's Special Envoy of the Minister of Foreign Affairs for Counter-Terrorism and Mediation in Conflict Resolution, 'Qatar's Policy and Experience in Mediation and Conflict Resolution', Doha Institute for Graduate Studies, Doha, Qatar, January 2021.
37. Al-Ra'i Agency, 'Al-Emadi: Qatar's Presence in Gaza Prevented War and Averted a Humanitarian Disaster' [in Arabic], Wikālat al-Ra'ī al-Filasṭīniyya, 19 September 2020, https://alray.ps/ar/post/219679
38. Dan Williams, 'Qatar Says Gaza Aid Spares Israel War, Shows Doha Does Not Back Hamas', Reuters, 22 February 2018, https://www.reuters.com/article/world/qatar-says-gaza-aid-spares-israel-war-shows-doha-does-not-back-hamas-idUSKCN1G62IG
39. Milton, Elkahlout, and Attallah, 'Shrinking Reconstruction Space'.
40. Ghassan Elkahlout (ed.), *Gaza's Cycle of Destruction and Rebuilding: Understanding the Actors, Dynamics, and Responses* (Cham: Palgrave Macmillan, 2024), https://doi.org/10.1007/978-3-031-67198-2
41. Al Jazeera, 'World Reaction to the Israel-Hamas Ceasefire in Gaza', Al Jazeera, 21 May 2021, https://www.aljazeera.com/news/2021/5/21/world-reaction-to-the-israel-hamas-ceasefire-in-gaza; MOFA, 'President of France-Qatar Friendship Group Thanks Qatar for Its Efforts to Reach Ceasefire in Palestine', Ministry of Foreign Affairs in the State of Qatar, 21 May 2021, https://www.mofa.gov.qa/en/all-mofa-news/details/1442/10/09/president-of-france-qatar-friendship-group-thanks-qatar-for-its-efforts-to-reach-ceasefire-in-palestine

42. Hady Amr, Ilan Goldenberg, Kevin Huggard, and Natan Sachs, 'Ending Gaza's Perpetual Crisis: A New U.S. Approach', Brookings, December 2018, https://www.brookings.edu/articles/ending-gazas-perpetual-crisis-a-new-u-s-approach
43. Interview with Mosa Abu Marzouq, Head of Hamas' office in Doha, Doha, Qatar, 7 October 2024.
44. Aras and Al Ansari, 'Standing Tall like Caesar?'
45. Yoel Guzansky and Ofir Winter, 'Two Are Better than One: The Role of Qatar and Egypt in Gaza', Institute for National Security Studies, 25 August 2022, https://www.inss.org.il/publication/qatar-egypt/
46. Interview with Mohammed Al-Aila, Secretary of the Hamas Office for International and Legal Affairs, Doha, Qatar, 19 April 2025.
47. Interview with Husam Badran, Qatar-based senior political officer and spokesman for Hamas, Doha, Qatar, 11 November 2024.
48. Ibrahim Fraihat and Mona Hedaya, 'Understanding the October 7th Hamas Attack on Israel and the War on Gaza', in Ghassan Elkahlout (ed.), *Gaza's Cycle of Destruction and Rebuilding* (Cham: Palgrave Macmillan, 2024), pp. 77–103, https://doi.org/10.1007/978-3-031-67198-2_5
49. Nimer Sultany, 'A Threshold Crossed: On Genocidal Intent and the Duty to Prevent Genocide in Palestine', *Journal of Genocide Research*, 9 May 2024, pp. 1–26, https://doi.org/10.1080/14623528.2024.2351261
50. Ahmad Jamil Azem, 'Qatar and the Repercussions of the October 7 War: Between Managing the Conflict and Solving It', Institute for Palestine Studies, 2024, https://www.palestine-studies.org/en/node/1655085
51. Congress of the United States, 'Letter to President Joseph R. Biden', Congress of the United States, 16 October 2023, https://d12t4t5x3vyizu.cloudfront.net/gottheimer.house.gov/uploads/2023/10/Israel-Hamas-Letter-to-Biden-.pdf
52. Giorgio Cafiero, 'Why Qatar Is the Go-to Mediator in the Gaza War, and Beyond', *The New Arab*, 29 April 2024, https://www.newarab.com/analysis/why-qatar-go-mediator-gaza-war-and-beyond
53. Prabhash K. Dutta, 'From Sudan to Ukraine to Gaza: How Qatar Has Emerged as the Master Mediator', Firstpost, 23 August 2024, https://www.firstpost.com/world/from-sudan-to-ukraine-to-gaza-how-qatar-has-emerged-as-the-master-mediator-13807411.html
54. Patrick Wintour, 'Why Is Qatar Often a Mediator and What Is Its Role in Israel-Hamas War?' *The Guardian*, 21 November 2023, https://www.theguardian.com/world/2023/nov/21/why-is-qatar-often-a-mediator-and-what-is-its-role-in-israel-hamas-war
55. Interview with Husam Badran.
56. Interview with Senior UN official involved in multi-party mediation in the Gaza Strip, Doha, Qatar, 2 December 2024.
57. STRATEGIECS Team, 'The Paths of Political Presence of Hamas Movement in Qatar', STRATEGIECS Think Tank, 28 April 2024, https://strategiecs.com/en/analyses/the-paths-of-political-presence-of-hamas-movement-in-qatar

58. Interview with Mosa Abu Marzouq.
59. Interview with Mohsen Abu Ramadan.
60. Yoel Guzansky and Ilan Zalayat, 'Indispensable Qatar?' Institute for National Security Studies, 27 November 2023, https://www.inss.org.il/publication/qatar-gaza/
61. Benjamin Barthe, Louis Imbert, Hélène Sallon, and Piotr Smolar, 'Israel-Hamas War: Who Are the Five Key Negotiators of the Unattainable Ceasefire?' *Le Monde*, 7 June 2024, https://www.lemonde.fr/en/international/article/2024/06/07/israel-hamas-war-who-are-the-five-key-negotiators-of-the-unattainable-ceasefire_6674144_4.html
62. Natalie Melzer and Wafaa Shurafa, 'Israel's Netanyahu Sends Mossad Director to Gaza Ceasefire Talks in Qatar in Sign of Progress', Associated Press, 12 January 2025, https://apnews.com/article/gaza-israel-palestinians-war-mossad-ceasefire-negotiations-63d38890b4628da8db75e58ba50d6ad9
63. Zena Al Tahhan, 'How Israel Has Repeatedly Rejected Hamas Truce Offers', Al Jazeera, 22 January 2024, https://www.aljazeera.com/features/2024/1/22/how-israel-has-repeatedly-rejected-hamas-truce-offers
64. Al Jazeera, 'Timeline: The Path to the Israel-Hamas Ceasefire Deal in Gaza', Al Jazeera, 19 January 2025, https://www.aljazeera.com/features/2025/1/19/timeline-the-path-to-the-israel-hamas-ceasefire-deal-in-gaza
65. Reuters, 'Israel–Hamas War: The Hostage Deal and Ceasefire Explained', Reuters, 27 November 2023, https://www.reuters.com/world/middle-east/israelhamas-war-hostage-deal-ceasefire-gaza-2023-11-22
66. Andrew Mills, 'How Qatar's Assertive Diplomacy Won a Break in the Gaza War', Reuters, 1 December 2023, https://www.reuters.com/world/middle-east/how-qatar-swayed-israel-hamas-make-truce-work-2023-11-30
67. Mills, 'How Qatar's Assertive Diplomacy Won a Break'.
68. Isabel DeBre, 'In West Bank, Palestinians Rejoice over Release of Women and Minors from Israeli Prisons', PBS News, 25 November 2023, https://www.pbs.org/newshour/world/in-west-bank-palestinians-rejoice-over-release-of-women-and-minors-from-israeli-prisons
69. Al Jazeera, 'Israel-Hamas Truce: How Much Aid Has Entered Gaza?' Al Jazeera, 29 November 2023, https://www.aljazeera.com/news/2023/11/29/israel-hamas-truce-has-it-helped-relieve-gazas-humanitarian-crisis
70. Al Jazeera, '"To Make Lives Easier": Aid Brings Relief in Gaza amid Israel-Hamas Truce', Al Jazeera, 25 November 2023, https://www.aljazeera.com/gallery/2023/11/25/to-make-lives-easier-aid-brings-relief-in-gaza-amid-israel-hamas-truce
71. Al Jazeera, 'The Israel-Hamas Truce Has Ended: What We Know so Far', Al Jazeera, 1 December 2023, https://www.aljazeera.com/news/2023/12/1/the-israel-hamas-truce-has-ended-what-we-know-so-far
72. Dalia Dassa Kaye and Sanam Vakil, 'Only the Middle East Can Fix the Middle East: The Path to a Post-American Regional Order', *Foreign Affairs*, 1 February 2024, https://www.foreignaffairs.com/middle-east/fix-middle-east-united-states

73. Kaye and Vakil, 'Only the Middle East Can Fix the Middle East'.
74. Patrick Wintour, 'Qatar and Egypt "Will Help Form New Palestinian Technocratic Government"', *The Guardian*, 27 February 2024, https://www.theguardian.com/world/2024/feb/27/qatar-and-egypt-will-help-form-new-palestinian-technocratic-government
75. Author observations from closed workshop with a leading Qatari mediator, Doha, Qatar, May 2024.
76. The New Arab, 'What is the Israel-Hamas Gaza Ceasefire Deal Presented by Joe Biden?' *The New Arab*, 1 June 2024, https://www.newarab.com/news/what-gaza-ceasefire-deal-presented-joe-biden
77. Victoria Kim, 'Why the World Fears a War Between Israel and Iran', *The New York Times*, 24 October 2024, https://www.nytimes.com/2024/10/24/world/middleeast/israel-iran-war.html; Jean-Philippe Rémy and Ghazal Golshiri, 'Fear of Regional War Heightens after Iran Missile Attack on Israel', *Le Monde*, 2 October 2024, https://www.lemonde.fr/en/international/article/2024/10/02/fear-of-regional-war-heightens-after-iran-missile-attack-on-israel_6727976_4.html
78. Asmahan Qarjouli, 'Qatar "Re-Evaluating" Mediation Role, Calls out "Exploitation and Abuse" of Efforts', *Doha News*, 17 April 2024, https://dohanews.co/qatar-re-evaluating-mediation-role-calls-out-exploitation-and-abuse-of-efforts/
79. Sultan Barakat, 'Priorities and Challenges of Qatar's Humanitarian Diplomacy', Chr. Michelsen Institute, 2019, https://www.cmi.no/publications/6906-priorities-and-challenges-of-qatars-humanitariandiplomacy
80. Philip Fabian, Nikolaus Harbusch, and Peter Tiede, 'Emir of Qatar in Berlin: Scholz Welcomes the Top Sponsor of Terror' [in German], *Bild*, 12 October 2023, https://www.bild.de/politik/inland/politik-inland/emir-von-katar-in-berlin-scholz-empfaengt-den-top-sponsor-des-terrors-85714334.bild.html
81. Robert Tait, 'US Asks Qatar to "Turn down the Volume" of Al Jazeera News Coverage', *The Guardian*, 27 October 2023, https://www.theguardian.com/media/2023/oct/27/us-asks-qatar-to-turn-down-the-volume-of-al-jazeera-news-coverage
82. Al Jazeera, 'Israel Bans Al Jazeera: What Does It Mean and What Happens Next?' Al Jazeera, 6 May 2024, https://www.aljazeera.com/news/2024/5/6/israel-bans-al-jazeera-what-does-it-mean-and-what-happens-next
83. Al Jazeera, 'Al Jazeera Refutes "Baseless" Israeli Allegations against Ismail Al-Ghoul', Al Jazeera, 1 August 2024, https://www.aljazeera.com/news/2024/8/1/al-jazeera-refutes-baseless-israeli-allegations-against-ismail-al-ghoul
84. Alon Pinkas, 'Qatar Is Part of the Solution to Israel's War in Gaza, Not the Problem', Haaretz.com, 18 April 2024, https://www.haaretz.com/israel-news/2024–04–18/ty-article/.premium/qatar-is-part-of-the-solution-to-gaza-war-not-the-problem/0000018e-f0c4-daad-a3de-fefff8c90000
85. Middle East Monitor, 'France, Germany, UK Join Calls for "Immediate Resumption of Negotiations" in Middle East', Middle East Monitor, 12 August 2024, https://www.middleeastmonitor.com/20240812-france-germany-uk-

join-calls-for-immediate-resumption-of-negotiations-in-middle-east; Qatar News Agency, 'UK, France, Germany, Italy Foreign Ministers Affirm Support for Gaza Mediation Efforts', Qatar News Agency, 17 August 2024, https://qna.org.qa/en/news/news-details?id=0035-uk,-france,-germany,-italy-foreign-ministers-affirm-support-for-gaza-mediation-efforts&date=17/08/2024

86. MOFA, 'Spokesperson for the Ministry of Foreign Affairs: Qatar's Efforts to Mediate between Hamas and Israel Are Currently Stalled', Ministry of Foreign Affairs in the State of Qatar, 9 November 2024, https://mofa.gov.qa/en/qatar/latest-articles/latest-news/details/2024/11/09/spokesperson-for-the-ministry-of-foreign-affairs--qatar's-efforts-to-mediate-between-hamas-and-israel-are-currently-stalled
87. The Peninsula, 'Lack of Serious Negotiations by Participating Parties Pushed Qatar to Suspend Gaza Mediation', *The Peninsula*, 20 November 2024, https://thepeninsulaqatar.com/article/20/11/2024/lack-of-serious-negotiations-by-participating-parties-pushed-qatar-to-suspend-gaza-mediation
88. David Gritten and Rushdi Abualouf, 'Hamas Leaders No Longer in Doha but Office Not Permanently Closed, Qatar Says', BBC News, 19 November 2024, https://www.bbc.com/news/articles/c86qd99nqgyo
89. Joe Inwood and Rushdi Abualouf, 'Qatar Suspends Role as Mediator between Israel and Hamas', BBC News, 9 November 2024, https://www.bbc.com/news/articles/c774d4p2mx6o; Min Jung Lee, Kylie Atwood, Jennifer Hansler, and Alex Marquardt, 'Qatar Agrees to Kick Hamas out of Doha Following US Request, Sources Say', CNN, 9 November 2024, https://edition.cnn.com/2024/11/08/politics/qatar-hamas-doha-us-request/index.html
90. Inwood and Abualouf, 'Qatar Suspends Role as Mediator'.
91. Al Jazeera, 'Qatar Has Suspended Mediation Efforts on Gaza, Foreign Minister Says', Al Jazeera, 9 November 2024, https://www.aljazeera.com/news/2024/11/9/qatar-suspends-mediation-efforts-on-gaza-officials-say
92. Humeyra Pamuk, 'Qatar Open to Reconsidering Hamas Presence in Qatar, US Official Says', Reuters, 27 October 2023, https://www.reuters.com/world/middle-east/qatar-told-us-it-is-open-reconsidering-hamas-presenceus-official-says-2023-10-27/
93. Khalid Al-Jaber and Patrick Theros, 'The Importance of Diplomacy: How Qatari Mediation Is Impacting Gaza', Middle East Council on Global Affairs, 13 June 2024, https://mecouncil.org/blog_posts/the-importance-of-diplomacy-how-qatari-mediation-is-impacting-gaza
94. Al-Jaber and Theros, 'The Importance of Diplomacy'.
95. Interview with Mr Mahmoud Al-Mardawi, senior Hamas leader, online, 24 April 2025.
96. The Peninsula, 'Lack of Serious Negotiations'.
97. Middle East Eye, 'Qatar to Withdraw as Key Mediator in Gaza Ceasefire Talks: Report', Middle East Eye, 9 November 2024, https://www.middleeasteye.net/news/qatar-withdraws-key-mediator-gaza-ceasefire-talks-report
98. Ibid.
99. Tomorrow's Affairs, 'Qatar's Withdrawal from the Peace Process—

Maintaining Influence as an Important Negotiator', Tomorrow's Affairs, 10 November 2024, https://tomorrowsaffairs.com/qatar-s-withdrawal-from-the-peace-processmaintaining-influence-as-an-important-negotiator

100. Irfan Bukhari, 'Gaza Ceasefire Talks in Final Stages: MOFA Spokesperson', *The Peninsula*, 15 January 2025, https://thepeninsulaqatar.com/article/15/01/2025/gaza-ceasefire-talks-in-final-stages-mofa-spokesperson
101. Arab Center Washington DC, 'Full Text of the Ceasefire Agreement That Hamas Has Accepted', Arab Center Washington DC, 6 May 2024, https://arabcenterdc.org/resource/details-of-the-ceasefire-deal-that-hamas-has-accepted/
102. Interview with Mohammed Al-Aila.
103. Al Jazeera, 'Hell Will Break Out: Trump Hints at Military Moves in Mideast, Americas', Al Jazeera, 7 January 2025, https://www.aljazeera.com/news/2025/1/7/hell-will-break-loose-trump-hints-at-military-moves-in-mideast-americas
104. Reuters, 'Israel, Hamas Reach Ceasefire Deal to End 15 Months of War in Gaza', Reuters, 16 January 2025, https://www.reuters.com/world/middle-east/gaza-ceasefire-appears-close-us-egyptian-leaders-put-focus-coming-hours-2025-01-14/
105. Steve Holland, 'Gaza Deal Emerged after Intense 96 Hours, US Officials Say', Reuters, 15 January 2025, https://www.reuters.com/world/gaza-deal-emerged-after-intense-96-hours-us-officials-say-2025-01-15/
106. Samy Magdy, Adam Geller, and Aamer Madhani, 'To Secure Gaza Ceasefire, Dealmakers Overcame Enemies' Deep Distrust', AP News, 23 January 2025, https://apnews.com/article/gaza-ceasefire-deal-negotiators-qatar-biden-trump-israel-hamas-e66fa514aa7215f249e5026b365b80d6
107. Ibid.
108. James Mackenzie and Nayera Abdallah, 'Israel Will Begin Negotiations on Next Phase of Gaza Ceasefire This Week, Minister Says', Reuters, 18 February 2025, https://www.reuters.com/world/middle-east/israel-begin-negotiations-second-phase-gaza-ceasefire-deal-minister-says-2025-02-18/
109. Raffi Berg, 'Is the War Starting Again in Gaza?' BBC News, 18 March 2025, https://www.bbc.com/news/articles/cy5klgv5zv0o
110. Organization of Islamic Cooperation, *Resolution of the Twentieth Extraordinary Session of the Council of Foreign Ministers on Palestine* (OIC/EXCFM-20/2025/Res.Final) (Jeddah: Organisation of Islamic Cooperation, 2025), https://bit.ly/444yiIG; Presidency of the Arab Republic of Egypt, *Cairo Statement Issued by the Extraordinary Arab Summit (Palestine Summit)*, Presidency of the Arab Republic of Egypt, 4 March 2025, https://bit.ly/4dYnu3f
111. Merve Gül Aydoğan Ağlarcı, 'UN Reports Nearly 400,000 Displaced after Gaza Ceasefire Collapse', Anadolu Agency, 7 April 2025, https://www.aa.com.tr/en/middle-east/un-reports-nearly-400–000-displaced-after-gaza-ceasefire-collapse/3530910
112. Lazar Berman and Jacob Magid, 'Witkoff Lands in Doha as Talks Resume with Aim of Extending Fragile Gaza Truce', *The Times of Israel*, 11 March 2025,

https://www.timesofisrael.com/witkoff-lands-in-doha-as-talks-resume-with-aim-of-extending-fragile-gaza-truce/

113. Ibrahim Khazen and Rania Abu Shamala, 'Egypt, Qatar Discuss Efforts to Stabilize Gaza Ceasefire', Anadolu Agency, 12 March 2025, https://www.aa.com.tr/en/middle-east/egypt-qatar-discuss-efforts-to-stabilize-gaza-ceasefire/3507826
114. MOFA, 'Joint Communique of the Five-Member Ministerial Committee on Gaza's Meeting with the US President's Envoy to the Middle East', Ministry of Foreign Affairs in the State of Qatar, 12 March 2025, https://mofa.gov.qa/en/latest-articles/statements/joint-communique-of-the-five-member-ministerial-committee-on-gaza-s-meeting-with-the-us-president's-envoy-to-the-middle-east
115. Julian Borger, 'Hamas Hands Over Six Hostages but Israel Suspends Release of 600 Palestinians', *The Guardian*, 22 February 2025, https://www.theguardian.com/world/2025/feb/22/hamas-releases-six-hostages-exchange-israel-gaza-ceasefire-deal; Qassam Muaddi, 'Netanyahu Suspends Release of 600+ Palestinian Prisoners over "Degrading" Handover Ceremony', Mondoweiss, 23 February 2025, https://mondoweiss.net/2025/02/netanyahu-suspends-release-of-600-palestinian-prisoners-over-degrading-handover-ceremony/
116. Reuters, 'Israel's Far-Right Finance Minister Withdraws Threat to Quit Coalition over Ceasefire Deal', Reuters, 27 January 2025, https://www.reuters.com/world/middle-east/israels-far-right-finance-minister-withdraws-threat-quit-coalition-over-2025-01-27/

8. QATARI MEDIATION AT THE HEART OF GLOBAL CRISES

1. Sansom Milton, Ghassan Elkahlout, and Sana Tariq, 'Qatar's Evolving Role in Conflict Mediation', *Mediterranean Politics* 30, no. 1 (16 October 2023), pp. 53–77, https://doi.org/10.1080/13629395.2023.2266665
2. AKM Ahsan Ullah, 'The Emergence of Qatar's Diplomacy in a Complex World: Balancing Soft Power in Regional Affairs', *World Affairs* 187, no. 4 (5 November 2024), pp. 532–44, https://doi.org/10.1002/waf2.12051
3. MOFA, 'His Highness the Amir Participates in the Opening of the 77th Session of the United Nations General Assembly', Ministry of Foreign Affairs in the State of Qatar, 20 September 2022, https://ny.mission.qa/en/media/news/detail/1444/02/24/hi-highness-the-amir-participates-in-the-opening-of-the-77th-session-of-the-united-nations-general-assembly
4. Al Jazeera, 'Somalia Cuts Diplomatic Ties with Kenya Citing Interference', Al Jazeera, 15 December 2020, https://www.aljazeera.com/news/2020/12/15/somalia-cuts-diplomatic-ties-with-kenya-citing-interferences
5. Desirée Custers, 'Qatar and Somalia-Kenya Relations: Projection of Mediation Power in the Horn of Africa', Stimson Center, 19 May 2021, https://www.stimson.org/2021/qatar-and-somalia-kenya-relations-projection-of-mediation-power-in-the-horn-of-africa

6. Yusuf Ali Mohammed, 'Maritime Border Dispute between Kenya and Somalia in the Indian Ocean', *Mersin University Journal of Maritime Faculty* 5, no. 1 (30 June 2023), pp. 1–6, https://doi.org/10.47512/meujmaf.1230643
7. Birgit Schwarz, 'Nothing to Go Back to—From Kenya's Vast Refugee Camp', Human Rights Watch, 26 May 2016, https://www.hrw.org/news/2016/05/27/nothing-go-back-kenyas-vast-refugee-camp
8. Interview with H.E. Ambassador Dr Mutlaq Al-Qahtani, Special Envoy of the Foreign Minister of the State of Qatar for Counterterrorism and Mediation of Conflict Resolution, Doha, Qatar, 2 August 2023.
9. Somali National News Agency, 'A Communique on the Resumption of Diplomatic Relations between the Republic of Kenya and the Federal Republic of Somalia', Somali National News Agency, 6 May 2021, https://sonna.so/en/a-communique-on-the-resumption-of-diplomatic-relations-between-the-republic-of-kenya-and-the-federal-republic-of-somalia/
10. David Herbling and Mohamed Sheikh Nor, 'Kenya Bans Somalia Flights Days after Qatar-Led détente', Bloomberg, 11 May 2021, https://www.bloomberg.com/news/articles/2021-05-11/kenya-suspends-somalia-flights-days-after-qatar-brokered-detente; Bernard Makong, 'Kenya Rubbishes Impending ICJ Judgment on Somalia Case as Flawed', Capital News, 7 October 2021, https://www.capitalfm.co.ke/news/2021/10/kenya-rubbishes-impending-icj-judgment-on-somalia-case-as-flawed/
11. Mohamed Kahiye, 'Somalia, Kenya Agree to Mend Strained Relations', Voice of America, 8 August 2021, https://www.voanews.com/a/africa_somalia-kenya-agree-mend-strained-relations/6209331.html; Mohamed Gaas, 'Too Early to Celebrate a Somalia–Kenya Rapprochement', Institute for Security Studies, 23 September 2021, https://issafrica.org/iss-today/too-early-to-celebrate-a-somaliakenya-rapprochement
12. Interview with H.E. Ambassador Dr Mutlaq Al-Qahtani.
13. Abdulkadir Khalif, 'Qatari Special Envoy in Somalia Over Electoral Impasse', *The EastAfrican*, 5 May 2021, https://www.theeastafrican.co.ke/tea/news/east-africa/qatari-special-envoy-in-somalia-over-electoral-impasse-3388734; Somaliland Chronicle, 'Breaking: Qatar Offered to Mediate Somaliland—Somalia Talks and Direct Flight of Qatar Airways to Somaliland', *Somaliland Chronicle*, 7 May 2021, https://somalilandchronicle.com/2021/05/07/breaking-qatar-offered-to-mediate-somaliland-and-somalia-talks-and-direct-flight-of-qatar-airways-to-somaliland/
14. Khalif, 'Qatari Special Envoy in Somalia Over Electoral Impasse'.
15. Al Jazeera, 'Somalia Elects New President after Long Overdue Elections', Al Jazeera, 15 May 2022, https://www.aljazeera.com/news/2022/5/15/somalia-elects-hassan-sheikh-mohamud-as-president
16. Altea Pericoli and Federico Donelli, 'Qatar's Foreign Aid and Political Strategies in the Horn of Africa: The Case of Somalia', *Global Policy* 15, no. 1 (26 October 2023), pp. 53–65, https://doi.org/10.1111/1758–5899.13294
17. Morris Kiruga, 'Kenya/Somalia: Is Thawing of Relations a Major Win for Qatar?' *The Africa Report*, 20 July 2021, https://www.theafricareport.com/86429/kenya-somalia-is-thawing-of-relations-a-major-win-for-qatar/

18. MOFA, 'Qatar Affirms that It Is Making Unremitting Efforts Through Mediation to Resolve Conflicts in Africa', Ministry of Foreign Affairs in the State of Qatar, 20 May 2021, https://mofa.gov.qa/en/qatar/latest-articles/latest-news/details/1442/10/08/qatar-affirms-that-it-is-making-unremitting-efforts-through-mediation-to-resolve-conflicts-in-africa
19. Lewis Mudge, 'Chad: How Much Longer Will the Military Council Stay?' Human Rights Watch, 20 April 2022, https://www.hrw.org/news/2022/04/20/chad-how-much-longer-will-military-council-stay
20. Milton, Elkahlout, and Tariq, 'Qatar's Evolving Role in Conflict Mediation'.
21. Interview with H.E. Ambassador Zayed bin Rashid Al Nuaimi, former Director of the African Affairs Department at the Ministry of Foreign Affairs in the State of Qatar, Doha, Qatar, 28 October 2023.
22. Qatar News Agency, 'Doha Peace Agreement: New Success for Qatar in International Mediation, Conflict Resolution', Qatar News Agency, 8 August 2022, https://www.gulf-times.com/story/722404/doha-peace-agreement-new-success-for-qatar-in-international-mediation-conflict-resolution
23. Michael Tantoh, 'Chad: Will the National Dialogue Resume?' AllAfrica.com, 5 September 2022, https://allafrica.com/stories/202209050491.html
24. United Nations, 'Secretary-General's Video Message to the Signing Ceremony of the Doha Peace Agreement between the Chadian Transitional Authorities and Politico-Military Groups', United Nations, 8 August 2022, https://www.un.org/sg/en/content/sg/statement/2022-08-08/secretary-generals-video-message-the-signing-ceremony-of-the-doha-peace-agreement-between-the-chadian-transitional-authorities-and-politico-military-groups-delivered
25. Al Jazeera, 'Deadly Clashes Between Rival Armed Groups Erupt in Libyan Capital', Al Jazeera, 27 August 2022, https://www.aljazeera.com/news/2022/8/27/armed-clashes-erupt-in-central-tripoli
26. United World International, 'Sisi's Visit to Qatar: A Step Towards Resolving the Libyan Crisis', United World International, 2022, https://uwidata.com/sisis-visit-to-qatar-a-step-towards-resolving-the-libyan-crisis/
27. Ibid.
28. Milton, Elkahlout, and Tariq, 'Qatar's Evolving Role in Conflict Mediation', p. 14.
29. Geneva Centre for Security Sector Governance, 'Exploring Armed Groups in Libya: Perspectives on Security Sector Reform in a Hybrid Environment', Geneva Centre for Security Sector Governance, 2020, https://www.dcaf.ch/sites/default/files/publications/documents/ExploringArmedGroupsinLibya.pdf
30. Sansom Milton and Abdulrauf Elgeroshi, 'Libya's Conflict Stalemate: Towards a Multitrack Approach to Stability and Peace', Center for Conflict and Humanitarian Studies Policy Briefing, October 2022, https://chs-doha.org/en/Publications/Pages/Libya-s-Conflict-Stalemate-Towards-a-multitrack-approach-to-stability-and-peace.aspx
31. Safa Alharathy, 'MP Daghim: Saleh Will Allow Parliamentary Elections if He Assumes Presidency of PC', *The Libya Observer*, 15 September 2022, https://

libyaobserver.ly/news/mp-daghim-saleh-will-allow-parliamentary-elections-if-he-assumes-presidency-pc

32. Reuters, 'Libyan Parliament Speaker Says Election Plan Approved', Reuters, 9 September 2021, https://www.reuters.com/world/africa/libyan-parliament-speaker-says-election-plan-approved-2021-09-09/
33. U.S. Embassy—Libya (@USEmbassyLibya), 'Status: 1611090046316077094', X (formerly Twitter), 5 January 2023, https://x.com/USEmbassyLibya/status/1611090046316077094
34. Giorgio Cafiero, 'Qatar's Careful Balance between Ukraine and Russia', *Doha News*, 9 August 2023, https://dohanews.co/qatars-careful-balance-between-ukraine-and-russia
35. Al Jazeera, 'Ukrainian Children Repatriated from Russia through Qatari Mediation', Al Jazeera, 16 October 2023, https://www.aljazeera.com/news/2023/10/16/ukrainian-children-repatriated-from-russia-through-qatari-mediation;' RBC, 'Katar Soobshchil o Posrednichestve v Peredache 4 Detey Iz Rossii Na Ukrainu' [in Russian], RBC Group, 16 October 2023, https://www.rbc.ru/politics/16/10/2023/652cef4c9a7947745bb4a19f
36. Al Jazeera, 'Ukrainian Children Repatriated from Russia through Qatari Mediation'.
37. International Criminal Court, 'Situation in Ukraine: ICC Judges Issue Arrest Warrants against Vladimir Vladimirovich Putin and Maria Alekseyevna Lvova-Belova', International Criminal Court, 17 March 2023, https://www.icc-cpi.int/news/situation-ukraine-icc-judges-issue-arrest-warrants-against-vladimir-vladimirovich-putin-and
38. Al Jazeera, 'Ukrainian Children Repatriated from Russia through Qatari Mediation'.
39. Andrew Mills and Max Hunder, 'Six Ukrainian Children to Be Returned from Russia through Qatari Mediation', Reuters, 5 December 2023, https://www.reuters.com/world/europe/embargoed-six-ukrainian-children-be-returned-russia-through-qatari-mediation-2023-12-05/
40. Mary O'Connor, 'Joy for Six Ukrainian Children as They Are Reunited with Their Families Following Qatar-Brokered Deal with Moscow 20 Months after They Were Snatched by Russia', Daily Mail Online, 5 December 2023, https://www.dailymail.co.uk/news/article-12827325/Joy-six-Ukrainian-children-reunited-families-following-Qatar-brokered-deal-Moscow-20-months-snatched-Russia
41. Qatar News Agency, 'Reuniting Ukrainian Families… Qatar Reinforces New Concept of Humanitarian Diplomacy', Qatar News Agency, 15 June 2024, https://www.qna.org.qa/en/newsbulletins/2024-06/15/0012-reuniting-ukrainian-families-qatar-reinforces-new-concept-of-humanitarian-diplomacy
42. Al Jazeera, 'Qatar Hails Mediation "Milestone" as It Hosts Freed Ukrainian, Russian Kids', Al Jazeera, 25 April 2024, https://www.aljazeera.com/news/2024/4/25/qatar-hails-mediation-milestone-as-it-hosts-freed-ukrainian-russian-kids
43. MOFA, 'Qatar Pledges USD 100 Million for Humanitarian Assistance to

Ukraine', Ministry of Foreign Affairs in the State of Qatar, 28 July 2023, https://mofa.gov.qa/en/qatar/latest-articles/latest-news/details/1445/01/10/qatar-pledges-usd-100-million-for-humanitarian-assistance-to-ukraine
44. Ibid.
45. MOFA, 'Qatar Announces $3 Million Commitment to Ukrainian Parliament Commissioner Office for Human Rights', Ministry of Foreign Affairs in the State of Qatar, 26 April 2024, https://mofa.gov.qa/en/qatar/latest-articles/latest-news/details/1445/03/05/prime-minister-and-minister-of-foreign-affairs-meets-venezuela's-foreign-minister
46. O'Connor, 'Joy for Six Ukrainian Children'.
47. Al Jazeera, 'Zelenskyy Thanks Qatar for Role in Returning Ukraine Children on Doha Visit', Al Jazeera, 5 June 2024, https://www.aljazeera.com/news/2024/6/5/zelenskyy-thanks-qatar-for-role-in-returning-ukraine-children-on-doha-visit
48. President of Russia, 'Meeting with Emir of Qatar Sheikh Tamim Bin Hamad Al Thani', President of Russia, 4 July 2024, http://en.kremlin.ru/events/president/news/74468
49. Cathrin Schaer, 'Israel-Hamas Ceasefire: Why Qatar Is Such a Good Negotiator', Deutsche Welle, 16 January 2025, https://www.dw.com/en/israel-hamas-ceasefire-why-qatar-is-such-a-good-negotiator/a-69995458
50. Al Jazeera, 'Qatar to Act as US Diplomatic Representative in Afghanistan', Al Jazeera, 12 November 2021, https://www.aljazeera.com/news/2021/11/12/qatar-to-act-as-us-diplomatic-representative-in-afghanistan
51. Imad K. Harb, 'Qatar's New Designation as US Non-NATO Ally Serves Multiple Purposes', Arab Center Washington DC, 4 February 2022, https://arabcenterdc.org/resource/qatars-new-designation-as-us-non-nato-ally-serves-multiple-purposes
52. Ali Bakir, 'Washington's Dilemma over Hamas in Qatar', Middle East Council on Global Affairs, 8 April 2024, https://mecouncil.org/blog_posts/washingtons-dilemma-over-hamas-in-qatar/
53. Christopher M. Blanchard, 'Qatar: Issues for the 118th Congress (Updated 15 February 2024)', Congressional Research Service, 2024, https://sgp.fas.org/crs/mideast/R47467.pdf
54. MOFA, 'Prime Minister and Minister of Foreign Affairs Meets Venezuela's Foreign Minister', Ministry of Foreign Affairs in the State of Qatar, 20 September 2023, https://mofa.gov.qa/en/qatar/latest-articles/latest-news/details/1445/03/05/prime-minister-and-minister-of-foreign-affairs-meets-venezuela's-foreign-minister
55. Al Jazeera, 'Venezuela, US Reach Prisoner Swap Deal as Tensions Ease', Al Jazeera, 20 December 2023, https://www.aljazeera.com/news/2023/12/20/venezeula-us-reach-prisoner-swap-deal
56. The Peninsula, 'Qatar's Successful Mediation Leads to US, Venezuela Prisoner Exchange', *The Peninsula*, 21 December 2023, https://thepeninsulaqatar.com/article/21/12/2023/qatars-successful-mediation-leads-to-us,-venezuela-prisoner-exchange

57. Tanner Manley and Leily Rossi, 'Mediating Multipolarity: Qatar's Role in U.S.-Venezuela Negotiations', Carnegie Endowment for International Peace, 5 September 2023, https://carnegieendowment.org/sada/2023/09/mediating-multipolarity-qatars-role-in-us-venezuela-negotiations?lang=en
58. Asmahan Qarjouli, 'Qatar and Venezuela Take on Bilateral Ties in Doha Meeting', *Doha News*, 9 October 2023, https://dohanews.co/qatar-and-venezuela-take-on-bilateral-ties-in-doha-meeting
59. Shaher Zakaria, 'Qatar's Mediation between the United States and Venezuela', *The Peninsula*, 18 July 2024, https://thepeninsulaqatar.com/opinion/18/07/2024/qatars-mediation-between-the-united-states-and-venezuela
60. Manley and Rossi, 'Mediating Multipolarity'.
61. Ibid.
62. Erick Viramontes, *Looking towards the South: Qatar's National Vision and Its Latin American Horizon*, Gulf Studies Center (Qatar University) Working Paper no. 2 (August 2021), https://www.qu.edu.qa/siteimages/static_file/qu/research/gulf%20studies/documents/working%20paper%202%20-%20erick%20viramontes%20-%202021.pdf; Qatar Chamber, 'Qatar Chamber Explores Cooperation Links with Latin American Countries', Qatar Chamber, 28 May 2024, https://www.qatarchamber.com/qatar-chamber-cooperation-latin-american-countries
63. Tanner Manley, 'Qatar's Next Diplomatic Step in Latin America?' Middle East Council on Global Affairs, 21 November 2023, https://mecouncil.org/blog_posts/qatars-next-diplomatic-step-in-latin-america
64. Jacqueline Anne Braveboy-Wagner, *The Venezuela-Guyana Border Dispute: Britain's Colonial Legacy in Latin America* (New York: Routledge, 2019); Janette Bulkan, 'The Limits of State Territorialisation: Geopolitics and Petroleum in Guyana', *Social and Economic Studies* 70, nos 3 & 4 (2021), pp. 72–105.
65. Sultan Al-Khulaifi, 'DRC's Conflict Demands a New Peace Model Rooted in Inclusion and Reform', Al Jazeera, 23 May 2025, https://www.aljazeera.com/opinions/2025/5/23/drcs-conflict-demands-a-new-peace-model-rooted-in-inclusion-and-reform
66. International Crisis Group, 'Fall of DRC's Goma: Urgent Action Needed to Avert a Regional War', International Crisis Group, 28 January 2025, https://www.crisisgroup.org/africa/great-lakes/democratic-republic-congo/fall-drcs-goma-urgent-action-needed-avert-regional-war
67. Obi Anyadike, 'Goma Capture Sparks Fears of Deeper Regional Conflict as Rwanda-Backed Rebels Push South', The New Humanitarian, 31 January 2025, https://www.thenewhumanitarian.org/news-feature/2025/01/31/drc-goma-capture-sparks-fears-deeper-regional-conflict-rwanda-backed-rebels-m23
68. Middle East Monitor, 'Tripartite Summit Brings Qatari Emir and Rwanda and Congo Presidents Together', Middle East Monitor, 19 March 2025, https://www.middleeastmonitor.com/20250319-tripartite-summit-brings-qatari-emir-and-rwanda-and-congo-presidents-together/
69. Al Jazeera, 'DR Congo, M23 Rebels Announce Ceasefire after Peace Talks in

Qatar', Al Jazeera, 24 April 2025, https://www.aljazeera.com/news/2025/4/24/drc-m23-rebels-commit-to-pause-fighting-amid-peace-talks

70. Andrew Mills and Ange Adihe Kasongo, 'Qatar Presents Draft Peace Proposal to Congo and M23 Rebels, Source Says', Reuters, 5 June 2025, https://www.reuters.com/world/middle-east/qatar-presents-draft-peace-proposal-congo-m23-rebels-source-says-2025-06-05/
71. Asmahan Qarjouli, 'DRC, Rwanda to Sign Peace Deal June 27 Following Qatar's Mediation', *Doha News*, 19 June 2025, https://dohanews.co/drc-rwanda-to-sign-peace-deal-june-27-following-qatars-mediation/; U.S. Department of State, 'Joint Statement on Peace Talks between the Democratic Republic of the Congo and the Republic of Rwanda, Mediated by the United States and Observed by the State of Qatar', U.S. Department of State, 18 June 2025, https://www.state.gov/releases/office-of-the-spokesperson/2025/06/joint-statement-on-peace-talks-between-the-democratic-republic-of-the-congo-and-the-republic-of-rwanda-mediated-by-the-united-states-and-observed-by-the-state-of-qatar/
72. Gulf Times, 'Qatar Attends Rwanda-DRC Peace Deal Signing', *Gulf Times*, 28 June 2025, https://www.gulf-times.com/article/706662/qatar/qatar-attends-rwanda-drc-peace-deal-signing
73. Colloquially referred to as the 2015 Iran nuclear deal or Iran nuclear agreement.
74. Al Jazeera, 'US and Iran Release Prisoners after $6bn Transfer', Al Jazeera, 18 September 2023, https://www.aljazeera.com/news/2023/9/18/five-americans-land-in-doha-after-release-in-us-iran-prisoner-swap
75. Arab News, 'Qatar Steps up Its Mediation Role in US-Iran Nuclear Negotiations', *Arab News*, 8 March 2022, https://arab.news/c4uhu
76. Al Jazeera, 'US and Iran Release Prisoners'.
77. Al Jazeera, '"Important Step": What We Know about Tentative US-Iran Prisoner Deal', Al Jazeera, 11 August 2023, https://www.aljazeera.com/news/2023/8/11/important-step-what-we-know-about-tentative-us-iran-prisoner-deal
78. Al Jazeera, 'Biden Thanks Qatar's Emir for Rare Iran-US Prisoner Swap Deal', Al Jazeera, 3 October 2023, https://www.aljazeera.com/news/2023/10/3/biden-thanks-qatars-emir-for-rare-iran-us-prisoner-swap-deal
79. Islamic Republic News Agency, 'Iran FM Thanks Qatar for Mediating Prisoner Swap with US', Islamic Republic News Agency, 21 September 2023, https://en.irna.ir/news/85235323/Iran-FM-thanks-Qatar-for-mediating-prisoner-swap-with-US; Al Jazeera, 'US and Iran Release Prisoners'.
80. Ministry of Foreign Affairs of the Islamic Republic of Iran, 'Statement by the Ministry of Foreign Affairs on the release of seized Iranian resources and the release of a number of prisoners illegally detained by the United States', Ministry of Foreign Affairs of the Islamic Republic of Iran, 3 August 2023, https://mfa.gov.ir/portal/NewsView/727109; Mardo Soghom, 'Iran Contradicts US, Denying Restrictions on Unfrozen Funds', Iran International, 12 August 2023, https://www.iranintl.com/en/202308122240

81. MOFA, 'Qatar Praises New Deal Between Iran, IAEA', Ministry of Foreign Affairs in the State of Qatar, 9 March 2024, https://mofa.gov.qa/en/qatar/latest-articles/latest-news/details/1444/08/16/qatar-praises-new-deal-between-iran-iaea
82. MOFA, 'Qatar Urges Iran, IAEA to Continue Cooperation to Resolve Standing Issues in Iranian Nuclear Program', Ministry of Foreign Affairs in the State of Qatar, 13 September 2023, https://mofa.gov.qa/en/qatar/latest-articles/latest-news/details/1445/02/28/qatar-urges-iran-iaea-to-continue-cooperation-to-resolve-standing-issues-in-iranian-nuclear-program
83. Middle East Monitor, 'Iran Concessions to IAEA Largely Hinge on Future Talks—IAEA', Middle East Monitor, 6 March 2023, https://www.middleeastmonitor.com/20230306-iran-concessions-to-iaea-largely-hinge-on-future-talks-iaea; Middle East Monitor, 'Qatar Praises New Agreement between Iran, IAEA', Middle East Monitor, 9 March 2023, https://www.middleeastmonitor.com/20230309-qatar-praises-new-agreement-between-iran-iaea
84. MOFA, 'Qatar Welcomes Hosting Indirect Talks between the United States and Iran in Doha to Revive the Nuclear Deal', Ministry of Foreign Affairs in the State of Qatar, 28 June 2024, https://mofa.gov.qa/en/statements/qatar-welcomes-hosting-indirect-talks-between-the-united-states-and-iran-in-doha-to-revive-the-nuclear-deal
85. Reuters, 'US Envoy Asked Middle East Foreign Ministers to Mediate with Iran', Reuters, 11 April 2024, https://www.reuters.com/world/middle-east/us-envoy-asked-middle-east-foreign-ministers-mediate-with-iran-2024-04-11/
86. Giorgio Cafiero, 'Gaza War Spotlights Qatar's Role as a Regional Mediator', *The New Arab*, 6 November 2023, https://www.newarab.com/analysis/gaza-war-spotlights-qatars-role-regional-mediator
87. Foundation for Defense of Democracies, 'Iran Appeals to Qatar, Oman to Revive Nuclear Talks', Foundation for Defense of Democracies, 15 June 2025, https://www.fdd.org/analysis/2025/06/15/iran-appeals-to-qatar-oman-to-revive-nuclear-talks/; Parisa Hafezi, Samia Nakhoul, and Andrew Mills, 'Iran Sought US Pressure on Israel for Ceasefire via Gulf States, Sources Say', Reuters, 16 June 2025, https://www.reuters.com/world/middle-east/iran-asks-gulf-arab-states-have-trump-press-israel-immediate-ceasefire-sources-2025-06-16/https://www.reuters.com/world/middle-east/us-envoy-asked-middle-east-foreign-ministers-mediate-with-iran-2024-04-11/; Asmahan Qarjouli, 'Iran Tells Mediators Qatar, Oman It Will Not Negotiate "While under Attack"', *Doha News*, 16 June 2025, https://dohanews.co/iran-tells-mediators-qatar-oman-it-will-not-negotiate-while-under-attack/;
88. Hafsa Adil, 'Calm Returns to Qatar Following Iran's Attack on Al Udeid Airbase', Al Jazeera, 24 June 2025, https://www.aljazeera.com/news/2025/6/24/calm-returns-to-qatar-following-irans-attack-on-al-udeid-airbase
89. MOFA, 'Advisor to Prime Minister and Official Spokesperson for Ministry of Foreign Affairs: Qatar Strongly Condemns Attack That Targeted Al-Udeid Air

Base', Ministry of Foreign Affairs in the State of Qatar, 23 June 2025, https://mofa.gov.qa/en/qatar/latest-articles/latest-news/details/2025/06/23/advisor-to-prime-minister-and-official-spokesperson-for-ministry-of-foreign-affairs--qatar-strongly-condemns-attack-that-targeted-al-udeid-air-base
90. PressTV, 'FM Says Iran Committed to Enhance Ties with Qatar after Retaliatory Strike on US Base', PressTV, 24 June 2025, https://www.presstv.ir/Detail/2025/06/24/750099/fm-says-iran-committed-enhance-ties-qatar-retaliatory-strike-us-base
91. Ravi Hari, 'Donald Trump Calls Iran's Missile Strike a "Very Weak Response", Praises Qatar's Emir', *LiveMint*, 24 June 2025, https://www.livemint.com/news/us-news/donald-trump-calls-iran-s-missile-strike-a-very-weak-response-praises-qatar-s-emir-11750709646382.html

9. PILLARS OF QATARI MEDIATION

1. The Amiri Diwan, 'The Constitution of the State of Qatar', The Amiri Diwan, https://www.diwan.gov.qa/-/media/Diwan-Amiri/Files/Constitution-EN.ashx?la=en (accessed 25 February 2025).
2. Interview with a senior official at the Qatari Ministry of Foreign Affairs (MOFA), Doha, Qatar, February 2020.
3. The Amiri Diwan, 'Sheikh Jassim Bin Mohammed Bin Thani', The Amiri Diwan, https://www.diwan.gov.qa/about-qatar/qatars-rulers/sheikh-jassim-bin-mohammed-bin-thani?sc_lang=en (accessed 25 February 2025).
4. The Peninsula, 'Qatar Consistent in Helping the Oppressed', *The Peninsula*, 23 October 2014, https://thepeninsulaqatar.com/article/23/10/2014/qatar-consistent-in-helping-the-oppressed
5. Interview with H.E. Ambassador Zayed bin Rashid Al-Nuaimi, former Ambassador of the State of Qatar to Lebanon (1991–2001), Eritrea (2005–11), and Bulgaria (2012–16), Doha, Qatar, 29 November 2023.
6. Interview with H.E. Mirdef Alqashouti, Chargé d'Affaires of Qatar for Afghanistan, Doha, Qatar, August 2023.
7. Sultan Barakat and Sansom Milton, '8 Qatar: Conflict Mediation and Regional Objectives', in Agnieszka Paczyńska (ed.), *The New Politics of Aid: Emerging Donors and Conflict-Affected States* (Boulder, CO: Lynne Rienner Publishers, 2020), p. 142, https://doi.org/10.1515/9781626378407-009
8. Interview with H.E. Mohamed bin Ahmad bin Abdullah Al-Misnad.
9. Interview with H.E. Ambassador Mohammed bin Ali Al-Nuaimi.
10. Interview with H.E. Ambassador Mohammad Al-Emadi, Qatari Envoy to the Gaza Strip and the Chairman of Qatar's Gaza Reconstruction Committee, Doha, Qatar, 3 January 2024.
11. Interview with H.E. Ambassador Ali bin Hassan Al-Hammadi, former Qatari Ambassador to Sudan, and former Secretary-General of the Qatar Red Crescent, Doha, Qatar, 14 August 2023.
12. Interview with H.E. Dr Hamad Mohammed Hussein Al-Muftah, Deputy Chief of Mission of the State of Qatar to the United States, Doha, Qatar, August 2024.

13. Interview with senior UN official involved in multi-party mediation in the Gaza Strip, Doha, Qatar, December 2024.
14. Mirdef Alqashouti, 'Qatar Mediation: From Soft Diplomacy to Foreign Policy', in Mahjoob Zweiri and Farah Qawasmi (eds), *Contemporary Qatar: Examining State and Society*, vol. 4 (Singapore: Springer, 2021), pp. 73–92, https://doi.org/10.1007/978-981-16-1391-3_6
15. Interview with H.E. Dr Hamad Mohammed Hussein Al-Muftah.
16. Ruslan Minich, 'Conflict Mediation: The Qatari Experience', *Historia i Polityka* 14, no. 21 (24 November 2015), p. 121, https://doi.org/10.12775/hip.2015.026
17. Ibrahim Karataş, 'Qatar's Return to Mediation Diplomacy: What Changed?' AlSharq Strategic Research, 21 June 2022, https://research.sharqforum.org/2022/06/21/return-to-mediation-diplomacy/
18. Sansom Milton, Ghassan Elkahlout, and Sana Tariq, 'Qatar's Evolving Role in Conflict Mediation', *Mediterranean Politics* 30, no. 1 (16 October 2023), pp. 1–25, https://doi.org/10.1080/13629395.2023.2266665
19. Interview with H.E. Dr Abdulaziz bin Mohamed Al-Horr, Director of the Diplomatic Institute, Ministry of Foreign Affairs of the State of Qatar, Doha, Qatar, October 2024.
20. Sansom Milton and Ghassan Elkahlout, 'Qatar's Multifaceted Humanitarian Role in Afghanistan since August 2021', *Development Policy Review* 43, no. 1 (8 July 2024), https://doi.org/10.1111/dpr.12793
21. Milton, Elkahlout, and Tariq, 'Qatar's Evolving Role in Conflict Mediation'.
22. Ignacio Álvarez-Ossorio and Leticia Rodríguez García, 'The Foreign Policy of Qatar: From a Mediating Role to an Active One', *Revista Española de Ciencia Política* 56 (26 July 2021), pp. 97–120. https://doi.org/10.21308/recp.56.04
23. Interview with H.E. Ambassador Zayed bin Rashid Al-Nuaimi.
24. Interview with H.E. Dr Majid Al-Ansari, Spokesperson for the Ministry of Foreign Affairs in the State of Qatar, Doha, Qatar, 1 August 2024.
25. Mehran Kamrava, 'Mediation and Qatari Foreign Policy', *The Middle East Journal* 65, no. 4 (1 September 2011), pp. 539–56, https://doi.org/10.3751/65.4.11
26. Sultan Barakat, 'Qatari Mediation: Between Ambition and Achievement', Brookings Doha Center, November 2014, https://www.brookings.edu/wp-content/uploads/2016/06/Final-PDF-English.pdf
27. Interview with H.E. Mirdef Alqashouti; Interview with Dr Mehran Kamrava, Professor of Government at Georgetown University-Qatar and Director of Iranian Studies Unit at the Arab Center for Research and Policy Studies. Doha, Qatar, 25 September 2023.
28. Interview with H.E. Mohamed bin Ahmad bin Abdullah Al-Misnad, National Security Advisor to the Emir of Qatar, Doha, Qatar, December 2024.
29. Ibid.
30. Interview with Zalmay Mamozy Khalilzad, former U.S. Special Representative for Afghanistan Reconciliation, Doha, Qatar, October 2024.
31. Al Jazeera, 'Qatar Lauded for Its Role in Afghanistan Evacuations', Al Jazeera,

30 August 2021, https://www.aljazeera.com/news/2021/8/30/qatar-emerges-as-key-player-in-afghanistan-after-us-pullout

32. Ghassan Elkahlout and Sansom Milton, 'The Evolution of the Gulf States as Humanitarian Donors', *Third World Quarterly* 45, no. 15–16 (10 July 2023), pp. 2246–65, https://doi.org/10.1080/01436597.2023.2229742

BIBLIOGRAPHY

Abdulfatah, Mohamed, 'Qatari Peace Mediation and Humanitarian Aid in Sudan: Lessons from the War in Darfur 2003–2022', *Journal of Peacebuilding & Development* 20, no. 1 (2025), https://doi.org/10.1177/15423166241312874

Abdullah, Abdulkhaleq, 'The Gulf Cooperation Council: Nature, Origin, and Process', in Michael Hudson (ed.), *Middle East Dilemma: The Politics and Economics of Arab Integration* (New York: Columbia University Press, 1999), pp. 150–70.

Aboudouh, Ahmed, 'The Fatah–Hamas Agreement Increases Chinese Influence in Palestinian Affairs. But the Road to Unity Is Rocky', Chatham House, 24 July 2024, https://www.chathamhouse.org/2024/07/fatah-hamas-agreement-increases-chinese-influence-palestinian-affairs-road-unity-rocky

Abu Amer, Adnan, 'Hamas Ties to Qatar Have Cost', Al-Monitor, 22 April 2013, https://www.al-monitor.com/originals/2013/04/hamas-qatar-relationship-independence.html

Abu-Nimer, Mohammed, 'Conflict Resolution Approaches', *The American Journal of Economics and Sociology* 55, no. 1 (January 1996), pp. 35–52, https://doi.org/10.1111/j.1536-7150.1996.tb02706.x

———, *Nonviolence and Peace Building in Islam: Theory and Practice* (Gainesville, FL: University Press of Florida, 2003).

Abu-Nimer, Mohammed, and Timothy Seidel, 'Culture, Religion and Politics in International Mediation', in Alexia Georgakopoulos (ed.), *The Mediation Handbook: Research, Theory, and Practice* (New York: Routledge, 2017), pp. 324–33, https://doi.org/10.4324/9781315648330

Abusalim, Jehad, 'The Great March of Return: An Organizer's Perspective', *Journal of Palestine Studies* 47, no. 4 (21 December 2020), pp. 90–100, https://doi.org/10.1525/jps.2018.47.4.90

Abushouk, Ahmed Ibrahim, 'Qatar: From a Tribal Confederacy to a Modern State', in Mahjoob Zweiri and Farah Al Qawasmi (eds), *Contemporary Qatar: Examining State and Society*, 1st edn (Singapore: Springer, 2021), pp. 9–22.

Adil, Hafsa, 'Calm Returns to Qatar Following Iran's Attack on Al Udeid Airbase', Al Jazeera, 24 June 2025, https://www.aljazeera.com/news/2025/6/24/calm-returns-to-qatar-following-irans-attack-on-al-udeid-airbase

BIBLIOGRAPHY

Africa Defense Forum, 'UAE Role in Sudan's Civil War Draws Criticism', *Africa Defense Forum*, 30 January 2024, https://adf-magazine.com/2024/01/uae-role-in-sudans-civil-war-draws-criticism/

African Development Bank Group, 'Sudan—Update of the Country Brief 2017–2019 to December 2021', African Development Bank Group, 1 December 2021, https://www.afdb.org/en/documents/sudan-update-country-brief-2017-2019-december-2021

———, 'Sudan Poverty Profile: Summary Results of the 2014–2015 National Baseline Household Budget Survey', African Development Bank Group, 2018, https://www.afdb.org/fileadmin/uploads/afdb/Documents/Publications/Brief-Sudan_Poverty_Profile_2014-2015_-_Key_Findings.pdf

African Studies Centre, 'Eritrea-Sudan: Text of Agreement Signed in Qatar, 5/4/99', University of Pennsylvania—African Studies Center, 3 May 1999, https://www.africa.upenn.edu/Hornet/irin_5499.html

African Union, 'Report of the African Union High-Level Panel on Darfur (AUPD)', African Union, 29 October 2009, https://archives.au.int/handle/123456789/8263

Akarli, Engin Deniz, *The Long Peace: Ottoman Lebanon, 1861–1920*, 1st edn (Oakland, CA: University of California Press, 1993).

Akkad, Dania, 'How Qatar Became the US-Taliban Mediator—and What Happens Next', Middle East Eye, 13 September 2021, https://www.middleeasteye.net/news/qatar-us-taliban-how-became-mediator-talks

Al Arabiya, 'Khalid Bin Salman: We Will Continue to Work with Allies to Reach Afghanistan Peace', Al Arabiya, 20 December 2018, https://english.alarabiya.net/News/gulf/2018/12/20/Khalid-bin-Salman-We-will-continue-to-work-with-allies-to-reach-Afghanistan-peace

Al Hassan, Omar, 'The GCC's Formation: The Official Version', Al Jazeera Centre for Studies, 30 March 2015, https://studies.aljazeera.net/en/dossiers/2015/03/201533011258831763.html

Al Jazeera, 'Al Jazeera Refutes "Baseless" Israeli Allegations against Ismail Al-Ghoul', Al Jazeera, 1 August 2024, https://www.aljazeera.com/news/2024/8/1/al-jazeera-refutes-baseless-israeli-allegations-against-ismail-al-ghoul

———, 'Analysts: Qatar Supports Gaza Not Hamas', Al Jazeera, 7 June 2017, https://www.aljazeera.com/features/2017/6/7/analysts-qatar-supports-gaza-not-hamas

———, 'Biden Thanks Qatar's Emir for Rare Iran-US Prisoner Swap Deal', Al Jazeera, 3 October 2023, https://www.aljazeera.com/news/2023/10/3/biden-thanks-qatars-emir-for-rare-iran-us-prisoner-swap-deal

———, 'Deadly Clashes Between Rival Armed Groups Erupt in Libyan Capital', Al Jazeera, 27 August 2022, https://www.aljazeera.com/news/2022/8/27/armed-clashes-erupt-in-central-tripoli

———, 'DR Congo, M23 Rebels Announce Ceasefire after Peace Talks in Qatar', Al Jazeera, 24 April 2025, https://www.aljazeera.com/news/2025/4/24/drc-m23-rebels-commit-to-pause-fighting-amid-peace-talks

———, 'Hell Will Break Out: Trump Hints at Military Moves in Mideast,

Americas', Al Jazeera, 7 January 2025, https://www.aljazeera.com/news/2025/1/7/hell-will-break-loose-trump-hints-at-military-moves-in-mideast-americas

———, '"Important Step": What We Know about Tentative US-Iran Prisoner Deal', Al Jazeera, 11 August 2023, https://www.aljazeera.com/news/2023/8/11/important-step-what-we-know-about-tentative-us-iran-prisoner-deal

———, 'Israel Bans Al Jazeera: What Does It Mean and What Happens Next?' Al Jazeera, 6 May 2024, https://www.aljazeera.com/news/2024/5/6/israel-bans-al-jazeera-what-does-it-mean-and-what-happens-next

———, 'Israel-Hamas Truce: How Much Aid Has Entered Gaza?' Al Jazeera, 29 November 2023, https://www.aljazeera.com/news/2023/11/29/israel-hamas-truce-has-it-helped-relieve-gazas-humanitarian-crisis

———, 'Photos: Mourners Pay Tributes at Ismail Haniyeh's Funeral in Qatar', Al Jazeera, 2 August 2024, https://www.aljazeera.com/gallery/2024/8/2/anger-calls-for-resistance-at-hamas-chief-haniyehs-funeral-in-qatar

———, 'Profile: Abdul Ghani Baradar, Taliban's Political Head in Qatar', Al Jazeera, 25 January 2019, https://www.aljazeera.com/news/2019/1/25/profile-abdul-ghani-baradar-talibans-political-head-in-qatar

———, 'Qatar Hails Mediation "Milestone" as It Hosts Freed Ukrainian, Russian Kids', Al Jazeera, 25 April 2024, https://www.aljazeera.com/news/2024/4/25/qatar-hails-mediation-milestone-as-it-hosts-freed-ukrainian-russian-kids

———, 'Qatar Has Suspended Mediation Efforts on Gaza, Foreign Minister Says', Al Jazeera, 9 November 2024, https://www.aljazeera.com/news/2024/11/9/qatar-suspends-mediation-efforts-on-gaza-officials-say

———, 'Qatar Lauded for Its Role in Afghanistan Evacuations', Al Jazeera, 30 August 2021, https://www.aljazeera.com/news/2021/8/30/qatar-emerges-as-key-player-in-afghanistan-after-us-pullout

———, 'Qatar Pledges Support to Lebanon', Al Jazeera, 22 August 2006, https://www.aljazeera.com/news/2006/8/22/qatar-pledges-support-to-lebanon

———, 'Qatar to Act as US Diplomatic Representative in Afghanistan', Al Jazeera, 12 November 2021, https://www.aljazeera.com/news/2021/11/12/qatar-to-act-as-us-diplomatic-representative-in-afghanistan

———, 'Russia Returns Six Children to Ukraine in Qatar-Brokered Deal: State Media', Al Jazeera, 22 May 2024, https://www.aljazeera.com/news/2024/5/22/russia-returns-six-children-to-ukraine-in-qatar-brokered-deal-state-media

———, 'Somalia Cuts Diplomatic Ties with Kenya Citing Interference', Al Jazeera, 15 December 2020, https://www.aljazeera.com/news/2020/12/15/somalia-cuts-diplomatic-ties-with-kenya-citing-interferences

———, 'Somalia Elects New President after Long Overdue Elections', Al Jazeera, 15 May 2022, https://www.aljazeera.com/news/2022/5/15/somalia-elects-hassan-sheikh-mohamud-as-president

———, 'Taliban Releases Austrian Far-Right Activist Held in Afghanistan', Al

Jazeera, 25 February 2024, https://www.aljazeera.com/news/2024/2/25/taliban-releases-austrian-far-right-activist-held-in-afghanistan

———, 'The Israel-Hamas Truce Has Ended: What We Know so Far', Al Jazeera, 1 December 2023, https://www.aljazeera.com/news/2023/12/1/the-israel-hamas-truce-has-ended-what-we-know-so-far

———, 'Timeline: The Path to the Israel-Hamas Ceasefire Deal in Gaza', Al Jazeera, 19 January 2025, https://www.aljazeera.com/features/2025/1/19/timeline-the-path-to-the-israel-hamas-ceasefire-deal-in-gaza

———, '"To Make Lives Easier": Aid Brings Relief in Gaza amid Israel-Hamas Truce', Al Jazeera, 25 November 2023, https://www.aljazeera.com/gallery/2023/11/25/to-make-lives-easier-aid-brings-relief-in-gaza-amid-israel-hamas-truce

———, 'Ukrainian Children Repatriated from Russia through Qatari Mediation', Al Jazeera, 16 October 2023, https://www.aljazeera.com/news/2023/10/16/ukrainian-children-repatriated-from-russia-through-qatari-mediation

———, 'US and Iran Release Prisoners after $6bn Transfer', Al Jazeera, 18 September 2023, https://www.aljazeera.com/news/2023/9/18/five-americans-land-in-doha-after-release-in-us-iran-prisoner-swap

———, 'Venezuela, US Reach Prisoner Swap Deal as Tensions Ease', Al Jazeera, 20 December 2023, https://www.aljazeera.com/news/2023/12/20/venezeula-us-reach-prisoner-swap-deal

———, 'World Reaction to the Israel-Hamas Ceasefire in Gaza', Al Jazeera, 21 May 2021, https://www.aljazeera.com/news/2021/5/21/world-reaction-to-the-israel-hamas-ceasefire-in-gaza

———, 'Zelenskyy Thanks Qatar for Role in Returning Ukraine Children on Doha Visit', Al Jazeera, 5 June 2024, https://www.aljazeera.com/news/2024/6/5/zelenskyy-thanks-qatar-for-role-in-returning-ukraine-children-on-doha-visit

Al Jazeera English, 'Nasrallah Addresses Lebanon—08 May 08', YouTube, 9 May 2008, https://www.youtube.com/watch?v=YrfxnCoPViI

Al Qahtani, Mutlaq Majed, and Dana Mansour Al-Thani, 'Qatar's Policy and Experience in Mediation and Dispute Settlement', *Siyasat Arabiya* 9, no. 51 (1 July 2021), pp. 7–22, https://doi.org/10.31430/muib3023

Al Tahhan, Zena, 'How Israel Has Repeatedly Rejected Hamas Truce Offers', Al Jazeera, 22 January 2024, https://www.aljazeera.com/features/2024/1/22/how-israel-has-repeatedly-rejected-hamas-truce-offers

Alarabeed, Wadee, 'Qatar's Approach across the Triple Nexus in Conflict-Affected Contexts: The Case of Darfur', *Third World Quarterly* 45, no. 1 (2023), pp. 6–23, https://doi.org/10.1080/01436597.2023.2215724

Al-Azami, Usaama, 'Yusuf Al-Qaradawi, the Muslim Scholar Who Influenced Millions', Al Jazeera, 27 September 2022, https://www.aljazeera.com/news/2022/9/27/yusuf-al-qaradawi-the-muslim-scholar-who-influenced-millions

Alharathy, Safa, 'MP Daghim: Saleh Will Allow Parliamentary Elections if He Assumes Presidency of PC', *The Libya Observer*, 15 September 2022, https://

libyaobserver.ly/news/mp-daghim-saleh-will-allow-parliamentary-elections-if-he-assumes-presidency-pc

Al-Jaber, Khalid, and Patrick Theros, 'The Importance of Diplomacy: How Qatari Mediation Is Impacting Gaza', Middle East Council on Global Affairs, 13 June 2024, https://mecouncil.org/blog_posts/the-importance-of-diplomacy-how-qatari-mediation-is-impacting-gaza

Aljamal, Yousef M., 'Hamas: A Terrorist Organization or Liberation Movement?' *Politics and Religion Journal* 8, no. 1 (1 June 2014), pp. 39–58, https://doi.org/10.54561/prj0801039a

Al-Khulaifi, Sultan, 'DRC's Conflict Demands a New Peace Model Rooted in Inclusion and Reform', Al Jazeera, 23 May 2025, https://www.aljazeera.com/opinions/2025/5/23/drcs-conflict-demands-a-new-peace-model-rooted-in-inclusion-and-reform

Al-Kuwari, Aisha, 'An Appraisal of Qatar Foreign Aid Effectiveness in Post-Conflict Affected Countries: From 2008–2017', Master's thesis, Hamad Bin Khalifa University, Doha, Qatar, 2020.

Alqashouti, Mirdef, 'Qatar Mediation: From Soft Diplomacy to Foreign Policy', in Mahjoob Zweiri and Farah Qawasmi (eds), *Contemporary Qatar: Examining State and Society*, vol. 4 (Singapore: Springer, 2021), pp. 73–92, https://doi.org/10.1007/978-981-16-1391-3_6

Al-Ra'i Agency, 'Al-Emadi: Qatar's Presence in Gaza Prevented War and Averted a Humanitarian Disaster' [in Arabic], Wikālat al-Ra'ī al-Filasṭīniyya, 19 September 2020, https://alray.ps/ar/post/219679

Alraouf, Ali A., 'Museums as a Catalyst for a New Urban and Cultural Identity in Qatar: Interrogating the Case of the Museum of Islamic Art', in Karen Exell and Sarina Wakefield (eds), *Museums in Arabia* (London: Routledge, 2016), pp. 151–66.

Altiok, Huzeyfe, 'Kuwait's Mediation in the Gulf Crisis: Dynamics of Kuwait's Foreign Policy Approaches', in Md Mizanur Rahman and Amr Al-Azm (eds), *Social Change in the Gulf Region: Gulf Studies*, vol. 8 (Singapore: Springer, 2023), pp. 597–618, https://doi.org/10.1007/978-981-16-1391-3_6

Álvarez-Ossorio, Ignacio, and Leticia Rodríguez García, 'The Foreign Policy of Qatar: From a Mediating Role to an Active One', *Revista Española de Ciencia Política* 56 (26 July 2021), pp. 97–120, https://doi.org/10.21308/recp. 56.04

Amin, Hira, Khoulood Sakbani, and Evren Tok, 'State Aspirations for Social and Cultural Transformations in Qatar', *Social Sciences* 13, no. 7 (5 July 2024), https://doi.org/10.3390/socsci13070359

Amnesty International, *Sudan: Scorched Earth, Poisoned Air: Sudanese Government Forces Ravage Jebel Marra, Darfur* (London: Amnesty International, 2016), https://www.amnesty.org/en/documents/afr54/4877/2016/en/

Amr, Hady, Ilan Goldenberg, Kevin Huggard, and Natan Sachs, 'Ending Gaza's Perpetual Crisis: A New U.S. Approach', Brookings, December 2018, https://www.brookings.edu/articles/ending-gazas-perpetual-crisis-a-new-u-s-approach

Antoniades, Alexis, Rafia Al-Jassim, and Khalique Gharatkar, 'The Blockade against

Qatar: A Blessing in Disguise?' *Journal of Arabian Studies* 11, no. 1 (2 September 2021), pp. 81–99, https://doi.org/10.1080/21534764.2021.1954354

Anyadike, Obi, 'Goma Capture Sparks Fears of Deeper Regional Conflict as Rwanda-Backed Rebels Push South', The New Humanitarian, 31 January 2025, https://www.thenewhumanitarian.org/news-feature/2025/01/31/drc-goma-capture-sparks-fears-deeper-regional-conflict-rwanda-backed-rebels-m23

Apsel, Joyce, 'The Complexity of Destruction in Darfur: Historical Processes and Regional Dynamics', *Human Rights Review* 10, no. 2 (6 September 2008), pp. 239–59, https://doi.org/10.1007/s12142-008-0099-6

Arab Center Washington DC, 'Full Text of the Ceasefire Agreement That Hamas Has Accepted', Arab Center Washington DC, 6 May 2024, https://arabcenterdc.org/resource/details-of-the-ceasefire-deal-that-hamas-has-accepted/

Arab News, 'Qatar Steps up Its Mediation Role in US-Iran Nuclear Negotiations', *Arab News*, 8 March 2022, https://arab.news/c4uhu

Aras, Bülent, and Majed Al Ansari, 'Standing Tall like Caesar? Qatar's Unwavering Voice for Palestine at the United Nations', *Third World Quarterly* 45, no. 9 (10 May 2024), pp. 1458–75, https://doi.org/10.1080/01436597.2024.2346214

Aras, Bulent, Burcu Fazlioglu, and Majed Al Ansari, 'Interest, Need, or Reputation? Determinants of Qatar's Foreign Aid', *Foreign Policy Analysis* 20, no. 4 (4 October 2024), p. orae027, https://doi.org/10.1093/fpa/orae027

Ardemagni, Eleonora, 'Still a Mediator: Qatar's Afghan Shot on the International Stage', Institute for International Political Studies, 3 September 2021, https://www.ispionline.it/en/publication/still-mediator-qatars-afghan-shot-international-stage-31542

Arsan, Andrew, *Lebanon: A Country in Fragments* (London: Hurst & Company, 2018).

Athanasiadis, Konstantinos, 'Re-Visioning "Lebanon": Power-Sharing during the Postwar Era (1990–2015)', PhD dissertation, Luiss University, Rome, Italy, 2017.

Aydoğan Ağlarcı, Merve Gül, 'UN Reports Nearly 400,000 Displaced after Gaza Ceasefire Collapse', Anadolu Agency, 7 April 2025, https://www.aa.com.tr/en/middle-east/un-reports-nearly-400–000-displaced-after-gaza-ceasefire-collapse/3530910

Azem, Ahmad Jamil, 'Qatar and the Repercussions of the October 7 War: Between Managing the Conflict and Solving It', Institute for Palestine Studies, 2024, https://www.palestine-studies.org/en/node/1655085

Baabood, Abdullah, 'Gulf Countries and Arab Transitions: Role Support and Effects', The European Institute of the Mediterranean (IEMed), 2014, https://www.iemed.org/publication/gulf-countries-and-arab-transitions-role-support-and-effects/

Bakir, Ali, 'The Evolution of Turkey—Qatar Relations amid a Growing Gulf Divide', in Andreas Krieg (ed.), *Divided Gulf: Anatomy of a Crisis* (Singapore: Palgrave Macmillan, 2019), pp. 197–215, https://doi.org/10.1007/978-981-13-6314-6_12

———, 'Washington's Dilemma over Hamas in Qatar', Middle East Council on

Global Affairs, 8 April 2024, https://mecouncil.org/blog_posts/washingtons-dilemma-over-hamas-in-qatar/

Bakr, Amena, 'Qatar Seeks Role as Gaza Mediator, Israel Wary', Reuters, 17 July 2014, https://www.reuters.com/article/world/qatar-seeks-role-as-gaza-mediator-israel-wary-idUSKBN0FM2GD/

Barakat, Sultan, 'Priorities and Challenges of Qatar's Humanitarian Diplomacy', Chr. Michelsen Institute, 2019, https://www.cmi.no/publications/6906-priorities-and-challenges-of-qatars-humanitariandiplomacy

———, 'Qatari Mediation: Between Ambition and Achievement', Brookings Doha Center, November 2014, https://www.brookings.edu/wp-content/uploads/2016/06/Final-PDF-English.pdf

———, 'The Qatari Spring: Qatar's Emerging Role in Peacemaking', Kuwait Programme on Development, Governance and Globalisation in the Gulf States, July 2012, https://www.brookings.edu/wp-content/uploads/2016/06/qatar-role-peacekeeping-barakat.pdf

Barakat, Sultan, and Sansom Milton, '8 Qatar: Conflict Mediation and Regional Objectives', in Agnieszka Paczyńska (ed.), *The New Politics of Aid: Emerging Donors and Conflict-Affected States* (Boulder, CO: Lynne Rienner Publishers, 2019), pp. 141–60, https://doi.org/10.1515/9781626378407-009

———, 'Qatar's Role in Conflict and Peace: An Assessment of Motivations and Influence', *Saferworld*, 20 September 2011.

Barltrop, Richard, *Darfur and the International Community: The Challenges of Conflict Resolution in Sudan* (London: I.B. Tauris, 2011).

Barthe, Benjamin, Louis Imbert, Hélène Sallon, and Piotr Smolar, 'Israel-Hamas War: Who Are the Five Key Negotiators of the Unattainable Ceasefire?' *Le Monde*, 7 June 2024, https://www.lemonde.fr/en/international/article/2024/06/07/israel-hamas-war-who-are-the-five-key-negotiators-of-the-unattainable-ceasefire_6674144_4.html

Baumann, Jonas, and Govinda Daniel Clayton, 'Mediation in Violent Conflict', *CSS Analyses in Security Policy* 211 (June 2017), pp. 1–2, https://doi.org/10.3929/ethz-b-000169653

Beardsley, Kyle C., David M. Quinn, Bidisha Biswas, and Jonathan Wilkenfeld, 'Mediation Style and Crisis Outcomes', *Journal of Conflict Resolution* 50, no. 1 (February 2006), pp. 58–86, https://doi.org/10.1177/0022002705282862

Bercovitch, Jacob, and Richard Dean Wells Jackson, *Conflict Resolution in the Twenty-First Century: Principles, Methods, and Approaches* (Ann Arbor, MI: University of Michigan Press, 2009), https://doi.org/10.3998/mpub.106467

Bercovitch, Jacob, and Su-Mi Lee, 'Mediating International Conflicts: Examining the Effectiveness of Directive Strategies', *International Journal of Peace Studies* 8, no. 1 (2003), pp. 1–17, http://www.jstor.org/stable/41852891

Berg, Raffi, 'Is the War Starting Again in Gaza?' BBC News, 18 March 2025, https://www.bbc.com/news/articles/cy5klgv5zv0o

Berman, Lazar, and Jacob Magid, 'Witkoff Lands in Doha as Talks Resume with Aim of Extending Fragile Gaza Truce', *The Times of Israel*, 11 March 2025, https://www.timesofisrael.com/witkoff-lands-in-doha-as-talks-resume-with-aim-of-extending-fragile-gaza-truce/

Biberman, Yelena, and Jared Schwartz, 'Pakistan Is Ready for Stability in Afghanistan', East Asia Forum, 29 March 2019, https://eastasiaforum.org/2019/03/29/pakistan-is-ready-for-stability-in-afghanistan

Bibolov, Aidyn, Tongfang Yuan, Sidra Rehman, and Ken Miyajima, '2022 FIFA World Cup', *Selected Issues Papers* 2024, no. 011 (February 2024), https://doi.org/10.5089/9798400267864.018

Björkdahl, Annika, 'Ideas and Norms in Swedish Peace Policy', *Swiss Political Science Review* 19, no. 3 (2013), pp. 322–37, https://doi.org/10.1111/spsr.12046

Black, Ian, 'Arab States Withdraw Ambassadors from Qatar in Protest at "Interference"', *The Guardian*, 5 March 2014, https://www.theguardian.com/world/2014/mar/05/arab-states-qatar-withdraw-ambassadors-protest

Blanchard, Christopher M., *Qatar: Background and US Relations* (Washington, DC: Congressional Research Service, 2010).

———, 'Qatar: Issues for the 118th Congress (Updated 15 February 2024)', Congressional Research Service, 2024, https://sgp.fas.org/crs/mideast/R47467.pdf

Blanford, Nicholas, 'Qatari Deal Defuses Lebanese Crisis', The Christian Science Monitor, 22 May 2008, https://www.csmonitor.com/World/Middle-East/2008/0522/p01s05-wome.html

Borger, Julian, 'Hamas Hands Over Six Hostages but Israel Suspends Release of 600 Palestinians', *The Guardian*, 22 February 2025, https://www.theguardian.com/world/2025/feb/22/hamas-releases-six-hostages-exchange-israel-gaza-ceasefire-deal

Bower, Leah, 'Gulf Could Gain from Thaw in Saudi-Qatar Relations', Gulf News, 8 July 2008, https://gulfnews.com/business/analysis/gulf-could-gain-from-thaw-in-saudi-qatar-relations-1.117086

Boyce, Sir Graham, 'Qatar's Foreign Policy', *Asian Affairs* 44, no. 3 (28 October 2013), pp. 365–77, https://doi.org/10.1080/03068374.2013.826003

Braveboy-Wagner, Jacqueline Anne, *The Venezuela-Guyana Border Dispute: Britain's Colonial Legacy in Latin America* (New York: Routledge, 2019).

Brewer, Cecily, *More States Are Vying to Mediate Conflict—What Does It Mean for Global Peace?* (Washington, DC: United States Institute of Peace, 7 October 2024), https://www.usip.org/publications/2024/10/more-states-are-vying-mediate-conflict-what-does-it-mean-global-peace

Brooking, Steve, 'Why Was a Negotiated Peace Always Out of Reach in Afghanistan? Opportunities and Obstacles, 2001–21', United States Institute of Peace, August 2022, https://www.usip.org/sites/default/files/2022-08/pw-184-why-negotiated-peace-always-out-of-reach-afghanistan.pdf

Brooks, Sean, 'Enforcing a Turning Point and Imposing a Deal: An Analysis of the Darfur Abuja Negotiations of 2006', *International Negotiation* 13, no. 3 (2008), pp. 413–40, https://doi.org/10.1163/157180608x365262

Bruno, Greg, 'Saudi Arabia and the Future of Afghanistan', Council on Foreign Relations, 10 December 2008, https://www.cfr.org/backgrounder/saudi-arabia-and-future-afghanistan#chapter-title-0–4

Bukhari, Irfan, 'Gaza Ceasefire Talks in Final Stages: MOFA Spokesperson', *The*

Peninsula, 15 January 2025, https://thepeninsulaqatar.com/article/15/01/2025/gaza-ceasefire-talks-in-final-stages-mofa-spokesperson

Bulkan, Janette, 'The Limits of State Territorialisation: Geopolitics and Petroleum in Guyana', *Social and Economic Studies* 70, no. 3 & 4 (2021), pp. 72–105.

Cafiero, Giorgio, 'Gaza War Spotlights Qatar's Role as a Regional Mediator', *The New Arab*, 6 November 2023, https://www.newarab.com/analysis/gaza-war-spotlights-qatars-role-regional-mediator

———, 'Qatar's Careful Balance between Ukraine and Russia', *Doha News*, 9 August 2023, https://dohanews.co/qatars-careful-balance-between-ukraine-and-russia

———, 'Why Qatar Is the Go-to Mediator in the Gaza War, and Beyond', *The New Arab*, 29 April 2024, https://www.newarab.com/analysis/why-qatar-go-mediator-gaza-war-and-beyond

Call, Charles T., 'Interests or Ideas? Explaining Brazil's Surge in Peacekeeping and Peacebuilding', in Emel Parlar Dal (ed.), *Rising Powers in International Conflict Management: Converging and Contesting Approaches* (London: Routledge, 2020), pp. 66–84.

Cavusoglu, Esra, 'From Rise to Crisis: The Qatari Leadership', *Türkiye Ortadoğu Çalışmaları Dergisi* 7, no. 1 (30 June 2020), pp. 81–110, https://doi.org/10.26513/tocd.624334

CBS News, 'Lebanon Factions Reach Deal to End the Crisis', CBS News, 21 May 2008, https://www.cbsnews.com/news/lebanese-factions-reach-deal-to-end-crisis

Cho, Jacqui, and Dana M. Landau, 'In Search of the Golden Formula: Trends in Peace Mediation Research and Practice', *Civil Wars* 25, no. 2–3 (15 December 2023), pp. 317–40, https://doi.org/10.1080/13698249.2023.2249326

Center for Conflict and Humanitarian Studies, 'Unprecedented Terrains: Deliberating US Policy on Afghanistan under the New Trump Administration and Considering Evolving Regional Dynamics', Workshop organized by the Center for Conflict and Humanitarian Studies, Doha, Qatar, 19–20 February 2025, https://chs-doha.org/en/Events/Pages/Unprecedented-Terrains-Deliberating-US-Policy-on-Afghanistan-under-the-new-Trump-Administration-and-Considering-Evolving-Re.aspx

Chr. Michelsen Institute, 'Developing Darfur: A Recovery & Reconstruction Strategy', Chr. Michelsen Institute, 2013, https://www.cmi.no/file/2320-Darfur-Development-Strategy-6–3–13.pdf

Cochrane, Logan, 'The United Arab Emirates as a Global Donor: What a Decade of Foreign Aid Data Transparency Reveals', *Development Studies Research* 8, no. 1 (2021), pp. 49–62, https://doi.org/10.1080/21665095.2021.1883453

Congress of the United States, 'Letter to President Joseph R. Biden', Congress of the United States, 16 October 2023, https://d12t4t5x3vyizu.cloudfront.net/gottheimer.house.gov/uploads/2023/10/Israel-Hamas-Letter-to-Biden-.pdf

Congressional Research Service, 'Qatar: Background and U.S. Relations', Congressional Research Service, 2014, https://www.everycrsreport.com/reports/RL31718.html#fn25

Cooper, Andrew F., and Bessma Momani, 'Qatar and Expanded Contours of Small

State Diplomacy', *The International Spectator* 46, no. 3 (September 2011), pp. 113–28, https://doi.org/10.1080/03932729.2011.576181

Courbage, Youssef, and Hala Naufal, *Palestinian Worldwide: A Demographic Study* (Doha/Beirut: Arab Center for Research and Policy Studies, 2020).

Crystal, Jill, 'US Relations with Qatar', in Robert Looney (ed.), *Handbook of US-Middle East Relations*, 1st edn (London: Routledge, 2014), pp. 391–402.

Custers, Desirée, 'Qatar and Somalia-Kenya Relations: Projection of Mediation Power in the Horn of Africa', Stimson Center, 19 May 2021, https://www.stimson.org/2021/qatar-and-somalia-kenya-relations-projection-of-mediation-power-in-the-horn-of-africa

Dabanga Radio, '"31,000 Ex-Rebel Combatants Demobilised so Far": Darfur DDR Commission', Dabanga Radio TV Online, 20 July 2015, https://www.dabangasudan.org/en/all-news/article/31-000-ex-rebel-combatants-demobilised-so-far-darfur-ddr-commission

Dakhlallah, Farah, 'The Arab League in Lebanon: 2005–2008', *Cambridge Review of International Affairs* 25, no. 1 (2012), pp. 53–74, https://doi.org/10.1080/09557571.2011.646241

Dana, Tariq, 'A Cruel Innovation: Israeli Experiments on Gaza's Great March of Return', *Sociology of Islam* 8, no. 2 (2020), pp. 175–98, https://doi.org/10.1163/22131418-00802003

Dandashly, Assem, and Christos Kourtelis, 'The Provision of Arab Gulf Aid: The Emergence of New Donors', *International Politics* 60, no. 2 (2023), pp. 406–27, https://doi.org/10.1057/s41311-022-00418-4

Dargin, Justin, 'Qatar's Natural Gas: The Foreign-Policy Driver', *Middle East Policy* 14, no. 3 (2007), pp. 136–42.

Day, Adam, 'Peacekeeping Without a Partner: A Review of UNAMID's Political Strategy in Darfur', in Adam Day, Aditi Gorur, Victoria K. Holt, and Charles T. Hunt (eds), *The Political Practice of Peacekeeping: How Strategies for Peace Operations Are Developed and Implemented* (New York: United Nations University, 2020), pp. 44–63.

De Carvalho, Benjamin, and Cedric De Coning, 'Rising Powers and the Future of Peacekeeping and Peacebuilding', NOREF: Norwegian Peacebuilding Resource Centre, November 2013, https://www.files.ethz.ch/isn/175234/f194e6326ee12f80c3705117b151ef78.pdf

De Waal, Alex, 'Sudan: A Turbulent Political Marketplace', in Mehran Kamrava (ed.), *Fragile Politics: Weak States in the Greater Middle East* (New York: Oxford University Press, 2016), pp. 171–96, https://doi.org/10.1093/acprof:oso/9780190246211.003.0008

———, *The Real Politics of the Horn of Africa: Money, War and the Business of Power* (Cambridge: Polity Press, 2015).

———, 'Who Are the Darfurians? Arab and African Identities, Violence and External Engagement', *African Affairs* 104, no. 415 (1 April 2005), pp. 181–205, https://doi.org/10.1093/afraf/adi035

De Waal, Alex, and Abdul Mohammed, *Defining the Crisis in the Sudans: Lessons from the African Union High-Level Panels for Sudan and South Sudan* (Johannesburg: Thabo

Mbeki Foundation, 2024), https://mbeki.org/wp-content/uploads/2024/10/TMF-Crisis-in-The-Sudans-Report-Digital.pdf

DeBre, Isabel, 'In West Bank, Palestinians Rejoice over Release of Women and Minors from Israeli Prisons', PBS News, 25 November 2023, https://www.pbs.org/newshour/world/in-west-bank-palestinians-rejoice-over-release-of-women-and-minors-from-israeli-prisons

Doha News, 'It's Official: Qatar Has Sent Troops to Bahrain', *Doha News*, 19 March 2011, https://dohanews.co/its-official-qatar-has-sent-troops-to-bahrain/

Doha Roots, 'Darfur Ruler Confirms That Qatar Has Provided Clear Support in Doha Document for the Peace of the Region', *Doha Roots*, 9 August 2021, https://doharoots.com/darfur-ruler-confirms-that-qatar-has-provided-clear-support-in-doha-document-for-the-peace-of-the-region

Duggan, Niall, Bas Hooijmaaijers, Marek Rewizorski, and Ekaterina Arapova, 'Introduction: "The BRICS, Global Governance, and Challenges for South–South Cooperation in a Post-Western World"', *International Political Science Review* 43, no. 4 (2022), pp. 469–80, https://doi.org/10.1177/01925121211052211

Dutta, Prabhash K., 'From Sudan to Ukraine to Gaza: How Qatar Has Emerged as the Master Mediator', Firstpost, 23 August 2024, https://www.firstpost.com/world/from-sudan-to-ukraine-to-gaza-how-qatar-has-emerged-as-the-master-mediator-13807411.html

Efremova, Ksenia, 'Small States in Great Power Politics: Understanding the "Buffer Effect"', *Central European Journal of International and Security Studies* 13, no. 1 (22 March 2019), pp. 100–21, https://doi.org/10.51870/cejiss.a130102

El-Affendi, Abdelwahab, *Azmat Darfur: Nazra fi'l-Judhur wa'l-Hulul al-Mumkina* [in Arabic] (Abu Dhabi: The Emirates Centre for Strategic Studies and Research, 2009).

Elayah, Moosa, and Hasan Al-Awami, 'Exploring the Preference for Bilateral Aid: Gulf Oil States' Aid to Yemen', *Third World Quarterly* 45, no. 15–16 (2024), pp. 2266–86, https://doi.org/10.1080/01436597.2024.2327451

ElEtreby, Basma Mahmoud, 'Qatari Foreign Policy and the Arab Spring: From Mediation to Intervention', Master's thesis, American University in Cairo, Cairo, Egypt, 2014.

Elkahlout, Ghassan (ed.), *Gaza's Cycle of Destruction and Rebuilding: Understanding the Actors, Dynamics, and Responses* (Cham: Palgrave Macmillan, 2024), https://doi.org/10.1007/978-3-031-67198-2

———, '"Hearts and Minds": Examining the Kuwaiti Humanitarian Model as an Emerging Arab Donor', *Asian Journal of Middle Eastern and Islamic Studies* 14, no. 1 (2 March 2020), pp. 141–57, https://doi.org/10.1080/25765949.2020.1728975

Elkahlout, Ghassan, and Sansom Milton, 'The Evolution of the Gulf States as Humanitarian Donors', *Third World Quarterly* 45, no. 15–16 (10 July 2023), pp. 2246–65, https://doi.org/10.1080/01436597.2023.2229742

El-Khazen, Farid, *The Communal Pact of National Identities: The Making and Politics of the 1943 National Pact* (Oxford: Centre for Lebanese Studies, 1991).

Elshabik, Mohamed, 'Sudan: Learning Lessons from the Past in Search of Peace',

World Economic Forum, 9 August 2024, https://www.weforum.org/agenda/2024/08/sudan-upcoming-geneva-talks-negotiators-peace/

Elzarov, Zurab, 'Community Stabilization and Violence Reduction: Lessons from Darfur', *Stability: International Journal of Security & Development* 4, no. 1 (23 February 2015), https://doi.org/10.5334/sta.ex

Eriksson, Mikael, and Roland Kostić (eds), *Mediation and Liberal Peacebuilding: Peace from the Ashes of War?* (Abingdon: Routledge, 2013).

Fabian, Philip, Nikolaus Harbusch, and Peter Tiede, 'Emir of Qatar in Berlin: Scholz Welcomes the Top Sponsor of Terror' [in German], *Bild*, 12 October 2023, https://www.bild.de/politik/inland/politik-inland/emir-von-katar-in-berlin-scholz-empfaengt-den-top-sponsor-des-terrors-85714334.bild.html

Feltman, Jeffrey, 'Hezbollah: Revolutionary Iran's Most Successful Export', Brookings, 17 January 2019, https://www.brookings.edu/articles/hezbollah-revolutionary-irans-most-successful-export/

Fenton-Harvey, Jonathan, 'Interests First: The UAE's India-Pakistan Imbalance', Gulf International Forum, 2 February 2023, https://gulfif.org/interests-first-the-uaes-india-pakistan-imbalance/

———, 'The UAE's Adaptive Relationship with the Taliban', *The New Arab*, 30 November 2021, https://www.newarab.com/analysis/uaes-adaptive-relationship-taliban

Fischer, Thomas, 'Switzerland's Good Offices: A Changing Concept, 1945–2002' *Eidgenössische Technische Hochschule (ETH Zürich)* 37 (2002), https://doi.org/10.3929/ethz-a-004445304

Foundation for Defense of Democracies, 'Iran Appeals to Qatar, Oman to Revive Nuclear Talks', Foundation for Defense of Democracies, 15 June 2025, https://www.fdd.org/analysis/2025/06/15/iran-appeals-to-qatar-oman-to-revive-nuclear-talks/

Fraihat, Ibrahim, 'Superpower and Small-State Mediation in the Qatar Gulf Crisis', *The International Spectator* 55, no. 2 (2020), pp. 79–91, https://doi.org/10.1080/03932729.2020.1741268

Fraihat, Ibrahim, and Mona Hedaya, 'Understanding the October 7th Hamas Attack on Israel and the War on Gaza', in Ghassan Elkahlout (ed.), *Gaza's Cycle of Destruction and Rebuilding* (Cham: Palgrave Macmillan, 2024), pp. 77–103, https://doi.org/10.1007/978-3-031-67198-2_5

France 24, 'Taliban Release Western Hostages in Prisoner Swap', France 24, 19 November 2019, https://www.france24.com/en/20191119-taliban-afghanistan-prisoner-haqqani-usa-king-weeks-australia-professor-khan

———, 'Thousands of Syrians Evacuated under Qatar-Iran Deal', France 24, 14 April 2017, https://www.france24.com/en/20170414-syria-four-towns-begin-evacuating-30000-qatar-iran-deal-madaya-zabadani

Freer, Courtney, *Interrogating Different Modes of GCC Conflict Mediation* (Edinburgh: PeaceRep: The Peace and Conflict Resolution Evidence Platform, 2022), https://peacerep.org/wp-content/uploads/2023/05/Freer-2023-Interrogating-Different-Modes-of-GCC-Conflict-Mediation-GT.pdf

———, 'Qatar and the UAE in Peacemaking and Peacebuilding', *LSE Middle East*

Centre Paper Series 60 (March 2022), https://eprints.lse.ac.uk/114561/3/Qatar_and_UAE_in_Peacemaking_and_Peacebuilding_1_.pdf

Fromherz, Allen James, *Qatar: Rise to Power and Influence* (London: Bloomsbury Publishing PLC, 2012).

Gaas, Mohamed, 'Too Early to Celebrate a Somalia–Kenya Rapprochement', Institute for Security Studies, 23 September 2021, https://issafrica.org/iss-today/too-early-to-celebrate-a-somaliakenya-rapprochement

Galal, Abdelraouf Mostafa, 'External Behavior of Small States in Light of Theories of International Relations', *Review of Economics and Political Science* 5, no. 1 (20 January 2020), pp. 38–56, https://doi.org/10.1108/reps-11-2018-0028

Gale, 'The Argentine Who Was Kidnapped for Eight Months in Afghanistan Speaks: "I'm Fine, Back with My Family"', Gale, 4 August 2024, https://link.gale.com/apps/doc/A803949626/IFME?u=anon~f0117489&sid=sitemap&xid=f3277512

Galeeva, Diana, *Qatar: The Practice of Rented Power* (Abingdon: Routledge, 2022).

Gangi, Yagoub Ali, and Alfadil Timan Idris, 'Qatar's Path to a Knowledge-Based Economy: A Content Analysis of Entrepreneurship Training Initiatives', *Business and Economic Research* 13, no. 4 (14 October 2023), https://doi.org/10.5296/ber.v13i4.21256

General Secretariat for Development Planning—Qatar, *Qatar National Vision 2030* (Doha: General Secretariat for Development Planning—Qatar, July 2008), https://www.npc.qa/en/QNV/Documents/QNV2030_English_v2.pdf

Geneva Centre for Security Sector Governance, 'Exploring Armed Groups in Libya: Perspectives on Security Sector Reform in a Hybrid Environment', Geneva Centre for Security Sector Governance, 2020, https://www.dcaf.ch/sites/default/files/publications/documents/ExploringArmedGroupsinLibya.pdf

Gengler, Justin, 'Society and State in Post-Blockade Qatar: Lessons for the Arab Gulf Region', *Journal of Arabian Studies* 10, no. 2 (2 July 2020), pp. 238–55, https://doi.org/10.1080/21534764.2020.1828023

Gengler, Justin J., Bethany Shockley, and Michael C. Ewers, 'Refinancing the Rentier State: Welfare, Inequality, and Citizen Preferences toward Fiscal Reform in the Gulf Oil Monarchies', *Comparative Politics* 53, no. 2 (1 January 2021), pp. 283–317, https://doi.org/10.5129/001041521x15903211136400

Geukjian, Ohannes, 'Political Instability and Conflict after the Syrian Withdrawal from Lebanon', *The Middle East Journal* 68, no. 4 (1 September 2014), pp. 521–45, https://doi.org/10.3751/68.4.12

Ginesta, Xavier, and Jordi San Eugenio, 'The Use of Football as a Country Branding Strategy: Case Study', *Communication & Sport* 2, no. 3 (25 April 2013), pp. 225–41, https://doi.org/10.1177/2167479513486886

Giustozzi, Antonio, 'The Taliban Beyond the Pashtuns', The Centre for International Governance Innovation, July 2010, https://www.files.ethz.ch/isn/121069/Afghanistan_Paper_5.pdf

Godal, Bjørn Tore, *A Good Ally: Norway in Afghanistan 2001–2014* (Oslo: Norwegian Ministry of Foreign Affairs and Ministry of Defence, 2016), https://www.regjeringen.no/en/dokumenter/nou-2016-8/id2503028/

Goetz, Andrew R., and Lucy Budd, *The Geographies of Air Transport* (London: Routledge, 2016).

Gray, Kevin, and Barry K. Gills, 'South–South Cooperation and the Rise of the Global South', *Third World Quarterly* 37, no. 4 (24 March 2016), pp. 557–74, https://doi.org/10.1080/01436597.2015.1128817

Gray, Matthew, 'A Theory of "Late Rentierism" in the Arab States of the Gulf', *CIRS Occasional Papers*, 18 August 2011, http://dx.doi.org/10.2139/ssrn.2825905

———, *Qatar: Politics and the Challenges of Development* (Boulder, CO: Lynne Rienner Publishers, 2013), https://doi.org/10.1515/9781626370784

Green, R., 'Solving the Darfur Crisis: The U.S. Prefers Qatar to Egypt as Mediator', Middle East Media Research Institute (MEMRI), 31 August 2009, https://www.memri.org/reports/solving-darfur-crisis-us-prefers-qatar-egypt-mediator

Greig, Michael J., and Paul Diehl, *International Mediation* (Cambridge: Polity Press, 2012).

Gritten, David, and Rushdi Abualouf, 'Hamas Leaders No Longer in Doha but Office Not Permanently Closed, Qatar Says', BBC News, 19 November 2024, https://www.bbc.com/news/articles/c86qd99nqgyo

Grix, Jonathan, and Paul Michael Brannagan, 'Sports Mega-Events as Foreign Policy: Sport Diplomacy, "Soft Power," and "Sportswashing"', *American Behavioral Scientist*, 23 July 2024, https://doi.org/10.1177/00027642241262042

Gulbrandsen, Anders, 'Bridging the Gulf: Qatari Business Diplomacy and Conflict Mediation', Master's thesis, Georgetown University, Washington DC, USA, 2010, https://repository.library.georgetown.edu/bitstream/handle/10822/552827/gulbrandsenAnders.pdf

Gulf Times, 'Qatar Attends Rwanda-DRC Peace Deal Signing', *Gulf Times*, 28 June 2025, https://www.gulf-times.com/article/706662/qatar/qatar-attends-rwanda-drc-peace-deal-signing

Guzansky, Yoel, and Ofir Winter, 'Two Are Better than One: The Role of Qatar and Egypt in Gaza', Institute for National Security Studies, 25 August 2022, https://www.inss.org.il/publication/qatar-egypt/

Guzansky, Yoel, and Ilan Zalayat, 'Indispensable Qatar?' Institute for National Security Studies, 27 November 2023, https://www.inss.org.il/publication/qatar-gaza/

Haddad, Simon, 'Lebanon: From Consociationalism to Conciliation', *Nationalism and Ethnic Politics* 15, no. 3–4 (11 December 2009), pp. 398–416, https://doi.org/10.1080/13537110903346684

Hafezi, Parisa, and Andrew Mills, 'Iran, US on Verge of Prisoner Swap under Qatar-Mediated Deal', Reuters, 11 September 2023, https://www.reuters.com/world/iran-us-verge-prisoner-swap-under-qatar-mediated-deal-2023-09-10/

Hafezi, Parisa, Samia Nakhoul, and Andrew Mills, 'Iran Sought US Pressure on Israel for Ceasefire via Gulf States, Sources Say', Reuters, 16 June 2025, https://www.reuters.com/world/middle-east/iran-asks-gulf-arab-states-have-trump-press-israel-immediate-ceasefire-sources-2025-06-16/

Hajjar, Sami G., 'The Convoluted and Diminished Lebanese Democracy', *Democracy and Security* 5, no. 3 (1 December 2009), pp. 261–76, https://doi.org/10.1080/17419160903304864

Hamid, Shadi, 'From the Arab Spring Comes a More Unified Gulf Cooperation Council', Brookings, 15 April 2011, https://www.brookings.edu/articles/from-the-arab-spring-comes-a-more-unified-gulf-cooperation-council/

Hamieh, Christine Sylva, and Roger Mac Ginty, 'A Very Political Reconstruction: Governance and Reconstruction in Lebanon after the 2006 War', *Disasters* 34 (30 November 2009), pp. S103–23, https://doi.org/10.1111/j.1467-7717.2009.01101.x

Hammond, Andrew, 'Saudi Arabia Hosts Taliban Talks to Bolster Pakistan', Reuters, 15 October 2008, https://www.reuters.com/article/idUSLF59145

Hamzawy, Amr, 'The Political Impact of the Israel-Hamas Ceasefire', Carnegie Endowment for International Peace, 6 December 2023, https://carnegieendowment.org/posts/2023/12/the-political-impact-of-the-israel-hamas-ceasefire?lang=en

Haqqani, Husain, 'Pakistan Reaps What It Sowed: How the Country's Support for the Taliban Backfired', *Foreign Affairs*, 23 May 2022, https://www.foreignaffairs.com/articles/afghanistan/2022-05-23/pakistan-reaps-what-it-sowed

Harb, Imad K., 'Qatar's New Designation as US Non-NATO Ally Serves Multiple Purposes', Arab Center Washington DC, 4 February 2022, https://arabcenterdc.org/resource/qatars-new-designation-as-us-non-nato-ally-serves-multiple-purposes

Hari, Ravi, 'Donald Trump Calls Iran's Missile Strike a "Very Weak Response", Praises Qatar's Emir', *LiveMint*, 24 June 2025, https://www.livemint.com/news/us-news/donald-trump-calls-iran-s-missile-strike-a-very-weak-response-praises-qatar-s-emir-11750709646382.html

Harris, Alistair, *Half Full or Half Empty: Assessing Prospects for Peace in Lebanon* (Washington, DC: United States Institute of Peace, 2008).

Hartwell, Leon, 'Conflict Resolution: Lessons from the Dayton Peace Process', *Negotiation Journal* 35, no. 4 (October 2019), pp. 443–69, https://doi.org/10.1111/nejo.12300

Hassan, Yousif, 'The Evolution of the Sudanese Authoritarian State: The December Uprising and the Unravelling of a "Persistent" Autocracy', in Ozgun Topak, Merouan Mekouar, and Francesco Cavatorta (eds), *New Authoritarian Practices in the Middle East and North Africa* (Edinburgh: Edinburgh University Press, 2022), pp. 252–75.

Hazan, Pierre, *Negotiating with the Devil: Inside the World of Armed Conflict Mediation* (London: Hurst & Company, 2024).

Heemsbergen, Luke, and Asaf Siniver, 'New Routes to Power: Towards a Typology of Power Mediation', *Review of International Studies* 37, no. 3 (1 September 2010), pp. 1169–90, https://doi.org/10.1017/s0260210510001002

Helali, Baryalai, *An Insider's View: Lessons from the Afghan Peace Process, 2001–2021* (Stockholm: Folke Bernadotte Academy, 2024), https://doi.org/10.61880/JNPH7128

Henne, Peter, 'The United Arab Emirates', in *Islamic Politics, Muslim States, and Counterterrorism Tensions* (Cambridge: Cambridge University Press, 2017), pp. 119–46, https://doi.org/10.1017/9781316534328.006

Herbling, David, and Mohamed Sheikh Nor, 'Kenya Bans Somalia Flights Days after Qatar-Led Detente', Bloomberg, 11 May 2021, https://www.bloomberg.com/news/articles/2021-05-11/kenya-suspends-somalia-flights-days-after-qatar-brokered-detente

Hill, Ginny, *Yemen Endures: Civil War, Saudi Adventurism and the Future of Arabia* (New York: Oxford University Press, 2017).

Hitti, Nassif, *The Foreign Policy of Lebanon: Lessons and Prospects for the Forgotten Dimension* (Oxford: Centre for Lebanese Studies, 1989).

Hoetjes, Gertjan, 'Stepping Out of the Shade: Qatari-Saudi Relations Amid the Rise of Cosmopolitan Qatar', in Thomas R. Klassen, Nara Park, and Ian Roberge (eds), *Asymmetric Neighbors and International Relations: Living in the Shadow of Elephants* (London: Routledge, 2023), pp. 175–88.

———, 'The Gulf Cooperation Council and the Failure of Peacebuilding in Yemen', *The International Spectator* 56, no. 4 (15 November 2021), pp. 151–66, https://doi.org/10.1080/03932729.2021.1987034

Holland, Steve, 'Gaza Deal Emerged after Intense 96 Hours, US Officials Say', Reuters, 15 January 2025,https://www.reuters.com/world/gaza-deal-emerged-after-intense-96-hours-us-officials-say-2025-01-15/

Holper, Anne, and Lars Kirchhoff, 'Rethinking the Professionalization of Peace Mediation', *Rethinking Peace Mediation*, 11 January 2021, pp. 355–72, https://doi.org/10.51952/9781529208207.ch017

Humaid, Maram, 'Fears of More Violence as Palestinians Protest in Gaza', Al Jazeera, 6 April 2018, https://www.aljazeera.com/news/2018/4/6/fears-of-more-violence-as-palestinians-protest-in-gaza

Human Rights Watch, 'Sudan: Imperatives for Immediate Change: The African Union Mission in Sudan', Human Rights Watch, 19 January 2006, https://www.hrw.org/reports/2006/sudan0106/sudan0106web.pdf

Ibrahimi, Yaqub, 'False Negotiations and the Fall of Afghanistan to the Taliban', *International Journal: Canada's Journal of Global Policy Analysis* 77, no. 2 (2022), pp. 168–87, https://doi.org/10.1177/00207020221135299

Institute for Economics & Peace, *Global Peace Index 2024: Measuring Peace in a Complex World* (Sydney: Institute for Economics & Peace, 2024), https://www.economicsandpeace.org/wp-content/uploads/2024/06/GPI-2024-web.pdf

Institute for Palestinian Studies, 'Prospects of Reconciliation after the "Doha Declaration"', Masarat Center, 2 June 2012, https://store.palestine-studies.org/en/node/1635965

International Criminal Court, 'Situation in Ukraine: ICC Judges Issue Arrest Warrants against Vladimir Vladimirovich Putin and Maria Alekseyevna Lvova-Belova', International Criminal Court, 17 March 2023, https://www.icc-cpi.int/news/situation-ukraine-icc-judges-issue-arrest-warrants-against-vladimir-vladimirovich-putin-and

International Crisis Group, 'Afghanistan Peace Talks Since 2018: A Timeline',

International Crisis Group, 11 August 2020, https://www.crisisgroup.org/asia/south-asia/afghanistan/afghanistan-between-february-2018-and-august-2020-timeline

———, 'Darfur Rising: Sudan's New Crisis', International Crisis Group, 25 March 2004, https://www.crisisgroup.org/africa/horn-africa/sudan/darfur-rising-sudans-new-crisis

———, 'Fall of DRC's Goma: Urgent Action Needed to Avert a Regional War', International Crisis Group, 28 January 2025, https://www.crisisgroup.org/africa/great-lakes/democratic-republic-congo/fall-drcs-goma-urgent-action-needed-avert-regional-war

———, 'Hizbollah and the Lebanese Crisis', International Crisis Group, October 2007, https://www.crisisgroup.org/middle-east-north-africa/eastern-mediterranean/lebanon/hizbollah-and-lebanese-crisis

———, 'Taking Stock of the Taliban's Perspectives on Peace', International Crisis Group, 11 August 2020, https://www.crisisgroup.org/asia/south-asia/311-afghanistan/taking-stock-talibans-perspectives-peace

———, 'The Rebels Come to Khartoum: How to Implement Sudan's New Peace Agreement', International Crisis Group, 23 February 2021, https://www.crisisgroup.org/africa/horn-africa/sudan/b168-rebels-come-khartoum-how-implement-sudans-new-peace-agreement

Inwood, Joe, and Rushdi Abualouf, 'Qatar Suspends Role as Mediator between Israel and Hamas', BBC News, 9 November 2024, https://www.bbc.com/news/articles/c774d4p2mx6o

Ishac, Wadih, 'Examining Sport Tourism Role in Fostering Social Sustainability: Qatar Youth Perceptions', *Frontiers in Sports and Active Living* 6 (31 May 2024), https://doi.org/10.3389/fspor.2024.1388123

Islamic Republic News Agency, 'Iran FM Thanks Qatar for Mediating Prisoner Swap with US', Islamic Republic News Agency, 21 September 2023, https://en.irna.ir/news/85235323/Iran-FM-thanks-Qatar-for-mediating-prisoner-swap-with-US

Jacobs, Anna, 'Gulf Arab Reconciliation Hides Simmering Tensions', International Crisis Group, 12 July 2023, https://www.crisisgroup.org/middle-east-north-africa/gulf-and-arabian-peninsula/qatar-saudi-arabia-united-arab-emirates/gulf-arab-reconciliation-hides-simmering-tensions

Jahshan, Khalil E., 'The Persistent Illusion of Palestinian Reconciliation', Arab Center Washington DC, 7 August 2023, https://arabcenterdc.org/resource/the-persistent-illusion-of-palestinian-reconciliation/

Jett, Jennifer, Abigail Williams, and Mushtaq Yusufzai, 'Two Americans Released from Afghanistan in Deal Struck in Biden's Final Hours in Office', NBC News, 21 January 2025, https://www.nbcnews.com/news/world/american-held-afghanistan-released-final-hours-biden-administration-rcna188496

Johnson, Thomas H., and M. Chris Mason, 'Understanding the Taliban and Insurgency in Afghanistan', *World Affairs* 51, no. 1 (2007), pp. 71–89, https://doi.org/10.1016/j.orbis.2006.10.006

Jones, Deiniol Lloyd, *Cosmopolitan Mediation? Conflict Resolution and the Oslo Accords* (Manchester: University of Manchester Press, 1999).

Kahiye, Mohamed, 'Somalia, Kenya Agree to Mend Strained Relations', Voice of America, 8 August 2021, https://www.voanews.com/a/africa_somalia-kenya-agree-mend-strained-relations/6209331.html

Kamrava, Mehran, 'Iran-Qatar Relations', in Anoushiravan Ehteshami, Neil Quilliam, and Gawdat Bahgat (eds), *Security and Bilateral Issues between Iran and Its Arab Neighbours* (Cham: Palgrave Macmillan, 2017), pp. 167–87.

———, 'Mediation and Qatari Foreign Policy', *The Middle East Journal* 65, no. 4 (1 September 2011), pp. 539–56, https://doi.org/10.3751/65.4.11

———, *Qatar: Small State, Big Politics* (Ithaca, NY: Cornell University Press, 2013).

Karataş, Ibrahim, 'Qatar's Return to Mediation Diplomacy: What Changed?' AlSharq Strategic Research, 21 June 2022, https://research.sharqforum.org/2022/06/21/return-to-mediation-diplomacy/

Kardaş, Saban, and Bulent Aras, 'What Drove Syria Back into the Arab Fold?' *Middle East Policy* 30, no. 3 (7 August 2023), pp. 70–80, https://doi.org/10.1111/mepo.12704

Kastner, Philipp, 'Glocal Peace Mediators as Norm Translators', *Swiss Political Science Review* 26, no. 4 (22 November 2020), pp. 364–83, https://doi.org/10.1111/spsr.12423

Katzman, Kenneth, *Qatar: Governance, Security, and U.S. Policy* (Washington, DC: Congressional Research Service, 2018).

Kaye, Dalia Dassa, and Sanam Vakil, 'Only the Middle East Can Fix the Middle East: The Path to a Post-American Regional Order', *Foreign Affairs*, 1 February 2024, https://www.foreignaffairs.com/middle-east/fix-middle-east-united-states

Khalif, Abdulkadir, 'Qatari Special Envoy in Somalia Over Electoral Impasse', *The EastAfrican*, 5 May 2021, https://www.theeastafrican.co.ke/tea/news/east-africa/qatari-special-envoy-in-somalia-over-electoral-impasse-3388734

Khan, Assad Mehmood, Nazim Rahim, and Muhammad Javed, 'Socio-Political and Socio-Economic Perspectives of Sudan with Special Reference to Darfur Conflict', *Global Social Sciences Review* 4, no. 4 (30 December 2019), pp. 451–59, https://www.humapub.com/admin/alljournals/gssr/papers/GB5D98qzsn.pdf

Khazen, Ibrahim, and Rania Abu Shamala, 'Egypt, Qatar Discuss Efforts to Stabilize Gaza Ceasefire', Anadolu Agency, 12 March 2025, https://www.aa.com.tr/en/middle-east/egypt-qatar-discuss-efforts-to-stabilize-gaza-ceasefire/3507826

Kim, Victoria, 'Why the World Fears a War Between Israel and Iran', *The New York Times*, 24 October 2024, https://www.nytimes.com/2024/10/24/world/middleeast/israel-iran-war.html

Kinninmont, Jane, 'The Gulf Divided: The Impact of the Qatar Crisis', Chatham House, May 2019, https://www.chathamhouse.org/sites/default/files/publications/research/2019-05-30-Gulf%20Crisis_0.pdf

Kiruga, Morris, 'Kenya/Somalia: Is Thawing of Relations a Major Win for Qatar?' *The Africa Report*, 20 July 2021, https://www.theafricareport.com/86429/kenya-somalia-is-thawing-of-relations-a-major-win-for-qatar/

Knipp, Kersten, 'Gaza Cease-fire', Deutsche Welle, 21 November 2012, https://www.dw.com/en/cairo-mediators-achieve-breakthrough-cease-fire/a-16397749

Kolenda, Christopher D., 'Slow Failure: Understanding America's Quagmire in Afghanistan', *Journal of Strategic Studies* 42, no. 7 (2019), pp. 992–1014, https://doi.org/10.1080/01402390.2019.1663179

Küçükkeleş, Müjge, *Arab League's Syrian Policy* (Ankara: The SETA Foundation, 2012).

Kuperman, Alan J., 'A Model Humanitarian Intervention? Reassessing NATO's Libya Campaign', *International Security* 38, no. 1 (July 2013), pp. 105–36, https://doi.org/10.1162/isec_a_00126

Kurtz, Gerrit, 'Power Relations in Sudan after the Fall of Bashir: From Revolution to War', *SWP Research Paper*, no. 5/2024 (Berlin: Stiftung Wissenschaft und Politik, May 2014), https://doi.org/10.18449/2024RP05

Kusumawijaya, Kresna, and Yon Machmudi, 'Qatar Foreign Policy in Middle East Conflict Mediation', *Journal of Middle East and Islamic Studies* 9, no. 2 (1 December 2022), https://doi.org/10.7454/meis.v9i2.149

Langlois, Alexander, 'The Gulf's Role in Lebanon's Political and Economic Crisis', Gulf International Forum, 16 August 2023, https://gulfif.org/the-gulfs-role-in-lebanons-political-and-economic-crisis/

Lanz, David, 'Sudan/Darfur, Abuja Negotiations and the DPA', in *Unpacking the Mystery of Mediation in African Peace Processes* (Zurich: Mediation Support Project, Center for Security Studies, Swisspeace, 2008), pp. 78–84.

Latif, Aamir, 'Taliban Reluctant to Meet US Officials in Pakistan', Anadolu Agency, 18 January 2019, https://www.aa.com.tr/en/asia-pacific/taliban-reluctant-to-meet-us-officials-in-pakistan/1368622#

Law, Bill, 'Egypt Crisis: Fall of Morsi Challenges Qatar's New Emir', BBC News, 5 July 2013, https://www.bbc.com/news/world-middle-east-23185441

Lebanese Parliament, *The Lebanese Constitution Promulgated 23 May 1926 with Its Amendments, 23 May 1926 (with 1995 amendments)* (Beirut: Lebanese Parliament, 1926), https://lp.gov.lb/backoffice/uploads/files/Lebanese%20%20Constitution-%20En.pdf

Lee, Min Jung, Kylie Atwood, Jennifer Hansler, and Alex Marquardt, 'Qatar Agrees to Kick Hamas out of Doha Following US Request, Sources Say', CNN, 9 November 2024, https://edition.cnn.com/2024/11/08/politics/qatar-hamas-doha-us-request/index.html

Lefebvre, Jeffrey A., 'Red Sea Security and the Geopolitical-Economy of the Hanish Islands Dispute', *Middle East Journal* 52, no. 3 (1998), pp. 367–85.

Lie, Jon Harald, 'The Humanitarian-Development Nexus: Humanitarian Principles, Practice, and Pragmatics', *Journal of International Humanitarian Action* 5, no. 18 (December 2020), pp. 1–13, https://doi.org/10.1186/s41018-020-00086-0

Liyew, Estifanos Balew, 'Shattering Impact of the Sudan Conflict on Regional Stability', *African Identities* (5 March 2025), pp. 1–16, https://doi.org/10.1080/14725843.2025.2473989

Lloyd Jones, Deiniol, 'Mediation, Conflict Resolution and Critical Theory', *Review of International Studies* 26, no. 4 (2000), pp. 647–62, https://doi.org/10.1017/S0260210500006471

Loeb, Jonathan, *Talking to the Other Side: Humanitarian Engagement with Armed Non-State Actors in Darfur, Sudan, 2003–2012* (London: Overseas Development Institute, 2013).

Luck, Taylor, 'Checkbook Diplomacy? How Qatar's Renewed US Ties Reshape the Gulf', The Christian Science Monitor, 12 August 2019, https://www.csmonitor.com/World/Middle-East/2019/0807/Checkbook-diplomacy-How-Qatar-s-renewed-US-ties-reshape-the-Gulf

Mackenzie, James, and Nayera Abdallah, 'Israel Will Begin Negotiations on Next Phase of Gaza Ceasefire This Week, Minister Says', Reuters, 18 February 2025, https://www.reuters.com/world/middle-east/israel-begin-negotiations-second-phase-gaza-ceasefire-deal-minister-says-2025-02-18/

Magdy, Samy, Adam Geller, and Aamer Madhani, 'To Secure Gaza Ceasefire, Dealmakers Overcame Enemies' Deep Distrust', AP News, 23 January 2025, https://apnews.com/article/gaza-ceasefire-deal-negotiators-qatar-biden-trump-israel-hamas-e66fa514aa7215f249e5026b365b80d6

Maizland, Lindsay, 'The Taliban in Afghanistan', Council on Foreign Relations, 19 January 2023, https://www.cfr.org/backgrounder/taliban-afghanistan#chapter-title-0–8

Makdisi, Samir, Fadia Kiwan, and Marcus Marktanner, 'Lebanon: The Constrained Democracy and Its National Impact', in Ibrahim Elbadawi and Samir Makdisi (eds), *Democracy in the Arab World: Explaining the Deficit*, 1st edn (London: Routledge, 2011), pp. 115–41.

Makdisi, Samir, and Marcus Marktanner, 'Trapped by Consociationalism: The Case of Lebanon', *Topics in Middle Eastern and North African Economies* 4, no. 3 (2009), pp. 1–33.

Makong, Bernard, 'Kenya Rubbishes Impending ICJ Judgment on Somalia Case as Flawed', Capital News, 7 October 2021, https://www.capitalfm.co.ke/news/2021/10/kenya-rubbishes-impending-icj-judgment-on-somalia-case-as-flawed/

Malejacq, Romain, *Warlord Survival: The Delusion of State Building in Afghanistan* (Ithaca, NY: Cornell University Press, 2020).

Maley, William, and Ahmad Shuja Jamal, 'Diplomacy of Disaster: The Afghanistan "Peace Process" and the Taliban Occupation of Kabul', *The Hague Journal of Diplomacy* 17, no. 1 (2022), pp. 32–63, https://doi.org/10.1163/1871191x-bja10089

Mamdani, Mahmood, *Saviors and Survivors: Darfur, Politics, and the War on Terror* (Dakar: Council for the Development of Social Science Research in Africa, 2010).

Mamiya, Ralph, and Wibke Hansen, *Assessing the Effectiveness of the United Nations-African Union Hybrid Operation in Darfur (UNAMID)* (Oslo: Norwegian Institute of International Affairs, 2020), https://bitly.cx/vIQG

Manley, Tanner, 'Qatar's Next Diplomatic Step in Latin America?' Middle East Council on Global Affairs, 21 November 2023, https://mecouncil.org/blog_posts/qatars-next-diplomatic-step-in-latin-america

Manley, Tanner, and Leily Rossi, 'Mediating Multipolarity: Qatar's Role in U.S.-Venezuela Negotiations', Carnegie Endowment for International Peace, 5 September 2023, https://carnegieendowment.org/sada/2023/09/mediating-multipolarity-qatars-role-in-us-venezuela-negotiations?lang=en

Marks, Jesse, 'China's Strategic Facilitation in the Persian Gulf Security Crisis', in *China and Conflict Mediation Series* (Washington, DC: Stimson Center, 2024), https://www.stimson.org/2024/chinas-strategic-facilitation-in-the-persian-gulf-security-crisis/

Marsden, Rosalind, 'Peacemaking in Darfur and the Doha Process: The Role of International Actors', in Sarah M.H. Nouwen, Laura M. James, and Sharath Srinivasan (eds), *Making and Breaking Peace in Sudan and South Sudan: The Comprehensive Peace Agreement and Beyond* (London: British Academy Scholarship Online, 2020), pp. 230–57.

Mashal, Mujib, and Fatima Faizi, 'Afghanistan to Release Last Taliban Prisoners, Removing Final Hurdle to Talks', *The New York Times*, 9 August 2020, https://www.nytimes.com/2020/08/09/world/asia/afghanistan-taliban-prisoners-peace-talks.html

Masters, Jonathan, and Mohammed Aly Sergie, 'The Arab League', Council on Foreign Relations, 25 May 2023, https://www.cfr.org/backgrounder/arab-league#chapter-title-0–4

Mawdsley, Emma, *Recipients to Donors: Emerging Powers and the Changing Development Landscape* (London: Zed Books, 2012).

Mazzucco, Leonardo Jacopo Maria, 'The Gulf States Weigh Trade-Offs of Engaging with the Taliban', Gulf International Forum, 24 November 2022, https://gulfif.org/the-gulf-states-weigh-trade-offs-of-engaging-with-the-taliban/

Mazzucco, Leonardo Jacopo Maria, and Kristian P. Alexander, 'Saudi Arabia and Qatar Are Cooperating with the Taliban. But Their Approaches to Afghanistan Are Different', Atlantic Council, 12 January 2023, https://www.atlanticcouncil.org/blogs/menasource/saudi-arabia-and-qatar-are-cooperating-with-the-taliban-but-their-approaches-to-afghanistan-are-different/

McDonald, Henry, 'We Can Persuade Taliban to Be Peaceful—Expelled EU Man', *The Guardian*, 16 February 2008, https://www.theguardian.com/world/2008/feb/16/afghanistan.terrorism

Melzer, Natalie, and Wafaa Shurafa, 'Israel's Netanyahu Sends Mossad Director to Gaza Ceasefire Talks in Qatar in Sign of Progress', Associated Press, 12 January 2025, https://apnews.com/article/gaza-israel-palestinians-war-mossad-ceasefire-negotiations-63d38890b4628da8db75e58ba50d6ad9

Mesfin, Berouk, 'Qatar's Diplomatic Incursions into the Horn of Africa', Institute for Security Studies, November 2016, https://issafrica.s3.amazonaws.com/site/uploads/ear8.pdf

Middle East Eye, 'Qatar Blockade: Top UN Court Rules in Favour of Doha in Airspace Case', Middle East Eye, 14 July 2020, https://www.middleeasteye.net/news/qatar-blockade-un-icj-rules-favour-aviation-saudi-uae

———, 'Qatar to Withdraw as Key Mediator in Gaza Ceasefire Talks: Report', Middle East Eye, 9 November 2024, https://www.middleeasteye.net/news/qatar-withdraws-key-mediator-gaza-ceasefire-talks-report

———, 'Rival Libyan Tribes Sign Peace Deal in Qatar', Middle East Eye, 25 November 2015, https://www.middleeasteye.net/news/rival-libyan-tribes-sign-peace-deal-qatar

Middle East Monitor, 'France, Germany, UK Join Calls for "Immediate Resumption of Negotiations" in Middle East', Middle East Monitor, 12 August 2024, https://www.middleeastmonitor.com/20240812-france-germany-uk-join-calls-for-immediate-resumption-of-negotiations-in-middle-east

———, 'Iran Concessions to IAEA Largely Hinge on Future Talks—IAEA', Middle East Monitor, 6 March 2023, https://www.middleeastmonitor.com/20230306-iran-concessions-to-iaea-largely-hinge-on-future-talks-iaea

———, 'Qatar Praises New Agreement between Iran, IAEA', Middle East Monitor, 9 March 2023, https://www.middleeastmonitor.com/20230309-qatar-praises-new-agreement-between-iran-iaea

———, 'Qatar: Hamas Office in Doha Cannot Be Closed Due to Its Importance in Ending the Conflict', Middle East Monitor, 30 October 2023, https://www.middleeastmonitor.com/20231030-qatar-hamas-office-in-doha-cannot-be-closed-due-to-its-importance-in-ending-the-conflict

———, 'Tripartite Summit Brings Qatari Emir and Rwanda and Congo Presidents Together', Middle East Monitor, 19 March 2025, https://www.middleeastmonitor.com/20250319-tripartite-summit-brings-qatari-emir-and-rwanda-and-congo-presidents-together/

Mills, Andrew, 'How Qatar's Assertive Diplomacy Won a Break in the Gaza War', Reuters, 1 December 2023, https://www.reuters.com/world/middle-east/how-qatar-swayed-israel-hamas-make-truce-work-2023-11-30/

Mills, Andrew, and Ange Adihe Kasongo, 'Qatar Presents Draft Peace Proposal to Congo and M23 Rebels, Source Says', Reuters, 5 June 2025, https://www.reuters.com/world/middle-east/qatar-presents-draft-peace-proposal-congo-m23-rebels-source-says-2025-06-05/

Mills, Andrew, and Max Hunder, 'Six Ukrainian Children to Be Returned from Russia through Qatari Mediation', Reuters, 5 December 2023, https://www.reuters.com/world/europe/embargoed-six-ukrainian-children-be-returned-russia-through-qatari-mediation-2023-12-05/

Milton, Sansom, and Abdulrauf Elgeroshi, 'Libya's Conflict Stalemate: Towards a Multitrack Approach to Stability and Peace', Center for Conflict and Humanitarian Studies Policy Briefing, October 2022, https://chs-doha.org/en/Publications/Pages/Libya-s-Conflict-Stalemate-Towards-a-multitrack-approach-to-stability-and-peace.aspx

Milton, Sansom, and Ghassan Elkahlout, 'Qatar's Multifaceted Humanitarian Role in Afghanistan since August 2021', *Development Policy Review* 43, no. 1 (8 July 2024), pp. 1–21, https://doi.org/10.1111/dpr.12793

Milton, Sansom, Ghassan Elkahlout, and Saba Attallah, 'Shrinking Reconstruction Space in the Gaza Strip: Rebuilding after the 2021 and 2022 Wars', *Conflict, Security & Development* 24, no. 1 (4 March 2024), pp. 49–78, https://doi.org/10.1080/14678802.2024.2314034

Milton, Sansom, Ghassan Elkahlout, and Sana Tariq, 'Qatar's Evolving Role in

Conflict Mediation', *Mediterranean Politics* 30, no. 1 (16 October 2023), pp. 53–77, https://doi.org/10.1080/13629395.2023.2266665

Minich, Ruslan, 'Conflict Mediation: The Qatari Experience', *Historia i Polityka* 14, no. 21 (24 November 2015), pp. 121–33, https://doi.org/10.12775/hip.2015.026

Ministry of Foreign Affairs of the Islamic Republic of Iran, 'Statement by the Ministry of Foreign Affairs on the release of seized Iranian resources and the release of a number of prisoners illegally detained by the United States', Ministry of Foreign Affairs of the Islamic Republic of Iran, 3 August 2023, https://mfa.gov.ir/portal/NewsView/727109

Mladenov, Nickolay, 'The Arab Approach to Mediation: Reshaping Diplomacy in a Multipolar World', The Washington Institute, Spring 2024, https://www.washingtoninstitute.org/policy-analysis/arab-approach-mediation-reshaping-diplomacy-multipolar-world

MOFA, 'Advisor to Prime Minister and Official Spokesperson for Ministry of Foreign Affairs: Qatar Strongly Condemns Attack That Targeted Al-Udeid Air Base', Ministry of Foreign Affairs in the State of Qatar, 23 June 2025, https://mofa.gov.qa/en/qatar/latest-articles/latest-news/details/2025/06/23/advisor-to-prime-minister-and-official-spokesperson-for-ministry-of-foreign-affairs--qatar-strongly-condemns-attack-that-targeted-al-udeid-air-base

———, 'HE the Foreign Minister Participates in Ministerial Meeting on Syria', Ministry of Foreign Affairs in the State of Qatar, 15 October 2016, https://mofa.gov.qa/en/qatar/latest-articles/latest-news/details/2016/10/15/he-the-foreign-minister-participates-in-ministerial-meeting-on-syria

———, 'His Highness the Amir Participates in the Opening of the 77th Session of the United Nations General Assembly', Ministry of Foreign Affairs in the State of Qatar, 20 September 2022, https://ny.mission.qa/en/media/news/detail/1444/02/24/hi-highness-the-amir-participates-in-the-opening-of-the-77th-session-of-the-united-nations-general-assembly

———, 'Joint Communique of the Five-Member Ministerial Committee on Gaza's Meeting with the US President's Envoy to the Middle East', Ministry of Foreign Affairs in the State of Qatar, 12 March 2025, https://mofa.gov.qa/en/qatar/latest-articles/latest-news/details/2025/06/23/advisor-to-prime-minister-and-official-spokesperson-for-ministry-of-foreign-affairs--qatar-strongly-condemns-attack-that-targeted-al-udeid-air-base

———, 'Le Monde: Qatar Gave the Afghan Refugees Park View Facilities before the World Cup Fans', Ministry of Foreign Affairs in the State of Qatar, 18 October 2021, https://ny.consulate.qa/en/media/news/detail/1443/03/12/le-monde-qatar-gave-the-afghan-refugees-park-view-facilities-before-the-world-cup-fans

———, 'President of France-Qatar Friendship Group Thanks Qatar for Its Efforts to Reach Ceasefire in Palestine', Ministry of Foreign Affairs in the State of Qatar, 21 May 2021, https://www.mofa.gov.qa/en/all-mofa-news/details/1442/10/09/president-of-france-qatar-friendship-group-thanks-qatar-for-its-efforts-to-reach-ceasefire-in-palestine

———, 'Prime Minister and Minister of Foreign Affairs Meets Venezuela's Foreign Minister', Ministry of Foreign Affairs in the State of Qatar, 20 September 2023, https://mofa.gov.qa/en/qatar/latest-articles/latest-news/details/1445/03/05/prime-minister-and-minister-of-foreign-affairs-meets-venezuela's-foreign-minister

———, 'Qatar Affirms that It Is Making Unremitting Efforts Through Mediation to Resolve Conflicts in Africa', Ministry of Foreign Affairs in the State of Qatar, 20 May 2021, https://mofa.gov.qa/en/qatar/latest-articles/latest-news/details/1442/10/08/qatar-affirms-that-it-is-making-unremitting-efforts-through-mediation-to-resolve-conflicts-in-africa

———, 'Qatar Announces $3 Million Commitment to Ukrainian Parliament Commissioner Office for Human Rights', Ministry of Foreign Affairs in the State of Qatar, 26 April 2024, https://mofa.gov.qa/en/qatar/latest-articles/latest-news/details/2024/04/25/qatar-announces--3-million-commitment-to-ukrainian-parliament-commissioner-office-for-human-rights

———, 'Qatar Calls on the International Community to Support Palestinian Reconciliation', Ministry of Foreign Affairs in the State of Qatar, 30 April 2014, https://mofa.gov.qa/en/qatar/latest-articles/latest-news/details/2014/04/30/qatar-calls-on-the-international-community-to-support-palestinian-reconciliation

———, 'Qatar Committee for Reconstruction of Gaza Affirms Qatar's Continuous Support for Palestinians', Ministry of Foreign Affairs in the State of Qatar, 4 February 2025, https://mofa.gov.qa/en/qatar/latest-articles/latest-news/details/1442/06/22/qatar-committee-for-reconstruction-of-gaza-affirms-qatar's-continuous-support-for-palestinians

———, 'Qatar Pledges USD 100 Million for Humanitarian Assistance to Ukraine', Ministry of Foreign Affairs in the State of Qatar, 28 July 2023, https://mofa.gov.qa/en/qatar/latest-articles/latest-news/details/1445/01/10/qatar-pledges-usd-100-million-for-humanitarian-assistance-to-ukraine

———, 'Qatar Praises New Deal Between Iran, IAEA', Ministry of Foreign Affairs in the State of Qatar, 9 March 2024, https://mofa.gov.qa/en/qatar/latest-articles/latest-news/details/1444/08/16/qatar-praises-new-deal-between-iran-iaea

———, 'Qatar, Turkey and Russia Affirm the Need to Preserve Sovereignty and Territorial Integrity of Syria', Ministry of Foreign Affairs in the State of Qatar, 11 March 2021, https://mofa.gov.qa/en/qatar/latest-articles/latest-news/details/1442/07/27/qatar-turkey-and-russia-affirm-the-need-to-preserve-sovereignty-and-territorial-integrity-of-syria

———, 'Qatar Urges Iran, IAEA to Continue Cooperation to Resolve Standing Issues in Iranian Nuclear Program', Ministry of Foreign Affairs in the State of Qatar, 13 September 2023, https://mofa.gov.qa/en/qatar/latest-articles/latest-news/details/1445/02/28/qatar-urges-iran-iaea-to-continue-cooperation-to-resolve-standing-issues-in-iranian-nuclear-program

———, 'Qatar Welcomes Hosting Indirect Talks between the United States and Iran in Doha to Revive the Nuclear Deal', Ministry of Foreign Affairs in the State of Qatar, 28 June 2024, https://mofa.gov.qa/en/statements/qatar-welcomes-hosting-indirect-talks-between-the-united-states-and-iran-in-doha-to-revive-the-nuclear-deal

———, 'Security Council Hails Qatar's Role in US-Taliban Negotiations', Ministry of Foreign Affairs in the State of Qatar, 11 March 2020, https://ny.mission.qa/en/media/news/detail/1442/04/16/security-council-hails-qatar's-role-in-us-taliban-negotiations

———, 'Spokesperson for the Ministry of Foreign Affairs: Qatar's Efforts to Mediate between Hamas and Israel Are Currently Stalled', Ministry of Foreign Affairs in the State of Qatar, 9 November 2024, https://mofa.gov.qa/en/qatar/latest-articles/latest-news/details/2024/11/09/spokesperson-for-the-ministry-of-foreign-affairs--qatar's-efforts-to-mediate-between-hamas-and-israel-are-currently-stalled

Mohammed, Yusuf Ali, 'Maritime Border Dispute between Kenya and Somalia in the Indian Ocean', *Mersin University Journal of Maritime Faculty* 5, no. 1 (30 June 2023), pp. 1–6, https://doi.org/10.47512/meujmaf.1230643

Mohtar, Rabi H., 'Opportunities and Challenges for Innovations in Qatar', *The Muslim World* 105, no. 1 (19 December 2014), pp. 46–57, https://doi.org/10.1111/muwo.12079

Mouin Rabbani, 'Qatar and the Palestinians', Jadaliyya, 1 December 2012, https://www.jadaliyya.com/Details/27510

Muaddi, Qassam, 'Netanyahu Suspends Release of 600+ Palestinian Prisoners over "Degrading" Handover Ceremony', Mondoweiss, 23 February 2025, https://mondoweiss.net/2025/02/netanyahu-suspends-release-of-600-palestinian-prisoners-over-degrading-handover-ceremony/

Mudge, Lewis, 'Chad: How Much Longer Will the Military Council Stay?' Human Rights Watch, 20 April 2022, https://www.hrw.org/news/2022/04/20/chad-how-much-longer-will-military-council-stay

Nagmeldin, Karamalla Gaiballa, 'The Qatari Efforts to Resolve the Armed Conflict in Darfur—The Challenges and Obstacles', *International Journal of Sudan Research* 7, no. 1 (15 January 2017), pp. 57–65, https://doi.org/10.47556/j.ijsr.7.1.2017.5

Nakhleh, Emile A., 'Labor Markets and Citizenship in Bahrayn and Qatar', *Middle East Journal* 31, no. 2 (1977), pp. 143–56.

Natsios, Andrew S., 'Darfur: A "Plan B" to Stop Genocide?' U.S. Department of State Archive, 11 April 2007, https://2001-2009.state.gov/p/af/rls/rm/82941.htm

———, *Sudan, South Sudan, and Darfur: What Everyone Needs to Know* (New York: Oxford University Press, 2012).

Nonneman, Gerd, 'The Gulf States and the Iran–Iraq War: Pattern Shifts and Continuities', in Lawrence G Potter and Gary G Sick (eds), *Iran, Iraq, and the Legacies of War* (New York: Palgrave Macmillan, 2004), pp. 167–92.

Nufal, Ahmad S., 'The Gulf States and the Crisis over Kuwait', *Arab Studies Quarterly* 13, no. 1/2 (1 January 1991), pp. 37–51, http://www.jstor.org/stable/10.2307/41858950?refreqid=fastly-default

Nuruzzaman, Mohammed, 'Gulf Cooperation Council (GCC), Qatar and Dispute Mediations: A Critical Investigation', *Contemporary Arab Affairs* 8, no. 4 (27 October 2015), pp. 535–52, https://doi.org/10.1080/17550912.2015.1078073

———, 'Qatar and the Arab Spring: Down the Foreign Policy Slope', *Contemporary Arab Affairs* 8, no. 2 (27 April 2015), pp. 226–38, https://doi.org/10.1080/17550912.2015.1024034

Nye, Joseph, *Soft Power: The Means to Success in World Politics* (New York: Public Affairs, 2004).

O'Connor, Mary, 'Joy for Six Ukrainian Children as They Are Reunited with Their Families Following Qatar-Brokered Deal with Moscow 20 Months after They Were Snatched by Russia', Daily Mail Online, 5 December 2023, https://www.dailymail.co.uk/news/article-12827325/Joy-six-Ukrainian-children-reunited-families-following-Qatar-brokered-deal-Moscow-20-months-snatched-Russia

Olsson, Ola, and Eyerusalem Siba, 'Ethnic Cleansing or Resource Struggle in Darfur? An Empirical Analysis', *Journal of Development Economics* 103 (July 2013), pp. 299–312, https://doi.org/10.1016/j.jdeveco.2013.02.004

Organization of Islamic Cooperation, *Resolution of the Twentieth Extraordinary Session of the Council of Foreign Ministers on Palestine* (OIC/EXCFM-20/2025/Res.Final) (Jeddah: Organisation of Islamic Cooperation, 2025), https://bit.ly/444yiIG

Oxford Analytica, 'Qatar's Rewarding Afghan Role Carries Future Risks', *Expert Briefings*, 23 September 2021, https://doi.org/10.1108/OXAN-DB264285

Paczyńska, Agnieszka, '"New" State Actors and Conflict-Affected States: Confronting Violence, Shifting Ambitions, and Adjusting Principles', *Frontiers in Political Science* 3, (7 May 2021), https://doi.org/10.3389/fpos.2021.663432

Pamuk, Humeyra, 'Qatar Open to Reconsidering Hamas Presence in Qatar, US Official Says', Reuters, 27 October 2023, https://www.reuters.com/world/middle-east/qatar-told-us-it-is-open-reconsidering-hamas-presence-us-official-says-2023-10-27/

Pericoli, Altea, and Federico Donelli, 'Qatar's Foreign Aid and Political Strategies in the Horn of Africa: The Case of Somalia', *Global Policy* 15, no. 1 (26 October 2023), pp. 53–65, https://doi.org/10.1111/1758-5899.13294

Peter, Mateja, and Haley Rice, *Non-Western Approaches to Peacemaking and Peacebuilding: State-of-the-Art and an Agenda for Research* (Edinburgh: PeaceRep: The Peace and Conflict Resolution Evidence Platform, 2022), https://peacerep.org/wp-content/uploads/2022/04/State-of-the-Art-Report-Digital-1.pdf

Petraeus, David, 'Afghanistan Did Not Have to Turn out This Way', *The Atlantic*, 8 August 2022, https://www.theatlantic.com/international/archive/2022/08/us-withdrawal-afghanistan-strategy-shortcomings/670980/

Pinfari, Marco, 'Nothing but Failure? The Arab League and the Gulf Cooperation Council as Mediators in Middle Eastern Conflicts', *LSE Crisis States Research Centre Working Papers* 45 (2009), https://www.files.ethz.ch/isn/98212/WP45.2.pdf

Pinkas, Alon, 'Qatar Is Part of the Solution to Israel's War in Gaza, Not the Problem', Haaretz.com, 18 April 2024, https://www.haaretz.com/israel-news/2024–04–18/ty-article/.premium/qatar-is-part-of-the-solution-to-gaza-war-not-the-problem/0000018e-f0c4-daad-a3de-fefff8c90000

Planning & Statistics Authority in Qatar, *Sustainable Development Goals in the State of Qatar 2022*, March 2023, https://www.npc.qa/en/media/Doc/Sustainable/SDG_Report_2022.pdf (accessed 15 June 2025).

Presidency of the Arab Republic of Egypt, *Cairo Statement Issued by the Extraordinary Arab Summit (Palestine Summit)*, Presidency of the Arab Republic of Egypt, 4 March 2025, https://bit.ly/4dYnu3f

President of Russia, 'Meeting with Emir of Qatar Sheikh Tamim Bin Hamad Al Thani', President of Russia, 4 July 2024, http://en.kremlin.ru/events/president/news/74468

PressTV, 'FM Says Iran Committed to Enhance Ties with Qatar after Retaliatory Strike on US Base', PressTV, 24 June 2025, https://www.presstv.ir/Detail/2025/06/24/750099/fm-says-iran-committed-enhance-ties-qatar-retaliatory-strike-us-base

Pronk, Jan, 'Darfur Agreement Is Severely Paralysed', *Sudan Tribune*, 28 June 2006, https://sudantribune.com/?p=16982&lang=en

Qarjouli, Asmahan, 'DRC, Rwanda to Sign Peace Deal June 27 Following Qatar's Mediation', *Doha News*, 19 June 2025, https://dohanews.co/drc-rwanda-to-sign-peace-deal-june-27-following-qatars-mediation/

———, 'Exclusive: Mass Evacuation of Afghans "Draining Afghanistan of Its Brains", Qatar's Lolwah Al Khater Says', *Doha News*, 29 August 2021, https://dohanews.co/exclusive-mass-evacuation-of-afghans-draining-afghanistan-of-its-brains-qatars-lolwah-al-khater-says/

———, 'Iran Tells Mediators Qatar, Oman It Will Not Negotiate "While under Attack"', *Doha News*, 16 June 2025, https://dohanews.co/iran-tells-mediators-qatar-oman-it-will-not-negotiate-while-under-attack/

———, 'Qatar and Venezuela Take on Bilateral Ties in Doha Meeting', *Doha News*, 9 October 2023, https://dohanews.co/qatar-and-venezuela-take-on-bilateral-ties-in-doha-meeting

———, 'Qatar Helps Facilitate Release of US Aid Worker from Taliban Custody', *Doha News*, 3 April 2022, https://dohanews.co/qatar-helps-facilitate-release-of-us-aid-worker-from-taliban-custody/

———, 'Qatar "Re-Evaluating" Mediation Role, Calls out "Exploitation and Abuse" of Efforts', *Doha News*, 17 April 2024, https://dohanews.co/qatar-re-evaluating-mediation-role-calls-out-exploitation-and-abuse-of-efforts/

———, 'Qatar Supports Students in Afghanistan with 60 Tonnes of Educational Material', *Doha News*, 19 April 2023, https://dohanews.co/qatar-supports-students-in-afghanistan-with-60-tonnes-of-educational-material/

Qarmout, Tamer, 'How the International System Failed', Middle East Eye, 2 February 2024, https://www.middleeasteye.net/opinion/israel-war-gaza-upended-region-what-comes-next

———, 'Predictable in Their Failure: An Analysis of Mediation Efforts to End the Palestinian Split', *International Peacekeeping* 31, no. 4 (15 April 2024), pp. 283–308, https://doi.org/10.1080/13533312.2024.2338410

Qatar-Afghanistan Mediation Archive, 'The Qatari Role in Operating Kabul Airport: A World Perspective', Qatar-Afghanistan Mediation Archive, 28 September 2024, https://qama.qa/2024/09/28/the-qatari-role-in-operating-kabul-airport-a-world-perspective/

Qatar Chamber, 'Qatar Chamber Explores Cooperation Links with Latin American Countries', Qatar Chamber, 28 May 2024, https://www.qatarchamber.com/qatar-chamber-cooperation-latin-american-countries

Qatar Charity, 'Qatar Charity Opens Taiba Education City for Orphans in Sudan', Qatar Charity, 29 June 2021, https://www.qcharity.org/en/global/news/detailsinternational/19378-qatar-charity-opens-taiba

Qatar Embassy in Dushanbe—Republic of Tajikistan, 'Qatari Mediation Succeeds in Releasing Four Tajikistani Soldiers', Qatar Embassy in Dushanbe—Republic of Tajikistan, Ministry of Foreign Affairs, 13 June 2015, https://dushanbe.embassy.qa/en/media/news/detail/2016/12/06/qatari-mediation-succeeds-in-releasing-four-tajikistani-soldiers

Qatar Foundation, 'Qatar Has Been the Gateway to a Better Life for Us, Says Captain of Afghan Robotics Team', Qatar Foundation, 1 August 2022, https://www.qf.org.qa/stories/qatar-has-been-the-gateway-to-a-better-life-for-us-says-captain-of-afghan

———, 'QF Volunteers Support Afghan Refugees in Qatar', Qatar Foundation, 13 September 2021, https://www.qf.org.qa/stories/qf-volunteers-support-afghan-refugees-in-qatar

Qatar Fund for Development, 'Qatar Fund for Development Annual Report 2016', Qatar Fund for Development, 2017, https://exsjwzu9tz6.exactdn.com/wp-content/uploads/2021/01/QFFD-Report-English.pdf

Qatar News Agency, 'Doha Peace Agreement: New Success for Qatar in International Mediation, Conflict Resolution', Qatar News Agency, 8 August 2022, https://www.gulf-times.com/story/722404/doha-peace-agreement-new-success-for-qatar-in-international-mediation-conflict-resolution

———, 'Palestinian PM to QNA: Qatar Provides Fundamental Political, Moral, Financial Support for Palestinian Cause', Qatar News Agency, 7 June 2021, https://qna.org.qa/en/news/news-details?id=0043-palestinian-pm-to-qna-qatar-provides-fundamental-political,-moral,-financial-support-for-palestinian-cause&date=7/06/2021

———, 'Qatar's Support for Palestinian Cause… Firm Principles, Noble Humanitarian Values', Qatar News Agency, 21 October 2023, https://www.qna.org.qa/en/News-Area/News/2023-10/21/0009-qatars-support-for-palestinian-cause-firm-principles,-noble-humanitarian-values

———, 'Reuniting Ukrainian Families… Qatar Reinforces New Concept of Humanitarian Diplomacy', Qatar News Agency, 15 June 2024, https://www.qna.org.qa/en/newsbulletins/2024-06/15/0012-reuniting-ukrainian-families-qatar-reinforces-new-concept-of-humanitarian-diplomacy

———, 'UK, France, Germany, Italy Foreign Ministers Affirm Support for Gaza Mediation Efforts', Qatar News Agency, 17 August 2024, https://qna.org.qa/en/news/news-details?id=0035-uk,-france,-germany,-italy-foreign-ministers-affirm-support-for-gaza-mediation-efforts&date=17/08/2024

Qatar Red Crescent Society, 'QRCS Commences Construction Works at QFFD-Funded Development Project in West Darfur', ReliefWeb, 19 January 2021, https://reliefweb.int/report/sudan/qrcs-commences-construction-works-qffd-funded-development-project-west-darfur-enar

———, 'QRCS Online Reporting for Projects in Afghanistan', Qatar Red Crescent Society, https://www.qrcs.org.qa/en/Pages/CountryDetails.aspx?CountryId=/5cV605IEqY=# (accessed 30 April 2025).

———, 'QRCS, KRCS Relieve Affected Population in Afghanistan', Qatar Red Crescent Society, 19 July 2022, https://www.qrcs.org.qa/en/News/Pages/QRCS,-KRCS-relieve-affected-population-in-Afghanistan.aspx?NewsId=51O5pbICUEM

Qatar's Gaza Reconstruction Committee, 'Grant of HH the Emir of the State of Qatar for the Relief of the Gaza Strip 2018' [in Arabic], Qatar's Gaza Reconstruction Committee, https://q-grc.ps/grants (accessed 5 November 2024).

Qazi, Shehzad H., 'The "Neo-Taliban" and Counterinsurgency in Afghanistan', *Third World Quarterly* 31, no. 3 (2010), pp. 485–99, https://doi.org/10.1080/01436597.2010.488484

Quadir, Fahimul, 'Rising Donors and the New Narrative of "South–South" Cooperation: What Prospects for Changing the Landscape of Development Assistance Programmes?' *Third World Quarterly* 34, no. 2 (March 2013), pp. 321–38, https://doi.org/10.1080/01436597.2013.775788

Rabi, Uzi, 'Qatar's Relations with Israel: Challenging Arab and Gulf Norms', *The Middle East Journal* 63, no. 3 (1 June 2009), pp. 443–59, https://doi.org/10.3751/63.3.15

Raz, Ido Gadi, 'China's New Mediating Role and the Palestinian-Israeli Conflict', *Israel Affairs* 30, no. 5 (2024), pp. 1090–112, https://doi.org/10.1080/13537121.2024.2394320

RBC, 'Katar Soobshchil o Posrednichestve v Peredache 4 Detey Iz Rossii Na Ukrainu' [in Russian], RBC Group, 16 October 2023, https://www.rbc.ru/politics/16/10/2023/652cef4c9a7947745bb4a19f

Reeves, Eric, 'UN Displacement Figures for Darfur: Assessment, Confused Guesses, or Dissimulation?' *Sudan Tribune*, 21 December 2015, https://sudantribune.com/?p=55817&lang=en

Refugees International, 'Sudan: Saving the Darfur Peace Agreement', Refugees International Bulletin, 21 August 2006, https://www.refworld.org/reference/countryrep/ri/2006/en/49658

ReliefWeb, 'Sudan, Armed Groups Agree to Resume Talks for Peace in Darfur', ReliefWeb, 7 December 2018, https://reliefweb.int/report/sudan/sudan-armed-groups-agree-resume-talks-peace-darfur

Rémy, Jean-Philippe, and Ghazal Golshiri, 'Fear of Regional War Heightens after Iran Missile Attack on Israel', *Le Monde*, 2 October 2024, https://www.lemonde.fr/en/international/article/2024/10/02/fear-of-regional-war-heightens-after-iran-missile-attack-on-israel_6727976_4.html

Republic of Lebanon—Ministry of Finance, *International Conference for Support to Lebanon—Paris III: First Progress Report* (Beirut: Republic of Lebanon—Ministry of Finance, 2007), https://www.finance.gov.lb/en-us/Finance/DC/AC/Documents/Paris%20III%20First%20Progress%20Report.pdf

Reuters, 'Israel, Hamas Reach Ceasefire Deal to End 15 Months of War in Gaza', Reuters, 16 January 2025, https://www.reuters.com/world/middle-east/gaza-ceasefire-appears-close-us-egyptian-leaders-put-focus-coming-hours-2025-01-14/

———, 'Israel–Hamas War: The Hostage Deal and Ceasefire Explained', Reuters, 27 November 2023, https://www.reuters.com/world/middle-east/israel-hamas-war-hostage-deal-ceasefire-gaza-2023-11-22

———, 'Israel's Far-Right Finance Minister Withdraws Threat to Quit Coalition over Ceasefire Deal', Reuters, 27 January 2025, https://www.reuters.com/world/middle-east/israels-far-right-finance-minister-withdraws-threat-quit-coalition-over-2025-01-27/

———, 'Libyan Parliament Speaker Says Election Plan Approved', Reuters, 9 September 2021, https://www.reuters.com/world/africa/libyan-parliament-speaker-says-election-plan-approved-2021-09-09/

———, 'Qatar Pulls off Mediation Coup in Lebanon Crisis', Reuters, 22 May 2008, https://www.reuters.com/article/world/qatar-pulls-off-mediation-coup-in-lebanon-crisis-idUSL22740435/

———, 'US Envoy Asked Middle East Foreign Ministers to Mediate with Iran', Reuters, 11 April 2024, https://www.reuters.com/world/middle-east/us-envoy-asked-middle-east-foreign-ministers-mediate-with-iran-2024-04-11

Richelieu, André, Yen-Chun Lin, and Ho Keat Leng, 'A Typology of Countries Using Place Branding through Sport', *Journal of Global Sport Management*, 19 September 2021, pp. 1–19, https://doi.org/10.1080/24704067.2021.1972431

Roberts, David B., 'Qatar and the UAE: Exploring Divergent Responses to the Arab Spring', *The Middle East Journal* 71, no. 4 (1 September 2017), pp. 544–62, https://doi.org/10.3751/71.4.12

———, *Reflecting on the GCC Crisis: Qatar and Its Neighbours*, 1st edn (London: Routledge, 2022).

———, 'Understanding Qatar's Foreign Policy Objectives', *Mediterranean Politics* 17, no. 2 (18 July 2012), pp. 233–39, https://doi.org/10.1080/13629395.2012.695123

Roggio, Bill, 'Taliban Calls Afghan Government "Impotent," Says Negotiating with It Is "a Waste of Time"', *Long War Journal*, 28 November 2018, https://www.longwarjournal.org/archives/2018/11/taliban-calls-afghan-government-impotent-says-negotiating-with-it-is-a-waste-of-time.php

Rowayheb, Marwan George, 'Political Change and the Outbreak of Civil War: The Case of Lebanon', *Civil Wars* 13, no. 4 (December 2011), pp. 414–36, https://doi.org/10.1080/13698249.2011.629871

Ruttig, Thomas, 'How Tribal Are the Taliban?' in Shahzad Bashir and Robert Crews (eds), *Under the Drones: Modern Lives in the Afghanistan-Pakistan Borderlands* (Cambridge, MA: Harvard University Press, 2012), pp. 102–35.

Sack, Mary, and Cyrus Samii, 'An Interview with Lakhdar Brahimi', *Journal of International Affairs* 58, no. 1 (Fall 2004), pp. 239–47, https://www.proquest.com/docview/220720597?sourcetype=Scholarly%20Journals

Sadiki, Larbi, and Layla Saleh, '"Writing" Small States: Contextualizing the Construct in the Arab Gulf', *International Politics* 60, no. 2 (27 July 2021), pp. 371–89, https://doi.org/10.1057/s41311-021-00335-y

Saeed, Sami, 'Darfur Dialogue: From War to Peace, Coexistence and Stability', *Idea International Journal*, 6 December 2023, https://doi.org/10.31752/idea.2023.91

Saidy, Brahim, 'Qatari-US Military Relations: Context, Evolution and Prospects', *Contemporary Arab Affairs* 10, no. 2 (1 April 2017), pp. 286–99, https://doi.org/10.1080/17550912.2016.1244902

Salamey, Imad, *The Government and Politics of Lebanon* (London: Routledge, 2013).

Salari, Fatemeh, 'Qatar Charity Partners with UN to Help Afghan Refugees', *Doha News*, 30 January 2022, https://dohanews.co/qatar-charity-partners-with-un-to-help-afghan-refugees/

Salmoni, Barak, Bryce Loidolt, and Madeleine Wells, 'Regime and Periphery in Northern Yemen: The Huthi Phenomenon', RAND Corporation, 14 April 2010, https://www.rand.org/pubs/monographs/MG962.html

Sawafta, Ali, 'Palestinian Rivals Agree to Form Unity Government', Reuters, 6 February 2012, https://www.reuters.com/article/world/palestinian-rivals-agree-to-form-unity-government-idUSTRE8150KX

Schaer, Cathrin, 'Israel-Hamas Ceasefire: Why Qatar Is Such a Good Negotiator', Deutsche Welle, 16 January 2025, https://www.dw.com/en/israel-hamas-ceasefire-why-qatar-is-such-a-good-negotiator/a-69995458

Schiff, Amira, 'The Boy Who Plugs a Dike with His Finger: UN Mediation in the Gaza-Israel Crisis, 2018–2019', *International Negotiation* 27, no. 3 (2022), pp. 386–417, https://doi.org/10.1177/23477970241298839

Schultz, Kenneth, *Great Power Mediation: Opportunities and Challenges for China* (Washington, DC: The Stimson Center, 2019), https://bit.ly/42NWn4e

Schwarz, Birgit, 'Nothing to Go Back to—From Kenya's Vast Refugee Camp', Human Rights Watch, 26 May 2016, https://www.hrw.org/news/2016/05/27/nothing-go-back-kenyas-vast-refugee-camp

Shad, Muhammad Riaz, and Sajid Iqbal, 'From Intervention to Exit: An Analysis of Post-9/11 US Strategies in Afghanistan', *Margalla Papers* 25, no. 2 (31 December 2021), pp. 23–34, https://doi.org/10.54690/margallapapers.25.2.70

Shalizi, Hamid, Abdul Qadir Sediqi, and Rupam Jain, 'Taliban Step up Attacks on Afghan Forces since Signing U.S. Deal—Data', Reuters, 1 May 2020, https://www.reuters.com/article/us-health-coronavirus-afghanistan-taliba/taliban-step-up-attacks-on-afghan-forces-since-signing-u-s-deal-data-idUSKBN22D5S7

Shams, Shamil, and Masood Saifullah, 'Ghani's Last-Ditch Effort to Stop Taliban Gains', Deutsche Welle, 24 June 2021, https://www.dw.com/en/biden-ghani-meeting-afghan-president-makes-last-ditch-effort-to-stop-taliban-gains/a-58034686

Sheikh, Mona, and Maja Greenwood, *Taliban Talks: Past, Present and Prospects for the*

US, Afghanistan and Pakistan (Copenhagen: Danish Institute for International Studies, 2013), https://www.diis.dk/files/media/publications/import/extra/rp2013-06-taliban-talks_web.jpg.pdf

Simmons, Mark, and Peter Dixon (eds), *Peace by Piece: Addressing Sudan's Conflicts* (London: Conciliation Resources, 2006).

Skånland, Øystein Haga, '"Norway Is a Peace Nation": A Discourse Analytic Reading of the Norwegian Peace Engagement', *Cooperation and Conflict* 45, no. 1 (2010), pp. 34–54, https://doi.org/10.1177/0010836709347212

Slim, Randa M., 'Small-State Mediation in International Relations: The Algerian Mediation of the Iranian Hostage Crisis', in Jacob Bercovitch and Jeffery Z. Rubin (eds), *Mediation in International Relations: Multiple Approaches to Conflict Management* (London: Palgrave Macmillan, 1992), pp. 206–31.

Soghom, Mardo, 'Iran Contradicts US, Denying Restrictions on Unfrozen Funds', Iran International, 12 August 2023, https://www.iranintl.com/en/202308122240

Somali National News Agency, 'A Communique on the Resumption of Diplomatic Relations between the Republic of Kenya and the Federal Republic of Somalia', Somali National News Agency, 6 May 2021, https://sonna.so/en/a-communique-on-the-resumption-of-diplomatic-relations-between-the-republic-of-kenya-and-the-federal-republic-of-somalia/

Somaliland Chronicle, 'Breaking: Qatar Offered to Mediate Somaliland—Somalia Talks and Direct Flight of Qatar Airways to Somaliland', *Somaliland Chronicle*, 7 May 2021, https://somalilandchronicle.com/2021/05/07/breaking-qatar-offered-to-mediate-somaliland-and-somalia-talks-and-direct-flight-of-qatar-airways-to-somaliland/

Sopko, John, and David Young, 'The Factors Leading to the Collapse of the Afghan Government and Its Security Forces', Special Inspector General for Afghanistan Reconstruction, 2 March 2023, https://www.sigar.mil/Portals/147/Files/News/Speeches/SIGAR_John_Sopko_David_Young_Berlin_Speech_2023-03-02.pdf

Spyer, Jonathan, 'Lebanon 2006: Unfinished War', *Middle East Review of International Affairs* 12, no. 1 (13 March 2008).

Stansfield, Gareth R.V., 'The 1995–96 Yemen-Eritrea Conflict over the Islands of Hanish and Jabal Zuqar: A Geopolitical Analysis', *Durham Middle East Papers* 66 (February 2001), https://durham-repository.worktribe.com/output/1699302

Steinberg, Guido, *Qatar's Foreign Policy: Decision-Making Processes, Baselines, and Strategies* (Berlin: Stiftung Wissenschaft und Politik, 2023).

STRATEGIECS Team, 'The Paths of Political Presence of Hamas Movement in Qatar', STRATEGIECS Think Tank, 28 April 2024, https://strategiecs.com/en/analyses/the-paths-of-political-presence-of-hamas-movement-in-qatar

Sudan Tribune, 'France Supports Qatari Efforts to Bring Peace in Darfur', *Sudan Tribune*, 12 September 2008, https://sudantribune.com/?p=28554&lang=en

———, 'JEM Holds Talks with Qataris over Darfur Peace Process', *Sudan Tribune*, 2 December 2008, https://sudantribune.com/?p=29369&lang=en

———, 'Qatar Proposed as Host to International Summit on Darfur', *Sudan Tribune*, 4 September 2008, https://sudantribune.com/?p=28463&lang=en

———, 'Qatar Says Ready to Participate Actively in Darfur Economic Development', *Sudan Tribune*, 5 June 2011, https://sudantribune.com/?p=38691&lang=en

———, 'Sudan Acknowledges Obstacles with Qatari Mediation, Blast France', *Sudan Tribune*, 1 January 2009, https://sudantribune.com/?p=29633&lang=en

Suhrke, Astri, *When More Is Less: The International Project in Afghanistan* (New York: Columbia University Press, 2011).

Sultany, Nimer, 'A Threshold Crossed: On Genocidal Intent and the Duty to Prevent Genocide in Palestine', *Journal of Genocide Research*, 9 May 2024, pp. 1–26, https://doi.org/10.1080/14623528.2024.2351261

Tait, Robert, 'US Asks Qatar to "Turn down the Volume" of Al Jazeera News Coverage', *The Guardian*, 27 October 2023, https://www.theguardian.com/media/2023/oct/27/us-asks-qatar-to-turn-down-the-volume-of-al-jazeera-news-coverage

Tantoh, Michael, 'Chad: Will the National Dialogue Resume?' AllAfrica.com, 5 September 2022, https://allafrica.com/stories/202209050491.html

Taulbee, James Larry, Ann Kelleher, and Peter C. Grosvenor, 'The Peace Engagement of a Peace Culture: Observations on the National Identity Foundations of Norwegian Foreign Policy', in *Norway's Peace Policy* (New York: Palgrave Macmillan, 2014), pp. 23–47, https://doi.org/10.1057/9781137429193_2

The Amiri Diwan, 'Sheikh Ahmad Bin Ali Al Thani', The Amiri Diwan, https://www.diwan.gov.qa/about-qatar/qatars-rulers/sheikh-ahmad-bin-ali-al-thani (accessed 18 February 2025).

———, 'Sheikh Jassim Bin Mohammed Bin Thani', The Amiri Diwan, https://www.diwan.gov.qa/about-qatar/qatars-rulers/sheikh-jassim-bin-mohammed-bin-thani?sc_lang=en (accessed 25 February 2025).

———, 'The Constitution of the State of Qatar', The Amiri Diwan, https://www.diwan.gov.qa/-/media/Diwan-Amiri/Files/Constitution-EN.ashx?la=en (accessed 25 February 2025).

The Economist Intelligence Unit, 'Qatari Mediation Still Needed for US-Taliban Deal', *The Economist Intelligence Unit*, 19 September 2019, https://country.eiu.com/article.aspx?articleid=1288456512&Country=Qatar&topic=Politics&subtopic=Forecast&subsubtopic=International+relations&oid=1858473769

The Enough Project, 'First Days at Doha', The Enough Project, 13 February 2009, https://enoughproject.org/blog/first-days-doha

———, 'The Darfur Peace Process: Recipe for a Bad Deal?' The Enough Project, 6 April 2010, https://enoughproject.org/reports/update-doha

The New Arab, 'Exclusive: How Iran, US Quietly Agreed to Negotiate in Oman', *The New Arab*, 8 April 2025, https://www.newarab.com/news/exclusive-how-iran-us-quietly-agreed-negotiate-oman

———, 'What is the Israel-Hamas Gaza Ceasefire Deal Presented by Joe Biden?'

The New Arab, 1 June 2024, https://www.newarab.com/news/what-gaza-ceasefire-deal-presented-joe-biden

The New Humanitarian, 'SUDAN-ERITREA: Reconciliation Agreement Signed', The New Humanitarian, 1 May 1999, https://www.thenewhumanitarian.org/news/1999/05/01/sudan-eritrea-reconciliation-agreement-signed

The Peninsula, 'Full Speech of Amir at the Opening Session of 77th UN General Assembly', *The Peninsula*, 20 September 2022, https://thepeninsulaqatar.com/article/20/09/2022/full-speech-of-amir-at-the-opening-session-of-77th-un-general-assembly

———, 'Lack of Serious Negotiations by Participating Parties Pushed Qatar to Suspend Gaza Mediation', *The Peninsula*, 20 November 2024, https://thepeninsulaqatar.com/article/20/11/2024/lack-of-serious-negotiations-by-participating-parties-pushed-qatar-to-suspend-gaza-mediation

———, 'Qatar Consistent in Helping the Oppressed', *The Peninsula*, 23 October 2014, https://thepeninsulaqatar.com/article/23/10/2014/qatar-consistent-in-helping-the-oppressed

———, 'Qatar's Successful Mediation Leads to US, Venezuela Prisoner Exchange', *The Peninsula*, 21 December 2023, https://thepeninsulaqatar.com/article/21/12/2023/qatars-successful-mediation-leads-to-us,-venezuela-prisoner-exchange

———, 'QFFD Signs Deal to Support 30,000 Afghan Students', *The Peninsula*, 22 March 2023, https://thepeninsulaqatar.com/article/22/03/2023/qffd-signs-deal-to-support-30000-afghan-students

———, 'Rubio Praises Qatar's "Reliable" Mediation in American Hostage Release', *The Peninsula*, 21 March 2025, https://s.thepeninsula.qa/nbkvsl

Tok, Mohamed Evren, 'Gulf Donors and the 2030 Agenda: Towards a Khaleeji Mode of Development Cooperation', Centre for Policy Research (United Nations University), 2015.

Tomorrow's Affairs, 'Qatar's Withdrawal from the Peace Process—Maintaining Influence as an Important Negotiator', Tomorrow's Affairs, 10 November 2024, https://tomorrowsaffairs.com/qatar-s-withdrawal-from-the-peace-process-maintaining-influence-as-an-important-negotiator

Touval, Saadia, and Jeffery Z. Rubin, 'The Superpowers as Mediators', in Jacob Bercovitch and Jeffery Z. Rubin (eds), *Mediation in International Relations: Multiple Approaches to Conflict Management* (London: Palgrave Macmillan, 1992), pp. 232–48.

Tran, Mark, 'Senior Afghan Taliban Leaders Arrested in Pakistan', *The Guardian*, 18 February 2010, https://www.theguardian.com/world/2010/feb/18/pakistan-market-bombing-orakzai

Tubiana, Jérôme, Victor Tanner, and Musa Adam Abdul-Jalil, 'Traditional Authorities' Peacemaking Role in Darfur', United States Institute of Peace, 8 November 2012, https://www.usip.org/publications/2012/11/traditional-authorities-peacemaking-role-darfur

Tür, Özlem, 'The Lebanese War of 2006: Reasons and Consequences', *Perceptions*, Spring 2007, pp. 109–22.

Türedi, Almula, 'Lebanon: At the Edge of Another Civil War', *Perceptions* 13, no. 1 (2008), pp. 21–36.

Ullah, AKM Ahsan, 'The Emergence of Qatar's Diplomacy in a Complex World: Balancing Soft Power in Regional Affairs', *World Affairs* 187, no. 4 (5 November 2024), pp. 532–44, https://doi.org/10.1002/waf2.12051

Ulrichsen, Kristian Coates, 'Kuwait as a Mediator in Regional Affairs: The Gulf Crises of 2014 and 2017', *The International Spectator* 56, no. 4 (2021), pp. 119–33, https://doi.org/10.1080/03932729.2021.1982293

———, 'Qatar and the 2022 FIFA World Cup: Soft Power, State Branding, or Nation Building?' in Simon Chadwick, Paul Widdop, and Michael M Goldman (eds), *The Geopolitical Economy of Sport: Power, Politics, Money, and the State*, 1st edn (London: Routledge, 2023), pp. 127–33.

———, *Qatar and the Arab Spring* (Oxford: Oxford University Press, 2014).

———, 'Qatar and the Arab Spring: Policy Drivers and Regional Implications', Carnegie Endowment for International Peace, 24 September 2014, https://carnegieendowment.org/research/2014/09/qatar-and-the-arab-spring-policy-drivers-and-regional-implications?lang=en

———, *Qatar and the Gulf Crisis* (London: Hurst & Company, 2020).

———, 'Qatar's Mediation Initiatives', The Norwegian Peacebuilding Resource Centre (NOREF), February 2013, https://www.files.ethz.ch/isn/160109/da1df25567ebd34af26d634892934b03.pdf

———, 'The Gulf States and the Iran–Iraq War: Cooperation and Confusion', in Nigel Ashton and Bryan Gibson (eds), *The Iran–Iraq War: New International Perspectives* (London: Routledge, 2012).

———, 'The Rationale and Implications of Qatar's Intervention in Libya', in Dag Henriksen and Ann Karin Larssen (eds), *Political Rationale and International Consequences of the War in Libya* (Oxford: Oxford University Press, 2016), pp. 118–33, https://doi.org/10.1093/acprof:oso/9780198767480.003.0007

UNAMID, '15 Oct 12—Communiqué of the Second Meeting of the Joint Commission of the Doha Document for Peace', United Nations–African Union Mission in Darfur, 16 October 2012, https://unamid.unmissions.org/15-oct-12-communiqu%C3%A9-second-meeting-joint-commission-doha-document-peace

———, 'Darfur Peace Agreements: Challenges and Opportunities', United Nations–African Union Mission in Darfur, 1 July 2012, https://unamid.unmissions.org/peace-process-0

———, 'Doha Document for Peace in Darfur', United Nations–African Union Mission in Darfur, 2011, https://unamid.unmissions.org/doha-document-peace-darfur

———, 'Final Communiqué International Donor Conference for Reconstruction and Development in Darfur', United Nations–African Union Mission in Darfur, 14 April 2013, https://unamid.unmissions.org/final-communiqu%C3%A9-international-donor-conference-reconstruction-and-developmentin-darfur-0

———, 'Five Hundred Attend Darfur Stakeholders Conference', United Nations–

African Union Mission in Darfur, 27 May 2011, https://unamid.unmissions.org/27-may-11-five-hundred-attend-darfur-stakeholders-conference

UNESCO, 'UNESCO—Majlis, a Cultural and Social Space', United Nations Educational, Scientific and Cultural Organization, 2015, https://ich.unesco.org/en/RL/majlis-a-cultural-and-social-space-01076

United Nations, 'At Five-Year Mark, Darfur Crisis Is Only Worsening—UN Aid Chief', United Nations, 22 April 2008, https://news.un.org/en/story/2008/04/256942

———, 'Eritrea v. Yemen (Award of the Arbitral Tribunal in the First Stage of the Proceedings between Eritrea and Yemen (Territorial Sovereignty and Scope of the Dispute))', in *Reports of International Arbitral Awards* (New York: United Nations, 1998), pp. 209–332, https://legal.un.org/riaa/cases/vol_xxii/209-332.pdf

———, 'Resolution 2148 (2014) / Adopted by the Security Council at Its 7152nd Meeting, on 3 April 2014', United Nations, 3 April 2014, https://digitallibrary.un.org/record/768033?ln=en&v=pdf

———, 'Secretary-General's Video Message to the Signing Ceremony of the Doha Peace Agreement between the Chadian Transitional Authorities and Politico-Military Groups', United Nations, 8 August 2022, https://www.un.org/sg/en/content/sg/statement/2022-08-08/secretary-generals-video-message-the-signing-ceremony-of-the-doha-peace-agreement-between-the-chadian-transitional-authorities-and-politico-military-groups-delivered

———, *The Taif Agreement*, negotiated in Ta'if, Saudi Arabia, September 1989, and approved by the Lebanese Parliament on 4 November 1989, https://www.un.int/lebanon/sites/www.un.int/files/Lebanon/the_taif_agreement_english_version_.pdf

———, 'United Nations, African Union Agree to Convene Renewed Peace Negotiations for Darfur in Tripoli, 27 October', United Nations, 10 September 2007, https://press.un.org/en/2007/sgsm11149.doc.htm

———, 'United Nations Guidance for Effective Mediation', United Nations, September 2012, https://unrcca.unmissions.org/sites/default/files/dpa_msu_guidance_english_web.pdf (accessed 26 December 2024).

———, *UNGA Resolution 43/177 (A/RES/43/177)* (New York: United Nations, 1988), https://www.un.org/unispal/document/auto-insert-184706/

United Nations Multi-Partner Trust Fund Office, 'Qatar Contributes 88.5 Million USD to UN Fund for Darfur', United Nations Multi-Partner Trust Fund Office, 23 September 2014, https://mptf.undp.org/news/qatar-contributes-88-5-million-usd-un-fund-darfur

United Nations Office for the Coordination of Humanitarian Affairs, 'High-Level Pledging Event on Supporting the Humanitarian Response in Afghanistan 2022', United Nations Office for the Coordination of Humanitarian Affairs, 31 March 2022, https://www.unocha.org/events/high-level-pledging-event-supporting-humanitarian-response-afghanistan-2022

———, 'Humanitarian News from Sudan: Monthly Digest—Jul 2007', United Nations Office for the Coordination of Humanitarian Affairs, 31 July 2007, https://www.unocha.org/publications/report/chad/humanitarian-news-sudan-monthly-digest-jul-2007

United Nations Peacemaker, 'Agreement of Good Will and Confidence-Building for the Settlement of the Problem in Darfur, Signed on 17 February 2009', UN Peacemaker: Mediation Support Unit, 5 July 2024, https://bitly.cx/5mrL

———, 'Doha Agreement on the Results of the Lebanese National Dialogue Conference', UN Peacemaker: Mediation Support Unit, 21 May 2008, https://peacemaker.un.org/sites/default/files/document/files/2024/05/lebanondohaagreement2008engl.pdf

———, 'Framework Agreement to Resolve the Conflict in Darfur between the Government of Sudan (GOS) and the Justice and Equality Movement Sudan (JEM), Signed on 23 February 2010', UN Peacemaker: Mediation Support Unit, 5 July 2024, https://bitly.cx/sKEk

———, 'Framework Agreement to Resolve the Conflict in Darfur between the Government of Sudan (GOS) and Liberation and Justice Movement (LJM), Signed on 18 March 2010', UN Peacemaker: Mediation Support Unit, 5 July 2024, https://bitly.cx/vmFA

———, 'Humanitarian Ceasefire Agreement on the Conflict in Darfur', UN Peacemaker: Mediation Support Unit, 2 April 2004, https://peacemaker.un.org/node/9516

United Nations Security Council, *Letter Dated 22 May 2008 from the Permanent Observer of the League of Arab States to the United Nations Addressed to the President of the Security Council (S/2008/392)* (New York: United Nations Security Council, 2008), https://digitallibrary.un.org/record/632576

United Press International, 'Qatar Mediates Yemen, Eritrea Dispute', United Press International, 20 December 1995, https://www.upi.com/Archives/1995/12/20/Qatar-mediates-Yemen-Eritrea-dispute/6433819435600/

United World International, 'Sisi's Visit to Qatar: A Step Towards Resolving the Libyan Crisis', United World International, 2022, https://uwidata.com/sisis-visit-to-qatar-a-step-towards-resolving-the-libyan-crisis/

U.S. Department of Defense, *Semiannual Report: Enhancing Security and Stability in Afghanistan ('1225 Report')*, U.S. Department of Defense, 2020, https://media.defense.gov/2021/Apr/23/2002626546/-1/-1/0/ENHANCING-SECURITY-AND-STABILITY-IN-AFGHANISTAN.PDF

U.S. Department of State, 'Joint Statement on Peace Talks between the Democratic Republic of the Congo and the Republic of Rwanda, Mediated by the United States and Observed by the State of Qatar', U.S. Department of State, 18 June 2025, https://www.state.gov/releases/office-of-the-spokesperson/2025/06/joint-statement-on-peace-talks-between-the-democratic-republic-of-the-congo-and-the-republic-of-rwanda-mediated-by-the-united-states-and-observed-by-the-state-of-qatar/

———, 'Meeting of U.S. Officials with Taliban Representatives', U.S. Department of State, 31 July 2023, https://2021-2025.state.gov/meeting-of-u-s-officials-with-taliban-representatives/

U.S. Embassy—Libya (@USEmbassyLibya), 'Status: 1611090046316077094', X (formerly Twitter), 5 January 2023, https://x.com/USEmbassyLibya/status/1611090046316077094

Vakil, Sanam, 'Understanding the GCC Collective Security Mindset', Chatham House, 30 November 2022, https://kalam.chathamhouse.org/articles/understanding-the-gcc-collective-security-mindset/

Viramontes, Erick, *Looking towards the South: Qatar's National Vision and Its Latin American Horizon*, Gulf Studies Center (Qatar University) Working Paper no. 2 (August 2021), https://www.qu.edu.qa/siteimages/static_file/qu/research/gulf%20studies/documents/working%20paper%202%20-%20erick%20viramontes%20-%202021.pdf

Wählisch, Martin, 'The Lebanese National Dialogue: Past and Present Experience of Consensus-Building', in *National Dialogue Handbook* (Berlin: Berghof Foundation, 2017).

Waldman, Matt, *Peacemaking in Trouble: Expert Perspectives on Flaws, Deficiencies and Potential in the Field of International Mediation* (Cambridge: Belfer Center for Science and International Affairs, Harvard Kennedy School, 2024).

Weber, Annette, 'Bridging the Gap between Narrative and Practice: The Role of the Arab League in Darfur', Fundación Para Las Relaciones Internacionales y El Diálogo Exterior (FRIDE), 2010, https://www.swp-berlin.org/publications/products/fachpublikationen/03._Arab_League_Weber1_ks.pdf

Weiss, Max, 'The Historiography of Sectarianism in Lebanon', *History Compass* 7, no. 1 (January 2009), pp. 141–54, https://doi.org/10.1111/j.1478-0542.2008.00570.x

Whitfield, Teresa, *Still Time to Talk: Adaptation and Innovation in Peace Mediation* (London: Conciliation Resources, 2024).

WikiLeaks, 'Doha's Gaza Summit—Qatar Lurches Toward the Radical Camp', WikiLeaks, 19 January 2009, https://wikileaks.jcvignoli.com/cable_09DOHA42

———, 'Qatar Outlines Darfur Strategy to SE Williamson', WikiLeaks, 14 December 2008, https://wikileaks.org/plusd/cables/08DOHA854_a.html

———, 'Qatar Will Consider Deposit in Lebanon's Central Bank, Mediation Role', WikiLeaks, 13 December 2006, https://wikileaks.org/plusd/cables/06DOHA1737_a.html

———, 'Qatari Minstate Al-Mahmoud Looks to Next Steps on Darfur Mediation, Says Qatar Wants No Part of ICC Postponement (Canonical ID:09DOHA100_a)', WikiLeaks, 9 February 2009, https://wikileaks.org/plusd/cables/09DOHA100_a.html

———, 'Reported Qatari Mediation in Formation of Lebanese Cabinet', WikiLeaks, 9 November 2009, https://wikileaks.org/plusd/cables/09DOHA664_a.html

———, 'Scenesetter for Special Envoy Williamson's Visit to Qatar', WikiLeaks, 20 November 2008, https://wikileaks.org/plusd/cables/08DOHA817_a.html

———, 'SUDAN/QATAR/BURKINA FASO—Qatari Minister Denies Exerting Pressure on Darfur Rebel Movements', WikiLeaks, 11 March 2013, https://wikileaks.org/gifiles/docs/67/672191_sudan-qatar-burkina-faso-qatari-minister-denies-exerting.html

Williams, Dan, 'Qatar Says Gaza Aid Spares Israel War, Shows Doha Does Not Back Hamas', Reuters, 22 February 2018, https://www.reuters.com/article/world/qatar-says-gaza-aid-spares-israel-war-shows-doha-does-not-back-hamas-idUSKCN1G62IG

Williams, Paul R., and Matthew T. Simpson, 'Drafting in Doha: An Assessment of the Darfur Peace Process and Ceasefire Agreements', in Melanne A. Civic and Michael Miklaucic (eds), *Monopoly of Force: The Nexus of DDR and SSR* (Washington, DC: National Defense University Press, 2011), pp. 41–58.

Wintour, Patrick, 'Qatar and Egypt "Will Help Form New Palestinian Technocratic Government"', *The Guardian*, 27 February 2024, https://www.theguardian.com/world/2024/feb/27/qatar-and-egypt-will-help-form-new-palestinian-technocratic-government

———, 'Why Is Qatar Often a Mediator and What Is Its Role in Israel-Hamas War?' *The Guardian*, 21 November 2023, https://www.theguardian.com/world/2023/nov/21/why-is-qatar-often-a-mediator-and-what-is-its-role-in-israel-hamas-war

Wirtschafter, Jacob, 'Qatar's Balancing Act in Middle East Is Mediation amid Crisis', Voice of America, 2 October 2024, https://www.voanews.com/a/qatar-s-balancing-act-in-middle-east-is-mediation-amid-crisis/7807833.html

Wódka, Jakub, 'Turkey's Middlepowermanship, Foreign Policy Transformation and Mediation Efforts in the Russia-Ukraine War', *Studia Europejskie—Studies in European Affairs* 2023, no. 4 (15 December 2023), pp. 215–33, https://doi.org/10.33067/se.4.2023.12

Worden, Scott, 'Breaking the Stalemate: Biden Can Use the U.S.-Taliban Deal to Bring Peace', United States Institute of Peace, 2021, https://www.usip.org/publications/2021/02/breaking-stalemate-biden-can-use-us-taliban-deal-bring-peace

World Bank, 'Population, Total—Qatar', World Bank, https://data.worldbank.org/indicator/SP.POP.TOTL?locations=QA (accessed 18 February 2025).

———, *Economic Monitoring Report to the Ad Hoc Liaison Committee* (Washington, DC: World Bank, 2016), https://documents1.worldbank.org/curated/en/474311473682340785/pdf/108205-V2-WP-PUBLIC-SEPT-14–2PM-September–2016-AHLC-World-Bank-Report.pdf

Wörmer, Nils, *Exploratory Talks and Peace Initiatives in Afghanistan: Actors, Demands, Germany's Role as Mediator* (Berlin: Stiftung Wissenschaft und Politik, 2012), https://www.swp-berlin.org/en/publication/afghanistan-peace-initiatives/

Worrall, James, '"Switzerland of Arabia": Omani Foreign Policy and Mediation Efforts in the Middle East', *The International Spectator* 56, no. 4 (8 December 2021), pp. 134–50, https://doi.org/10.1080/03932729.2021.1996004

Worth, Robert F., 'Qatar, Playing All Sides, Is a Nonstop Mediator', *The New York Times*, 9 July 2008, https://www.nytimes.com/2008/07/09/world/middleeast/09qatar.html

Worth, Robert, and Nada Bakri, 'Deal for Lebanese Factions Leaves Hezbollah Stronger', *The New York Times*, 22 May 2008, http://www.nytimes.com/2008/05/22/world/middleeast/22lebanon.html?_r=1&

Yacoubian, Mona, *Facing the Abyss: Lebanon's Deadly Political Stalemate* (Washington, DC: United States Institute of Peace, 2008), https://www.usip.org/publications/2008/02/facing-abyss-lebanons-deadly-political-stalemate

Yadav, Stacey Philbrick, 'Lebanon's Post-Doha Political Theater', *Middle East Report*, 23 July 2008, https://merip.org/2008/07/lebanons-post-doha-political-theater/

Ylönen, Aleksi, 'Is the Horn of Africa's "Cold War" Over? Abiy Ahmed's Early Reforms and the Rapprochement between Ethiopia and Eritrea', *African Security Review* 27, no. 3–4 (25 January 2019), pp. 245–52, https://doi.org/10.1080/10246029.2019.1569079

Young, Karen E., 'Sovereign Risk: Gulf Sovereign Wealth Funds as Engines of Growth and Political Resource', *British Journal of Middle Eastern Studies* 47, no. 1 (2020), pp. 96–116, https://doi.org/10.1080/13530194.2020.1714866

Zakaria, Shaher, 'Qatar's Mediation between the United States and Venezuela', *The Peninsula*, 18 July 2024, https://thepeninsulaqatar.com/opinion/18/07/2024/qatars-mediation-between-the-united-states-and-venezuela

Zartman, William I., 'Structuring in a Vacuum: Negotiating in the Current World Disorder', *International Negotiation* 25, no. 1 (2020), pp. 5–17, https://doi.org/10.1163/15718069-25131236

Zartman, William I., and Saadia Touval, 'International Mediation: Conflict Resolution and Power Politics', *Journal of Social Issues* 41, no. 2 (1985), pp. 27–45, https://doi.org/10.1111/j.1540-4560.1985.tb00853.x

Zureik, Elia, 'Qatar's Humanitarian Aid to Palestine', *Third World Quarterly* 39, no. 4 (6 November 2017), pp. 786–98, https://doi.org/10.1080/01436597.2017.1392087

INDEX

INDEX